W9-CRK-639

Great Walls of Discourse and Other Adventures in Cultural China

Harvard East Asian Monographs 212

Great Walls of Discourse and Other Adventures in Cultural China

◆

Haun Saussy

Published by the Harvard University Asia Center
and distributed by Harvard University Press
Cambridge (Massachusetts) and London 2001

Printed in the United States of America

The Harvard University Asia Center publishes a monograph series and, in coordination with the Fair-bank Center for East Asian Research, the Korea Institute, the Reischauer Institute of Japanese Studies, and other faculties and institutes, administers research projects designed to further scholarly understand-ing of China, Japan, Vietnam, Korea, and other Asian countries. The Center also sponsors projects ad-dressing multidisciplinary and regional issues in Asia.

Library of Congress Cataloging-in-Publication Data

Saussy, Haun, 1960–
    Great walls of discourse and other adventures in cultural China / Haun Saussy.
        p. cm. -- (Harvard East Asian monographs ; 212)
    Includes bibliographical references and index.
    ISBN 0-674-00859-6 (cloth : alk. paper) -- ISBN 0-674-00860-x (paper : alk. paper)
    1. China--Civilization. 2. China--Historiography. I. Title. II. Series.

DS 727.S28 2001
951'.007'2--dc21   2001039652

Index by Janet Russell

⊗   Printed on acid-free paper

Last number below indicates year of this printing
11 10 09 08 07 06 05 04 03 02 01

For Paul and Didi Farmer

Always and always, the difficult inch,
On which the vast arches of space
Repose, always, the credible thought
From which the incredible systems spring . . .
　　　　—Wallace Stevens, "The Sail of Ulysses"

The Mind, that Ocean where each kind
Does streight its own resemblance find . . .
　　　　—Andrew Marvell, "The Garden"

物相雜古曰文
　　—易經, 繫辭

Information is a name for the content of
what is exchanged with the outer world as
we adjust to it, and make our adjustment felt
upon it.
　　　　—Norbert Wiener, *The Human
　　　　Use of Human Beings*

Acknowledgments

The cover image appears by courtesy of the Art Library, Stanford University. Illustrations on pp. 51–52 and 85–86 appear by the gracious permission of the Beinecke Library, Yale University; the Biblioteca Apostolica Vaticana; the University of Indiana Libraries; and the Stanford University Libraries.

Chapter Two: I thank Roland Greene, Hent de Vries, Sam Weber, Bill Rowe, and Neil Hertz for giving me occasions to learn from audiences what to do with earlier versions of this piece. Permission to reprint from an earlier version of the essay ("In the Workshop of Equivalences," in Hent de Vries and Samuel Weber, eds., *Religion and Media*, Stanford: Stanford University Press, 2001), copyright by the Board of Trustees of the Leland Stanford Junior University, is gratefully acknowledged.

Chapter Three: An early version of this paper was presented at the panel "*Wen*: The Nature of Chinese Language and Writing," Association for Asian Studies Annual Meeting, Boston, March 1994, and a fuller version published as number 75 of *Sino-Platonic Papers* (February 1997). Zhang Longxi was the panel's main organizer and I have benefited from discussing these issues with him over the years. I thank Pauline Yu, Justine Stillings, Anthony Yu, Eugene Eoyang, Thomas Hare, Stephen Owen, Lionel Jensen, Martin Svensson, James Marshall Unger, and several anonymous scholars for comments and suggestions. Particular thanks are due Victor Mair, editor and publisher of *Sino-Platonic Papers*, for permission to reprint the chapter in this expanded version. Passages quoted from the Pound Archive (Beinecke Library, Yale University), copyright © 2001 by Mary de Rachewiltz and Omar S. Pound, are used by permission of New Directions Publishing Corporation.

Chapter Four: An earlier version of this section was first published in Lydia Liu, ed., *Tokens of Exchange: The Problem of Translation in Global Circula-*

tions (Durham: Duke University Press, 1999), pp. 107–23. I gratefully acknowledge the comments and advice of Lydia Liu, Ken Wissoker, and Q. S. Tong. I thank Duke University Press for their generous permission to print the revised version.

Chapter Five: Steven Shankman, Stephen Durrant, Hyong Rhew, and Anand Yang provided forums in which I presented earlier versions of this paper and put me in front of hard-to-please audiences. A preliminary version of the argument was published in Steven Shankman and Stephen Durrant, eds., *Thinking Through Comparisons* (Albany: State University of New York Press, 2001). SUNY Press's permission to reprint is hereby gratefully acknowledged.

Chapter Six: Most of this essay is a revised version of one published originally in Wen-hsin Yeh, ed., *Cross-Cultural Readings of Chineseness* (Berkeley: Institute of East Asian Studies, 2000), pp. 128–58; another section was first written as a paper for the conference "China Ten Years After Tian'anmen" held by the Joint East Asian Studies Center of the University of Toronto and York University, in June 1999. I thank Wen-hsin Yeh for asking me to expand into a paper some off-the-cuff remarks at a panel discussion, and Tim Brook for inviting me to Canada to discuss memory and repression during the *furore* over the Belgrade embassy bombing; thanks are also due to Berkeley's Institute of East Asian Studies for their permission to reprint.

Chapter Seven: A previous version of this chapter saw the light in *Modern Language Notes* 115 (2000), pp. 849–91; thanks are due to Richard Macksey, editor of *MLN*, for his encouragement, and to Johns Hopkins University Press for permission to republish. Earlier versions were presented at the Comparative Literature Seminar of the University of Chicago, thanks to Anthony Yu and Michael Murrin; at the "Workshop on Literature / Theory / China / Japan" organized by Ivo Smits and Michel Hockx at the School of Oriental and African Studies, University of London, June 1999; and in a seminar for the Humanities Center at Johns Hopkins University, thanks to Neil Hertz and Michael Fried. A part of the argument has also appeared in *Zhongguo xueshu* 中國學術, edited by Liu Dong 劉東, whom I thank for the opportunity to think my way through the issues again in another language. For the translations from the Russian, I am greatly indebted to Marilena Ruscica.

Revisions to this book were carried out during a pleasurable stay at the City University of Hong Kong, where my hosts were Professors Cheng

Chin-chuan and Zhang Longxi. Two anonymous readers for the Press kindly suggested improvements; John Ziemer has been both a tough critic and a loyal editor, the best combination an author could desire. Janet Russell compiled the Index. My students have contributed in untold ways—usually by asking annoying and irrelevant questions that, of course, were anything but. The staffs of the Beinecke Library, Yale University, and the East Asia Collection, Stanford University, have been a great help. The Brown and Radway families' gifts to Stanford University have helped me carry out my research. The list of people not yet mentioned to whom I am indebted should by rights be impossibly long. Here let me mention the benefit I have received from conversations with Bob Batchelor; E. Bruce Brooks, Taeko Brooks, and the Warring States Working Group; Chris Bush; John Cayley; Nahum Chandler; Charles Egan; Chang Hao; Pei-kai Cheng; Lothar von Falkenhausen; Paul Farmer; Tom Hare; Roger Hart; Eric Hayot; Tim Lenoir; Mao Liang; David Porter; David Quint; Boris L. Riftin; Teemu Ruskola; David Schaberg; Helen Tartar; Wang Hui; Steve Yao; and Henry Yiheng Zhao. Yulin, Juliana, and Caleb provided a larger context of happiness and a much-needed counterpoint to my narrow and frantic musings.

HS

Contents

Illustrations

Great Walls of Discourse
and Other Adventures in
Cultural China

Introduction:
Group Tours and Swimming
with Schools

Solitary visitors to museums have every reason to dislike tour groups. They are loud; they are in a hurry; they look only at the single most famous picture in every room; they get between you and whatever you are looking at. Above all, they are hard to ignore. A serious museum-goer knows how to ignore people ("As if in the whole world, there were nothing but God and me" is how Leibniz described it, before there were proper museums). You wait out the human wave, and then return to your looking. An accomplished pickpocket could tell us which generally absorbs more attention, the focus on a work of art or the effort not to perceive a bustling group.

An epistemology solely concerned with the relation between perceiver and perceived object would be like the museum-goer who succeeds in blocking out the presence of the crowd; I ask the reader to imagine a more easily distracted perceiver. To follow this perceiver's perceptions, we would have to keep track of the artworks, the perceptions of them by the solitary observer, and the way other observers impinge (often annoyingly) upon that observer's awareness. We would thus be bringing the actions of other subjects and their perceptions (however imagined or anticipated) into the description of what it means to perceive. Transferred to the domain of literary culture, such an account would examine the ways in which the translation, interpretation, usage, and day-to-day life of texts involve not just a monadic observer but a plurality of subjects.

This book is about the career of China as an object of knowledge. But its account of knowing is not object-centered; it considers knowledge as *peripheral*, *reciprocal* and *mediated*.[1] That knowledge in the humanities is not simple or impersonal is by now widely admitted. Our interpretations are not fresh but layered. Case upon case teaches us that contextual pressures, the influence of schools of thought, unconscious preferences, analogical reasonings, societal prejudice, and so forth keep us from getting to the truth about things. The problem is what to do about that admission.

In Chinese studies, the "subjectivity problem" (as we might call it) takes specific, historically inflected forms. Like many people, I was drawn to Chinese studies because I was dissatisfied with my shaky education up to that point and saw in this field a promise of intellectual discipline. In the negative mode common to ascetic religions, backwoods camping, and the Cartesian project, I would have to put aside my habitual words and implicit ways of thinking, and learn to make sense—relearn what sense-making was—in a new language. It was a matter not of "becoming Chinese" but of overcoming the instinctive self-centeredness so well captured by Montesquieu in his question "How is it possible to be Persian?"[2] It was not an identification but an attempt to discriminate; to put it in somewhat exaggerated terms, it was an experiment in altering the conditions of linguistic and semantic experience. In the course of becoming (to whatever degree) a cultural bilingual, however, I found that the gesture of "putting aside" carried particular connotations and implications. It became necessary to question these as well.

An awareness of the mediated character of knowledge is familiar in the field of Chinese studies, but mainly as a danger to be guarded against. Mediation becomes visible as preconception or bias—Western, religious, metaphysical, Communist, imperial, didactic, modernist, and so forth. The purpose of calling it to attention is to remove it, since such mediation is thought always to get in the way. A nice anthology could be made of scholarly arguments taking the form *Confucius* (for example) *had no concept of X; therefore all readings of Confucius that assume the relevance of X are inauthentic.* Some such historical criticism is necessary when one is dealing with a long-lived, layered text that has been through many different hands and appropriated by many interests; I am here, however, talking about one side-effect of this critical attitude, which seems to me to set the tone for much study of traditional China. The self (as it materializes in unnoticed anachronisms such as the concept of X) is an obstacle; the experiment in thinking differently requires a certain denial of self. Nor is having to take our knowledge in mediated form a problem for moderns alone. The traditional narrators of the Chinese past are frequently unreliable guides who, like the obligatory tour leaders of recent mainland memory, subject one to an itinerary of carefully selected monuments and an insistently thesis-driven commentary. So the reader is in an uneasy position, forewarned against "doing what comes naturally" in interpretation and suspicious of the Potemkin-village realities that serve the needs of tour organizers.

The distrust of mediation is further complicated by the presence, in the wings, of ghostly Orientalists who proclaim that modern Chinese are completely out of touch with their classical past and modern Chinese who cannot imagine that anyone not Chinese has anything worthwhile to say about it. (I suspect that a great many readers of this book, following one or the other lead, will think that it addresses the errors that foreign or modern observers of China, being foreign or modern, necessarily make.) All the more reason, then, to adopt an attitude of aggressive modesty, to focus on one's document and try to make oneself its mouthpiece. Hence the model of scholarship that most students of China find most convincing: the faithful translation, into either modern Chinese or some other language, of an authentic document.

In this book, however, I adopt the view that we are always in the midst of mediation, that mediation is our authenticity—whoever "we" may be. (The predicament of the foreign student of China is, I hold, merely indicative of a general situation.) To make this view convincing, I will have to find mediation everywhere. That is not hard to do, if we are willing to shrink ourselves to a scale at which languages, cultures, and histories fade away by their very hugeness and formerly trivial details of interpretation loom large. Let us put the big categories on the defensive and measure authenticity and identity by the differences they (imperfectly) conceal. Dialogue is an uninterrupted process of translation between idiolects, and translation becomes the normal condition of language; translation being—as every bilingual knows—as much transformation as transfer. We can all recover the to-and-fro that goes into the simplest act of translation. To get a sentence right, you have to invoke a great deal of peripheral knowledge: awareness of connotation, of the weave of the text you are working with, of the many ways your reader might be led astray. The pull of two languages in one head is reciprocal, a balancing play of forces: "That word is a little severe, I need a word that doesn't imply an excess; but the other possibility suggests something else entirely, so let's go back to the original term and see if there isn't a connotation that will raise an idea." Or I hesitate to use a word because, although exact, it is not the sort of word I would use (and who exactly am "I" in the language I am translating into?). All this work is social, as we parry and trade with anticipated others, shuttle back and forth among possible outcomes. The crowd outside is disruptive because it competes with the crowd inside.

The work is social in yet another sense: in translating, we invoke or establish networks of mutual intelligibility. These needed to be built at some time and must continually be maintained. Once the received translation for a term is in place (let us consider the relatively problem-free equivalence of "space" and *kongjian* 空間), the legitimacy of their match is constantly undergoing subtle recalibrations, as the terms undergo independent modifications in their languages of origin, as they enter into compounds and contexts and distinctions (space heater, personal space, spacewalk . . .). The received equivalence of the terms can itself become a source of modification if there is a great deal of traffic between the languages: consider the figurative extensions of "space" that have become unremarkable in English over the past thirty years, and note how many of them occur as well in the present-day Chinese of particular milieux: scholarly articles, movie columns, real estate advertisements, call-in talk shows. Consider the ways social actors use the term "space" to vehicle their ideas about not only geometry and physics but also such things as subjective autonomy and interpersonal contact. The equivalence of any two mutually translatable terms holds for a small area of their connotations, which beyond that focus ramify indefinitely and independently. As a relation established among points on relational networks, translation—even of single terms—is highly contingent, something that must be made to happen. The truth of translation is therefore never simple, permanent, and unique. But this does not mean that translation is arbitrary or subjective. It is as complicated as it is precisely because it is mediated, peripheral, and reciprocal.

Certain seminar-room scenarios for demonstrating that translation is indeterminate seem to head toward the verdict of willfulness. W. V. Quine gives the example of the exclamation "Gavagai!" provoked by . . . well, what? The observant yet reflective linguist in the field runs over "Rabbit," "There's a rabbit," "Now we see a rabbit," "Lo! rabbithood again," but realizes that the apparatus of nouns in the English equivalent-sentences has trapped her into ascribing certain notions of quantity and identity to the conceptual scheme of the language being translated. Is that really how the natives think? "The obstacle to correlating conceptual schemes," says Quine, "is that any one intercultural correlation of words and phrases, and hence of theories, will be just one among various empirically admissible correlations, whether it is suggested by historical gradations or by unaided analogy; there is nothing for such a correlation to be uniquely right or wrong about."[3] Even with the important qualifier "uniquely," Quine's way of setting up the problem does not much resemble the social world in which most translation happens, for people are interested in the outcomes of translation and deem them to be right or wrong. They react to paraphrases, argue with them, replace them. Having in mind the possible recipients of a translation, as well as what a translation may do in the world once it gets out there, cures us of the too easy idea that translations are arbitrary or indifferent. But you would not arrive at that realization if you were to take the thing to be named and the set of its possible equivalent names as the only factors to be considered. Translation is not indeterminate, it is just other-determined—that is, it is not fully determined by the items registered in a narrowly linguistic and cognitive definition of translation. Considering the social side of the business does not require that we deny the epistemic legitimacy of translation, its power to communicate whatever is the case; it only gives us a more adequate understanding of what we are doing, since we are doing something more complex than correlating shouts of "Gavagai!" with rabbit appearances.[4]

A definition of translation as the substitution of equivalent terms in different languages correlates with an account of knowledge that restricts itself to the dyadic relation of subject and object, and an account that describes translation as a negotiation among many possible acts of meaning in several languages correlates with a description of the intersubjective, mediated character of knowing. Moreover, there is no necessary opposition between these two perspectives: the multipolar account of translation or perception can include the bipolar account as a subpart of its own investigation, a partial understanding or necessary illusion. That is what I have tried to do here, under various conditions and in differing contexts.

♦

Translation is a complicated business that we often treat as simple by ignoring its peripheral dimensions. In the interpretation of prestige-bearing cultural objects, even whole societies, the presence of peripheral interests is harder to ignore. The knowledge belonging to the "communities of practice" created by intercultural situations is often blamed for being *too* peripheral, too self-involved, too much a self-confirming belief system. Think of the Old China Hands, of the mission compounds, or of the scholars and policymakers described in Edward Said's *Orientalism*: in these expatriate circles "a whole experience . . . with its own integral history, cuisine, dialect, values, and tropes more or less detached itself from the teeming, contradictory realities [surrounding it]. . . and perpetuated itself."[5] Half the case to be made against Orientalist scholarship is simply that it held together to the point of repetition, that it constituted a community so tight that (such is Said's charge) no new knowledge could have penetrated it.[6] If this is what it means to be influenced by what is *around* one—if this is peripheral and mediated knowledge—then it is no surprise that even to talk about the non-Chinese contexts of our knowing about China is considered tactless. Indeed, the first idea that comes to mind is that such an investigation would have to be a critique. Such a history provides the presuppositions that look so unfavorably on presupposition.

My eye rests on Chinese life with undiminished fascination, but I have permitted myself to steal a glance or two at the China watchers. What critique there is in this book is directed not at the fact that people belong to social networks and are influenced by them (that is not a crime, even against objectivity), but at our habit of ignoring them. And so this book is not an attack on anything; rather, it is an attempt to replace limited perspectives with more comprehensive ones. The difficulty I repeatedly allege is that we misplace our understanding—we think that we are thinking about things as they are when we are actually thinking about things as they appear to us (and the people we speak with), things into which we have put a great deal of ourselves. There is nothing wrong with thinking subjectively; the problem lies in supposing that we are not doing so. (A paragraph of cant about how no one believes in the Cartesian subject any more will not remove the difficulty; that is like a legal release that does not stop problems happening but merely deprives the reader of recourse.) To look forward to an example that appears in a later chapter: when we translate a sentence of Huron or Chinese into a choppy pidgin-English, we are not representing how that sentence sounds to a speaker of Huron or Chinese. Instead we are distorting our English to show how distorted the Huron or Chinese sounds to us (as speakers of English). That can be a useful exercise, as an illustration (perhaps of the limits of English?), but if we say that *that is how Huron or Chinese is*, we have promoted the intersubjective effects of translation to the status of subjectless realities. Much of the knowledge that circulates under the heading of "China" (never mind the particular disciplinary field) is, to my mind, vitiated by this sort of presentation—wrong insofar as it is uncontextualized. By being restated as an effect of reciprocal, mediated reinscription, however, it can point us toward a more adequate knowledge about a whole set of interrelated things, only a few of which were available to us when the statement was thought to be adequate as it stood.

In Chinese studies, so far, the habitual ways of acknowledging (and, typically, bewailing) subjective influence are simply too stark. The experience of cultural difference, as well as theories of cultural relativism, teach us to allow for our biases in accounting for our judgments, not just of what is right and wrong but of what there is. But even the attempt to state our biases involves us in a twisted loop: the representations we make to ourselves of our identities and interests relate not to our selves but to our self-concepts, and these in turn rely on many further kinds of interests (somewhere among these we find an interest in honesty). The statement of our biases and interests is just one further element of the negotiation between us and the world, it is not that negotiation itself. We always learn our singular unity and group identity from others. But why do we suppose that we are subjects situated in this or that way and not some other? Forms of collective selfhood, whether strong or weak, binding or optional, emerge from conversations and persuasions of long standing. To invoke a group identity is, therefore, to refer back to a set of negotiations, and these must be investigated if we are not primarily interested in stopping conversations. "Belonging" does not insulate one against the feedback loops of intersubjectivity; it is merely one particular form of interaction developed to dampen them, and the degree to which it succeeds depends on other social determinants.

The strategy, then, is to represent facts as outcomes of interactions, not (simply) as evidence or givens of knowledge. Indeed, the fullest representation of an interaction will include knowledge (not discounting self-knowledge) as one of the effects of a large field of consequences. If we want to understand these, the tool for the job is the bent crowbar of the question mark, not the round period or the straight exclamation point.

As the historians say, "All history is the history of the present," a history of the things that stay active in memory.[7] It is a tautological saying, but a good reminder. Research on anything is also research on the idea that we have about it. One of the things Freud learned from his patients was that, however traumatic, deeply held, or powerfully repressed their narrated memories were, their pasts were also creations of the present: whatever the felt reality of these pasts, they had nevertheless emerged as constructions of the analytic situation and took on a meaning as episodes in a negotiation with Dr. Freud. That is, they had to be interpreted as side-effects of a "transference," a relationship that superimposed itself on the ostensible subjects of discussion during the analytic hour; they were evidence of the patient's desire to be a "good" patient, of an overwhelming relationship to an ego-ideal, signs of resistance, or attempts to take control of the conversation; they were gifts made to Dr. Freud, not just anybody. Had they been interpreted as raw data from the past having primary explanatory value, the analysis (and the history of psychoanalysis) would have taken a different course.[8] It may have been useful in the course of analysis for Dr. Freud to present himself as a scientist, an expert, the man with answers and an extraordinary ability to ferret out the truth—a qualified objective knower, in short—but Freud had to contend with his countertransference too, his own involvement in and distortion of the relationship. Contending with it was his contribution to the relationship. "Everyone possesses, in his own unconscious, an instrument with which he can interpret the expressions of the unconscious of others."[9]

I do not know enough about psychoanalysis to derive from it anything more than a metaphor, but the reconception of *actual* events in the *other* person's *past* as something we can understand only as a *present-tense* interaction that *we both* contribute to *making* strikes me as the germ of a program for accounting for what goes on in translation, interpretation, and the critique of these activities. I do not endorse agnosticism about the past or the other; rather, I would encourage a redirection of attention toward the nearer things through which the remoter things let themselves be spoken. To steal another analogy from a subsequent chapter: it is not a matter of determining what the difference between Western and Chinese concepts of meaning *is*, but of asking *how* there comes to be such a problem, who contributed (or contributes) to its life as a problem, and where the answers have been sought. Things begin to make sense not as things in themselves but as signs of relations, even of relations to further relations (as, in yet another chapter, the Jesuits' translation-strategies for China, their *ratio studiorum Sinicorum*, crystallized under the influence of the friends they had made among small dissident groups of scholar-officials). The translation (*Übersetzung*) works as a transference (*Übertragung*); it generates a countertransference (*Gegenübertragung*) or countertranslation (*Gegenübersetzung?*) in the measure that the semantics of the target language receive and reshape what was to be translated (the pidgin-effect). Reciprocity bedevils a stable economy of meaning: what the Jesuits, as translators, made the Chinese language say was "not Chinese" for a moment, but it quickly affected the rest of the Chinese language, as far as the small community that spoke with them was concerned. Because of the particular content and stakes of the psychoanalytic conversation, it is hardly an exaggeration to see it as the model case of the mutual constitution of subject and object that is my subject here.

If we are used to thinking of knowledge as power (as proof of our command over an object or the means to gaining it), this kind of knowledge will often feel like helplessness. Fresh from the wartime investigations that launched the first digital computers, Norbert Wiener saw little hope for measurable knowledge in the social sciences and humanities:

All the great successes in precise science have been made in fields where there is a certain high degree of isolation of the phenomenon from the observer. . . . In the social sciences we have to deal with short statistical runs, nor can we be sure that a considerable part of what we observe is not an artefact of our own creation. An investigation of the stock market is likely to upset the stock market. We are too much in tune with the objects of our investigation to be good probes.[10]

Being "too much in tune" and engaging unbidden "artifacts"—these are Freud's "countertransference" and "transference."

The distancing devices of professional interpretation have the purpose, George Devereux has suggested, of reducing anxiety in the face of too much reciprocity and negotiation. But that is a losing battle: you cannot eliminate subjective involvement; you can only try to ignore it. Perhaps the ideal of noninterference—of recounting the alien without bias—which has been one of the more unpredictable consequences of the reception of Said's *Orientalism*, stems from some such anxiety. But shame is not the only way to handle anxiety, and far from the best. (Changing one's name and seeking to deny one's old friends, as Orientalism as a profession has done, testifies to a degree of shame.) Devereux again, commenting on his work in psychiatric ethnography:

Instead of deploring the disturbance created by our presence in the field or in the laboratory and instead of questioning the objectivity of behavioral observations, we should tackle the problem constructively and find out *what positive insights—not ob-*

tainable by other means—we can derive from the fact that the presence of an observer (who is of the same order of magnitude as that which he observes) disturbs the observed event.[11]

In Devereux's case, this meant observing others, keeping an eye on his observations, and attempting to notice the ripples he caused in his subjects' lives and they in his. "It is countertransference, rather than transference, which is the most crucial datum of all behavioral science, because the information derivable from transference can usually also be obtained by other means, whereas that provided by the analysis of countertransference is not."[12] Or, as Devereux memorably put it, "Every rat experiment is also an experiment performed on the observer."[13]

Remembering the inequalities of authority and control that much study of "non-Western peoples" has assumed and reinforced (people are not rats, but there are ways of categorizing them that attempt to put them in that position), I shall re-examine a number of inconclusive rat experiments as successful experiments on rat scientists. A certain reversal of perspective comes with my method: if one way of investigating things yielded unreliable knowledge, I would like to see if the same investigation can be interrogated anew to produce knowledge of a different kind. "The best—and perhaps the only—way of attaining a simplicity congruent with the facts is to attack the greatest complexities frontally, by means of the extremely practical device of treating the difficulty *per se* as a fundamental datum, not to be evaded, but to be exploited to the utmost—not to be explained, but to be used as an *explanation* of seemingly simpler data."[14]

A reflexive method, then, with a call to self-awareness: but does not a reflexive method simply entrench the very differences between observer and observed that were such a problem in the earlier investigations? If we give up examining China in favor of examining sinology, have we gained anything thereby? To take the program in a narrow way would be to conflate self-absorption with self-awareness; but a relational model of knowledge ought to make us see more, not less, of the world around us.

China studies in the United States have taken their isolation from the object of study for granted and attempted to overcome it rather than notice the many ways in which self and other (not as "things-in-themselves," but as mutually reinforcing and refocusing feedback loops) are always in too close contact. In a conscious reaction to these presuppositions, each of the studies in this volume starts from a traditional problem and attempts to reformulate it. The reformulations in every case are subjective or countertransferential—

which does not, I hope, mean that I am interested primarily in myself. Once we know how to look for the transferential dimension of interactions among third parties, it is instructive and an aid, or so I contend, to forming more comprehensive explanations. That perspective contributes to my attempted reframing and critique of intellectual attitudes brought to particular problems by earlier observers.

As the reader will discover, this book is an attempt to come to terms with some repeated themes in the study of China—both as themes and as repetitions. It should not be taken as a polemic against "sinology"; I acknowledge that what I do is (however imperfectly) formed by the efforts of past sinologists and *hanxuejia* 漢學家, Chinese and other. If by "sinology" we mean the effort to understand, through texts, documents, artifacts, and interviews, the vast Chinese civilization, I see nothing reprehensible in this project; if we mean by it exclusively the efforts of "foreigners" to achieve such an understanding, then I do not see what purpose is served by the national or ethnic specialization of the title. To repudiate sinology, it seems to me, amounts to repudiating cross-cultural research, which is not to say that cross-cultural research is always disinterested or virtuous.

Nor is the book (to take up a second likely misunderstanding) a repudiation of "theory." I cannot honestly say that I know what "theory" is. Certain studies, arguments, and examples, historically connected to one another and often in mutual conflict, have led me to ask certain questions about the way we understand literary texts and other artifacts. To proclaim, with hasty triumph, that "theory" is wrong or inapplicable to Chinese objects is hardly my aim. The name of my game is to be sought at a lower level of generalization. If I often find myself interrogating the premises of a typological comparison between cultures by recovering an empirical moment of contact between the cultures or between elements within a culture, it would be immodest to style that interrogation a victory of "history" over "theory." A historical way of looking at a question can destabilize a theoretical investigation in just the same way and measure that a theoretical approach can destabilize a historical one. In every case, the lesson my case histories have taught me has to do with the difficulty (and the necessity) of thinking inclusively on the basis of variegated materials.

✦

The observers I study in subsequent chapters were, of course, wanderers through a certain landscape—not just a physical setting, but an imaginary one too: a China bounded by oceans, mountains, rivers, walls, and words. "Cultural China," according to Tu Weiming 杜維明, comprises three zones: the historic homeland itself (now under more than one distinct political dispensation); the diaspora of Chinese living abroad (many of them now for several generations); and a third, bafflingly amorphous, zone consisting of people who engage with China by studying or writing about it, trading with it, or conducting diplomacy with it.[15] Population figures for the three zones show how far each matters: Zone 1 has one-and-a-quarter billion people; Zone 2, an estimated thirty-six million; and Zone 3, perhaps a few hundred thousand who are not already counted in the other zones.

My discussions here involve relations within and among these three dimensions of "Cultural China." They are necessarily and always relations of translation, or relations of otherness, but this is not *because* they connect "Chinese" people, texts, or traditions with others who are not. Each time "Chinese" or its various antonyms appears here, it is as a marker relevant to a specific discussion, tied to documents, issues, or positions, and in all such discussions there are several positions available to differently situated observers within all the "Chinas." I am not assuming that to be Chinese is a simple or a single thing, nor, obviously, would I think the same of being "non-Chinese"; and, of course, being Chinese does not preclude being a thoughtful observer of China.

Nonetheless, the reader will encounter a great deal of "we" and "us" and see from the context that the implied speaker is someone coming to China from the outside. I do this for two reasons, and the reasons need to be explained (they are not self-evident). One is to be honest: this book was written by a particular person at a particular time, and there is no point hiding that. The other is to adopt the role and play it to its point of inconsistency, to turn it inside out—for this, one has to start by getting inside it. If my provisional adoptions of the "we"/"they" epistemological barrier succeed in making it unpersuasive, that will be a good thing. It happens that the marker "Chinese" is applied or grasped in various ways. These ways are a part of my subject, not the answer to its questions; the question is "How does 'Chinese' come to have a specific value in this situation?" and not "What are the properly, characteristically Chinese features of this situation?" These clarifications may be necessary, because I do occasionally have hard things to say about particular people, institutions, reasonings, or events, and I would think it the worst possible outcome of a comparative study if the properties of particular examples were taken as reinforcing illimitably big categories. There is not much help here for anyone who wants to know what makes the West different from China, or vice versa, but there is some encouragement for the person who is ready to start unlearning such distinctions.

♦

Great Walls of Discourse consists of several originally independent essays, rethought and rewritten in light of common problems as these gradually became clear to me. Chapter 5 ("No Time Like the Present") offers a historical (and historiographical) introduction to the comparative problem as I see it; Chapters 3 and 4 ("The Prestige of Writing," "Always Multiple Translation") cast it in more or less linguistic or semiotic terms; Chapters 2, 6, and 7 ("In the Workshop of Equivalences," "Postmodernity in China," "Outside the Parenthesis") deal with the anthropology of mediation and argue (not always dispassionately) about the ways in which cultural "bilinguals" affect the societies whose periscopes they are. Readers will notice that the chapters in the second half of the book deal increasingly with political phenomena. Not that I think I have any special insight into politics (much less Chinese politics), nor that political arguments necessarily clarify questions of literature and philology; but the political-social domain is where we see intersubjectivity most conspicuously played out, and for that reason its language, like the language of literature, invites a close analysis.

Having taken shape as essays, the chapters of this book retain some characteristics of the essay form. They are incomplete, provisional, and argumentative; they seek to posit terms, engage questions, and suggest lines of thought about the topics they discuss. Total coverage and conclusive verdicts are beyond their scope, although it would not displease their author to see others deal more fully (whether *pro* or *con*) with the views expressed in them. There is thus a great deal of blank space around the topics of the different chapters. A history of sinological knowledge, a comparative historiography of modernity, or a sociology of the humanities would not be able to tolerate such gaps, but an essay writer makes more modest claims of coverage and enlists the talents of an active reader to make good the difference between what is merely sketched and what is drawn in detail. All the subjects deserve fuller treatment; I hope only to have demonstrated relationships among a number of things usually discussed in isolation and urged the adoption of ways of thinking that are equal to the task of understanding those relationships.

2

In the Workshop of Equivalences: Translation, Institutions, and Media in the Jesuit Re-formation of China

We hear a great deal these days about globalism and multiculturalism. Niklas Luhmann seems to dispense with both in his view, declared in 1982, that in modern times

society becomes a global system. For structural reasons there is no other choice. . . . Under modern conditions . . . only one social system can exist. Its communicative network spreads over the globe. . . . It provides one world for one system; and it integrates all world horizons as horizons of one communicative system. The phenomenological and the structural meanings [of "world"] converge. A plurality of possible worlds has become impossible.[1]

A person whose main academic training (not to mention segments of intellectual capital, context of signification, and personal narrative) occurred in a discipline calling itself "comparative literature" is bound to feel a chill on encountering these words. What—if Luhmann is right (or simply prescient)—does comparison mean? Is comparison still significant, can comparison still discover anything, when the "plurality of possible worlds" has shrunk to one? What would the inner organization of that world be like? Does it mean anything to discern local variances of texture in the one communicative world? What is the definition, or the benchmark, of "communication"? Is it still useful to search out test cases in which "communication" may or may not have occurred? What about initial conditions—do they matter? The scale of interchange? The work of establishing a common basis? What is the sense of Luhmann's present tense—does it, for example, retrospectively cover what we can know about the premodern era, or do the old rules remain in effect there? And finally, how should we approach this global situation—joyfully, warily, with resignation? With Luhmann's horizon of horizons before us, I would like to consider a challenging test case: seventeenth-century China's place in the history of global media.

Global communication suggests a condition, or at least the possibility, of constant interchange of artifacts and meanings among what used to be known as distinct cultures. But merely to mention the category of culture seems to beg the question of culture's (and cultures') continued existence or pertinence. Even if we fight shy of Luhmann's merciless reduction, we must admit that culture bears little weight next to the wide circulation patterns of capital and information that also go under the name of globalism.[2] In any case, for many "culture" has become a leftover category—the name for the irrational residues so far unappropriated by the patterns of behavior thought to be economically or communicatively normative, or a name for a certain market of leisure activities. As for the cosmopolitan patchwork, the reconciling pluralism, that is sometimes advanced as the form of a progressive global culture—not only does such cultural globalism look small beside its financial and cybernetic namesakes, but it also gives a misleading impression of the interests and dynamics involved.

The current concern about globalism can be described—admittedly rather tritely—in the dramatic terms of a struggle between two principles, *ubiquity* and *jurisdiction*. As the national economies of the world become linked to such an extent that none of them can control its own fate and as information becomes both instantly and generally available, the familiar notion that *territory* is the mediating category whereby people and actions are made subject to law has been deprived of much of its force.[3] Of course, this has been true for as long as there has been communication across borders—to some extent and for some people: there have always been smuggling and emigration, no society has been airtight. But perhaps that point has been hard to see for the past three hundred years of history, a history that people have experienced and recounted to each other through the device of the state as protagonist. That is, the fit of jurisdiction and territory appeared to be the normal and typical state of affairs, broken by illegality, rebellion, dissent, or other exceptional circumstances. But if we are looking for evidence of the porosity of jurisdiction, then the efforts of a handful of Jesuit missionaries, for the most part Italian and Portuguese, to win converts among the educated elite of seventeenth-century China furnishes a wonderful and concentrated set of examples.[4] Here you have—in the prime vigor of the state-idea in its European form—an interaction between two vast and complex cultural ensembles, each built up over thousands of years, communicating through the tiny pipeline of a few priests—no more than twenty or so resident in China at any one time—and their Chinese interlocutors. The interaction forms, to my mind, a precious starting point for investigating the history and value of information networks. It gives us not only a suggestive model of the global interrelationship of cultures but also an alternative history to the triumphalism of information exchange so often found in the study of social interactions.

And finally, it is an episode in the history of print media that inverts some of the relations typically described in European accounts of the Gutenberg era.

♦

The following is an explanation of the role of printing and the circulation of ideas in Western Europe circa 1620, as narrated by a Jesuit missionary to his friend, an inquisitive Chinese scholar of the late Ming dynasty.

[*Missionary:*] It is the custom of the Western countries to put an extremely high value on teaching through books, and for this reason, the state becomes the ears and eyes of the people.[5] Where the convictions (*xin zhi* 心志) of the people are concerned, once a single falsehood has been given currency, nothing is free of falsehood. So our former sages took special pains to guard against error. Those who are in charge of doctrine must be the sages and worthies of the time, elevated far beyond the mass of people in intelligence, discrimination, and learning. Whatever books are to be circulated must first undergo the examiners' personal inspection, and only when they are seen to be free of the slightest flaw are they given to the press. Printing [in the Western countries] is an art of the greatest refinement and extremely expensive; only those with great resources can command it. Commoners are not allowed to possess this power; for rather, each country punishes the crime of private publication with the heaviest pains, even that of death. For this reason there has never been such a thing as the printing of unauthorized books; the law does not permit it, and the people would not tolerate it.

Reply: I am amazed at what I hear and can hardly believe it. In our country of China, there are many who chatter away in writing and spread it about through private printing, and the state is still unable to forbid the unlicensed publication of books, so that their number increases daily.[6]

The source of this quotation is a book of questions and answers about Roman Catholic doctrine composed by a layman convert named Yang Ting-yun 楊廷筠 (1557–1621) and issued under the title *Dai yi pian* 代疑篇, *A Treatise for Removing Doubts*. In this passage we find, along with a number of extraordinary inaccuracies, a delectable anticipation of many motifs of contemporary globalism, including the "yes, but" many of us feel about the Internet as a repository of knowledge. Behind this passage lies a history of converging technologies.

As many readers will know, printing was a Chinese invention. Movable type, the technical refinement on whose basis printing in alphabetic languages became economically feasible, was either a Chinese or a Korean invention, but one that for practical reasons remained dormant in China until the nineteenth century. From the eleventh century to the nineteenth, the dominant publishing technology was that of the incised board. Like many Chinese inventions, it combined simplicity with flexibility.[7] A fair copy of the text to be printed is written on paper and then pasted, written side down, on a slab of hard wood; the blank areas inside and between characters are carved away, leaving a mirror image of the text in relief. To print a copy of the page, one has only to ink the block and press paper against it. Once the blocks are carved, they can serve to print one copy or thousands. The skills required for carving the blocks are quite rudimentary; even an illiterate can do the carving once the paper has been pasted down.

As a result of this technology, Chinese books were cheap and plentiful—indeed, from a Ming dynasty perspective, getting cheaper all the time, with surplus labor in outlying regions contributing low-cost products to the metropolitan markets. Matteo Ricci (1552–1610), the founder of the Jesuit mission in China, noted "the multitude of books that are printed in this kingdom, everyone [publishing] in his own house"—an exaggeration to be sure, but accurate as to potential.[8] Since there was no need to hire and train specialist labor or to invest in complex machinery, and no need to calculate press runs before distributing and reusing the type, publishing in early modern China could be a cottage industry, decentralized and impossible to control except through penalties and confiscations of already published books.[9]

Comparatively speaking, then, there is some truth to Yang Tingyun's statement that in Europe, "printing is an art of the greatest refinement and extremely expensive, and only those with great resources can command it." This is what the Chinese scholar of his dialogue has in mind when he says admiringly: "In our country of China, there are many who chatter away in writing and spread it about through private printing, and the state is still unable to forbid the unlicensed publication of books, so that their number increases daily." The problem, as stated, is that the impossibility of controlling a low-cost form of publication leads to the multiplication of heterodox doctrines. The state has its own printing workshops, of course, and controls education through its monopoly on the rewards of education; from the state's point of view, however, official publications are too easily crowded out through the operations of an informational version of Gresham's Law. The missionary speaker responds to this felt absence of authority by constructing for his Chinese hearer a Western utopia in which the power of the press is restricted to those who possess governmental and moral authority, "the sages and worthies of the time, elevated far beyond the mass of people in intelligence, discrimination, and learning." Anyone not so qualified who dares to issue books is put to death.

As these two speakers, channeling through their dialogue a vast global exchange, represent their native economies of information distribution to each other, one has the disorienting sense of four centuries of history that might have been quite different. If this little dialogue had become the foundation of East-West cultural exchange, we might now be in the habit of contrasting Chinese free enterprise and liberty of information with European despotism.[10] Maybe that ignores too many contributing factors. At the very least, we can recognize, mirror-fashion, in this forgotten dialogue the despotic model against which later political thinkers will build up their profile of Western freedom. Here despotism is lauded as a Western achievement in centralization and efficiency against which China falls lamentably short. Here, perhaps for the first time, the idea of Europe is mobilized for the purpose of influencing Chinese cultural politics, and part of the piquancy of the situation is that we cannot know whether the inventor of this intercultural gambit was "Chinese" or "European."

In this dream of centralized intellectual control, the university plays a prominent part. Church and state in this account are indistinguishable, and the justification as well as the means for state censorship derives from the structure of the university as the institutional form of the hierarchy of sciences. The dialogue's Chinese speaker expresses astonishment at the bibliographic claims made for the libraries of Europe—in particular, that the religious theories expounded by the Jesuit missionaries are backed up by more

than ten thousand works of moral philosophy.[11] In response to his amaze-
ment, the European scholar explains:

Now the scholars of the Western countries consider that morals and principle are
the food whereby the inmost nature (*xing* 性) is nourished and believe that exhaustive contemplation is the means of attaining Heaven—a saying honored by all in our
home countries, without distinction of age, sex, or rank. Therefore morals and principle daily expand their scope, and the teaching of books daily extends its reach. The
greatest science of all is the *Study of Heaven*, called *Theologia*. This study is based on a
book called the *Summa*. . . . All the doubts that obstruct the human mind, it collects,
analyzes, and decisively refutes. You can well imagine how many volumes are taken
up by this science alone. Next comes the *Study of Men*, or *Philosophia*: the task of this
science is the investigation of things and the examination of reasons, and the books
devoted to it are almost as many as those of the Study of Heaven. Next come charters and laws; next calendars and computation; next medicine; next [? ? two characters missing]; of these several sciences, some are theoretical (*shuo li* 說理), some historical (*ji shi* 記事). Whatever in them can benefit the lives of the people is applied
to their daily needs. Poetry, rhapsodies, lyrics, and essays are also gathered into
books, but those in authority do not use these as a means of recruiting officials, and
scholars do not use them as a means of attaining renown.

Someone said: The crushing mass of publications today mostly consists of these
very poems, rhapsodies, lyrics, and essays. You tell me, however, that these productions are not recognized by the state; there must, then, not be much variety of literary composition in your countries. Or is it that unauthorized writings are allowed to
multiply, and unlicensed editions are scattered among the rest?

And thereupon, as an answer, follows the elucidation of the advantages of
expensive European publishing. Note the chain of ideas. From the question
about the number of books, the speaker glides into the institutional position
of books, writing, and teaching. The thought of the institution is for our
speaker inseparable from the hierarchy of sciences, recognizable as the model
of the medieval university divided into a higher faculty of theology and the
lower faculties of humanistic and practical learning. The identification of the
superior faculty with the highest authority then leads immediately to the
power to publish and condemn, the state becoming (through the faculty of
theology) "the ears and eyes of the people." Nowhere is it suggested that the
interests of church and state might diverge, or that the university, the Inquisition, and the political censors might derive their authority from different
sources. Yang Tingyun's Western utopia treats all these as a single power. In
its context of 1621, the nostalgia is many-layered and rich.

We would be selling Yang Tingyun short if we attributed his inaccuracies to a lack of direct information; to see them as strategically calculated false-hoods planted by his missionary informants would be only slightly better. Rather, we have here a coincidence of many desires and failures. Yang's ac-count dreams of a Europe in which the Protestant Reformation, that series of shocks to the solidarity of university, church, and state in which unli-censed publication played an obvious and central role, never occurred, and where the temporal powers wait upon the bidding of the spiritual authorities. By 1621, I doubt that even the most committed proponent of the Counter-Reformation expected to see a return to that idealized *status quo ante*, unless, of course, a miracle should make it possible in China.[12]

Or perhaps a miracle would not be necessary. For the flattering depiction of the European book trade and censoring agencies corresponds to an ob-served desire on the Chinese side and amounts to a proposal for an alliance on the basis of common interests. The proliferation of unauthorized books and, through them, the influence of heterodox schools of thought was a par-ticular vexation for certain intellectuals in late Ming China. The *Dai yi pian* misses no opportunity to hit the "hot buttons" of this group's dissatisfaction. When the personages of Yang's dialogue chafe at "those who chatter away in writing and spread it about through private printing," the reader of 1621 would have known exactly whom they meant and so, too, with a little his-torical summary, may we.

First, a word about the institutional specifics of Chinese thought or phi-losophy. A thinker in traditional China was above all an expounder of texts—and the texts that most mattered to most people in that world were the Confucian classics, works of history, ethics, ritual, statesmanship, and natural philosophy originating between the fifth and second centuries B.C. Both the moral legitimacy of the ruling dynasty and the cultural authority of the scholar-official class grew out of mastery of this canon: the analysis of set passages and the citing of precedents were the basic ingredients of the ex-amination essays whereby one qualified to obtain office.[13] The same norms furnished the yardstick by which one's performance in an official post would be judged. Of course, in any given period, the Classics, or classicism, spoke through a consensus of interpretation. Examinations elicited and guided that consensus. The manias and sympathies of examiners at the various levels were remarked on and discussed, not to mention anticipated by candidates eager to succeed; indeed the examination hall was traditional China's main arena for public debate on ideas and policy, however decorous and gradual the process might be.[14] An inspired thinker with a powerfully coherent vision of the message of the Classics might alter the shared understanding by training students who, after winning approval for a certain style of interpretation, would climb the ranks of officialdom and pass judgment on their younger colleagues, but the system was clearly not designed for promoting innovation.

The hundred or so years preceding the publication of Yang Tingyun's *Treatise for Removing Doubts* had been a time of particular philosophical ferment, which in the end overflowed the narrow bounds set by the examination system and the administrative career. Late Ming thought is a landscape of local schools, many of them centered on a charismatic individual and directed not toward transmitting learning or the wisdom of experience but toward inducing a kind of enlightenment that reveals the morality of the sages and the workings of the world. The historical starting point of this new orientation is usually said to be Wang Yangming's 王陽明 (1472–1529) rejection, circa 1506, of the "knowledge of information" in favor of the innate "knowledge of the mind."[15] Wang's many and diverse followers are thus collectively known as the "school of the mind," or *xinxue* 心學, as opposed to the officially endorsed "school of objective reason," or *lixue* 理學. The mind, in Wang's view, was the source of knowledge rather than a medium that passively awaited knowledge to come to it from outside. Under the heading of "knowledge" were morality and its expression in action.

This redefinition of the mind carries with it a revaluation of the reason for pursuing learning in books, even the Confucian classics. The Classics might instantiate the enlightenment attained by their authors, but the mere study of texts was not the truly philosophical activity. Wang's followers and imitators continued to cite and lecture on Confucian works, but they saw no obstacle to introducing concepts and criteria from Taoist and Buddhist sources. In fact, this was for them a necessary enlargement of the Way.[16] Here, however, one runs into the problem of professional competencies, for the Buddhist and Daoist canons had never been part of the official reading list. Moreover, the recognition of Buddhist or Daoist thought by the examining authorities would require a thorough revision of the values in whose name the state ruled, and that was no trivial undertaking. So when some of Wang's radical disciples, for instance Wang Ji 王畿 (1498–1583) and Wang

Gen 王艮 (1483–1541), attracted to themselves the label of "mad Zen" (*kuang chan* 狂禪) philosophers, the tone of the remark was partly dismissive, partly edgy.[17] To get the sense of "Zen" right, we must imagine what the term would have implied for a member of the Confucian academy. "Zen" stands for some rather scandalous postulates: a rejection of book learning and indeed of any knowledge that could be put into words, a hierarchy of goods that puts enlightenment above study or practical benevolence, and the claim that every man, even in his most banal undertakings, could achieve sagehood. "Mad Zen" sentiments amounted to a rejection of the whole meritocratic scaffolding of upper-class Ming social life—the examination system, the administration of justice in accordance with Confucian principles, the bonds of family and academic lineage.

The years around 1600 would have been the right time to opt out, for the meritocracy's ability to deliver rewards had begun to falter. The power of the traditional ruling class, the literate gentry, was on the wane, as emperors abandoned their authority and governmental business was increasingly transacted by eunuchs and other palace retainers in defiance of the long-standing distribution of powers.[18] The loss of opportunities left a great many intellectuals feeling empty-handed and frustrated; those who stayed in office saw themselves as "righteous elements" duty-bound to resist all challenges to their collective position.[19] The righteous elements had a great deal to complain about, in particular the privileges accorded to palace favorites and the danger that irregular philosophical schools might aspire to the position of national orthodoxy, as reflected by the recognition awarded to syncretic views in the judging of examination essays—two causes of dissatisfaction that generated systematic, coordinated protests. In 1599, to cite a famous incident, the Shenzong emperor (r. 1572–1619) entrusted a major tax-gathering mission to a group of palace eunuchs "with great authority and the power to act absolutely, without answering to any of the mandarins of the government."[20] The eunuchs' rapacity, together with indignation at the emperor's disregard for the constitutional powers of the mandarinate, led to numerous written protests. One of the protesters was Yang Tingyun, subsequently the author of the *Treatise for Removing Doubts*, but in 1599 provincial inspector of Jiangxi province and energetically involved in a Buddhist lay movement for moral reform.

The political crisis of 1599 gave form to a sense of peril among traditionally minded officials. Many veterans of the 1599 campaign—Yang Tingyun again prominent among them—are found in the years 1608–25 among the adherents of the Donglin 東林 Academy, a political and intellectual movement whose designated targets were the palace faction in government and the syncretic movements in philosophy.[21] It is also a crucial, though rarely noticed, episode in the history of Catholicism in China. The narration of that crisis in the *Journals* of Matteo Ricci, founder of the Jesuit mission, is strongly pitched in favor of the mandarin resistance and gives the first hint that Ricci is taking sides as a participant in local struggles, not just observing China as a visitor and theological showman. And as a consequence, the meaning of Catholicism in China—its Chinese meaning—was redefined.

The early history of the Chinese mission is dominated, and understandably so, by the extraordinary cultural adaptability of Father Ricci, who adopted Chinese dress, manners, and language and went forth to try to win over the intellectual leaders of his day.[22] Ricci was a remarkable man, whose flexibility has only recently received general approval—in his own day he was suspected by his fellow missionaries of compromising the essentials of the faith in order to gain converts more easily. But what did he represent to his Chinese acquaintances? How did he win the attention of someone like Yang Tingyun?

If, during the first years of Ricci's dialogue with Confucian texts and other scholars, his doctrine had any place in Chinese society, it would have been seen as the teachings of a small syncretic academy—deemed harmless so long as it consisted of a few padres lecturing on the manner of pursuing virtue. As the *Ming Dynastic History* puts it, "Ricci's books were such as the Chinese had never encountered before, and so, for a time, those desirous of strange and new things (*hao yi zhe* 好異者) gave him their approval."[23] The trademark, as it were, of this strange and new thing was a little book Ricci composed in 1595, called *Jiaoyou lun* 交友論, or *On Friendship*.[24] The book circulated widely, gaining Ricci a measure of fame and many curious visitors. Now, in late Ming China "friendship" had become something of a code word, as many of the levelers and ranters of *xinxue* claimed that the hierarchical relations of father and child, ruler and subject, elder and younger, husband and wife, were corrupt and should be replaced by friendship, a relation among equals entered into by personal choice.[25] To promote friendship was to look benevolently on a society without structure. Ricci's circle of visitors naturally

included many philosophical independents, of whom two merit special mention in his journals:

> At this time [early 1599] there lived in Nanking a *zhuangyuan* 狀元 who . . . having
> lost his office, stayed at home in great comfort, venerated by all.[26] He was given to
> preaching [the syncretic doctrine of] the three sects of China, in which he was
> learned. He kept in his house one of the most famous men of our time in China,
> named Li Zhuowu 李卓吾 [i.e., Li Zhi 李贄], who, having previously held high of-
> fice in the government and having served as governor of a region of many cities,
> abandoned his office and family and shaved his head, living as a Buddhist monk.
> And, because of his erudition . . . he had earned great fame and was followed by
> many disciples in a new sect of his own founding. . . . These two scholars welcomed
> Father Ricci. . . . [Li Zhi] received him with many other scholars of his sect, and
> they debated the moral law, except that Li Zhi would not dispute with Ricci or con-
> tradict him, for he said that our law was true.[27]

It is a pleasant scene of harmonious multiculturality and possible only because of the marginality of all the participants. Li Zhi could express approval
of Ricci's doctrines because he, as a philosophical outsider, was not in the
business of restricting the possession of doctrinal authority; nothing he advocated had to be denied to make room for Ricci. Ricci, in turn, was careful
to restrict the discussion to ethics. A few years later, when Li Zhi reappears
in the *Journals*, it is with a different role to play.

> But God with his divine Providence suddenly came to our aid, reproving his and our
> enemies. The occasion was given by that mandarin who abandoned his office,
> shaved his head, and became a monk, Li Zhi. Now that he was completely caught
> up and engulfed in his desire to leave a great name for himself and his doctrine, he
> went about acquiring disciples and writing many books, in which, to show his clev-
> erness, he rebuked those ancient Chinese who were considered saints and exalted
> those who were considered evil.[28] For this reason, since Li was staying in a city near
> Peking with the intention of presenting himself at court, where many desired his
> presence, one of the court advisors submitted a very strongly worded memorial to
> the Emperor, asking that Li be flogged and his books burned.[29]
>
> The Emperor ordered that Li be brought immediately to Peking and that the
> woodblocks of all his works be confiscated.
>
> So this man came to Peking in great fear. And seeing himself in such dishonor
> despite his great age (for he was over seventy years old), while in the prison and be-
> fore receiving any punishment, he cut his throat with a knife and died, thus misera-
> bly escaping from the hands of his enemies.

On this occasion Feng [Qi] 馮琦, the president of the Board of Rites,[30] submitted to the emperor a most strongly worded memorial against those mandarins and scholars who, abandoning the doctrine of their master Confucius, followed the doctrine of the idols [i.e., Buddhism] and created a scandal in the court. . . .

On receiving [the Emperor's] favorable answer, the president of the Board of Rites issued a proclamation to all the schools and tribunals that gave examination for academic degrees (of which he is the superintendent), in which he ordered that examination essays should make no mention of the [Buddhist] idols unless it be to refute them; no degree would be awarded to anyone who should do otherwise. And with this the Court seemed to have changed its face and to enter on a new age.[31]

Why should the syllabus for the Chinese civil-service exam matter to Matteo Ricci? Between 1599 and 1602, Ricci clearly took the Confucian conservatives' side in the Chinese political controversies—and it seems to me that from the Chinese point of view, as opposed to the Roman, that sort of partisanship mattered more than the compatibility or incompatibility of Catholic faith and Confucian morals. The test of Ricci's partisanship is his analysis of the political situation, in which he is clearly speaking as if he were one of those who stood to lose something by a broadening of the examination syllabus. He was not, of course; we need to see this as an imaginative self-projection. As a consequence of that investment, Ricci now describes grasping eunuchs and heterodox philosophers as "God's enemies, and ours." The force of that condemnation should not lead us to forget that it was only from the Donglin perspective that those two groups were linked. Eunuch rule and "mad Zen" philosophizing were not the same thing at all, but from a traditionalist point of view they were twin effects of a single cause—the Confucian scholar-gentry's loss of dominance.[32] Eunuch rule deprived them of the power to interpret the emperor's will; syncretic schools sidestepped their authority to interpret the words of the sages. Ricci now begins to present himself as having a remedy to these problems. For these eminently political reasons, then, his friendly coexistence with such free thinkers as Li Zhi is at an end. And Ricci's own aims change. Having removed any possible confusion, or so he may have thought, between his teaching and those of the late Ming new religions, Ricci will take aim at bigger game. No longer simply seeking to have Christianity tolerated as a minority sect, he will aspire to see it integrated with the most prestigious of majority doctrines.[33]

Yang Tingyun's conversion was itself a result of Ricci's choosing to make the cause of literati discontent (soon to crystallize as the Donglin Academy) his own. Another interpretation of globalism by Yang Tingyun rings variously according to whether we take it as Catholic theology or as Confucian statecraft:

Everyone knows that in China are found the two heresies (*yiduan* 異端) of Buddhism and Taoism, but not everyone is aware that the wide world contains a great many religions like these, with various names and doctrines. Some enjoy favor for a brief moment of time, others are honored in a limited space; some are attached to schools of thought, others derive from one man's private desires. As a result, what one religion establishes as true another religion cannot accept; what this one proclaims that one cannot believe. No such teaching can be called a truly catholic faith (*gong jiao* 公教, "universal teaching"). There is only one Lord (*zhu* 主); just as the ten thousand different kingdoms all live under one heaven, so they should all worship one Lord. My bodily shape is that of a man; the ten thousand things are given me so that I may care for my body; this body is also endowed with a spiritual nature (*ling xing* 靈性) that is the body's lord (*zhu* 主), and I seek moral philosophy so as to perfect my spirit. The ten thousand kingdoms are no different from this! Whatever has life, has it as a gift from the Lord; so each must be grateful and never tolerate the thought of rebelling.

The analogies of the passage are familiar from the Chinese discourse on monarchy—just as there is one sky over our heads, one sun in the sky, one head on the body, so the world should have one ruler, to wit, the emperor of China.[34] Note also the logical link between the universal spread of a religion and the universal nature of its object of worship; each guarantees the other. Now for the contrary case, in the dialogue's section on the history of Buddhism:

The members of the Society of Jesus travel far and wide to spread their religion. Many of them have been to India and are familiar with the religion of the country and have studied its books. The moral reasoning of the Indian books is gross and superficial; the believers are low and common people; it is really rather a cult (*si jiao* 私教) than a religion. None of the kingdoms around India honors the Buddhist religion; rather, each has its own worship. There are exceeding many of these, and none of them matches the others. Who would have thought that on entering China this religion would be honored by all? No one in its land of origin could have believed this.

Yang Tingyun continues his criticisms: Chinese Buddhism, for all its glorious reputation, is the result of unsupervised literary activity. When the Buddhist scriptures were first brought to China around 300 A.D., no one was found who could understand them. The sutras were translated roughly, by guesswork, and there was no one to correct the drafts. . . . Afterwards, as the paths [between India and China] became better known and the understanding of scholars improved, Buddhism adopted elements of the philosophies of Laozi 老子 and Liezi 列子 and the Pure Conversations [of early Taoism]. Continually under the threat of invasion by the five barbarian tribes, the emperors of the Six Dynasties ruled over a tiny parcel of territory. Lacking an enlightened sovereign or sagely lord, the scholars responsible for preserving the continuity of learning went into retirement or pursued futile discussions. Unhealthy doctrines began to proliferate. . . . So the Buddhist doctrines contain wisdom and folly, the ideas of worthy men and those of good-for-nothings, all intermingled.[35]

The unhealthy textual corpus of Buddhism is explained by the lack of political order in the China that proved so hospitable to its half-understood message. In the absence of an enlightened prince, there are no zealous scholars and no consistent doctrine. That is to say, the most nearly universal jurisdiction produces the most nearly universal religion. Crumbling empires produce incoherent, patchy cults. And the porosity both political and intellectual of early China (as Yang depicts it) plainly refers by analogy to the crisis of the present, when the integrity of Confucian teaching is menaced even in the citadel of the examination system by an indiscriminate syncretism. For Yang, it is obvious that the *gong jiao* of Catholicism is of a different species altogether from the *si jiao* that a maverick like Li Zhi might concoct.

Yang's praise of costly European printing is thus no incidental remark: it connects directly to the unmentioned core of what the Jesuits can offer China, namely, a rationale for unlimited jurisdiction over communications (including the examination system as a form of communication). That would assure the political supremacy of specialists in doctrine—scholars, priests, professors. Yang makes Catholicism the ideal image of Confucianism, inwardly solid and unlimited in authority. And it is surely relevant, too, that the ecclesiastical authorities in Yang's imagined Europe rule through the power of writing, teaching, the university, the faculty of theology. They directly possess the powers that the literate class of China exercises only by the special favor of the emperor.

In institutional terms, the attitudes of the Donglin group were most frequently translated into action by the members of the censorial service, those reviewing officials whose task was to serve as the "ears and eyes" of the emperor. And in 1621, as the Donglin faction seemed to be climbing into the command posts of the administrative apparatus, once again men who had come into prominence through the censorate were taking the initiative.[36] At a moment of instability, indeed crisis, in the Chinese ordering of jurisdictions, Yang Tingyun proposes the model of jurisdiction that most radically answers the prayers of the Donglin community and of its activists, the officials of the censorate. Monotheism and its realization on earth—namely, the universal church—come to patch the tattered garments of late Ming Confucian orthodoxy.

To summarize this lengthy labor of contextualization: Yang Tingyun's descriptions of European religious authority exemplify a media-centered globalism in several senses, some of which are bound to react in an unstable way with other senses. His description instantiates a form of global culture because, first and most obviously, it calls on information from widely separated areas of the world and links them in a comparison by drawing from various streams of human experience lessons about the historical process.[37] It involves claims to global authority in a second sense, for the reason that it brings together the strategies of two groups, Catholic priests and Confucian statesmen, who see themselves as radiating outward from their capitals to reform the whole world. And finally, Yang's comparative enterprise has as its midpoint the phantasm of a ubiquitous and already global jurisdiction, a "regime of truth." It accomplishes the considerable feat of aligning the figures through which two cultures think about authority—the emperor, the sage, the church universal, the Inquisition, the examination system, the Confucian classics, the Almighty.

Read as a political treatise, Yang's dialogue amounts to an invitation to the Confucian hierarchy to reform itself on the model of Catholicism. Does its persuasiveness not rest, however, on an ambiguity? To offer the fable of Europe as a model or analogy for China was one thing. But if Yang's readers had understood him as proposing the *extension* of the universal jurisdiction of the pope to the Chinese empire, then the possibilities of harnessing Donglin dissatisfaction would surely have vanished: the interest of the Confucians did not lie in adding another, remoter, emperor to the imperial system they already had. Papal authority is good to think with, to dream on, even in some respects to imitate, but no more. (The same could be said, *mutatis mutandis*, for European imaginings of the Chinese emperor or Great Khan.)[38] That is, the alien forms of authority are acceptable as figure, metaphor, model, analogy, or ideal, but as a basis for practical action they lose their charm. A certain form of cultural globalism lives and dies between these two conditions.[39]

In the European context of 1620, too, Yang's account has a dreamlike simplicity. After the Edict of Nantes (1598) and James I's adoption (1603) of the Act of Supremacy, the most vigorous defender of papal authority, Cardinal Robert Bellarmine, had no higher claim to vindicate than the Vatican's right to exert *indirect* temporal power.[40] No European sovereign could aspire to the Chinese emperor's undivided spiritual and temporal competence. Hobbes may have argued that "it is the Civill Soveraign, that is to appoint Judges, and Interpreters of the Canonicall Scriptures: for it is he that maketh them Laws. . . . In summe, he hath the Supreme Power in all causes, as well Ecclestiasticall, as Civill,"[41] but he was trying to impose consistency on a fractured landscape of rights and allegiances (fractured even before the English Civil War). Yang's portrait of the European reign of virtue joins the theories of both Chinese and European polity at precisely those points where each fails to fulfill its role. This multiple ambiguity around the notion of power—the discrepancy between theories of authority and its effective exercise, joined to the unresolved question of whether the instances of power described are to be seen as analogous or continuous—is the medium in which Yang's Confucian-Catholic hybrid lives.

What do these extremely restricted conditions tell us about global culture?

The early history of the China missions has recently been the subject of several books written with the aim of clarifying, through so salient an example, the history and possibilities of intercultural understanding—of a hybrid global culture, if you will.[42] Jacques Gernet's *Chine et christianisme* (China and the Christian impact) offers the richest documentary backing, with exquisitely chosen excerpts from anti-Christian polemics and notations by puzzled bystanders. Gernet reaches a skeptical conclusion suited to the temper of our times. Ricci's enterprise was doomed, says Gernet, because the frames of moral and philosophical reference, the very ontologies proper to China and early modern Europe, were too far out of kilter. Describing the adoption of certain Christian practices by sympathetic eighteenth-century Chinese, Gernet observes that "thanks to purely formal modifications, certain transferences between old and new have taken place while leaving the traditional ways of thought intact. The missionaries may have believed that their converts had become Christians, but it is permissible to doubt the existence of the radical change of mind that a true conversion implies."[43]

The language of appearance and reality shows where Gernet stands. He conceives of the contact between the Catholic missionaries and their Chinese listeners in the very way that the Roman curia did—principally as a matter of translation, and of one-way translation at that.[44] "Genuine conversion" for Gernet involves accepting a set of beliefs; beliefs are grounded in words, and since translation results in ambiguities, conversions achieved through translations are not trustworthy. The implicit standard is that of equivalence between native and foreign semantics, an equivalence that any attentive semanticist can quickly dissolve. So we are left with a linguistic determinism aspiring to philosophical status, and that is ultimately what Gernet delivers: "Our Reason is no more universal than is the grammar of our languages."[45]

The equivalence model seems a poor footing from which to begin to think about translation in cases like this, however, in which even simple lexical equivalences have to be made, not discovered. Do not these conditions oblige us to think about "universality" in a different way, a way closer perhaps to Yang Tingyun's vision of religion as institution than to Gernet's disappointed ecumenicism? When, for example, Matteo Ricci translated *sanctus* by the term *sheng* 聖, the habitual epithet for Confucius and other sages of antiquity and also a frequent qualifier for the emperor's majesty, he was surely not arguing that the two words meant the same thing, since they obviously do not. Rather, he was aspiring to harness some of the energies of the Chinese term to the new situations in which he would henceforth use it.

That is to say, the job of the translator is not reproductive, representing a pre-existing meaning in a new milieu, but rather expository and applicational—the task of making something mean something to somebody.[46] Its political counterpart would be not jurisdictions but alliances. Now, alliances do not have a good reputation in political theory, perhaps because it is in their nature to arise where jurisdictions come to an end. The word "unprincipled" perhaps expresses their uneasy moral and cognitive status. But for that very reason alliances deserve to be prominent among the models and metaphors of cultural contact, because it is through choosing sides that emissaries become participants in the civilization they have come to visit. There is an affinity between such participation and the notion that translations are acts, not discoveries. If translation is to be seen not as a matter of finding equivalences between vocabularies but as one of making the meanings of one speech community mean something to another speech community, then we should give our first attention to the pragmatic intervenings and meddlings that prepare the way for exchanges of meanings—the workshop, in short, of equivalences. Global culture, if there is to be such a thing, will be interesting, not primarily as a problem-free network of access to cultural goods but as a landscape of point-for-point *ad hoc* settlements.

So, for example, even the language of omnipotence has to be brokered with small specific interests. When we see Yang Tingyun doing that, we should put out of our minds the notion of an identity or compatibility between Confucianism and Catholicism and think, instead, of the model of the *pun*—that instant of ambiguity whereby two meanings are suspended in a single signifier and two speech communities can coincide in their language, although not in their frames of reference. A connected series of such puns is an *allegory*.[47] What Yang Tingyun proposed to his readers, in the guise of universal jurisdiction, was an allegory connecting various points of the Chinese and European imaginations of power. Its viability could be sustained (and this is true of the literary allegories as well) only so long as its readers did not see themselves obliged to choose between its coincident meanings. The allegory is unstable, suspenseful, loosely related to facts, latently contradictory—and so, as I see it, it furnishes a model for a global media culture that addresses everybody all the time but does not stop to integrate all the responses.

♦

The history of religions is, one could easily argue, the history of the media. The prohibition of idols, the periodic bouts of iconoclasm within Christianity, the mutual recognition of the three Peoples of the Book, the symbiosis of Protestantism and printing, radio, television, and other devices for "broadcasting"[48] (a term inspired by the Parable of the Sower, which is also and originally a parable of the mediatic address): there is certainly enough in these ruptures, these shifts from one vehicle to another, to suggest a history not of doctrines but of the relations between doctrine and its material or technical substratum. A broader view of this issue would have to go beyond Europe and take in the role of books, images, printing, and now television in the expansion of other religious traditions, particularly East Asian Buddhism. "Globalatinization" there may be, but it is well to remember that Latin is also a character-set, and one transmitted through particular technologies.[49]

It might well be otherwise, but I suspect that the story of religion told through media would necessarily be haunted by the religious story-pattern of a repeated, ongoing dematerialization. For media dematerialize: they uproot practices and practitioners from the immediacy of a place, an idol, a sacred saying, a relic, and put them on the path of replication and universalization, "unto the ends of the earth." The more sophisticated a medium is, the more effectively it transfers the important truths of the teaching (those that will come to be seen as the important truths) to the new vehicles, to the new converts; the religious tie is reformulated in just this way by each of its successive realizations. This chain of transferences not only echoes in form the logic of dematerialization common to many religions, it determines the role of the media as means whereby the teachings are spread. However great the role ascribed to the breakthroughs in media, however necessary and intimate the relation between teaching and the means of teaching, the doctrine remains the pre-existing thing to which this or that arrangement of communicative technique subsequently happened.

That is a particular understanding of the relations of religious messages and their media—just how particular, these pages are meant to show. For as if to perturb this order, the story of the Jesuits coming to grips with Chinese printing gives us an instance of an expanding religion encountering a technology that was *too advanced* for it. To exert the kind of control over media that the Jesuits' allies ascribed to the authorities of their half-imagined Europe, they would have had to possess the levers of the examination system, the imperial library, and the rewarding of degree holders—the outcomes of literacy rather than its supply network. Two powerful and tireless Manchu emperors—Kangxi 康熙 (r. 1661–1722) and Qianlong 乾隆 (r. 1736–96)—made as good a job of that assignment as could be made, and not even they could intercept all "unhealthy doctrines." (Qianlong's inquisition, the most comprehensive of its kind, banned the works of both Li Zhi and his antagonists in the Donglin group, the one for unorthodoxy, the others for partisan spirit.)[50] Indeed, the technology was too advanced for any of the players to control, which may explain why the reactive mode of censorship has become habitual for Chinese readers and rulers—a customary price to pay for social order—in the centuries since Yang Tingyun wrote.

As an ideology of communication, globalism looks forward to its definitive realization—its apocalypse—when all obstacles to circulation, be it of information or of merchandise, will have disappeared: an informational space both pure and unbounded. The fortunes of global communication at the juncture represented by Ricci and his successors suggest a less sanguine prediction: that the effort to extend communicative space itself generates impurities and limits, and that it is chiefly these, more than some presumably unvarying content, that are communicated. The relation between worldwide informational networks and all-seeing censorship that founded the seventeenth-century dialogue between China and Europe would be, then, one case of a broader paradox in the sociology of communication.

3

The Prestige of
Writing: 文, Letter, Picture,
Image, Ideography

Mais ne point posséder la clé, n'être point instruit des règles, des signes, des correspondances, ne pouvoir deviner le sens de ce que l'on voit,—n'est-ce point réduire ce qui se voit à ce qui se voit,—*à la figure et au mouvement?*—Rien de plus cartésien, je pense?
—Paul Valéry, "Le Retour de Hollande"

. . . because they hold that all existents differ among themselves only through figure, order or orientation: thus A differs from N in figure, AN from NA in order, Z from N in orientation.
—Aristotle, *Metaphysics* 985 b 18

The disparagement of writing is a motif possible in any tradition that has writing.[1] Writing is most often faulted as being inadequate to represent speech or thought. One response to the inadequacy of writing has been to exalt some other kind of writing—occasionally a language reformer's pet project, but more frequently the writing of the angels, of the citizens of some utopia, of the scholars of some faraway kingdom, or of the forces of nature. Imagined writings of this sort telescope critique and critique's wishful compensation. They attribute wonders—*praestigia*—to a medium most often noticed for its falterings.

Since Chinese writing became known in Europe, it has often been pressed into service as the model of this perfected writing.[2] This enthusiasm must appear outlandish to those whose "native" writing-system is Chinese.[3] But this difference in opinion is not enough to show that the indigenous and foreign perceptions of Chinese writing are at variance or even that the tales told of Chinese script do not stand up to linguistic scrutiny: there is an inventive element to all intercultural interpretation, a fit between its observations and the intellectual needs of its proponents, that expert testimony simply shoves aside. The proper way to analyze an intellectual tangle of this sort is not, it seems to me, to hold it to the standard of specialist univocity but to situate it ethnographically among the conceptions it echoes or answers. Perhaps by doing this we may be able to distinguish the elements of these utopias that still beckon to us from those that have become fodder for intellectual historians.

The Power of Wen

The sixth-century literary critic Liu Xie 劉勰 never set out to diagnose what might cause twentieth-century Europeans and Americans to fall in love with Chinese literature, but in the "Yuan dao" 原道 (Tracing the Way) chapter of his *Wenxin diaolong* 文心雕龍, he certainly put his finger on it. "The power of *wen*," wrote Liu Xie, "is great indeed: for was it not born together with heaven and earth? . . . The mind comes into existence, and words are established; words are established, and *wen* gives forth its brilliance—the very way of nature" 文之爲德也大矣，與天地並生者何哉！. . . 心生而言立，言立而文明，自然之道也.[4] The passage and its predecessors and variants throughout the Chinese tradition have inspired eloquence, subtlety, etymological zeal, and much sympathetic imagination.[5] Liu Xie was certainly no disparager of writing—if he measured the writing of humans against the majestic writing of nature, it was to enlarge the former. *Wen* 文, the word I have hesitated to translate, smoothes the path of Liu's argument. It combines in its several meanings many of the attractions of Chinese literature. *Wen* is (to cite several dictionaries at once) "markings; patterns; stripes, streaks, lines, veins; whorls; bands; writing, graph, expression, composition; ceremony, culture, refinement, education, ornament, elegance, civility; civil as opposed to military; literature (specifically belletristic prose in its distinction from poetry)." The coexistence of these various meanings is suggestive; to say "*wen* is *wen*" is never just a tautology.[6] Indeed a great deal of writing about the Chinese language and Chinese literature (mostly but not exclusively by nonnative speakers) has said exactly this by drawing on textual evidence and close reading to amplify the assertion that, for example, "*wen* in sense 16 is really or ultimately the same thing as *wen* in sense 7." The most frequent variant is that *wen* in the sense of literary writing is best illumined by analogy to one of the other senses: literary writing as inherent pattern, writing as civilization, literature as an outgrowth of the Chinese writing system.

It is this last possibility—surrounded by overtones of some of the others—that will occupy the ethnographer of literary culture. For it is notable that, despite the decay of many simplistic illusions about the singularities of the Chinese written language, the motif of a *contrast* between alphabetic writing and ideogrammatic writing as modes of representation survives to direct many accounts of the contrasts between "Chinese" literature and "Western" literature. (This level of generality comes with the territory, unfortunately; maybe after a few more decades of mutual research, the geographical blocs will melt.) It is as if the initial error about writing systems, now discredited, has had to migrate into considerations of style, genre, ideology, philosophy, and so forth. Accordingly I shall not insist on a genealogical connection among my exhibits, only a chain of related homologies; although I may have skeptical words for this or that instance of the contrast of which I speak, not all instances are equally pernicious or unfounded.

First, Chinese writing versus the alphabet. Most writings on the concept of *wen* subscribe to a view that Chinese writing is directly semantic and symbolizing in nature: unlike the alphabetic transcription of a word, which breaks down into letters without intrinsic meaning—*cenemes*, in Louis Hjelmslev's terminology—a Chinese term, already meaningful, can, in the view of those I shall call ideogrammatists, always be split or traced to simple *pleremes*, or inherently meaning-bearing units.[7] At the level where the pleremes of Chinese writing break down into mere strokes, there is nothing left for the theory of writing and language associated with the word *wen* to discuss. And yet that is the level at which writing appears as pure syntax, as figures about which it is appropriate to ask how they are put together, not what they stand for. The "syntactic" interrogation of writing holds gratifications that are no less great for being delayed. ("Syntax," the reader will have surmised, is here taken in the broadest sense. In Greek the term meant "composition of parts into a whole"; its use by some modern linguists to denote word-order relations is a narrow one that obscures the word's place in intellectual history.)[8] I shall first discuss the theory of plerematic writing in some of its more baroque forms and end by arguing that the eventual fading-out of the pleremes into pure cenematic structure is not the end of *wen*, or of civilization either for that matter; that is, I will try to argue for the interest of the strokes *as strokes*, not primarily as signs *of* anything, and I will work to win some of the authoritative classical texts over to my side.

"It Passes Between Two Terms"

My first example will be drawn from a book that nobody interested in the American understanding of China can ignore, Ernest Fenollosa's *The Chinese Written Character as a Medium for Poetry*.[10] (Fenollosa [1858–1908] taught in the Imperial University in Tokyo. His essay, originally a lecture series given in the United States in 1904–5, was first published in *The Little Review* in 1919, in an adaptation by Ezra Pound.) Having a professional interest in Chinese literature, I know I expose myself to trouble simply for having mentioned Fenollosa's name. As we learn very early in our training, Fenollosa was an enthusiast: in his wonderment at the Chinese language, he vastly over-estimated the number of primary pictograms in the writing system and saw images and parables where a more sober palaeographer would have seen combinations of phonetic clues. The profession has never forgotten his error.[11] The profession is in this case right, but since the profession's response to Fenollosa's ambitious surmising has always been empirical—carried out on the level of examples and presupposing the interpretation of those exam-ples—it may be useful here to present the system of Fenollosa's ideas so that they may provoke a principled, and not merely an atomistic, answer. From a different quarter, Jacques Derrida has cited Fenollosa/Pound as an example of grammatology on nonphonetic, nonphonologocentric principles—not, perhaps, a wise choice.[12] For Fenollosa's rejection of phonetic writing repro-duces in particularly unequivocal terms the very intuition-grounded episte-mology that Derrida's critique of phonetic theories of writing was meant to undermine. Fenollosa's 1904–5 lectures thus have enjoyed a rich afterlife, be-ing variously denounced as the expression of a massive cultural mistake and adopted as the prophecy of poetic developments that their author could not have anticipated and would probably, if given the chance, have rejected.[13]

Fenollosa could not find words enough to praise the Chinese character, which for him was "something much more than arbitrary symbols. It is a vivid shorthand picture of the operations of nature. . . . Chinese poetry . . . speaks at once with the vividness of painting and with the mobility of sounds. . . . In reading Chinese we do not seem to be juggling mental counters, but to be watching *things* work out their own fate" (8–9).[14] In explaining how this can be so, Fenollosa with remarkable subtlety and prescience swerved away from the usual definition of the "ideograph," the definition that makes the character a picture of a thing.

The picture has long had a place in Chinese epigraphy. The great etymologist Xu Shen 許慎 (A.D. 30–124), in the preface to his dictionary *Shuo-wen jiezi* 說文解字, put near the top of his list of character-formation techniques that of *xiang xing* 象形, the "imaging and shaping" of the thing a character referred to.[15] *Xiang xing* was preceded in the list only by the *zhi shi* 指事, or "self-designating," type of character. Xu Shen lived in a time of controversy about the reading of classical texts: when manuscripts from earlier times or outlying regions were transcribed into the standard script the Han dynasty had inherited from the Qin dynasty's script reforms, disagreements could and did ensue. Thus Xu's careful distinction among types of character composition; thus, perhaps, too, a powerful urge to root the methods of etymology in unimpeachable classical sources. The label *xiang xing* is a case in point. It derives from the "Appended Verbalizations" chapters of the *Yi jing* 易經, or *Book of Changes*. In such a context the connotations of "image and shape" easily reach beyond etymology into cosmogony, as a passage of the *Da Dai li ji* 大戴禮記, one of several ritual compendia from the Han, confirms: "Transformation by light and darkness, *imaging, shaping,* and sending forth—that is known as 'generation' or 'life.'"[16]

Later philologists have followed Xu Shen's lead, seeking out or supposing from comparative evidence a primitive picture-writing system as the ancestor of the by now highly conventionalized characters.[17] Writing must have begun as drawing—an idea commonly held of alphabetic scripts as well. But where pictography is most vestigial, the movement *away from* it provides the principle to interpret writing's history. So Hegel in his *Encyclopedia* could easily dismiss the Chinese language as a backward medium of thought because, as he sensibly pointed out, most of the things worth thinking about are not representable in pictures.[18]

Fenollosa, however, as Donald Davie points out, turns the discussion in a new direction.[19] He takes the root meaning of any Chinese character (and thus the root impulse in the elaboration of the writing system) to be the verb, a step in the direction both of greater linguistic sophistication and of a more insistent claim for the character's iconic virtues. The picture writing with which Fenollosa's name is forever associated could not do what Fenollosa saw Chinese writing as doing—transmitting the intuition of force. All nature, according to Fenollosa, is really a vast interplay of verbs, not of nouns; nouns or things are merely "the terminal points, or rather the meeting points, of actions" (10).[20] The European languages of today, "thin and cold," have lost their "primitive sap"; they are "cut and dried as a walking-stick." (24)[21] One can recover the vital energy of the primitive verbs, says Fenollosa, by going back to the roots of the Aryan proto-language: in them we see what must count for Fenollosa as the perfect linguistic situation, expressions "forced upon primitive men by nature itself."[22] But the patchiness of the Aryan record only heightens the importance of the study of Chinese ideograms as a means of "throwing light upon our forgotten mental processes" (21).

By centering his theory of the ideogram on the verb, Fenollosa reintroduces syntax, long absent from discussions of Chinese that had taken as their starting point the character as picture. Pictures are "put together," to be sure, but their "syntax" is not an *ordering* of parts into a sequence or sentence, as Lessing had long before observed in his influential essay *Laocoön*.[23] The sentence is for Fenollosa a category that the Chinese language and nature share. "The type of sentence in nature is a flash of lightning. It passes between two terms, a cloud and the earth" (12).[24] So, too, the Chinese sentence: subject–verb–object. Fenollosa makes Chinese syntax, on precisely the same principles as the ideogram, an image of nature: it is semantic, or meaningful, through and through, and that is the reason behind its particular uncluttered excellence.[25] Ideogrammatic qualities reside not only in the individual Chinese character but in the Chinese sentence, which Fenollosa sees as depicting pictographically a complex of natural actions and relations laid out in a causal line.

Fenollosa's primitivism may strike us as naïve, misguided, potentially vicious, but to be fair we must admit that it is in the service of a linguistic-critical project, a project of desedimentation. Fenollosa's essay moves across the same territory as Nietzsche's essay "On Truth and Lie in the Extra-Moral Sense"—an influential essay in the history of literary theory, if anything is.[26] "So what is truth?" asked Nietzsche. He answered his own Pontius Pilate question with: "A mobile army of metaphors, metonymies, anthropomorphisms, in a word a sum of human relations that have been poetically and rhetorically heightened, translated and ornamented, and after long use come to seem canonical and obligatory to a people: truths are illusions of which one has forgotten that they are illusions."[27] A decade or two later, Fenollosa asked himself the same question and answered: "a flash of lightning pass[ing] between a cloud and the earth." By just such a lightning-stroke, the sentence-form was forced on primitive men by nature. "All truth has to be expressed in sentences because all truth is *the transference of power*" (12), Fenollosa went on to say, glossing himself in strikingly Nietzschean language.[28] The ideogram (and consequently the sentence as an expanded ideogram, an ideogrammatically ordered series of ideograms) is true for Fenollosa because it depicts truly; that is, it depicts, with a transference of power, the operations of nature, which are always transferences of physical force.

There is little point in summoning up the thunder and lightning of present-day criticism to attack such naïve epistemic realism. Naïve it is, and self-proclaimedly so: for Fenollosa, as for Emerson or Wallace Stevens in some of his antinominalist moods, the primitive man is the benchmark of perceptual accuracy because he sees naïvely, sees things as they are without the fog of culture, theology, or artifice.[29] And for the primitivist, the authors of Chinese writing—being, in this nostalgic reconstruction, similarly endowed with the gift of simplicity—point the way back to the truth of undisguised appearances. This hardly merits criticism, but those who like to array their enemies in one United Front will be comforted by the close cousinage of Fenollosa's epistemic standard with the bad habits of ethnographic (and colonial) exoticism. The Chinese—like their written language—are (1) alien, alien because uncivilized, and hence (2) praiseworthy; if they were less unlike us, there would be less reason for the primitivist to hold them up as the model of poetic knowledge.

In Fenollosa's enthusiasm for Chinese word order, we may even see a double exoticism, a European nostalgia complicated by a Japanese one. He had come to Chinese through Japanese teachers, and word order is the main thing that literate speakers of Japanese must consciously train themselves to relearn when they begin reading Chinese texts (as opposed to Japanese texts with a heavy Chinese-character component). Japanese word order, Fenollosa seems to suggest, is an imposition on or rearrangement of that natural scheme of things that Chinese (he believes) more directly reflects, and so the Japanese medium of his training in Chinese poetry disappears. Indeed, language itself disappears: when a sentence's syntax is identical to nature's, it does nothing that things that are not sentences do not do; the "sentence" becomes merely an instance of natural symbolism and disappears as a distinct category of event. Presumably this could not have happened in Japanese, where phonetic writing coexists with logographic writing and word order is both more complex and more demanding of attention (at least to an English speaker).

The Lines of Force

Fenollosa and Pound knew Chinese as a collection of ideograms—snapshots made into metaphors. So did Sergei Eisenstein, who appealed to ideograms as the predecessor of his method of cinematic montage. Mercifully, the word "ideogram" is falling out of our vocabulary: most linguists now prefer "logogram" or some more easily pronounceable regional term such as *kanji* 漢字.[30] Indeed there is room for clarity in the discussion of Chinese writing, especially among scholars of literature. I shall attempt to distinguish among classes often taken as equivalent. By *pictogram* is meant a conventional, usually highly schematized, graphic element whose interpretation is based on a claim of visual resemblance between the graph and its referent.[31] *Logograms* represent the words, or—to acknowledge the vagueness of the term "word"—the distinct meaning-bearing units of a language through a corresponding vocabulary of distinct signs. (The scholarly consensus at present is to consider Chinese characters a mainly logographic system.)[32] In English we spell, or at least we think we do, by matching alphabetic signs with sounds, but it has long been observed that in reading we usually grasp words and simple sentences as unanalyzed wholes, that is, logogrammatically. One test for logogrammatic qualities might be the persistence of a core of reference despite a wide variety of regional or functional pronunciations (as Chinese characters are not said to change their meaning in being pronounced differently by speakers of Mandarin, Cantonese, and so on; or as a single Chinese character used in Japanese may have widely different pronunciations according to whether it is used as part of a noun, a verb, an idiom, a citation in literary language, and so forth). Here too, however, allowance might be made for the role of writing in preserving the continuities of etymology through differences of dialect and period even among European languages: to adopt a panchronic point of view and say that Latin *Caesar* [kai:sar], *Kaiser, tsar, czar, César,* English *Caesar* [see:zer], and so forth are historically the "same" word is indeed to use an etymological root (cloaked in the vagaries of spelling and dialect) as a kind of translinguistic logogram, an interpretant, a mediator of identity among diverse things.[33]

Part of the ignominy attached to *ideogram* derives from the way it is used loosely as a synonym for both the visual and semantic types of reference, a conflation that tends to suggest that all true ideograms or logograms are really pictograms—Fenollosa's thesis, more or less. An antidote would be to proclaim mathematical or logical notation the model for ideography. No one would say that *p* and *q* resemble propositions, particularly since we can form reasonings about *p* and *q* with no definite propositions *p* and *q* in mind. And yet *p* and *q* do for logical notation exactly what an ideogram is supposed to do: they mark the places of ideas.[34] (Moreover, what more challenging example for the classification of writing types than the place-marking symbol "o," which stands in no necessary relation to any particular linguistic or phonetic realization, but can hardly be considered a visual representation of its referent—perhaps a representation of a representation of emptiness?) Pictorial quality accounts for very little of what attested ideograms allow us to do. Symmetrically, histories of writing typically separate the two phases, casting the picture stage as a forerunner of alphabetism and algebra as one of the alphabet's special technical consequences.

As a reference point for the historical development of the concept of ideogrammatic writing, note that the *Encyclopédie* of Diderot and d'Alembert describes Chinese writing as a hieroglyphic writing that has lost consciousness of (or concern for) its pictographic roots and grown accustomed to treating its characters as conventional "marks" for ideas. Praising exactly that advance toward abstraction which Fenollosa condemned, they say: "Chinese writing has gone one step beyond [hieroglyphic]. It casts aside the *images*, and keeps nothing but their abbreviated *marks*, which then proliferate in prodigious number."[35] So ideography is not necessarily pictography: the eighteenth century, at least, was able to see the distinction between an "image" and a "mark." Another case would be the ideographic yet alphabetic languages of such seventeenth-century projectors as Lodwick, Beck, Dalgarno, Kircher, and Wilkins.[36] Those languages assigned to each letter of the alphabet a place on a table of categories: a word, once analyzed into its letter-components, was a set of directions for locating its own meaning. But examples of such idea-writing without pictures may be found closer to hand: punctuation, capitalization, distinctive spellings, quotation marks, parentheses, and so forth modify the import of words and sentences in ways that may have no grammatical or prosodic equivalents in speech.

Ideograms on this pattern are distinct from pictograms: resemblance is not the only clue to their meaning, nor does an ideogram have to be immediately intelligible to earn its name. Fenollosa's investment in the "picture" (and in the sentence as picture) is thus responsible for a deeper misunderstanding about the nature of Chinese writing than those to which China scholars often object. It is a matter of the nature of picto-ideograms, not their frequency or etymological importance. The fact that a Chinese graph seems to stand not for a sound but for a "meaning" or "thing" allows commentators like Fenollosa to believe that it directly represents that thing instead of an intermediate object, say a concept, which for linguistics would take on reality only after it had been expressed in vocal or written form. Ideogrammatism conveniently obliterates history and returns us to the intellectual purity of the caveman's awe at the lightning bolt.

The trouble, however, is that one must become a primitive in order to appreciate the pictographic quality of Chinese writing fully. I find that price a little high and propose a reformulation that restores to consideration the things Fenollosa, with his devotion to lively pictures and juices, had to ignore. If there is a place for the notion of "ideogram"—the writing that posits and makes available for subsequent reference an idea—that place should be everywhere in language, for phonemes, letters, and words, too, are ideal and only conceivable as idealities.[37] Yet "ideas" are knowable not as ideas but through having taken physical (verbal, graphic) form. The bandwidth assigned to the category "ideogram" swells to fill most of the available definitional space as our linguistic skepticism becomes less hospitable to wordless concepts and self-defining phonemes. Perhaps a braver grammatologist will someday propose a definition of "ideography" that includes alphabetic writing as one of its subsets (and a poor cousin no doubt). That move, however, would do away with the everyday category of "ideogram" in opposition to "phonetic writing." All types of writing, indeed all linguistic sound-forms, will then be graphs or enduringly inscribed forms of ideas. "Marks," as the *Encyclopédie* called them. Would we have lost anything valuable?

'The Images of Cogitations'—With and Without Likeness

Thus the term "ideogram," which at one time may have seemed a useful typological classification, has become a thing needing an explanation. The question is no longer What is an ideogram? but rather How did the term "ideogram" come into currency? What was required for the distinction—now part of our linguistic common sense—between phonetic writing and conceptual writing to be made? On what reservoirs of linguistic thought does it draw?

The term itself entered modern European languages with the diffusion of Champollion's decoding of ancient Egyptian script, announced in the *Lettre à Monsieur Dacier* of 1822 and presented more fully in the *Grammaire égyptienne* of 1836–41. Champollion there speaks of "ideographic writing, that is, writing that depicts the ideas and not the sounds of a language" and adds: "The Chinese also use an ideographic script."[38] Champollion established three functional classes for Egyptian characters: *caractères mimiques*, which depict or imitate the objects to which they refer; *caractères tropiques ou symboliques*, which depict an object having a meaningful relation to the thing or idea to which the character refers; and *caractères phonétiques*, used merely to represent or cue for sounds. The first two classes Champollion inherited from the ancient tradition of speculation on Egyptian writing. For centuries it had been customary to treat the Egyptian writing system as entirely pictographic or symbolic. To decipher an inscription was to unfold the meanings of the pictures it contained: thus an eye was held to represent the knowledge of God, the snake biting its tail represented the universe, and so forth. The difference between mimetic and symbolic characters was the same as that between literal and metaphorical speech: one represented immediately, the other represented something through which another thing was represented. But both mimetic and symbolic characters were interpreted without stepping outside the space of meanings: to take an extreme case, "Horapollo" glossed Egyptian writing for Greeks and Romans while scarcely mentioning the Egyptian language.[39] When Matteo Ricci began learning Chinese in the 1580s, the writing system appeared to him to be organized in just this manner, as a system of symbolic cross-references like heraldry, rebus, or emblematics (the domains most closely related to Egyptian hieroglyphics in the visual world of sixteenth-century Rome). By introducing phonetic characters, that is, characters whose functions in writing are not always to convey a meaningful content, into the decipherment of Egyptian, Champollion disrupted this purely semantic interpretive method. And that is the point at which the ideogram becomes conceivable in all its specificity.

Ricci's description of Chinese "characters in the style of the Egyptian hieroglyphics" would have suggested, for a contemporary observer, a visual language in which writing blended into painting; but one could argue on art-historical grounds that the kinds of visual representation in which "hieroglyphics" were prominent actually reduced painting to a form of writing.[40] When the Encyclopédistes and Warburton had depicted the Chinese written language as departing, for intellectual reasons, from the pictorialism of its origins, they, too, were situating the characters on a scale of greater or less sensory immediacy. (Bouvet's emphasis on the visual analysis of the characters, in his "hieroglyphic" attempt to discover prophecies of Christianity in the earliest Chinese texts, ran counter to the practice of the missionaries of his day, who typically referred to the characters as "letters.") Champollion's discovery of the phonetic values of the Egyptian hieroglyphics altered the grammatological landscape, and not only for Egyptologists. The decipherer of an Egyptian text now faced a choice among three possible values (two based on meaning and one on sound: "mimetic," "tropic" or "phonetic") for the reading of each character. No single alternative could have served as the overall label for a writing system so obviously mixed as Egyptian hieroglyphic; interpretation necessarily included them all. But when, in a parenthetical remark ("the Chinese also use an ideographic script"), Champollion adapted his own triple classification of symbolic values to the description of East Asian scripts, the alternatives were taken as labels for the whole (the spirit?) of a writing-system. "Phonetic" or "ideographic" no longer stood for strategies used by scribe and reader to communicate through an inventory of quasi-pictorial signs; they operated as mutually exclusive designations of the nature of writing-systems. Champollion's great advance in Egyptology sent Chinese studies back to Aristotle, whose semiology had furnished the means for the first European interpretation of the Chinese character.

For in classifying Chinese writing as "ideographic," nineteenth-century grammatologists repeated Francis Bacon's view of Chinese "Characters Real," which is to say, they repeated Aristotle. In 1605 Bacon observed of the Chinese character:

For the organ of tradition, it is either Speech or Writing: and Aristotle saith well, *Words are the images of cogitations, and letters are the images of words*; but yet it is not of necessity that cogitations be expressed by the medium of words. . . . And we understand further that it is the use of China and the kingdoms of the high Levant to write in Characters Real, which express neither letters nor words in gross, but Things or Notions; insomuch as countries and provinces, which understand not one another's language, can nevertheless read one another's writings, because the characters are accepted more generally than the languages do extend.[41]

Bacon's reference for the idea that "words as the images of cogitations" is the short treatise *On Interpretation* attributed to Aristotle, a work that assumes that writing is inescapably the transcription of sound. *On Interpretation* sets up a double parallelism between words and things centering, asymmetrically, in the soul: "spoken sounds are symbols of affections in the soul, and written marks symbols of spoken sounds. And just as written marks are not the same for all men, neither are spoken sounds. But what these are signs of— affections of the soul—are the same for all; and what these affections are likenesses of—actual things—are also the same."[42]

For Bacon, Chinese writing brought the possibility of eliminating one of the levels of mediation through which the *De Interpretatione* had constructed its picture of mind, language, and world. If indeed words symbolized (conventionally) affections in the soul and phonetic writing symbolized words, then a writing that symbolized affections in the soul would symbolize things themselves, since both things and affections were "the same for all." Such a writing would no longer refer indirectly (by a sign, σημεῖον) to "things" belonging to an altogether different order of representation but would be linked to a mental image that in turn linked directly (as a likeness, ὁμοίωμα) with things. (For further evidence that Aristotle uses "likenesses" to indicate a more powerful form of representation than "signs," see *Politics* 1340 a 33.) Given the possibility of making that direct link, it did not matter much how it was to be achieved. Bacon divided such "Notes of Cogitations" into "two sorts: the one when the note hath some similitude or congruity with the notion; the other *ad placitum*, having force only by contract or acceptation," and he put Chinese characters into the latter category—as indeed did most European writers on China before Fenollosa. For Bacon, at least, ideogrammatism does not imply resemblance.

The fortunes of the "Chinese model" of writing promoted by Bacon—the direct notation of reality, through conventional characters, without the interference of spoken words—have been explored by Rossi, Derrida, Slaughter, and Eco.[43] Resurfacing in the guise of the ideogrammatic/phonetic distinction drawn by Champollion in 1830, however, it carried new and different implications. For the earlier attempts to mimic the supralinguistic reach of Chinese writing had been meant to ensure problem-free communication among all people; "Characters Real" were presumed necessarily to lead to "a Universal Character." But when Champollion assigned Chinese writing to the category of "ideographic script," he was read as offering a restrictive definition, a definition that marked the peculiar, nonuniversal features of that writing. Subsequent discussions about whether Chinese writing does or does not consist of "ideograms" have assumed precisely that landscape of meaning: "ideographic" holds for a whole writing system or not at all, and the function of the term is to designate what singles out Chinese writing, instead of what in it might furnish a model for a possible universal writing.

Although Egyptian writing, in Champollion's account, retains its multiple basis, functioning simultaneously as sound-clue, picture, and rebus, Chinese writing is defined, with a look backward to the Aristotelian tradition, as "ideographic" in the precise sense of "nonphonetic." The politicized discipline of world history in the early nineteenth century is no doubt partly responsible for the currency of Champollion's simplified adaptation of his own typology—more influential, at any rate, than linguistics (for which discipline the salient feature of Chinese was rather its "monosyllabism": see Chapter 4 below). It had not yet occurred to Bacon's contemporaries that they were "ahead" of their Far Eastern counterparts in the rush to scientific or political perfection, or that Asian civilizations were childish and unchanging. Such connotations could be attached to "ideography"—and they indisputably were—only after they had become commonplaces in nineteenth-century European culture.

Bacon, then, with debts to Aristotle, initiates a nonphonetic and potentially wholly conventional model of writing, for which Chinese script serves as the chief ethnographic example, seconded by gesture and numbers. Bacon supposed that a universal character might, but need not necessarily, express some "similitude or congruity" with the things signified. For a rival understanding of universal conceptual writing in Bacon's period and afterwards, however, convention was inadequate, because no set of conventional marks could ever equal the power of a language grounded in a prior kinship between signified and signifiers. Etymology, wrote Claude Duret in 1613, depends entirely "on the resolution of words into syllables and letters, wherein consists the representation of the essence of the things that one wishes to name by their correct names"; his model for etymology is a roughly understood Kabbalah.[44] By searching out the word origins of a modern language, one can get back not only to the full utterance of its original speakers but also to the proto-language, forced on men by nature and thus common to all nations. Etymology (like Fenollosa's "character") is the model of a pre- or counter-Babelic language.[45] Agrippa of Nettesheim cites "the Platonists" (meaning the neo-Platonists) as his authority for the view that "when a noun or a verb is formed, the force of the thing [to which it refers] dwells in its articulations, like a kind of life hiding beneath the things it formally signifies."[46] The ordinary speech we use is a degenerate form of "sacred or divine letters, self-identical and permanent in every nation and language."[47] References to such letters in Renaissance texts almost always lead back to the *Corpus Hermeticum*, a set of late-classical initiatory writings in Greek attributed to the Egyptian god Thoth or "Hermes Trismegistus." It was generally assumed that Egyptian hieroglyphics were the prototype of these "sacred or divine letters," vehicles of mysterious wisdom. Thoth predicts in one of the treatises assigned to him, entitled "Definitions," that his books are doomed to become "entirely unclear when the Greeks eventually desire to translate our language to their own, and thus produce in writing the greatest distortion and unclarity. . . . The very quality of the speech and the [? sound] of Egyptian words," on the other hand, "have in themselves the energy of the objects they speak of" (ἐν ἑαυτῇ ἔχει τὴν ἐνέργειαν τῶν λεγομένων).[48] In Egyptian, then, one has the true ideograms—energeiograms?—of Hermes's thought; translate them into Greek, and they become impoverished markers—"sapless" Fenollosa/Pound would call them—of their original fullness. Note, however, the obtuseness of the Greeks even in their quest for exotica. The thing that strikes us most about Egyptian writing, its hieroglyphic or pictorial quality, is missing from the Hermetic description of its uncanny "powers." Power resides for Hermes in spoken words, not written marks.

The Hermetic praise of hieroglyphics evidently made its mark on the Jesuit proto-scientist and seeker into strange things, Athanasius Kircher, who wrote an early and oft-cited description of the Chinese writing system. Kircher traced Chinese writing back to the original script of the Egyptian Thoth or Hermes himself, known in China—according to Kircher's typological chronology—as Fu Xi 伏犧.[49] Fu Xi bequeathed to his Chinese descendants a "Serpent Book" in which the letters were formed by "serpents wonderfully intertwined and made to take different forms representing the diversity of things signified by them."[50] But—precisely as in the passage from the "Definitions"—their removal from Egypt impoverished these characters. The Egyptian sign for the sun, for example, represented

the hidden powers exerted, not merely by the material Sun in this world of sensation, but also those of the archetype of the Sun in the world of ideas. . . . All of this is missing from the construction of Chinese characters, inasmuch as the latter were instituted precisely in order to indicate the simple concepts of words and names, with no other mystery latent in them.[51]

Chinese writing for Kircher imitates nature without revealing its secrets. Of course, Kircher knew of Chinese characters only what a dictionary told him and was utterly misled as to the meaning of Egyptian hieroglyphs.[52] His readiness to believe that the original forms of the Chinese characters echoed natural forms and that these forms lingered in the abbreviated modern characters led Kircher to offer proof in the form of a Chinese book that had found its way to the libraries of Rome. Its chronological table of the evolution of Chinese characters out of nature, as joyfully adopted by Kircher, is shown in Figure 3.1; for his Chinese source, see Figure 3.2; for some pages from a related calligraphic curiosity, see Figures 3.3 and 3.4.[53]

Nature and convention mark the difference between these two ways of conceiving of the universal idiom, of which the Chinese character was, for early modern Europe, one ancient attempt at realization. (Duret's *Thrésor* of 1613 was one of the first European books to include a page of Japanese writing.) Although Bacon would have been content to see an agreed-upon code serve as the "Characters Real" for a new ideogrammatic language, this second group of writers would have settled for nothing less than a participation (via "force") of the symbol in the thing symbolized. Mere mimesis is too weak a word for the relation they wished to establish between sign and referent. Relevant to the distinction between these two visions of writing (because historically indebted to them) is the Romantics' critical commonplace of a distinction between sign and symbol or between allegory and symbol. "An allegory simply signifies a general concept or an idea that is distinct from it, whereas the symbol is the idea itself in sensory, bodily form."[54] Fenollosa relocated this commonplace, moving it from the domain of theology or art

II. Forma.   IV. Forma.   III. Forma.

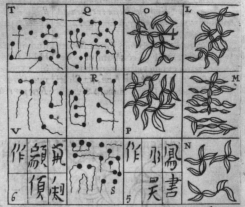

E eee

IV. Literarum forma.

Quarta priscorum characterum forma exhibetur signis Q R S T V, ex ostreis & vermiculis constructa, ita Sinici characteres signati numero 6, totidem literis eos explicant:

Li teù chuen kim çò, hoc est, *notæ ostrearum & vermiculorum*, quos *Chuen kim Rex fecit*, & librum hisce & similibus exaravit. Vide columnas binas suprà exhibitas.

VII. Forma.   VI. Forma.   V. Forma.

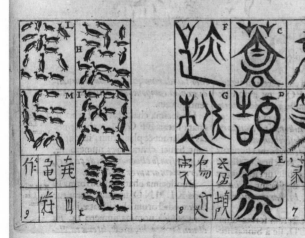

V. Literarum forma.

Quinta characterum vetustorum forma exhibetur literis X Y Z A B, ex herbarum radicibus composita; & hisce prisci utebantur, in literis & libris

F f 3

3.1 The "primitive characters" of the Chinese language. From Athanasius Kircher, *China illustrata* (1667), p. 229.

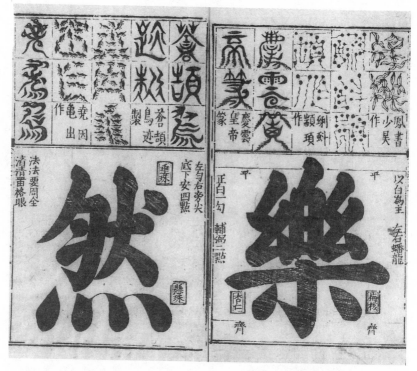

3.2 Kircher's "primitive characters" in their original setting, a calligraphy manual incorporated in the late Ming almanac *Tianxia bianyong Wenlin miaojin wanbao quanshu* 天下便用文林妙錦萬寶全書. Vatican Library, Barb. orient. 139. © Biblioteca Apostolica Vaticana

history to that of geography: the languages of Europe are cold and thin, the European alphabets inexpressive, medieval logic and that inveterate tribal totem, the verb "to be," dead weights on the mind of Europe.[55] The Chinese character would serve as a "medium" not only for poetry but for infusing new life into the dry veins of the West.

The examples from seventeenth-century Europe help to make more obvious something that might reasonably have been asserted about the twentieth-century interpretations of Liu Xie's sixth-century utterances about *wen*: namely, that "nature" is a variable, rather than a constant. It is hard to imagine Bacon and Duret agreeing on the definition of "representation" or "the correct names of things," because they inhabit differently constituted cosmoses. For Bacon, words serve to name things; for the Hermetic tradition to which Duret, like many another Renaissance magical thinker, belongs,

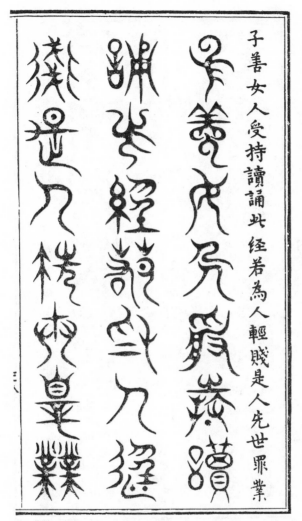

子善女人受持讀誦此経若為人輕賤是人先世罪業

3.3 "Bird-track script." From *Sanshi'er zhuanti Jin'gang jing* 三十二篆體金剛經 (The Diamond Sutra in thirty-two styles of seal-character calligraphy, ca. 1600), p. 78a.

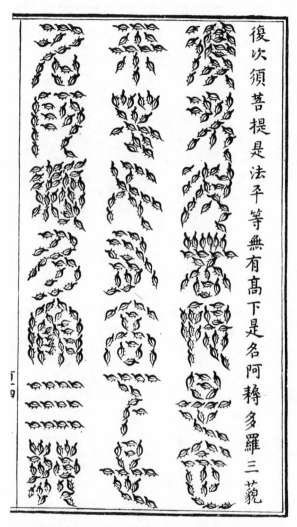

後次須菩提是法平等無有高下是名阿耨多羅三藐

3.4 "Tortoise script." From *Sanshi'er zhuanti Jin'gang jing* 三十二篆體金剛經 (The Diamond Sutra in thirty-two styles of seal-character calligraphy, ca. 1600), p. 104a.

words are packets of "energy" passed from a source within things to the properly empowered initiate, who alone can release these energies in speech. Fenollosa appears at a moment in the history of ideas at which "energy" has re-emerged as a basic category of natural philosophy, but has not yet been worked into a convincing picture of matter, time, and change; so his use of terms such as "power" and "energy" looks back, like New Age ontology, to gnostic initiatory traditions while struggling to establish a relation with more recent thermodynamics.[56] The basic semantic attitude of Fenollosa—his longing for a lightning bolt of natural meaning—is that of the neo-Neoplatonics; his dissatisfaction with patchwork of idioms put together by humans is theirs, too. Their common imagery of currents, flows, bonds, and magnetic forces speaks their desire for a language that will be "something much more than arbitrary symbols." But can this double imagination of a language that participates in nature and a nature endowed with intrinsic meaningfulness guide the idea of writing in the same way as Liu Xie's cosmos realized itself in written patterns?

Syntax Versus Semantics, or the Alphabetic Ideal

The visions of natural force that inspired Fenollosa have (or such is my intermediary conclusion) a long European history and a flickering resemblance with those expressed by Liu Xie. The arguments made for the superiority of ideogram-like characters often invoke a pictorial, even a talismanic, logic; symmetrically enough, those whose linguistic ideal resembles the alphabet have in common a pragmatic, technicist vocabulary and a concentration on certain operations of the mind. If the perfect writing in Fenollosa's view is one that devotes all its resources to the acting-out of meaning, the anti-Fenollosa sees writing as a kit of parts and rules.

Ideographic-logographic writing and alphabetic writing are often contrasted in terms of their structure, with the central exhibit being the distinction (found in any articulated language) between semantics and syntax, a distinction in which alphabetic writing systems have a certain constitutive stake. Chinese characters are vehicles of meaning; alphabetical characters, meaningless in themselves, combine to form complexes (words) that are vehicles of meaning. A frequent analogy in philosophical linguistics holds that syntax, or the capacity of building new sequences from preordained elements and rules, is the hallmark of life (as opposed to the dead letter of an inscription, in Plato's *Phaedrus* [264 b 3 – e 1, 275 d 6]), of the human (as op-posed to the animal, in Descartes' *Discourse on Method*),[57] or of free will, as opposed to biological or political determinism (as Chomsky argued in *Carte-sian Linguistics*). Alphabetic writing carries the syntactic principle from the level of the sentence to that of the individual word.[58] In the other direction, the theory of the ideogram raises semantic power to the extreme. The ideo-gram-as-pictogram is supposed to make visible the very concept to which it refers, without the mediation of sound, and reduces to a redundancy the grammar of the language in which it occurs. Ideogrammatic theories of Chi-nese writing thus correlate with the idea that the Chinese language has "no grammar." (Whether the ideogram's power is thought to compensate for the alleged lack of grammar or whether the theory of the ideogram depends on willfully ignoring what grammar there is in Chinese is the question treated in Chapter 4.)

A picto-ideogrammatic language is (or, rather, *would be*) a rather mon-strous case of specialized overdevelopment—a motif running through countless descriptions of the time required by children to learn thousands of distinct characters and the ground for Hegel's famous pronouncement that "alphabetic writing is in and for itself the more intelligent."[59] Given the long-standing association between syntactic arrangement and intelligence and the labor-saving ideal of alphabetic spelling systems, it is hard to see how Hegel could have thought otherwise. Cave Beck, the author of an alphabetic yet ideographic universal language, neatly combines all the faults of pictographic writing in his vigorous critique: a picture-script fails to represent objects with intuitive accuracy, it too often depends on devices of the local languages it is supposed to supersede (puns, metaphors, word associations), and it re-quires heroic efforts of memory:

The *Egyptians* of old, had a Symbolical way of writing by Emblems and Pictures which might be read by other Nations instructed in their Wisdom, but was so hard to learn, and tedious in the practice, that Letters soon jostled them out of the world. Besides, most of their Hieroglyphicks were so catachrestical (the Picture showing one thing to the eye, and a quite different sense imposed upon it) that they justified the Printer who drew a misshapen Cock upon a Sign-board, and wrote under it, 'This is a bull.'

That the *Chinois* have a general Character, which serves themselves and their Neighbors, though of different languages, is affirmed by some that have been there, and brought some scrawls of it, which are such for their fashion, that an European with his one Eye (which they afford him) would think they shut both theirs (they so much boast of) when they drew the shapes of those Characters: there being no Proportion or Method observed in their form, which causes them to spend many years, beginning in their childhood, in learning of it, and this may be the Reason none of our travellers have been able to bring away any competent skill in that way of writing.[60]

The very existence of ideograms in the strong sense (Fenollosa's sense) of the word is thus challenged by illiteracy, by the fact that people can fail to make sense of the system. That should not happen when a writing system or art form delivers "the idea itself in sensory, bodily form," but, of course, it does. You say *niao* 鳥 (or even its archaic form, shown to the right) is a picture of a bird; I say it is a conventional mark that readers are trained to read as meaning the word "bird." There is something to be said for both accounts, but the first case is harder to make, since it requires agreement on a number of linguistic and vaguely experiential issues (What would constitute a picture of a bird? What would not count as a picture of a bird? What defines "being a picture of something"? Is the seeing of marks as pictures not a matter of conventional training?—and so on). The test that would permit us to verify that a representation is a true "likeness" of its content and "the same for all" (whether conventionally or naturally) is a determinate account of the relation between linguistic meaning and reference. Such an account is less to be hoped for, the more reference to extra-linguistic objects is involved. (The situation in mathematics is less desperate because mathematics does not require the existence of its objects.) There is clearly room for an account of the Chinese character that does not assume meaningfulness as an ingredient (as the notion of the "ideogram" does) but asks how meanings and references come to be attached to graphic complexes.

Like any concept, the term "ideogram" derives its meaning from a semantic network and cannot be thought in isolation from its implicit partner-terms—"phonetic writing," "picture," "convention," "mark," and so forth. Moreover, the system of terms has grown up over a considerable history over which the relations among the terms have been in constant movement: the set of relevant terms expands or shrinks, the definitions of the terms change, new implications impose themselves from unexpected quarters. A term makes sense to a prepared understanding. A term such as "ideogram" appears to function as the name for a thing, when more properly it condenses our readiness to think about things in a certain way. The aim of this exercise in historical semantics has been to spread out and distinguish the elements of that preparation.

All Chinese Poems Are True

The opposition of ideographic and alphabetic writing was a grand simplification and highly vulnerable to fact. Nowadays *The Chinese Written Character as a Medium for Poetry* is apt to look quaint: every undergraduate learns to distrust ideas of immediate natural signification, and even a superficial knowledge of Chinese is enough to show that many of Fenollosa's etymologies, indeed the drift of his whole enterprise, belong to the realm of the imagination. But what Fenollosa thought held for the Chinese *written* language often still appears, in diluted and distanced form, in the frequent characterization of the Chinese *poetic* language as "something much more than arbitrary symbols." In part this must relate to the influence (through Ezra Pound) of Fenollosa's ideas on modern poetry in English—an influence that has not been entirely a bad thing. (Good art can always accommodate absurd philology.) In part, too, prolonging the ideogrammatic theme is a fitting expression of gratitude on the part of the Europeans and Americans who have become acquainted with the Chinese tradition: to utter straightforwardly what Liu Xie said in hyperbolic mode about the *wen* of heaven, earth, and man is very good manners indeed. For the idea that writing, in its most sublime manifestations, speaks with the authority of nature is both inspiring to people in the Chinese tradition and impressive to people out of it. "Nature" is, after all, the one thing that ought to hold constant across differences among "cultures." But what happens when a pattern of thought—even thought about Nature—crosses into a new context of ideas? The next stage to which the term *wen* (as italicized and appropriated into European languages) leads is a certain articulation, held to be naturally, culturally, or historically guaranteed, of the things signified by the characters, when those characters meet in a representative Chinese poem.

Fenollosa's attack on classical logic denounced it as bound to the forms of language, when it ought to be bound to the forms of nature (25–29). His proposal was therefore to cast aside one form of mimesis, seen as artificial and obstructive, in favor of another, supposedly natural and transparent, one. Although the classical Chinese poets and critics never had a chance to be amused or challenged by Greek theories of mimesis, their modern-day expositors invariably open the discussion by *rejecting* the idea that literature (like artifice in general) imitates a prior reality.[61] Stephen Owen made some of the crucial linkages in this rejoinder to Aristotle. The Chinese poem does not imitate or feign reality but follows from it; whereas "metaphor is fictional and involves true substitution," the categorical correspondences one finds in Chinese poetry are "'strictly true,' based upon the order of the world." "The traditional Chinese reader had faith that poems were authentic presentations of historical experience," because the writing of poetry was conceived of as "a virtual transfer of substance" from experience to words and from words to reader, "an organic process of manifestation."[62]

Communication an "organic process"? The semiotic eyebrow rises. Anticipating such a skeptical reaction, Owen sites the idea of "organic . . . manifestation" in the "faith" of the "traditional reader" and thus brackets a certain nature (traditional Chinese nature) within culture. "We speak here of the inclinations of readers and of a poet's anticipation of those inclinations: the actual truth or untruth of poems, authentic presentation or manipulation for art's strange motives, is not in question—these, in fact, are usually beyond recovery."[63]

In other writers the power of culture to set the terms under which nature will be understood is taken for granted, indeed left unspoken. Pauline Yu presents the Chinese literary universe as one in which "there are no disjunctures between true reality and concrete reality, nor between concrete reality and literary work." A Chinese poem is typically seen not as a representation but as "a *literal reaction* of the poet to the world around him and of which he is an integral part."[64] For Michael Fuller the Western problematics of subject and object (deeply connected to the theory of mimesis via the correspondence theory of truth and perception)[65] simply do not hold for the Chinese reader, who is able to say: "On a certain day at a certain place a poet encountered a certain situation and wrote the poem. . . . In the classical Chinese tradition, all poems are true by their very existence; the only questions are *how* they are true and if their truth is of any significance."[66] What is special about Chinese literature, according to the modern theorists of the classical tradition, is its hyperreality: as we shall see, the claim is that Chinese representation, unlike Greek mimesis, is always true. (Or efficacious, if "truth" seems to involve too Greek a claim of correspondence between word and thing.) Moreover, the truth of the representations is guaranteed by the means of representation. Joseph Roe Allen radically condenses this synecdochical poetic: "One might even say that *wen* is itself the cosmos, not a sign in place of something else, but a sign that is the very thing to which it refers."[67] The "not . . . but . . ." structure of the formula summons the student of Chinese literature whose training is European to make a choice: either Aristotelian metaphor and the Saussurean sign or the Chinese symbol, which signifies by unveiling a corner of its real referent.

At a time when the foremost buzzword in other branches of the humanities was "sign" with its predicates "arbitrary," "differential," and "constructed," scholars of Chinese poetry, wary of semiotics with its Aristotelian genealogy, deliberately turned to an account of Chinese literature that emphasized the opposite qualities. They insisted, above all, on the lack of disjunctures among things Western theories had disjoined. The commentatorial language of metaphor gave way to the language of literal meaning and, beyond that, of empirical reference. The *shi* 詩 poem, with its associations of sincerity, occasional composition, and emotional release, took the prime place among Chinese literary genres to become their "dominant," the genre that guides the interpretation of literature in general.[68] One should remember that these critics belong collectively to the first moment at which Chinese literature entered (circa 1975) into the ambit of comparative poetics, which meant, at that juncture, taking a typological and categorical look at their materials rather than a historical one.[69] This chronological fact helps explain the cognitive clash, for it is not certain what the preparatory groundwork for typological study would be. The only certainty is that it involves a departure from the questions one can ask and solve from within a single literary history.

A shift occurs in the reports of these scholars from Fenollosa's and Pound's universalistic "nature" (natural signs are the same for all and immediately recognizable to anyone) to a delimited one (the relations between nature and culture in traditional China differ from ours; nature is an aspect of culture and claims legitimacy because it is cultural). But the shift often appears as an ambiguity. Critics should be, and in normal circumstances are, able to discuss views that somebody considers to be true without taking a stand on whether or not they are true. In scholarly discourse, that is, the truth-value of a statement such as "Literature expresses the *dao* of nature" should be subordinate to the syntax of a sentence such as "Liu Xie believed that literature expresses the *dao* of nature." The contents of the object-language are relevant to scholarship only as they are bracketed and filtered by the meta-language of quotation and paraphrase.

And yet in the study of Chinese poetics, we find a case of incompatibility between the semantics of the quoted language and its place in a quoting syntax. The object-language must at least threaten to break through the meta-language's syntactic frame, for one mission of such cultural comparison is to call into doubt the assumption that our meta-language (typologically "Western," "modern") enjoys a superordinate, theoretically capable, status and is entitled to determine what "true" means. "Construction" and its whole family of concepts (fabrication, fiction, metaphor, persona, imaginary) represent, for the group of critics being discussed here, a contemporary Western set of preoccupations that must not be allowed to run the whole show. One might phrase the issue faced by these comparatists thus: acknowledge the constructedness of the concept of "construction" without seeming to fall back into an unreflective concept of nature. This possibly insoluble imperative surfaces in symptomatic form. An example is the quotation marks Owen puts around the phrase "strictly true," evidence of true discomfort with the language of truth. What is *strictly true* should, strictly, appear in quotation marks only once it has been deemed no longer strictly true—true perhaps for some other, but not for the speaker or his audience. The quoted matter says, "This is the way things are!" and the practice of quotation says, "One way of putting the way things are is, 'This is the way things are.'" That is to say, the reading of traditional Chinese literature obliges twentieth-century people to entertain (at least) two logics. We set up a frame of language and convention (cultural relativism) to enclose authenticity and immediacy (cultural absolutism). The frame has to be there, but its role is to dissolve and leave us with the "transfer of substance." The total result is a heterocosm of the sort imagined by Zhuangzi, Pu Songling, or Marguerite Yourcenar.[70]

Translating on the Empty Mountain

Obviously, Ernest Fenollosa and contemporary literary scholars are not talking about precisely the same things. Rather, they are talking about different things in the same way. Running through Fenollosa's praise of the ideogram and the praise of Chinese poetics in present-day literary studies is a common thread of admiring sympathy for a system of representations that can present its claim to truth so powerfully. The nonmimetic version of Chinese literary theory contrasts with Western attitudes in exactly the same way that the ideogram triumphs, for Fenollosa, over the defective logics and alphabets of Europe. "Something more than arbitrary symbols" indeed! For the reader lucky enough to endorse all these interpretive programs at once, Chinese writing would be anchored in the vital representation of things, Chinese poetic speech in nonfictionality, and the lexical meaning of Chinese poems in inevitable empirical reference (authenticity guaranteed by cultural reflex). Chinese would be the language that "simply HAD TO STAY POETIC; simply couldn't help being and staying poetic in a way that a column of English type might very well not stay poetic."[71]

Pound's gift for picking out glints of promise in the ruins of world culture notwithstanding,[72] the Chinese language has needed the steady work of generations of translators to become, "be, and stay poetic" for English speakers. And it is Pound who has taught us what to look for, what to value, what to avoid. Here a third level of the reception of Liu Xie's *wen* emerges, the level at which perception and verbalization are deemed one (as if in paraphrase of Liu's "words are established and *wen* gives forth its brilliance—the very way of nature"). Wai-lim Yip appeals to a Fenollosan set of virtues in presenting the eighth-century poet Wang Wei as "the quietest poet in Chinese and perhaps in all literary history."

Wang Wei is Nature (Phenomenon) as it is: no trace of conceptualization. . . . In Wang Wei, the scenery *speaks* and *acts*. The poet has become, even before the act of composition, Phenomenon itself and can allow the things in it to emerge *as they are* without being contaminated by intellectuality. The poet does not step in; he views things as things view themselves. . . . Wang Wei is Phenomenon itself: no trace of conceptualization.[73]

As tautologous as the critical gesture whereby Yip establishes Wang Wei as the poet of "Phenomenon itself," the Wang Wei poem exhibits "no disturbance of intellectual impositions, no hurry-scurry to establish causal relations, each object is given its fullest chance to emerge in spotlighting distinctiveness." The "spotlight" image rapidly matures into the praise of a "cinematic distinctiveness."[74] And for Yip, to read one of these poems is to follow "the visual order of his images . . . [which] follows naturally the cuts and turns of our experiencing the fluctuations of Phenomenon."[75] Reading melts into seeing.

If that is what Wang Wei is all about, Wai-lim Yip foresees difficulty in showing readers of English poetry why they should read him. As he puts it, "the process of conceptualization seems to have dominated much of English poetry," and the normal course of an English or even European poem is that of working through "historical, cyclical and human meanings" projected onto the phenomenal objects of experience. The place where we see the two modes hinging or impinging on each other, but irregularly, is in translation—or the failures of translation. Yip sets his own translation of Wang Wei against a predecessor's. Speaking once more of the "cinematic" quality of the poet's "visual order" of images, he stipulates that

any violation of this order in translation will deface Wang Wei's unique mode of presentation, as one example will show.

Empty mountains; no man (is visible)

becomes, in Witter Bynner's hand,

There seems to be no one on the empty mountain....

The analytical or explanatory 'There seems to be no one . . . ' has destroyed completely the dramatic presentation of the two phases of perception and putting 'no one' ahead of 'empty mountain' violates the stance or consciousness of the poet in that unique moment.[76]

Translation is a pliant witness: if "the emptying out of intellectual interference" is one's model, then one has only to choose stark concrete nouns and plant them in a rudimentary syntax to confirm the thesis. The idea that Wang Wei "is Phenomenon itself" depends somewhat on our willingness to see a certain style of translation as Translation itself. And our acceptance of that style of translation relies on thoughts and attitudes that precede our encountering the poem—very possibly, among other possibilities, thoughts about the difficulty of articulating "Not Ideas About the Thing But the Thing Itself" (to cite a Stevens title invoked by Yip as a yardstick for measuring Wang Wei). The chain of associations in which connotative literalness is connected to syntactic starkness, syntactic starkness to phenomenal concreteness, and concreteness to cinematic (observerless) visuality has been a long time in the making; that it should take this particular shape in English-language poetry is a matter of multiple inheritance, in which David Hume, Ralph Waldo Emerson, Ernest Fenollosa, T. E. Hulme, Ezra Pound, and Ludwig Wittgenstein, among many others, fashion the channels through which we can receive messages from Zhuang Zhou, Han Shan, and Wang Wei.[77]

However much a method of translation owes to influences beyond the text and however unsatisfying it is to appeal to the "accuracy" of a translation *sans plus*, there is no point denying that translations are determined by something and that they form historical series and rankings: it is by being the sort of historical players we are that we can feel the rightness or wrongness of a translation, judge a translation as being "for us" or not. A chronological series of translations can show what potentials in the original become entrenched over time and which ones simply read as "dated." And just such a series is the main exhibit of Eliot Weinberger's pithy and instructive *Nineteen Ways of Looking at Wang Wei*. It is as if "Wang Wei poems in English" constituted a genre with its own law or tendency of development. Critical judgments about the original and about the success or failure of translations attempt to state this law, although they always state it as judgments rooted in the object rather than as side-effects of the evolution of taste. In this sense, the voice of Wang Wei in English at this or that moment is almost logically deducible from the diffusion of Imagist precepts at the time. Take point A (the meeting point of Witter Bynner and a Wang Wei poem in 1929), draw a line from it through point B (Burton Watson's 1971 translation of the same poem), and going farther along on the same line, you may predict Gary Snyder's 1978 translation.

空山不見人
但聞人語響
反景入深林
復照青苔上

—Wang Wei

There seems to be no one on the empty mountain . . .
And yet I think I hear a voice,
Where sunlight, entering a grove,
Shines back to me from the green moss.
—Witter Bynner and Kiang Kang-hu

Empty hills, no one in sight,
only the sound of someone talking;
late sunlight enters the deep wood,
shining over the green moss again.
—Burton Watson

Empty mountains:
no one to be seen.
Yet—hear—
human sounds and echoes.

Returning sunlight
   enters the dark woods;
Again shining
   on the green moss, above.

               —Gary Snyder[78]

Weinberger's slender anthology, a sampling of successive renditions of this one short poem, positions Snyder's translation, number nineteen, as crown and arrival point. (The stealthy editor actually works twenty-two or twenty-three variants of the poem into the book.) Along this line several co-ordinated things happen, all of which add up to the identity of Chinese poetry in English today: the narrator vanishes steadily away, a cluttered syntax turns bare, prosy rhythms consolidate into a few strong beats, verbal parallelism comes more sharply into focus, and the aim of making the reader "see" a scene (although a scene of which there are several defensible versions) becomes paramount. Wang Wei in English, from 1919 to 1978, works toward a form of Imagism. No fuller proof could be desired of Ezra Pound's "invention of Chinese poetry for our time." Yet between the invention and its reduction to practice, as the career of this one quatrain shows, some sixty-five years elapsed.

And that is just when the "naturalness" argument about Chinese poetry began to re-emerge as an interpretive position. The path then runs from a theory about Chinese writing (Fenollosa) to a practice of translation and a poetic canon (Watson, Yip, Snyder, and many others) to an ethnographically inflected attitude about the reception of literature (Owen, Yu, and others). The historical influence is indirect, filtered, and moderated (a direct appeal from the brash Fenollosa would most likely have been ignored, and Yip's statements on behalf of Wang Wei omit any consideration of the "traditional reader"), but it is through this process that Chinese poetry has come to have a voice in English. "A voice," not "its voice": for one inevitable outcome of tracing a history is that we can begin to see the alternative paths branching out on right and left. Thus, then, the link from a graphic poetics to a conception of the poet as witness to an undeceiving world. The positions should not be confused, but neither should their near or far resemblances be denied. Knowing that one's family tree includes Fenollosa, Emerson, Hulme, or Nietzsche helps to explain the persuasiveness of some concepts that citizens of other literary disciplines may find puzzling.

Syntax Within Semantics

The problem with the theory of the ideogram and its correlates in literary study is not that they mislead or involve dubious presuppositions (both forgivable flaws, since literary understanding is not a straight deduction from axioms), but rather that they direct our attention to certain objects and make other objects hard to conceive. Indeed, as long as the discussion about *wen* remains within the province of reference and semantics, it tends to founder on problems of representation—claims that representation can be direct, faithful, adequate, sincere, and so on, versus claims that it cannot. I will therefore try to shift the discussion to new ground: rather than conceive of *wen* as a writing that differs from alphabetic writing or Aristotelian representation through having a more immediate relation to things or ideas, I shall try to capture its specificity in its expression of part-to-whole relations, that is, in the syntax of the sign—not what it means but how it is put together. (Traditional etymological studies, beginning with Xu Shen's six classes, are not incompatible with this model: note how much less arbitrary it is to rank characters in terms of the complexity of their part-to-whole relations than it is to sort them subjectively on a scale of pictographic qualities.) This involves putting the shoe on a wrong or at least inhabitual foot, since accounts of *wen* that emphasize semantic power have tended to ignore syntax or to reduce it (as did Fenollosa) to another means of semantic representation.[79] Fenollosan signification fits into this scheme as a claim that there are representations that are simply *caused* and not at all, or very minimally, put together; a counterargument will have only to show how much (and exactly what) every reading of an object as simply caused has to leave out.

What would it mean to read ideograms (and their poetic counterparts) not ideographically but syntactically and contextually? Would that not compel us to give up the power and majesty of cosmic writing, to abandon the specifically Chinese patterns of thought about writing and meaning? Liu Xie's praise of *wen* has often been interpreted in a Fenollosan sense, that is, as proclaiming the unity of Chinese writing with the universe it emulates. My counter-citation (and route of return to Liu Xie) will be the definition and etymology of *wen* found in the *Shuowen jiezi*—a fairly inconspicuous text but one into which a reading of the very classical texts cited by Liu Xie is compressed. Xu Shen's original entry for the character reads merely: *Wen, cuo hua ye* 文 , 錯畫也: "*Wen* is crossing lines."[80] Crossing lines? That sounds strangely weak and vague. The great eighteenth-century philologist Duan Yucai 段玉裁 added a commentary drawing on examples from the classical-period texts that Xu would have consulted in making his dictionary:

Cuo 錯, "cross," here stands for [its homonym] *cuo* 造, "meet." "Meeting lines" are lines that cross and join. When the *Kaogongji* 考工記 [Record of Artificers] section of the *Zhou li* 周禮 [Rituals of Zhou] says, "Green set beside red: this we call *wen*," it gives a case of meeting lines, and such meeting lines are the etymon of *wen*.

錯當作造 . 造畫者 , 交造之畫也 . 考工記曰 . 青與赤謂之文 . 造畫之一耑也 . 造畫 , 文之本義 .

Lines cross or meet most strikingly in the juxtaposition of designs and colors in an artifact. And not just any artifact either: the passage Duan cites gives instructions for the ornamentation of the sovereign's clothes, an inevitably meaningful and meaning-conferring kind of artifact. On the evidence of this passage, writing is like a mark: a mark of distinction, an elaboration, an addition to the plainness of whatever is without *wen*.

But then Duan goes on to give a second example from an even more prestigious text—so prestigious that it does not even need to be named, for it is the *Book of Changes*.

The Yellow Emperor's scribe, Cang Jie 倉頡, perceiving the tracks left by the claws of birds and animals, understood that their distinct patterns [*li* 理] could be used as the basis for differentiating them into classes. So he began to make tallies and writings, producing images and shapes according to the kinds [of the things represented] 依類象形. Thus the name of writing is *wen*.[81]

This second example shows us writing as reading, interpretation, tracking of causes, even (incidentally) imitation of something given in the natural world: just as a track of a certain shape signifies that animal and no other, so a certain sign represents and singles out a certain meaning. Not composition but causality provides the rationale whereby the "writing" of animal spoors transmits information. Reading, in this version, is none other than perception (and note the similarity between this model of writing and Aristotle's account of perceptual "impressions").

Taken as semiotic fable, the second example corresponds antithetically to the first: as nature pairs off with artifice and causation with composition, so the inherently meaningful sign stands in relation to decorative outwardness. If the *Yi jing* passage gives us the original scene of semantics, the *Zhou li* passage gives us that of syntax (the embroiderers' *wen* is made by putting "green together with red," and the meaning of this *wen* is to be sought not in either color but in their combination). A fuller citation from the *Kaogong ji* will complete the story of how *wen* comes to inhabit the artifact. "The embroiderers' task is to combine the Five Colors," says the text. "The color of the East is green; that of the South is red," and so on through the four directions plus heaven and earth. "Green and white follow each other or go on top of each other (*ci* 次); red and black follow each other; dark and yellow follow each other." "Following each other" or "overlying each other" is the name for the relation of polar opposites: north and south, east and west, heaven and earth. These "overlying" pairs seem to be colors suitable for robes to be worn in a given season, as the Son of Heaven takes up residence in a certain quarter of his Mingtang (Hall of Lights). But combinations of "neighboring" colors are more unusual, more specialized: each gets its own name and is associated with a definite pictorial shape. "The combination of green and red is called *wen*. That of red and white is called *zhang* 章 [boundary]. That of white and black is called *fu* 黼 [axe-head shape]; that of black and green is called *fu* 黻 [double-bow shape]."[82] The *Kaogong ji* gives a "grammar of ornament" (if I may reuse with new emphasis a fine nineteenth-century title)[83]—a set of rules and forms appropriate to the adornment of a Zhou king. The colors may be meaningful, whether naturally or by convention; the shapes embroidered on the robe certainly are. But it is the syntax, or combination, of the meanings of the different background colors and the different shapes chosen for the foreground that gives the artifact as a whole its character as an "inscriptional object" in the broadest sense, or *wen wu* 文物. The *Kaogong ji* account relates, unlike the "bird-track" story, the generation of meanings and meaningful things out of meaningless things. When we are talking about nature as opposed to culture, clothes are a particularly loaded subject. If one wanted to emphasize the doubleness of the signifier *wen*, one would say that the imperial attire, if truly inhabited by *wen*, imprints kingliness on the human animal chosen to wear it, rather than the kingly qualities somehow exuding from man to robe. To reason from bird track to bird shows good woodcraft; to reason from the signs of authority to the basis of authority betrays unfamiliarity with the ways of the world. If the two kinds of know-how were identical, perhaps culture would finally become transparent, ideogrammatical—which is doubtless what the fashioners of Chinese culture have always wanted it to be. Who can blame them for that?

But the two kinds of know-how are not identical, and their nonidentity is the very milieu of meaning in which all social actors live and move. Consider this speech from the *Zuo zhuan*, in which a learned advisor, an expert in ritual and history, upbraids a duke who has just received the gift of a venerable cauldron belonging to a neighboring state's ruling family:

A lord of men must exhibit (*zhao* 昭) virtue to block misdeeds; he must illuminate (*zhao* 照) his many officers. Always fearing that he may somehow fail, he exhibits (*zhao* 昭) his charismatic virtue so that it may be visible to his sons and grandsons. For this reason his Pure Temple is covered with thatch; his grand chariot has a mat of knotted grass; his ceremonial soup is without flavorings; the grain he eats is not polished. All these display (*zhao* 昭) his thriftiness. His clothing . . . displays (*zhao* 昭) his sense of degree. . . . The flame patterns and dragon patterns, the axe symbols and bow symbols, woven into his clothing display (*zhao* 昭) his civilizing power (*wen* 文). The Five Colors in their contrasting pattern-color combinations emblazon (*zhao* 昭) his regalia (*wu* 物). . . . Now, when one whose virtues are thrift and carefulness, and who conscientiously ascends and descends [in the course of ritual enactments], employs *wen* 文 and *wu* 物, patterns and sumptuary articles, to mark his [attainments] and calls on sounds and splendid sights to proclaim them—when such a one reveals himself (*zhao* 照) in the presence of his many officials, the many officials, chastened and fearful, do not dare alter what he has caused to be set down and made a standard.[84]

The crucial thing about an instituted sign is that, unlike a natural one, it can fail to mean. If the lord of men is to show charismatic power by wielding the appropriate objects, the objects demand that he live up to the claims they make on his behalf. Thus a classical Chinese reflection on the nature of signs encompasses both sides of what, in most Western writing on the subject, are presented as alternative Chinese and Western conceptions. Western accounts of the philosophical background of Liu Xie's description of *wen* tend to present only one side of the Chinese evidence, the side of the "natural image" or "ideogram," and moreover tend to stress that side's essential Chineseness.[85] We have at least broken down that polarizing simplification.

Indeed, a closer look at the range of activities whose accomplishment is named *wen* helps to situate the kind of *wen* of which Liu Xie spoke: a cultural ideal, a wish grounded in belief and, as such, endowed with a different sort of power from that which an iconic reading of his description would give it. It also provides us the outline of a contrapuntal reading of Liu's praise of *wen*, a reading that would see it above all as a *composition*. (A shift toward the latter style of reading is one of the great virtues of Owen's 1992 discussion over that of 1985.) With this way of reading, Liu Xie's page begins to swarm with covert quotation marks. *Wen* displays the evidence of itself in the world for the semantic eye to see and read, as difference, analogy, pattern. But to reproduce the actions of *wen* in writing, Liu Xie must trim, align, compose: for those whose ears are trained in the vocabulary of the music section of the *Records of Ritual*, the differences and analogies he notes as relevant are those crucial to the building of the Chinese social order and its artistic monuments (*tian, di; gao, bei* 天, 地; 高, 卑), differences that must be understood *as differences* rather than as atomic positions (the ritual texts are quite firm on the idea that without one element of a polar pair, the other cannot be thought).[86] "Sounds that form a complete pattern (*cheng wen* 成文) are called music," says the "Record of Music," which further prescribes: perfect musical-dramatic performance is achieved when "the Five Colors [or just possibly: the five elements with their corresponding sounds] form a pattern (*cheng wen*) and make no havoc, the Eight Timbres follow their modal rules without trespassing."[87] The pattern of *wen* may originate in nature, but emulating it takes effort—havoc and trespassing may always occur. A reading that aimed at preserving both the content of Liu Xie's writing and its construction could take it as an act of translation—the persistent relaying of natural predicates into cultural and textual ones, of the differences that the hands and eyes perceive into the differences that the educated mind sees. Liu allows a place for that translation to occur, namely the mind, that focal creation that reconstitutes the order of nature in perceiving it. If that is Liu's course, it is quite opposite to that set by Fenollosa, even if the two paths may pass by some of the same landmarks.

And the direction of travel—the order of operations, the implied syntax of composition—makes all the difference. If ideology (an ugly term, but one sure to appear wherever literary criticism is done nowadays) denotes the practice of disguising facts of history as facts of nature, then a piece of writing like Liu Xie's presents pitfalls. Read it as an image of the semantic universe of its writer, and it is pure Chinese imperial ideology; read it as an act of *cheng wen*—the syntactic alternative I have been developing here—and it becomes a manual for constructing imperial ideology. In the embroiderer's eye, the cloud-rending dragon dissolves into a field of tiny, separate stitches. That may be the price of finding out where dragons come from. But that is also how reading becomes not merely the reading of what is written but the reading of the writing process and the whole cumulative series of writing processes invoked by every instance of writing. That is why a semantic account of the Chinese character is incomplete (and never so incomplete as in the pure theory of the ideo-pictogram); that is also why the theory of Chinese writing as the immediate perception of cosmic order, while gratifying to contemplate in texts as eloquent as Liu Xie's, leaves us with a partial and plotless apprehension of what the text is trying to do.[88] It was a mistake (though a predestined one) to seek the opposite of a "Western" tradition of analytic artifice in a Chinese "natural" poetics and semiology, when both sides could have discovered the same counterarguments at home.

Rhythm, or Sequence Without Semantics

Benedict Anderson seeks the trigger for the development of modern nationalisms in the moment when "three fundamental cultural conceptions, all of them of great antiquity, lost their axiomatic grip on men's minds." These were the beliefs in a sacred script, in divinely ordained kingship, and in "a conception of history in which cosmology and history were indistinguishable, the origins of the world and of men essentially identical."[89] Anderson sees the crumbling of the cosmos as a gradual nineteenth-century event. It is unlikely, in my view, that these three conceptions were "axiomatic" for educated Chinese of Liu Xie's time, who had seen, in recent centuries, a parade of dynasties of various origins, some "barbarian," each of them claiming one or another type of legitimacy and none of them possessing the unchallenged reach in space or time that would belong to a genuine "Son of Heaven." Nor, of course, do twentieth-century readers find these conceptions of writing, power, and nature axiomatic. An uneasy awareness that sense is made in society and that the social order most densely packed with meanings is not necessarily the best surfaces in recent half-disavowals of the theory that the Chinese cultural order is a natural and inevitable reading from experience.[90] Are these the alternatives—the celebration of a social order's confidence in itself as the one right order and the suspicion that any attempt to ground social order in nature is only the wish-fulfilling dream of the powerful? Let us suppose they are. How will we who are bound to Chinese literature answer those alternatives through the techniques of reading?

The direction of this essay has been to develop the artificer's point of view and draw the reader's sympathies toward it. A rhetoric whose job is to ground the categories of art in those of nature is by the terms of its own argument committed to not recognizing its own handiwork in some of its objects. There has to be a nature with which art can productively contrast, or the grounding has no ground to stand on. But no such rule of limited responsibility (or limit to self-knowledge) applies to a rhetoric that sees itself as splicing art onto art, (perceived) order onto (presumed) order. To say that the Chinese (or the ancient Chinese) believe, or want to believe, in dragons does not really put the difference between dragons and embroidery to rest. After all, we owe what we know about dragons to those who could both embroider them and tell us about the process—for example, Liu Xie.

But adopting the embroiderer's point of view—or adopting a social-constructivist platform for interpreting the networks of meaning in Chinese literature—is not necessarily the end of alienation and an instant refutation of all authority. Liu Xie can show us as much, for in China perhaps more than anywhere else, a vigorous social mythology has grown up around the idea that writing (or kingship) is a matter of tempering or weaving together the stuffs that brute nature provides.[91] By opting for a poetics of manufacture, one does not automatically put imperial rule and its charters behind one. One may indeed have done no more than express one's need for a master of works.

Our time is most comfortable with the social-constructivist option, even to the point of admitting the natural semiosis of the Chinese literary universe only as an example of a world constructed by a different set of social imperatives. But before we congratulate ourselves too heartily for being on the side of progress and civilization (postmodern civilization at that!), I should like to point out that the social-constructivist view in its specifically post-Enlightenment form is nothing new in Chinese thinking or new to non-Chinese students of China. Who could provide a more subtly historical and social reading of Liu Xie's praise of heavenly *wen* than Marcel Granet, the pupil of Durkheim and teacher of Lévi-Strauss? Granet, it is true, has often been taken to task for having presented a synoptic, ahistorical picture of Chinese culture.[92] But when we read Granet as a ritualist commenting on ritual documents, an artificer attempting to reproduce an earlier process of artifact making, perhaps the tenseless, categorical time of his telling of history will fall into place as a made time, a historical "representation" that yet shapes historical experience. Here is one example to show the way—Granet on the genesis of *yin-yang* 陰陽 and *wuxing* 五行 cosmologies:

The representation of Time and Space [in early China] . . . derives, not from simple individual sensations or from the observation of nature, but from purely social activities. Its elements are taken from the image of two teams clashing, under particularly moving circumstances, in a ritual joust. . . . A duple rhythm, based on simple opposition and simple alternance, presided over the organization of society. And thus it dictated the twin representations of Time and Space. . . . This rhythmic constitution [of time and space], based on the principle of antithesis between periods of dispersion and concentration, was first expressed through the correlated ideas of simple opposition and alternation, and the representation of Time and Space was from the first linked to the feeling of a difference of value between two sorts of distance and duration. . . . The idea that distances and durations were not all of equal value led to the idea that intervals of time, like intervals of space, possessed differing natures. This step forward was accomplished once the leading representation of Space was no longer the spectacle of two groups of warrior bands standing face to face, but rather a square formation in which the axial line separating the two groups had transformed itself into a center occupied by a Chief.[93]

Granet's reconstruction of the history of Chinese time (an ambitious project) puts social organization in the position of an agency determining the representation of nature. This much a quick and opportunistic reading of Granet's historical fable will give us. But a closer look finds rhythm—syntax in a pure form, a syntax prior to all content—"presiding over" the social reality. "A duple rhythm, based on simple opposition and simple alternance, *presided over* the organization of society [and] *dictated* the twin representations of Time and Space." Granet's seeming ahistoricality represents an attempt to derive history from something that is not yet history. "Alternance" and "opposition" are curious terms, straddling the realms of linguistics and politics. A term or a phoneme may "alternate" with another element having similar functions; in certain contexts, alternation permits us to perceive difference and thus functional opposition ("*pig* versus *big*" demonstrates the opposition *p/b*, voiced and unvoiced). Political "alternance" permits the orderly transfer of power from a ruling power to an opposition (as happens in certain groups with a ritual moiety structure or in electoral democracies). Granet's story now appears as a three-layered one: the story of the generation of a natural order out of a social order, which in turn is a specification, a semantic investment, of an order of merely potential signifiers. Like the *Kaogong ji*, Granet derives meaning from mere form (difference, repetition, rhythm, sequence). Both tell of an ensemble of complex forms emerging out of simpler ones and thus becoming available for semantic investment. In Fenollosa the natural event of the lightning bolt impresses itself so powerfully on an observer that he mimes it in pictorial writing, and the image reverberates down the centuries: the very pattern of semantic contagion. In Granet's story of the constitution of imperial order, the shapes come first and then their contents. The invention of meaning follows the invention of rhythm—a temporal syntax awaiting a content.[94] The regime of alternating opposites gives way to a period in which the axis of difference, that line without area, "transforms itself" into a space that a chief can inhabit. Liu Xie put writing, crowned with the attributes of divine kingship, into just such a spatialized center. To continue the passage cited at the outset of this chapter:

> Now Azure and Yellow intermingle their colors,
> the square and the round differentiate their forms;
> sun and moon in their recurrent orbs display the symmetrical
>   images of heaven,
> mountain and river in brilliant patternwork spread forth the
>   ordered shapes of earth;
> —all this the *wen* of *dao*.

> 夫玄黃色雜, 方圓體分;
> 日月疊壁, 以垂麗天之象;
> 山川煥綺, 以鋪理地之形;
> 此蓋道之文也.

Syntactic reading can find the *wen* that interests it in similar processes— orderings and intervals that are not to be found in the red or the green but only in what happens when they are put together. No longer to see the sun and moon but only the distinction between them—this sounds like a hard discipline for readers of Chinese poetry, but it is worth straining a bit to be a participant in the making of *wen*.

4

Always Multiple Translation: Or, How the Chinese Language Lost Its Grammar

If this were a "just-so" story, we would have to tell not only how the Chinese language lost its grammar but how it got it back. But then "it," the thing lost and found, would become the focus of a problem, for Chinese lost its grammar in one sense and recovered it in another. It was, to be more precise, a change in the accepted definition of "grammar" rather than new facts brought before an unchanging structure of assumptions that revealed the error as such.[1] Such stories reveal the history of linguistics to be discontinuous and improvised, an instance of "gypsy urban planning," to quote Umberto Eco's joke; and that realization should send us back to the tentmakers, to the definers of the tacit body of theory that rings a scholarly discipline.[2]

It is no longer current to say that Chinese "has no grammar," and it would be quixotic to argue against an idea so thoroughly discredited. The reason for looking into the history of the "error" is twofold: by reconstructing its history, we may recover some of the conceptual context in which the great nineteenth-century comparative linguists discussed the Chinese language, and we may also learn something about the act of comparison. My examination of theories about the Chinese language leads to two recommendations for comparative work. We should, I think, always keep in mind two questions. Are the facts about the object of study neutral givens, or are they produced by the interaction between the investigator and the object? If the latter, the comparatist's task is then redefined as the exploration of interactions—a project that seems to me far more interesting than the evaluation of similarities and differences.[3] Second, when we have located an interaction, are we sure we have brought into play all the relevant centers of influence? Too often we in China studies tend to counterpose an unalterable China with a "West" fixed in the attitudes of the imperially expanding nations of Europe circa 1900 and then generalize about their differences. This dyad makes for easy discussion, but it may, as I think is the case with the "grammar" controversy, omit consideration of indispensable third parties. At first glance, translation similarly seems to involve two parties and no more: the source language and the target language. The history of ideas about Chinese grammar demolishes that simplification. Even the plainest typological contrasts, even the most obviously binary categorizations in this story, emerge from multiple and layered interactions.

Interactions

In discussing the Chinese language, seventeenth- and eighteenth-century Europeans concentrated on what to them was its unique feature—the system of characters with its mix of phonetic and semantic clues. No one bothered to notice what rules bound these marvelous characters in sentences.[4] When, in the early nineteenth century, grammar became a central concern of this discussion, the views of Western scholars toward China had changed—China was no longer a high civilization with much to offer but a society seriously deficient in the virtues that the West saw itself as possessing. What had been the bountifulness of the Chinese language now appeared to be a lack. The replacement of the search for a general or universal grammar by historical and comparative philology as the central linguistic discipline also contributed to a re-evaluation of the Chinese language. It is important to note that this re-evaluation was not based on new sources of information; the Western knowledge of Chinese remained more or less stable between 1750 and 1820.[5]

Passages from the great American linguist William Dwight Whitney's cycle of lectures, *Language and the Study of Language*, first delivered at the Smithsonian Institution in 1864, reveal what happens when the description of a language is founded on an absence. Whitney wanted to impress on his audience the strictly monosyllabic character of the classical Chinese language, which, he said,

may be in some measure seen by comparing a Chinese sentence with its English equivalent. The Chinese runs, as nearly as we can represent it, thus: 'King speak:

Sage! Not far thousand mile and come; also will have use gain me realm, hey?' which means, 'the king spoke: O sage! Since thou dost not count a thousand miles far to come (that is, hast taken the pains to come hither from a great distance), wilt thou not, too, have brought some thing for the weal of my realm?'[6]

The quoted sentence is almost the first in one of the most influential works of philosophy in the Chinese tradition, the *Mencius: Wang yue: Sou bu yuan qian li er lai, yi jiang you yi li wu guo hu!* 王曰 : 叟不遠千里而來, 亦將有以利吾國乎! Whitney's choppy impersonation was obviously meant to startle his hearers. For a more decorous Victorian rendering of the philosopher's meaning, see James Legge's translation, published three years before Whitney's lecture: "The king said, 'Venerable sir, since you have not counted it far to come here, a distance over a thousand *li*, may I presume that you are provided with counsels to profit my kingdom?'"[7] Whitney and Legge were inserting Mencius into different generic and institutional frames, and these frames determine what is noteworthy in a translation. Legge wanted the king to speak in the fashion appropriate to a participant in philosophical dialogue—and so he does *chez* Legge, in a close match to the urbane conversation of Socrates and his Athenian friends as fluently Englished by Benjamin Jowett in the 1860s and 1870s.[8] A common language and style forms a precondition (as well as an ultimate objective) for cosmopolitan philosophizing. To bring Mencius into the world of European thought barking like a savage would only have put more barriers in the way of the mutual cultural recognition that Legge worked so hard to bring about.

But Whitney's purpose is not philosophical assimilation. If anything, the linguist needs to show Mencius as unassimilable to the common educated discourse. (Whitney's debt to August Schleicher and Friedrich von Schlegel, which will become apparent below, reveals the geopolitical heritage of the differential description of grammars.) This is translation for the sake of difference. Why? Whitney's description of his own translation method as putting the original into English "as nearly as we can represent it" opens up a specifically ethnographic ambiguity. Word-for-word translation aims at a surpassing *nearness*, a one-for-one correspondence between signs of the original and of the rendition, no fuzziness or paraphrase permitted. Even so, the translator is unable to promise everything, only to depict "as nearly as we can" thought processes that must remain alien. The more convincingly the translator observes the protocols of "nearness," the more exquisite the reader's sense of strangeness, of distance from the original text. If Legge's policy anticipates the global commonsense of Basic English, Whitney is opening the way to Benjamin Whorf, and these two styles of translation intend to make one another impossible.

The excessive "nearness" of the linguist's pidgin—its forcible transfer of not only the meaning but also the syntax of foreign sentences into another language—gives us a specific object of investigation, both morphological and historical: the "literal" translation. It was with deliberate perversity that Walter Benjamin declared "the interlinear paraphrase of the sacred text" the "archetype or idea of all translation" and cited Goethe's complaint about translators, that "they want to turn Indic, Greek, English into German, instead of Indicizing, Hellenizing, Anglicizing German. They have far more respect for the linguistic habits of their own community than for the spirit of the foreign work."[9] Benjamin and Goethe had at heart the interests of a cosmopolitan idea of the German language as a language that would live and grow in and through translations.[10] But that would have seemed dangerously romantic to the academic linguists of the nineteenth century. Too much hospitality to foreign constructions signified a failure to acknowledge the special character and genius of the home language. Ideologically speaking, this is the appearance in linguistics of the chasm between democratic and conservative romanticism, between aspirations to universal freedom and the legitimation of the traditional order, between the early Wordsworth, Coleridge, and Schlegel and their later selves.

For most readers, unidiomatic translation hardly counts as translation; even in the special case of sacred texts, the interlinear rendering demands a further paraphrase to fill in the gaps. Pidgin translation exhibits its own incompleteness as an unequal relationship between normal speech in the target language and the halting, misarticulated, or excessive speech of the source language it represents. Although these differences and asymmetries can be described formally, the pidgin style came into its own under the special conditions of the nineteenth century, conditions that may be marked with a sequence of proper names: Rousseau, Herder, Friedrich von Schlegel, Wilhelm von Humboldt, Franz Bopp. The procedures underlying it—calque, diglossia, imperfect second-language acquisition—must be nearly as old as language itself.[11] The Scythian policemen in Aristophanes' *Thesmophoriazousai*, to take the earliest example I know, talk in "me Tarzan, you Jane" style, mangling the verbs and cases of Greek—but always, as Wilhelm Dindorf first observed, in perfect meter. Rousseau saw no reason why a savage should see his two feet as forming a pair or falling under the scope of the single noun "foot." (It is a pity Rousseau never attempted an extended description of the world from this refreshing perspective; to do so might demolish our concept of "language.") The translation of sacred texts, as Benjamin points out, required close comparisons between the sentences of the source and target languages. Those comparisons inspired compensatory gestures: so, for example, the Authorized Version of the Bible produced under King James I uses italics for all words that do not correspond to terms in the original. But the age of linguistic typologies and comparative grammar brought forth projects to which pidgin could contribute a firm foundation and legitimation. Pidgin stands for—it makes audible and visible—the incommensurability of languages. The discussion of Chinese, that "grammarless" language, gives pidgin its greatest representational license.

To return to Whitney: his efforts on behalf of Chinese are not intended to expand the boundaries of English; rather, his purpose was to show how little Chinese and other languages have in common. At this point in his lecture series, Whitney was going around the globe and classifying the different human languages for his audience. Coming to the languages of eastern continental Asia, he pointed out that

the distinctive common feature of these tongues is that they are all monosyllabic. Of all human dialects, they represent most nearly what, as we have already seen reason for concluding, was the primitive stage of the agglutinative and inflective forms of speech. They have never begun that fusion of elements once independently significant into compound forms which has been the principal item in the history and development of all other tongues. The Chinese words, for example, are still to no small extent roots, representing ideas in crude and undefined form, and equally convertible by use into noun, verb, or adverb. . . . Not very much requires to be said in explanation of the structure and history of a language so simple—a language which might be said to have no grammatical structure, which possesses neither inflections nor parts of speech, and which has changed less in four thousand years than most others in four hundred, or than many another in a single century.[12]

Pidgin translation is full of gaps—the hiccups caused by local, structural inequalities between English and Chinese. Whitney wants to persuade us that those gaps correspond to historical absences. Other languages have moved on from monosyllabism or, like English, back toward it, but the "scanty and crippled" Chinese language stays right where it began, with no need, potential, or opening for change.[13] The rendering of Mencius into pidgin is thus an imaginative tunnel through which we journey back to a primitive state, the state at which all words are roots and nothing but roots. Formal parataxis is the representation in present speech of a history that should have taken place, but never did, leaving the Chinese in "the primitive stage" preceding the fusions and inflections of linguistic history.[14] And because for those of us who have a history, it is a journey backwards, the paraphrase affords us a historicizing experience that would be unavailable to a Chinese reader, unless of course this reader had previously entered history by learning a language with morphology and a history of development. The historically determined translation therefore accomplishes an asymmetrical transaction: it shows us, who have more grammatically speaking, how much less the others have. Gaps in Chinese grammar ("no grammatical structure . . . neither inflections nor parts of speech") are as plain as the holes in a beggar's clothes, whereas the things Chinese speakers have that we English or German speakers lack (the tonal separation of otherwise identical syllables, for example, or a semantically based writing system with forty thousand distinct signs) become invisible, filtered out by the translator's technique.

Pidgin translation generally works only in one direction, from richer to poorer. There are structural reasons for this. If we were trying to represent the word-for-word meanings of a language with finer grammatical articulations than ours, what would we put in the gaps between our own words? When translating from Chinese, Schleicher and Whitney insert a palpable absence or incorrectness to mark points of linguistic difference. But translation from a richer language stumbles over too many signs, outstripping the resources of linear speech, as in the examples from Whorf shown in Figures 4.1 and 4.2.

Incommensurability arguments take quite different forms according to the language described and the language of the description. With isolating languages (to use a typology I will shortly criticize), the thoughts expressed by native thinkers are typically held to ignore some distinction thought essential in the investigator's language. With agglutinating languages or the more morphologically complex inflectional ones, the investigator notes either subtleties or superfluities of thought;[15] the copious whirl of particles that must be laid out in translated equivalents becomes a quantitative basis for saying that we simply cannot make ours the thought processes of people with such exotically complex ways of saying things.

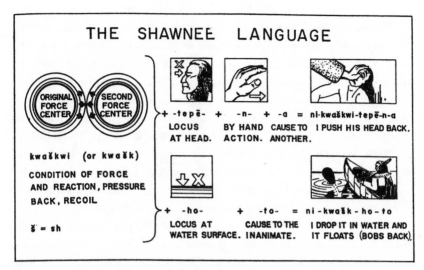

Figure 16. The English sentences 'I push his head back' and 'I drop it in water and it floats' are unlike. But in Shawnee the corresponding statements are closely similar, emphasizing the fact that analysis of nature and classification of events as like or in the same category (logic) are governed by grammar.

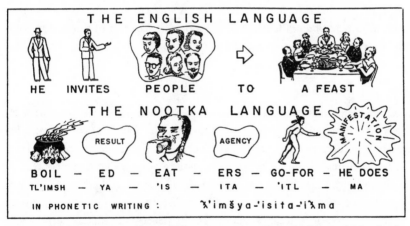

Figure 17. Here are shown the different ways in which English and Nootka formulate the same event. The English sentence is divisible into subject and predicate; the Nootka sentence is not, yet it is complete and logical. Furthermore, the Nootka sentence is just one word, consisting of the root *tl'imsh* with five suffixes.

Translation, then, creates asymmetries and incommensurabilities while allowing us to think of these as intrinsic to the objects of study, not to the process. While purporting to give a view of Chinese "as nearly as we can represent it," Whitney, like any literal translator, is actually synthesizing a new language whose properties come to exist only in relation to an earlier, in his case fuller, language. His Chinese is a dialect of English: only when set against English does it prove the incompleteness of the original; only the expectation of something else makes Chinese seem "scanty." To turn around the anthropological ambiguity alluded to earlier: if the "nearness" of the translation created, for Whitney's original hearers, an effect of distance, that effect could be achieved only with materials that lay close to home.

This is not to say that Whitney's description of Chinese is false or merely parochial. It is not necessarily wrong to say that Chinese "possesses neither inflections nor parts of speech" and therefore has no "grammar." It is wrong, however, to present these comparative judgments without making explicit the standard to which Chinese is being held, thereby allowing the question whether this is a meaningful standard of comparison to be raised. Had Whitney said *Chinese is poor insofar as / in those respects in which / on the assumption that English is rich*, he would have left us an accurate depiction of an interaction instead of a tendentious description of an artifact of translation technique as the simple truth about Chinese.

Evolutions

In Whitney's case, then, the judgment on Chinese resolves into a mirror effect of the pidgin-style translation into English. (Much of comparative literature reduces to mirror or seesaw effects.) The remark that Chinese lacks a grammar has, however, to be understood in a somewhat larger context. A contrast with English alone is inadequate to reconstructing that context, nor can the consequences of the remark be discerned without introducing at least one more interacting element. To the poverty of Chinese corresponds not only the relative richness of the idiom—English or German or whatever—used by the translator but above all the imagined glories of Sanskrit or Proto-Indo-European. These are the relations into which the story of "how Chinese lost its grammar" resolves.

The "isolating" character of the early Chinese language, its monosyllabic cadence, and freedom from morphological markers are frequently remarked by nineteenth-century linguists, whether their scholarly interest in Chinese was active or not. All their divisions of languages into types according to grammatical structure have as their "degree zero" the Chinese language, the absence of grammar. Friedrich von Schlegel's 1808 essay *On the Language and Wisdom of the Indians* at one point divides all languages into two groups: those that show grammatical relationships by modification of word roots, and those in which the roots remain unchanged but take on external affixes. Chinese is the paradigm of Schlegel's second type.

A noteworthy example of a language completely lacking inflections, in which everything that other languages express through inflection is indicated by means of separate words that already have meanings of their own, is Chinese: a language that, with its unique monosyllabism, and on account of its thoroughness or rather complete simplicity of structure, aids us greatly in understanding the whole world of language.[16]

The system of two genera was too crude, inasmuch as it lumped together morphologically complex languages such as Turkish and Hungarian with the far simpler Chinese. Friedrich von Schlegel's brother August Wilhelm von Schlegel seems to have been the first to replace it with what subsequently became the classical scheme of three types: "languages with no grammatical structure, languages that employ affixes, and languages with inflection." As before, Chinese is the primary example of the first type, a language "containing only one class of words, incapable of receiving either development or modification. It might be said that all its words are roots—but sterile roots producing neither plants nor trees. In these languages are found no declinations, no conjugations, no derivations, nor any word compounds save by simple juxtaposition."[17]

Wilhelm von Humboldt's vast *On the Variety of Human Language Structures* proposes, "apart from the Chinese language, which dispenses with all grammatical forms, three possible forms of language: the inflectional, agglutinative, and incorporative."[18] For all the favorable things Humboldt found to say about the Chinese language in this work and in his letter to Jean-Pierre Abel-Rémusat,[19] Chinese is, in the grand scheme of world languages, a pole with which all grammars are, *qua* grammars, to be contrasted. "Of all known languages, Chinese and Sanskrit stand in the most decisive opposition. . . . The Chinese and Sanskrit languages stand as the two extremes in the field of known languages, not perhaps comparable in their suitability for the development of the mind, but certainly so in the internal consistency and perfect execution of their systems."[20] "The development of the mind" connects Humboldt's anthropology with his linguistics. Humboldt insisted that language is, rather than the expression of a prior thought, the organ through which thinking becomes possible. Because Chinese leaves so much of its grammar unexpressed in sound, realized only as relations of proximity and word order, Chinese occupies, in Humboldt's classification, the lower reaches of the category "language."

It is hardly to be expected that an existing language family (or one language from such a family) should correspond in every point to the perfect form of language; in any case, such perfection lies beyond our experience. But the Sanskrit language family comes closest to this perfect form. In it the spiritual cultivation of the human race has reached its happiest development in the long series of its progresses. We can therefore establish the Sanskrit languages as a firm point of comparison for all the others.[21]

Under the conditions of nineteenth-century philology, then, to say that Chinese is a language without grammar necessarily involves it in a relationship with the supremely grammatical language, Sanskrit or Indic, and secondarily in a relationship with the languages that can claim a relation to Indic, the Indo-European family. That relationship can—must—be both direct and distant. Whitney's source for the *Mencius* example, August Schleicher's *Languages of Europe in Systematic Review*, crowns this tradition by placing Chinese in a class of its own, the "monosyllabic language" as distinguished from the "flexional" and "agglutinating" languages. The book's organization segregates monosyllabism even more strongly from the other two language types: the monosyllabic language, Chinese, appears only in the last section of the "Introduction," which is separated from the work proper by a second title. One of the three recognized language-types is somehow not a part of the book that includes it in a "systematic review" of languages, European and other (the title is more restrictive than the work's actual contents). The opening pages of Schleicher's "Introduction" explain this curious play of boundaries with a metaphor that gives a new weighting to the standard linguistic typology based on grammatical properties. In a language like Chinese,

the word is not in the least articulated; it is yet a strict unity previous to all difference, as is the *crystal* in the world of nature. These languages, which vocally express meaning but not relation, form the first language class, which we may most suitably

Inhaltsübersicht.

———

✳) Die mit einem ✳ bezeichneten Sprachen sind ausführlicher behandelt.

4.3 The "monosyllabic order of languages," that is, Chinese, inserted between the introduction and the main body of August Schleicher's *Die Sprachen Europas in systematischer Übersicht* (1850).

call the monosyllabic languages. . . . In the second class, that of the agglutinating languages . . . the word is articulated into parts (thus, a distinction from the first class), but these parts are not molded into a new whole, rather the word is still a collection of several individual lexical units (and this distinguishes the second from the third class). "The single, whole individual is still the ground [for several individual lexical units] rather than a subjective unity of members" as is the case, among natural organisms, for the *plants*. . . . The inflectional languages stand at the top of the ladder of language: here at last a genuine articulation of members develops in the organism of the word, the word is the unity-in-multiplicity of its members, corresponding to the *animal organism*, which has this same particularity.[22]

Inhalt des erſten Bandes.

4.4 "Oriental Philosophy" placed between "Introduction" and "Part One" of Hegel's *Lectures on the History of Philosophy*, from *Vorlesungen über die Geschichte der Philosophie* (1833).

The unreferenced internal quotation comes from Hegel's *Encyclopedia*, the middle third of which, the *Philosophy of Nature*, seems to have given Schleicher a program to follow even to the uttermost details.[23] With this set of connotations at work, the tripartite division cannot be evenly balanced. It has to be scanned mineral//vegetable/animal, for both agglutinating and inflectional languages stand opposite Chinese, just as all living things are distinct from dead things. The contrast with monosyllabic languages relativizes the differences between agglutinating and inflectional classes. Indeed, it puts them into a narrative relationship, since they alone, and not the monosyllabic languages, are capable of historical development.

It becomes apparent to us that the prehistoric development of languages corresponds perfectly to the system [of typology] and displays in the most perfect languages—the inflectional ones—the three periods of monosyllabicity, agglutination, and flexion. Not every language has worked its way up to the highest stages, the system shows us, just as not every organic substance has raised itself to the level of the animal organism; parts of the vocal substance are stalled at every stage and substage, just as parts of organic substance are at every stage of the scale of organic life.[24]

Whitney, too, accepted this broad picture of linguistic history, in which Chinese was a relic of the very oldest past and could hardly be anything else because of its unalterable crystalline structure. It was so much a commonplace that Whitney's great enemy, Max Müller, repeated it in precisely the same terms. And Otto Jespersen, toward the end of the century, created a stir by suggesting that languages evolved not away from the condition of Chinese but toward it, as had English.[25] (One result of Jespersen's activity was a clearer recognition of the legitimacy of word order as a grammatical principle: that is how Chinese got its grammar back.)[26]

The Wobbling Pivot

What nineteenth-century European and American linguists had to say about Chinese has little to do with Chinese and a great deal to do with something few contemporary scholars of China learn about in their training—another sign of the "gypsy urban planning" under which we conduct our careers. If Indic was so important as to dictate the terms under which Chinese was studied and discussed for over a century, what accounts for its attractiveness? What projects did Sanskrit uphold? And what happened to them?

The split between Chinese and Sanskrit is nowhere made more insistently than in Friedrich von Schlegel's *On the Language and Wisdom of the Indians*. It is surprising that so insubstantial and topical a work should have had such lasting influence, but Schlegel established, as we have seen, the framework in which it was common knowledge that Chinese had no grammar and no history, and it is his understanding of grammar and history that is at issue here.

Schlegel's praise of Sanskrit depends on a rejection of what he calls the Manchu language family (including predominantly Chinese). The two language families have opposite properties and distinct origins—indeed property and origin here intertwine in truly mythic fashion. The Manchu-Chinese languages originated, Schlegel holds, in onomatopoieia and imitation, *Klangnachahmung*, whereas the Indic languages arose from *Besonnenheit*, understanding.[27] "Manchurian" languages have no structure because they are not principally products of the mind but rather of human animals reacting to environmental stimuli. In contrast, the structure of Indic languages derives from the "pure thought world" of the first speakers, whose thoughts were "not in the form of pictures, but expressed themselves with immediate clarity." Rather like Revelation, which was supposed to have landed on certain peoples but not on others, this *Besonnenheit* grants the Indo-Europeans a "clear outlook," "exquisite feeling," "a sensitive and creative mind." It is never made clear how this correlates to Indic grammar—whether there is a causal relation one way or the other between them. Causality might detract from the purpose, after all.

Schlegel wants to combat the idea, prevalent in France since Condillac and in England since Locke, that humanity had worked its way up from sense perception to the naming of objects to grammatical categories. That way lies mechanism, materialism, and atheism. The completeness and exquisite organization of Sanskrit grammar—none of it "imitative"—is for Schlegel evidence of a separate creation. There are indeed languages that have developed in the way Locke and Condillac imagined them, and even in the way Rousseau and Herder imagined, but these are precisely not the languages we should study and imitate. "Many other languages appear to us, in truth, not as an organic artwork of meaningful syllables and fruitful nuclei, but as consisting for the most part of various sound-imitations and sound-plays, of raw emotional shrieks, signals, shouts, and directions, to which habit brought an ever more conventional understanding and arbitrary definition."[28] A language with a natural origin—imitation—stays in the realm of nature. The miraculous language begins, remains, and thinks in its own, properly supranatural realm.

This typological duality is founded on Schlegel's horror at the outcome of the French Revolution. What he calls Chinese is a language that Locke, Condillac, Rousseau, and de la Mettrie might have thought up, a mechanical system of signs founded on imitation, repetition, and reinforcement. And what he calls Indic is the spiritual converse of the mechanical languages. The center of the system of mid-century language typologies, Indic, turns out to be a reflection, the wishful projection, of a disgruntled ex-republican.

Schlegel was a brilliant dabbler, but a real philologist was soon at work filling out the indications he had left. *On the Conjugation-System of the Sanskrit*

Language, Franz Bopp's first publication, showed the original Indo-European tongue to have been a perfect language in the sense of Leibniz's or John Wilkins's philosophical projects and to have been sent down from the heavens by a benign personification as well. In Sanskrit conjugation-endings, Bopp saw the remnants of earlier Indo-European pronouns. Nothing is wasted, nothing is meaningless. "When the Genius of the language has painstakingly and thoughtfully represented the simple concepts of persons with simple signs, and when we see that the same concepts are expressed similarly, with wise economy, in both verbs and pronouns—then it becomes obvious that the letter originally had a meaning, and that it remained true to its original meaning."[29] This is historical restitution in a different mode altogether from the crude primitivism of Whitney's Chinese, and it should be, because Bopp, in this a good disciple of Schlegel, treats the earliest form of Indo-European as the most perfect one. Chinese, and languages assimilated to it typologically or historically, did not begin as a structured whole but as a collection of isolated signs maintained as a set only by the coercive operations of culture.

Ancestors and Inheritors

Indic supplied Schlegel a historical story about transcendence; it also supplied him and many others with a brand-new set of prestigious ancestors. The attempt to split Indic off from the merely natural "languages of imitation" could not stand up to critical examination, but the imagined community of Indo-Aryanism was a far more durable invention. What remained after the memory of the revolutions and restorations in France faded, carrying with it the immediate polemical purpose of Schlegel's account of "Manchurian" languages, were the idealized Indians. Whitney's account of his present moment calls on them to explain world history and, in the process, curiously dissolves nations, empires, and enmities into a vast spreading of grammatical competence.

One source of the special interest which we feel in the study of Indo-European language lies in the fact that our own tongue is one of its branches. . . . But we are further justified in our somewhat exclusive interest by the position which our languages, and the races which speak them, hold among other languages and races. . . . [The Indo-European race's] first entrance as an actor into what we are accustomed to call universal history . . . was in the far East, in the Persian empire of Cyrus and his successors. This founded itself upon the ruins and relics of more ancient empires and cultures, belonging to other peoples, in part Semitic, in part of obscurer kindred. . . . The Persian empire, in its conquering march westward, was first checked by one of these humble communities, the little jarring confederation of Greek states and cities, destined to become, notwithstanding its scanty numbers, the real founder of Indo-European prëeminence. . . . Rome, appropriating the fruits of Greek culture, and adding an organizing and assimilating force particularly her own, went forth to give laws to all nations. . . . And if Christianity was of Semitic birth, Greeks and Romans gave it universality. . . .

The Semites, inspired with the furious zeal of a new religion, Mohammedanism, broke from their deserts and overran the fairest parts of Asia and Africa. . . . They recoiled, at last, before the reviving might of the superior race, and the last and grandest era of Indo-European supremacy began, the era in the midst of which we now live. For the past few centuries, the European nations have stood foremost, without a rival, in the world's history. They are the enlightened and the enlighteners of mankind. . . . The network of their ability embraces the globe; their ships are in every sea between the poles, for exploration, for trade, or for conquest; the weaker races are learning their civilization, falling under their authority, or perishing off the face of the land, from inherent inability to stand before them. . . . They have inherited from its ancient possessors the sceptre of universal dominion . . . and they are worthy to hold it, since their sway brings, upon the whole, physical well-being, knowledge, morality and religion to those over whom it is extended.[30]

The idea that the Aryans acted as a people—at a time when, probably within hearing of the Smithsonian lecture hall, the majority Indo-European speakers of America were destroying each other over the question of how best to conduct their "sway" over members of a fellow race—must have struck Whitney as inspiring, a compensatory adjustment. Worse would come in the name of pan-Aryanism. Of course, Indo-European philology does not reduce to an ethnic propaganda exercise (*pace* Bernal), nor did it contribute anything indispensable to the militarizations and dehumanizations of the last two hundred years. And yet, and yet. . . . The phrase *corruptio optimi pessimum* (the worst thing is the corruption of the good man) comes to mind. Friedrich von Schlegel's influence on European thinking about tribes and selves is more subtle and insinuating than the classic racism of Gobineau, the racism of blame.[31] Does the praise of grammatical beauty create ugliness? Does the thought of noble ancestors prompt ignoble actions? Not necessarily, of course; but the observation of interactivity serves to point out what is at stake.

5

No Time Like the Present:
The Category of Contemporaneity
in Chinese Studies

Throw overboard the word "exoticism" and all its stale, threadbare implications. . . . Cast aside its tropical connotation, merely geographical. Exoticism is not just given in space, but in time as well. And then quickly define, set down the sensation of Exoticism: which is nothing other than the notion of the different; the perception of the diverse; the knowledge that something is not oneself; and the power of exoticism, which is nothing but the power of conceiving otherwise.

— Victor Segalen, *On Exoticism*

In every work of genius we recognize our own rejected thoughts: they come back to us with a certain alienated majesty.

— Emerson, "Self-Reliance"

The distance to be overcome is a recurrent motif of pathos in studies of traditional China. The pathos may be misplaced; after all, if there is one thing we know in the humanities today, it is that "what is well known is not known, just because it is well known."[1] What is not well known, moreover, keeps falling into the category of the already well known, of becoming exotic (or rather generically "exotic") and thereby predictable.[2] So the truly unknown, not only the new thing but the thing we cannot reduce to our pre-existing frameworks of knowledge, becomes a rare and valuable commodity, the apex of an angle of which the two sides are epistemology and ethics. Those of us who work on non-Western cultures—especially those of China and Japan—are frequently asked to furnish a taste of that strangeness. Indeed, curiosity about different ways of fashioning cultural spaces is often precisely what attracts newcomers into this field of study, and no matter how world-weary we become, the wonder, and the challenge, of Chinese texts is the impossibility of predicting exactly what will turn up on the next page.[3] But it is limiting to deal in curiosities, rather than essentials. Having got our foot in the door, we want to contribute to the big conversations. Arnaldo Momigliano put this well: "I hope it is not simply an ancient historian's prejudice to say that the new exploration in the field of ideas seems up to now more rewarding when remote cultures are its primary object. . . . But when we come to our own society we need to know what we can believe rather than what is believed."[4]

The modern concept of culture—of human ways of life as encapsulated in cultures, but not a pan-human category of Culture—is at the root of some of the trouble. For cultures define themselves by reciprocal difference; to champion a certain "culture" is (typically) to contend that it makes sense on its own and does not need to be suppressed by or merged with another.[5] The notion that preserving, not reducing, the otherness of others is our most demanding ethical task is a recent addition to the catechism, and it runs counter to millennia of moral training. In all traditions, I think I can say without too much exaggeration, the way you make others into people for whom you have legitimate moral concern is by making them neighbors, fellow tribesmen, part of your own flock. (Anthropologists often tell us of peoples whose self-designation does double duty as the term for "human beings." For such peoples, easy enough: to be a member of their group is to be human, and to be human is to be a member of their group.) The concept of humanity as it developed in the European seventeenth and eighteenth centuries was meant as just such an extension of the tribe, and it would have been difficult for its proponents to see what was wrong with "universalism" since they had before them so many examples of immoral actions based on particularisms of religion, race, or political obedience. People may be from Samaria, but that does not keep them from doing good; the otherness of Samaritans matters less (or such is the force of the parable) than the choice of one of them to behave toward the unfortunate stranger as a neighbor would.[6] However, one has to be rather confident about the extensibility of the concept of goodness and sure of recognizing it in far-flung places and guises for a moral economy of this kind to function.

There is a distance to be traveled between otherness as a moral or political condition and otherness as a logical category, but some have tried to make the trip: for Hegel, "otherness," however discovered, was the sign of an unresolved contradiction needing to be worked through and reduced to a local difference within the process of thought thinking itself. "Every operation of Spirit is [according to the Delphic command to 'Know Thyself'] thus only an effort of Spirit to grasp itself, and it is the aim of all genuine knowledge to bring Spirit to recognize itself in everything between heaven and earth. For Spirit, something wholly Other is simply not at issue [*vorhanden*: available, given, present]."[7] This is to make the reduction of otherness the whole (and unavoidable) business of thinking, likened by Hegel to the process whereby we eat external things and change them into our own flesh and blood.[8]

Perhaps unfortunately, certainly uncomfortably, confidence in such reductions now eludes those of us whose thinking leads us beyond the products of our immediate time and nation—which means all of us. It is not obvious that we can accomplish the assimilation of alien ideas and practices to ourselves, nor, indeed, that that is what we are meant to do. It is as if we have discarded Hegel and taken for our prophet the more demanding Emmanuel Levinas, for whom the face of the other, summoning us to an infinite responsibility, is the primary datum of consciousness. "The foreignness of the Other," says Levinas in a characteristic passage, "his irreducibility to the I, to my thoughts and my possessions, is precisely accomplished as a calling into question of my spontaneity, as ethics."[9] "The Other, qua Other, is not only an alter ego. He is that which I am not."[10] And from responsibility to this Other, for Levinas, flow all moral *and* cognitive obligations. These are perhaps most neatly bound together in the "ethical dealing" of language:

> The relationship of language implies transcendence, radical separation, the strangeness of the interlocutors, the revelation of the other to me. In other words, language is spoken where community between the terms of the relationship is wanting, where the common plane is wanting or is yet to be constituted. It takes place in this transcendence. Discourse is thus the experience of something absolutely foreign, a *pure* 'knowledge' or 'experience,' *a traumatism of astonishment.*[11]

Surely the combination of such a stance with the project of knowing about others is an extremely unstable one.

Acknowledging from the start that there may be no way to close off the angle, that the morality of dealing with others and the epistemology of knowing them may never meet, that the difficulty will always remain, I would like to examine some of the ways in which philosophical ethnography inflects the linked concepts of otherness, commonality, and time. In particular, I will look at ways of stating one's relation to those others who are Chinese—particularly premodern Chinese. Contemporary critical parlance may lead the reader to suppose that the talk of "others" and "otherness" in the foregoing derives from an ethnic context—that I am preparing to discourse on the relations of "Chinese" and "Westerners," each a *feiwo zulei* 非我族類, a (racial) other, to the other.[12] But that is a hypothesis I prefer to do without. The discontinuities that matter to my discussion emerge from time and the building of histories along time lines: in these we are all, as modern people indebted to various forms of self-definition, caught up.[13]

Anamnesis and Reconnaissance

Anthropology often poses as an agency of understanding, a bridge-building discipline. Johannes Fabian's *Time and the Other: How Anthropology Makes Its Object* turns this claim around. Fabian diagnoses an ethical trap in the use of terms like "primitive," "traditional," or "premodern." The trap begins with the trick of putting the societies usually described with such words on a time line where they occupy places formerly held by ancestral versions of Western societies: they are backward because they are (a) behind us and (b) treading the same path. Fabian's great exhibit is, appropriately and inevitably, Hegel's *Philosophy of History*, in which we are told that the attested civilizations of the world form a series, from least free to most nearly free, and the series maps itself more or less neatly onto the Eurasian landmass, with the earlier, more spiritually impoverished societies yielding to more forward-looking ones in a procession from East to West.[14]

Time is the category by which Hegel marks off the separateness of others yet draws their history into that of the human species. For Hegel each society has its day in the history of the world, its moment of realizing the maximum of freedom then possible; after its glory has passed, it disappears, ossifies, or falls under a more advanced neighbor's sway, although traces of its achievements survive it. Hegelian history—like its offshoot, the Marxist history of "modes of production"—is basically a means of telling what time it is: of establishing where the most advanced societies have got to and estimating how long it will take the others to catch up with them. "World history, we see, is generally the unfolding [*Auslegung*: also "exposition," "interpretation"] of Spirit in time, just as the idea as Nature unfolds itself in space."[15] Time (which, incidentally, on earth correlates with a daily east-to-west motion, the same path followed over the millennia by human history) is the medium of the internal differences of Spirit.

Hegel uses time so forcefully to exhibit differences that mere chronology suffers: from reading the *Philosophy of History*, you would never notice that Confucius was contemporary with the Persian wars and Aeschylus. China comes very early in Hegel's account because of its having so primitive a state formation, based, as he believes, on the family, that quasi-natural relation. The description of the Chinese stage of world history is followed by chapters on the increasingly sophisticated worlds of India, Persia, Judaea, and Egypt: thousands of years seem to have passed when in fact the "epochs" have been purely notional, and the "Oriental World" is a catalogue of types rather than a series. Although Hegel's project is outwardly historicist, chronology, it turns out, serves the needs of typology. Time keeps civilizations distinct: when a citizen of Prussia in 1830 looks at China, he sees (if he sees rightly) not the China of the present but the China of its formative period, when its institutions led the world. Essential China is historical China, just as the essential Greece is the Greece of Pericles and the essential England is the England of the worldwide mercantile empire. And what essential China brought to the world is something that lies deep in the past of historical Prussia, and of all humanity.

Fabian's name for this strategy is the "denial of coevalness. By that I mean *a persistent and systematic tendency to place the referent(s) of anthropology in a Time other than the present of the producer of anthropological discourse.*"[16] In Hegel's case, there is little room for argument: the historian is able to do Hegelian history by virtue of belonging to a different time from the others, a time a little closer to the eventual self-understanding of Spirit. For Fabian, this amounts to a serious ethical lapse. By putting the objects of anthropological study into the past—a past that in some sense belongs to us as observers, even if no direct causal link between our history and that of our objects of study can be shown—we consolidate our right to deal with those objects as we wish. (A horrific case in point, not mentioned by Fabian, is the National Socialist plan to turn Prague's Altstadt into a historical museum of Jewry, once all the Jews had been exterminated.) "In short, *geopolitics* has its ideological foundations in *chronopolitics.*"[17] A proper ethical relation, Fabian urges, begins with the recognition of coevalness. When we realize that we and the people we study are separated by many differentials, all of which nonetheless operate in the medium of contemporary history, our privileges and consequent responsibilities ought to come into view. We ought "to perceive anthropology as an activity which is part of what it studies," as a realm of praxis, and seek opportunities for "concrete, practical contradiction between coeval research and allochronic interpretation."[18]

That studying China and making statements about it may have practical effects will come as no surprise to those working in contemporary fields, particularly economics and politics: recall the names and divergent careers of Owen Lattimore and John King Fairbank.[19] Students of modern China have no problem in recognizing that all of us inhabit "the same time." Since the late nineteenth century the modernizers, whether political reformers, literary radicals, or builders of railways and arsenals, have been stirred to action by the realization that time, ticking away elsewhere, was passing China by; to modernize was to bring China from its "antique" or "immemorial" *status quo* to the present.[20] Mao Zedong's boast that the Great Leap Forward would lead to China's outstripping Britain in ten years was not just a matter of national output statistics; it was correlated to a race run along a time line, as if to make up by 1970 a lag perceptible since 1842. More recently, the process of market-directed reform in China since 1978 has given a new lease of life to the language of "backwardness" and "catching up," as by repudiating socialism China is deemed to have put itself back on the one historical track.[21] How many newspaper headlines have announced that "China Takes Steps to Join the World" in this or that respect! (The phrase is not the exclusive property of those who think of themselves as representing "the world." "Moving Toward the World," 走向世界, is also the title of a recent series of reprints of nineteenth-century Chinese travel writings.)[22] All this is familiar to the point of banality, but it shows how deeply a cliché can take root in the minds of people who may disagree on everything else. The relations of "advanced" and "developing" economies follow, at least ideologically, the very pattern of differentiated steps on an identical path that Fabian sees as permitting "the denial of coevalness," but with the significant difference that the parties are in continual communication. Differences in stage of industrialization (and the cost of labor, which is not necessarily the same thing) inflect and direct these communications, as has been observed since Adam Smith.[23]

The crude economic measures of "advanced" status, the notion that political evolution takes place as a series of irreversible stages (whether communism or liberal democracy is held to be the end point), the Weberian expectation that the processes set in motion by Protestantism in Western Europe set the pattern for a modern ethics, social structure, and economics—all these and more ways of putting the problems of recent world history show that the present, in China, is apt to be a haunted time, where what is done locally is always shadowed by its equivalence (or mismatch) with what goes on elsewhere.[24] For people whose modern history is strongly inflected by invasions and domestic haplessness, the fact that one lives in the same time with others is probably less a discovery and more the normal condition of awareness.

It takes no special virtue to share the present with China. Indeed, since Leibniz's *Novissima Sinica* (1697), that is what we intermediaries do best. The "coevalness" of civilizations is one of the givens of our field; it underwrites our brand of cultural pluralism. "I consider it a singular plan of the fates," says Leibniz, "that human cultivation and refinement should today be concentrated, as it were, in the two extremes of our continent, in Europe and in Tschina.... Perhaps Supreme Providence has ordained such an arrangement, so that as the most cultivated and distant peoples stretch out their arms to each other, those in between may gradually be brought to a better way of life."[25] Rather than a time line, with the Western present streaking away into the future, the favored figure of East-West philosophical chronology has been the intersection. Crucially, however, the intersection is the spot at which the interpreter appears. Without intermediaries, no mediation, only missed appointments. And this is where we see variation. The state of shared contemporaneity, although always possible, has to be attained through mutual explanations. It also requires some strategic manipulation of the relevant pasts and presents, so they will line up neatly with the point of convergence.

Matching the Pieces

The poetic function projects the principle of equivalence from the axis of selection into the axis of combination. Equivalence is promoted to the constitutive device of the sequence.

—Roman Jakobson[26]

What of a history that would make coevalness not the exceptional circumstance but the ordinary condition of a grouping of civilizations? Fabian talks of Marx's "radical presentism which . . . contained the theoretical possibility for a negation of allochronic distancing." The theme of praxis, Fabian shows, brings out the cotemporality in Marx and, even more than that, the idea that groups affect each other by what they do, "the materialist connection among human beings which is conditioned by their needs and the mode of production and is as old as mankind itself."[27] The historian of connections needs to see all the parts of the world moving through time as one great whole, but what mechanism will underwrite that intuition? Marx, of course, saw capitalism as burning its way through all territories of "precapitalist economic formations," bringing "dissolution" to all pre-existing types of social relations in its expansive drive.[28] Convergence happens, then, as a side effect of capitalism. But that leaves most of history—everything prior to the creation of the "world-system," however we date that—a set of unconnected provincial narratives.[29]

Again, one might follow Karl Jaspers in dating the efflorescence of the major civilizations from a single "axial age," the period of Buddha, Moses, Confucius, Zoroaster, Socrates, and Jesus, each of whom expressed (and whose successors gave institutional form to) a tension between the mundane and the transcendental orders.[30] How this series of "breakthroughs" came about, in what ways they were connected, and how their subsequent histories are to be interpreted in relation to one another are problems deriving from the understanding of the various axial-age civilizations as consequences of the "same" transhistorical moment.[31] But the multiple places, times, and meanings of the axial breakthroughs complicate, to say the least, the thought of a common origin.

One experimenter with synchronous history on a large scale was Giuseppe Ferrari (1811–76), sometime revolutionary agitator in the Italian uprisings of 1848 and thereafter resident in France, where he taught philosophy. His La Chine et l'Europe, published in 1867, attempts to do world history without the hierarchy of times or of agencies, and without the hypostatized categories, that accounted for the meaning of Hegel's. Indeed Ferrari's presentation has every appearance of having been designed as the anti-Hegel.

Hegel's world history was the narrative of the development of Spirit, *one spirit realizing itself in all the populations of the world successively*. From a study of Machiavelli, Ferrari derives a different explanation for historical change: every people in the world is involved in war, hot or cold, with all its immediate neighbors, and the slightest improvement in arms in one state is quickly adopted by all its competing states, and then by their neighbors. "Time" and "the Other" are indeed intimately linked—one is trying to stay one step ahead of the Other all the time. The form of government is also a weapon, but here, says Ferrari, not parity but distinction is the motive for change.

Universal war condemns peoples to exploit the soil, the climate, the population, and the whole variety of natural dispositions, so as to extract from them a force equivalent to that of their adversaries. The equivalence of force must be exact, on pain of death . . . if one of two neighboring states had the slightest advantage, it would enslave its neighbor.[32]

The [principle of the] equivalence of peoples explains the variety of political forms, all of them turned outward as instruments of eternal rivalry. . . . Does the enemy's land give him the resources to organize from the center, to have his seat in a mighty capital, to lead a trained army? Then the response will be a ring of federations, republics, tiny principalities, quasi-nomadic barbarians, pastoral peoples who will nag and harass and fatigue him. Or should the enemy's strength be freedom, one's answer will lie in the advantages of mysterious silence, passive obedience, permanent armies, and the caprices of despotism, so that monarchy makes a mockery of the plans of those who are condemned to debates, parliaments, scandalous revelations, and open shows of discord as a way of life.[33]

"Equivalence" produces diversity. This notion not only flies in the face of the idea of a one-way evolution of governments from despotism to freedom on which Hegel's story depends but also answers its representative logic: rather than being the institutional realization of the strengths, the essential spirit, of a people, the state is formed in anticipation of the neighboring state's weakness. For Ferrari, then, there will be no "end of history," since no type of state-formation can avoid stimulating, through its own successes, the growth of its diametrically opposed form.[34]

Since every state is involved in the universal arms race, and the internal constitution of each is a form of weapon as well, Ferrari sees the history of a single state as a matter of interrelated cyclical loosenings and tightenings of the despotic grip. Every state has neighbors and rivals to which it must respond and which will respond to its own actions. Ferrari considers (without filling in all the gaps) that this network of relations is all that is needed to synchronize history across the Eurasian continent. He settles on a term of 120 years (four generations) as representing the cycle of a completed revolution.

A four-stage period is the unit of measure for all histories; wherever men think, act, fight, and win, they must necessarily fall into a sort of four-act Chinese drama, which allows us to compare among themselves the most far-flung and opposed peoples. It matters little whether this one proclaims a monarchy and that a republic, or whether this one centralizes and that federalizes; just as with affirmation and negation, the forms have meaning only relative to the error being questioned, refuted, discussed, or resolved, and the fall of Troy may correspond to the founding of a dynasty at Luoyang.[35]

And with this Ferrari embarks on the synchronous, relative, "equivalent" history of the parallel ages of Europe and China, dividing history into cycles of 120 and 500 years, and picking out the events and personages that are supposed to reproduce themselves at the two ends of the continent— contemporaneously, or as nearly so as slow communications and information decay will allow. Some examples will show the nature of his comparative thinking.

After the reforms of the state of Qin in 375 B.C., it became possible for a man to occupy, cultivate, sell, or bequeath his fields. . . . [Private] property first gave the hegemony to the Qin, then to Xiang Yu's reaction, then to the Han. . . . Now in 375, 24 years after Socrates' death, we find Plato writing in his *Republic* against private property, calling it the vice of his time, the sickness of societies, the cause of all disorders, the great obstacle that stands in the way of rule by philosopher-kings. . . . But it was in vain that Plato evoked the memory of Sparta, glorified the castes of Egypt and India, and, in a word, gave Hellenic form to the ancient paternalism of China [in his *Republic*]. Aristotle, Plato's near-contemporary, answers him with the very words of Gongsun Yang [at the Qin court]: "No one," he says, "cares to cultivate the common field; without the motive of self-interest, the lands lie fallow; and equality no longer distinguishes between the useful and the useless man." With these words, the debate ceases, and Aristotle is without a doubt the chief philosopher of his time.[36]

In this parallel Ferrari seems to anticipate an economic history of modes of production, one in which regimes of landholding supply the conditions for political events (changes of dynasty, military victories). But this motive holds Ferrari's attention only in the immediate context: the real issue is establishing the cycles of 120 years, the logical steps by which the Chinese and Greco-Roman civilizations move from a patrician form of government to an empire. Once the empire is achieved, it is shaken by (identical) challenges from within.

In 1069 China arrives at the explosion of Wang Anshi, the atheist prime minister, the friend of the people, the great commentator of Confucius; at the same time Europe arrives at the revolution of the bishops and the pontificate of Gregory VII, and in 1077 the Emperor Henry IV is at the pope's feet in the castle of Canossa. . . . Wang Anshi's reforms encounter in 1084 the reaction of a narrowly learned literatus [presumably Sima Guang 司馬光 is meant], who wishes to separate the people from learning. Shall we say that the Roman pontiffs met with no opposition from the philosophers? Does not Gregory VII die in exile? Does not Henry IV win his battles? Does not his son Henry V imprison Pope Pascal II? How many imperially sponsored bishops turn against the bishops nominated by the Holy See! And this war of investitures is nothing more or less than the war of the Chinese scholars against the reformer of the empire, with the same altercations, the same confiscations on both sides, the same importance newly granted to theological opinions in the ruling of the world.[37]

Ferrari is not contending that medieval Catholicism and Song *daoxue* 道學 are identical in any substantive way, but rather that they frustrate their respective secular authorities in similar fashion. That is, the quarrel between religious and political authority may take different forms, but the fact of a quarrel generates ripples at either end of the continent that are soon felt at the other. China's internal organization, strong or weak, authoritarian or collegial, provokes a response by the neighboring powers, ever seeking the antidote to China's present situation; and the neighbors of these neighbors, acting similarly, convey the original impulse in upright or inverted form across the continent. (Ferrari omits these medial stages, considering that the outcomes at each end vouch for the reliability of the mechanism.) Ferrari sees inevitability, or at least predisposition, in the simultaneous appearance of Roscelin, William of Champeaux, Abelard, Wang Anshi 王安石, Zhu Xi, Avicenna, and Averroës.

In later chapters Ferrari yokes together the Ming dynasty and the Italian Renaissance, the Manchus and the German Reformation, the Taipings and the French Revolution. China sometimes pushes events, sometimes is pushed by them. At the time of writing, the 1860s, China is, as so many of Ferrari's contemporaries held, "belated" in comparison to Europe—but by a mere thirty to seventy years according to Ferrari's calendar of parallels. The Taiping rebels have been enacting the events that Europeans know as 1789, 1830, and 1848, but with the foreseeable difference that where the European rebels were philosophical rationalists, the Taipings raised a messianic religious army against the bureaucratic-rational Qing state. In the next period, lasting from 1875 to 2000, China may well make up the difference: "China has so often passed from the most violent phases to the most peaceful ones that we can expect to see her annotate her Thirteen Classics with the aid of our physical sciences before we reach the reign of the philosopher-bureaucrats."[38]

As an account of world history, Ferrari's story sits oddly alongside the ef-forts of Kant, Hegel, and Marx: formalistic rather than teleological, cyclical rather than linear, it does not so much explain as arrange. If anything, it re-calls the phases and alternations of *Yi jing*–inspired historiography, although that resemblance, too, must be put down to a parallel rather than an influ-ence.[39] Ferrari's history is entirely human—it does not await a theological justification—but does not quite answer to human purposes; the cycles of history dictate which purposes have a chance of being realized and which do not, and yet it would be futile to probe these cycles for their meaning. China and Europe are simply the spatial endpoints of a field of reverberations. Without Providence, but ineluctably, they "stretch out their arms toward each other."

The Squirrel Cage

What is missing in Ferrari's parallel history is an attempt to work out the milieu in which the reverberations occur, the stages and mechanisms of transmission. This silence is all the more deafening when we consider the period of his interest in Chinese affairs, precisely the years of the "open-ing" of the Far East to English, French, and American soldiers, traders, and diplomats. Ferrari mentions the Anglo-French expedition of 1860 but only to dismiss it as mere epiphenomenon.[40] Perhaps the conceptual architecture of Ferrari's history derives too directly from the use, by Voltaire and the other *philosophes*, of China as a parallel world, a counter-cosmos to Europe's.[41] Intervening in such an experiment would, like setting a thumb on the scales, vitiate the results. Ferrari's adventurous contemporaries had no such qualms, nor did they need much theory to ground their practical interventions: they themselves were the milieu of their com-munications with China, working through ballistics, investment, medicine, journalism, and sundry other modes of action to change the place. The "interpretive work" of the intercultural relationship consisted in translating books, attacking sinocentric prejudices, educating a new class of people, reshaping the syllabus of texts worth learning from, converting the heathen, opening minds, and so forth.[42] The resulting hybrid culture has been tagged a "colonial" or "translated" modernity.[43] The failed reforms of 1898 and the polymorphous vitality of prerevolutionary Shanghai are its main historical exhibits.

A copious literature has grown up to describe the process of "China's response to the West"—a formulation that canonizes, it hardly needs to be pointed out, the belatedness, the secondariness, of the response vis-à-vis the stimulus.[44] Some of this writing presents the newness of the situation in the late imperial and modern periods as a conversion from one mode of time to another—from a cyclical to a linear consciousness of time and history.[45] The very idea of a cyclical pattern of time suggests the autonomy of a national history that finds all the resources it needs already within itself and can only be sent in new directions by a violent impulse from outside (a *contingent* or *tangent* force). This is precisely how missionary scholars saw Chinese traditional learning and their impact upon it. The American missionary and interpreter of China S. Wells Williams, explaining for an English-speaking audience the traditional Five Elements 五行 theory of cyclical phases in nature, calls it

a satisfactory explanation to Chinese philosophers of the changes going on in the visible universe, for no possible contingency can arise which they are not prepared to solve by their analysis of the evolution of its powers. Through their speculations by this curious system they have been led away from carefully recording facts and processes, and have gone on, *like a squirrel in a cage, making no progress* toward the real knowledge of the elements they treat of.[46]

To adopt Fabian's typology of temporalities, the meeting of East and West would be an encounter between time and nontime. (This is a simplification, of course: it would be more accurate to say that the encounter produced the contrasts, which contemporary anxieties and polemics then pulled into the shapes of antithetical linear and cyclical time.) Native modernizers, then, put all their weight into gaining narrative control of linear, evolutionary, history. It was part of the process whereby they took over from "the West" the office of transforming China. But such a view of history, it has been argued, led necessarily in the application to a radical exclusivity, an anticipatory triumphalism by those who saw themselves in possession of the future "present," genuine modernity.[47] Co-temporality is, under these conditions, unthinkable: it would be like allowing two parallel lines to pass through the same point. The authority of the comparative scholar in the early twentieth century (in many cases, an astonishingly young activist) amounts to the power to say where the two lines (Chinese culture, Western culture) go and at what point they may, or may not, meet.[48]

Patching up the World

Linearity is, then, a game with only one possible winner, and it seems to predict the vanishing of all other temporalities (among them, traditional China). A rather different attempt to arrange "the meeting of East and West" took place in the book of that name, published by F. S. C. Northrop, a Yale professor of philosophy and comparative law, in 1946.[49] Writing out of the experience of World War II and the new position of leadership that had recently fallen to the United States, Northrop attempted to combine cultural pluralism with a political theology of convergence.

Northrop is convinced that the Orient and the Occident (particularly America, the Occident of the Occident) are hastening toward each other, but he emphasizes their different starting points and holds that even in their meeting they will remain distinct. The question is how to manage that distinctness. The modes of experience of the cultures are irreducible to each other, in Northrop's view. His job is to describe the conditions for a meeting in which each keeps its own and gracefully concedes to the other the other's own—a blueprint for the new world that is to follow the next peace. As with Leibniz, providence is a looming shadow of implication, for the aptitudes of the various civilizations line up crisply to form, as a body, the perfect universal man.

The meaning of Oriental civilization—that characteristic which sets it off from the West—may be stated very briefly. The Oriental portion of the world has concentrated its attention upon the nature of all things in their emotional and aesthetic, purely empirical and positivistic immediacy. . . . The Orient, for the most part, has investigated things in their aesthetic component; the Occident has investigated these things in their theoretic component. Consequently, each has something unique to contribute.[50]

The two civilizations are "different yet complementary." Northrop's West is defined through monotheism in religion, mathematical modeling in natural science, and express laws defining the scope of the individual's action in society. His East is a positivistic yet also aesthetic savoring of the particularities of family life (particular relations to particular persons), of nature (particular aspects of which are to be viewed or captured in art), and of wisdom (the sum of a life of experiences, not to be distilled into doctrine). Cultures under the auspices of these two great civilizations, East and West, modify their central attributes without negating them: thus Mexico for

Northrop tempers monotheism with the cult of the Virgin, steers pioneer capitalism in the direction of social ownership, experiences time qualitatively not quantitatively, but cannot for all that be confused with an "Oriental" nation. Northrop's explanatory analogy is to identify civilizations with particular faculties of the mind:

> For the Chinese, the ethical is grounded in the aesthetic. . . . Always, for the Chinese, knowledge and the Chinese ethics which is rooted in this knowledge have to do with warm, vivid, personal experiences filled with aesthetic content, such as the crunching of bamboo sprouts between one's teeth, the enjoyment of the flavor of sharks' fins, or the quiet aesthetic intuition of the fragrance and the flavor of a cup of tea, together with a feeling for and an appreciation of the beauty and the ritual of all the ceremonies associated with the drinking of it.[51]

For Northrop, "aesthetic experience" is sensory, immediate, pretheoretical: the "undifferentiated aesthetic continuum" is a primary datum from which theoretic calculations emerge. Theory builds itself up by negating the particularities of the former intuitions, for example by reducing the individuality of vision to a mathematical formula valid for any possible viewer (as in perspective). Although theory and mathematics are also capable of shaping sensory experience (as in the example just given), one could not say in the same way that the theoretic forms the basis for the aesthetic. In any case, the Oriental observer has not yet reached the stage of theory: his perception is one of "aesthetic immediacy by way of the immediately apprehended aesthetic continuum of which he is a part, from within, instead of as a partially postulated, geometrically proportioned, common-sense external object."[52] (The difference between a virtue and a limitation is, in Northrop, often hard to ascertain.) And so the necessity for the theoretic cultures to lead the way into the future is, as it were, objectively demonstrated. Northrop was not writing in a moment at which it could be predicted that the technology, law, morals, and beliefs of the West might yet be reinterpreted as baseless aesthetic show. His "solution of the world problem," as he calls it, is for the theoretic cultures to continue seeing things theoretically, to manage technology and infrastructure for the rest of the world; for the aesthetic cultures to continue seeing things aesthetically, building on their traditions of immanent spiritual cultivation; and for each to come to appreciate the other as a necessary part of the whole reality of things. "Thus the ideal society must return to the primitive intuition of the past with respect to its aesthetically grounded portion and advance to the sophisticated science of the present with respect to its theoretically based part."[53] The future, in short, belongs to the United States, which will have the wisdom to preserve the other countries of the world in their old habits of thought—most and best of all the nations of Asia, which can best show us (yes, unambiguously, *us*) how to "return to the primitive intuition of the past" and experience aesthetically satisfying moments in the course of our otherwise technicist, goal-driven lives.

The temporal structure of Northrop's plan for world order is original: neither Hegel's series of consecutive stations nor Ferrari's sequence of global instantaneous waves, but an eschatological fulfillment-of-history under the restrained guidance of cultural pluralists. For Northrop, when East meets West, history stops short—it ceases to be a linear development and becomes a spatial order of coexistences: museum, anthology, or zoo. Conflict, in previous history, arose from partiality. The *pax Americana* will transcend such pettiness. The various cultures represent aspects of the whole nature of man and, Northrop holds, are necessary to one another: both world-denying Calvinists and this-worldly Daoists will recognize in their fellows a complementary piece of the human puzzle. The coming world order will set forth a "criterion of the good" that everyone, within his or her cultural limits, will be able to endorse. It will answer, or so Northrop thinks, to the demands of democratic process and to those of universal reason, so long as both of these are inflected in culturally appropriate ways, that is, translated into Eastern and Western idiom.[54]

Northrop's wished-for convergence of complementarities depends on definitions of cultures as determinate starting points. It is because of having certain features (sets of characteristics that hold together in some essential way, so that from Japanese ethics you might deduce Japanese painting or business practices) that China or Japan or Mexico can enter the new world order as necessary "components" (to use one of Northrop's favorite words). Each representative people has already, through history, come to its definition (the Western peoples who attained modernity having done this most recently), and the future pluralist world will orchestrate this multiplicity of givens. To look at this scheme from an Asian point of view certainly changes its import. Not unusually for his place and time, Northrop's cultural references are cosmopolitan but conservative in the Chinese context—Lin Yutang 林語堂, the Soong 宋 family as presented by the Luce magazines, the New Life movement; and these are to be eternalized in the new world order.

The Chinese do not have to become modern; the Americans will do that for them and spare them the agony. What Northrop is saying about the peoples of the East is that their history is indeed their destiny, and that departing from that history would turn them into another sort of people and deprive the world of a precious spiritual resource. Northrop did not, to the best of my knowledge, succeed in shaping the foreign policy of the United States, but his handling of the "world problem" in its philosophical aspects has remained with us to shape the "culture" component of "cultural relativism."

Nakamura Hajime's *Ways of Thinking of Eastern Peoples* (first edition 1947), written partly in reaction to Northrop, is less obsessed by convergence and more by differentiation. Looked at from fifty years' distance, the book is flawed in many ways. It gives too much respectability to stereotypes (the Indians are otherworldly and fond of myth and poetry; the pragmatic Chinese believe in the reconciliation of opposites; the Japanese put too much stress on obedience but love evanescent nature). Its advance over an East-West theory like Northrop's lies in the care with which Nakamura distinguished the nations of "the Orient" from one another and the allowance he made for some measure of historical change: the spread and acculturation of Buddhism in four East Asian countries furnishes Nakamura his test case for deep national traits. It was undoubtedly necessary to challenge the idea that the people of the "Orient" are at bottom interchangeable, that differences among them are unimportant. The book was written during the U.S. Occupation, when the future of "Japaneseness" was an open question, and a silent, omnipresent concern with this "other" forms the background to which the "characteristics" of the Eastern peoples are pinned. More often than not, these features are summoned onto the page by a tacit contrast with a "modern," "Western" norm of philosophical thinking: "Disregard for the Individual and the Particular Appearing in Language," "Lack of Common Sense Concepts of Time," "Lack of the Notion of Order in the Objective Natural World," "Nondevelopment of Natural Sciences," "Lack of Consciousness of Universals," "Nonlogical Character of Verbal Expression and Thought," "Lack of Conscious Use of General Laws," "Nondevelopment of Free Thought," "Nondevelopment of Metaphysics," "Nonformation of Religious Sects," "Overstressing of Social Relations," "Weak Awareness of Religious Values," "Indifference to Logical Rules," "Tendency to Avoid Complex Ideas," just to give a few examples from the table of contents.[55] None of these could be a characteristic, *per se*—they presuppose a context against which a "way of thinking" is measured and found wanting. What is left out of the book is, of course, a theory of the "Way(s) of Thinking of Western Peoples." Or does that not need defining?

Cultural typologies are temporally ambiguous. They assume, as a necessary background, a present (milieu of interaction and canon of reason) into which the various cultural patterns are collected and to which they are logically subordinated. The patterns belong indifferently to the past (that is where the source material is found) or to the now (they are presented as diagnostically valid for members of this or that culture, past, present, or future). But this omnitemporality hides a larger difficulty. As with Northrop, typologies attempt to "solve the problem" of the coexistence of different cultures—a problem that has yet, for all its public notoriety, to be created. A critical review of the ways in which differences are produced (discursively, I mean) is not part of their task. The "differences" are sufficient to doing the job they are created to do, which is to discover and confirm cultural identities. But what if that is not the point?

Constructing the Present: Le contraire absolument contraire[56]

Bernard Williams holds that "in important ways, we are, in our ethical situation, more like human beings in antiquity than any Western people have been in the meantime. More particularly, we are like those who, from the fifth century and earlier, have left us traces of a consciousness that had not yet been touched by Plato's and Aristotle's attempts to make our ethical relations to the world fully intelligible."[57] Contemporaneity returns us to the situation of a remote past; it is as if the past twenty-five hundred years have been spent on a project whose collapse leaves us no better off than we were before we started. Williams returns then to Homer and Aeschylus for guidance, looking to talk with people who do not automatically know what one means by words like "moral" or "legitimate" or "selfish." He discusses their ways of making sense, with the goal of "putting them, or bits of them, to modern uses." Modern or, as some would say, postmodern.

Just such a search for a starting point that would not lead through the history of philosophy as we know it draws many people to Chinese texts.

Beginning with publications by Angus Graham in the early 1980s, an argument has been raised again and again to the effect that all the early philosophers of China are postmodern figures, or at least candidate postmoderns, because their thinking does not require the foundational hypotheses of substance, truth, or a transcendental origin. Because they are concerned with the effective, the probable, and the consensual, and because they lack absolute reference points for morality or argument, Confucius, Zhuangzi 莊子, and a host of others are suddenly promoted to the status of being our contemporaries. These accounts attempt to construct the present moment as a moment of coevalness, of philosophical convergence, between Chinese thinking and Western thinking, something that their authors claim is only now becoming imaginable. The different times in which the thinkers thought and the different paths by which they arrived at their purportedly congruent thoughts are overcome by present possibility.

David Hall and Roger Ames, for example, speak of surveying "the fragmentation of the modern self and the late modern celebration of that fragmentation as a means, *finally*, of *preparing* ourselves to understand the Chinese senses of self."[58] "The movement from representational to nonrepresentational understandings of knowledge and truth might well provide an appropriate bridge to the consideration of classical Chinese sensibilities." *Knowledge* and *truth* are, in fact, among the chief obstacles to understanding, since Chinese philosophy is not much concerned with either.

Historians of Chinese philosophy used to apologize for the tradition's gaps in philosophical preparedness. They pulled Mohist logic, Gongsun Long's 公孫龍 dialectical paradoxes, Wang Chong's 王充 skepticism, and Buddhist argumentation from their obscure corners and tried to integrate them into the thought of modern China.[59] Now it appears that the lack of interest in epistemology was a good thing. The dwindling of theology in the West creates opportunities for "mystical experience" and "empirical spirituality," just in time for us to appreciate types of Chinese religious experience that do not require "notions of cosmological unity and divine transcendence."[60] It is surely out of place to speak of providence, but some historical confluence has placed us, according to these witnesses, at a present where we are beginning to think like the early Chinese. (Or, at any rate, finding it hard to think like early modern Europeans.) Just as with Bernard Williams's recourse to Homer and early tragedy, it is our own destitution that sends us to learn from the people who have always "done without" the things we have just discovered missing.

François Jullien returns, in several of his books (*La Propension des choses, Fonder la morale, Traité de l'efficacité*) to that absence of the "ontological edifice" that makes Chinese thought the model for those shaken by late-modern tremors.[61] The Chinese think not God but nature, not morality but know-how, not teleology but propensity—there are many variations but one essential theme. Jullien is a sensitive, persuasive, and well-read scholar of traditional China, able to pursue the thread of an argument or the changing connotations of a word through dozens of authors, genres, and centuries. His readings deliver something to the European doorstep: not satisfied merely to parse the alien text, Jullien builds arguments in the contrastive mode, making further meanings emerge from the parallels and differences among canonical writings and assumptions. The point of these experiments in intercultural reading is to uncover alternatives to the set problems of a tradition. A remark lifted at random (indeed, it can be quite random since the device is so frequent) will show Jullien's contrastive method at work: "The price to pay for having conceived 'objectivity' in such rigorous fashion [in the seventeenth-century West] was that one would always be in danger of falling into the opposite error of *subjectivizing*. Chinese thought escapes this trap because it thinks in terms of process, where the subject dissolves; it thinks in terms of the 'way,' of function."[62]

Jullien frequently replaces, in this way, an antithesis crucial to the European formulation of a problem (a *or* b) with a Chinese ambiguity (a *and* b). An issue eludes the grasp of Westerners pursuing it with the too widely separated prongs of an alternative (objectivity/subjectivity); the Chinese, wise beyond wisdom for not having constructed the alternative in the first place, have never lost sight of the thing itself (process, the way, function).[63] Westerners hypostatize entities with a supposed explanatory power, such as God or the subject, and then have trouble maintaining them in good running order; the Chinese, by sticking to contextual terms and anecdotal arguments, keep their preternatural investments to a minimum. In the course of any one of Jullien's books, a fairly regular table of contrary values emerges. Consider the following, drawn from a series of Europe-versus-China arguments in his book on the term *shi* 勢, "propensity" or "disposition":

EUROPE	CHINA
being	becoming
cause	tendency
individual entity	relation
deductive chain	configuration of elements
metaphysical postulates	natural propensity

the Good, seen as goal	autoregulation
freedom	spontaneity
antagonism	correlative interaction
myths	rites
heroism	conformism[64]

This is anything but a table of translation equivalents ("for X, read Y")—and to use it as one would create some scandalous paraphrases. The correlated items are rather, in Jullien's view, the rough approximations that we must avoid at all costs lest our interpretations miss the point of all Chinese thinking.[65] So many points, however, assemble a definite profile, and as the polarities accumulate it begins to seem that Jullien's China is what we might call an "own other," a reversed image of his Europe—*that which I am not*, in Levinas's words, but (precisely) not in his sense.[66] Is the point of the Chinese case to furnish the counterfactual to a story made and told elsewhere? (It is useful, as with Northrop, to wonder what would become of the meaning of these books if they were translated into Chinese.) Is reading Zhuangzi or Wang Fuzhi 王夫之 still somehow a "response to the West"? Overall the relationship is not a symmetrical one: the constructs listed on the left column of the table above are all hypotheses for which the Chinese "had no need."[67] "Westerners" could know this; "Chinese" could not know it about themselves. The empire that "has no need" of any external thing is, of course, a powerful and prestigious myth about China entertained both there and abroad; future scholars may see in Jullien's philosophical China the latest refinement of this tradition. By application of Occam's Razor, then, Chinese thought is found superior, more economical, less compromised with metaphysics. But there is no guarantee that the opposite conclusion will not be drawn, namely, that Chinese culture is missing something important that the Europeans were lucky enough to find and develop.[68] Only the contemporary diagnosis of the "end of philosophy" directs us to interpret the absences as freedoms; contrastive philosophical typology (compare Nakamura's categories) cannot decide that value on its own.

The difference between postmodern praise and modern contempt (or patronizing indulgence) is just this slender—a matter not of comparisons but of the ends for which they are performed. The question for contrastive philosophy is whether it tells us much beyond restating the conditions under which it occurs (the conditions may well be quite fascinating): if Chinese thought "lacks" moral absolutism or logocentrism, is that a discovery about

Chinese thought or about the expectations of its observer? Here it may appear that the more results Jullien's method produces, the more his principle of contrastive reading totters. The production of regular, correlated oppositions transforms "the other" into "our other," which is to say, into a negative portrait of ourselves (or of a certain understanding of ourselves). In this transformation the allure of the unknown risks turning into a roundabout form of narcissism.

Jullien seems at moments to want to answer this objection, that the encounter of traditions results only in an accumulation of self-reflexive methodological artifacts. At one point, evoking the old missionary question about the supposedly "materialist" orientation of Chinese culture, he pursues:

> But the question [—materialist or not?—], visibly, is too deeply marked by our own conceptions to stand a chance of encountering the other culture and making sense on its ground; that is why it has remained without an answer. . . . Hence the problem of method that arises as one attempts to make the comparison *pertinent*. How else might one proceed . . . than by seeking to go far enough back into the establishment of our frames of thought as to discover *the point at which the split* [between the Chinese and Western categories] *takes place* and chart its direction? Moreover, that would be possible only if one began by establishing a point of effective mutual understanding, situated "upstream" from the split, a point from which one might observe the emergence of difference and upon which one might reconstruct that difference. Not, of course, with a view to composing a history, that realist project, but rather in keeping with the demands of a theoretical *genealogy*.[69]

The wording here acknowledges the danger of tautology in contrastive description. The word "pertinence" seeks to disavow random or irrelevant interpretation but denotes, precisely, the danger of narcissistic interpretation. What is *pertinent* to a comparison is what seems to be identical but hides a different field of implications (for example, the role of the president in the French Fourth Republic and in the Fifth Republic).[70] "Pertinence" is both a relation and a difference—more precisely, a difference within a relation.

A language, as Saussure put it and as information theory restated it, is made up of distinctions, (sensory) "differences that make a" (semantic) "difference."[71] Exposure to a language trains the ears and the mind to recognize differences through massively parallel arrays of analogous alternatives, rather as one polarizes a lump of iron by rubbing it against an already polarized magnet. But a universe composed of more than one language, or more than one semantic system, is apt to be less tidy, abounding in ambiguous signals and sheer "noise" (in fact no language can be successful in excluding the noninformational from its domain). When one is comparing European and Chinese thought (however those objects are to be determined), the sheer randomness of unorganized differences threatens to overwhelm the investigation. In principle, no contrasts at this level need be meaningful, because in intercultural studies the "system" that would create the distinctiveness, and thus the information value, of elements of utterance is precisely what is not given in advance. So the issue of "pertinence" is, first, How does one establish a context in which differences matter—in which a distinction amounts to a choice?

Jullien's solution is to seek an area of "effective understanding," an imaginary shared philosophical "state" or "time." Once this is posited, he will chart the different courses taken by the traditions, measuring their divergence from the suppositional common ground. The result would be, as he says, a logical genealogy but emphatically not a historical account: it would serve to explain how the concepts participating in a single tradition need (imply) each other, and how traditions are constituted as systems of needs (relays of implications). This "area of effective understanding" has to be constructed as a phantasm, the original point of emergence of the differences that are now (perhaps) converging as Western civilization winds down. But why not extend the domain of the phantasmatic to contain the milieu in which the antithetical characteristics of Europe and China are discovered? In other words, why not acknowledge the strategic purposes, the constructed nature, the "presentness" of the oppositions? If the Chinese thinkers are the antithesis (or the antidote) of the Greeks, it is we who make them so. (Things would be different if the thinkers of one tradition were reacting to the other, but that cannot yet be shown.)[72] The Chinese "lack of metaphysics" is no more a property of Chinese thought than the "lack of grammar" (or, for that matter, of the ablative case) is a property of the Chinese language. The lack (beneficial or crippling) emerges from a comparative project. There is nothing wrong with comparative projects, but they are not Maxwell's demon, they need to be acknowledged as partakers in what they describe. One is reminded of the compulsion, ably analyzed by James Peck and Bruce Cumings, of American scholars of Asia to make Asian history mysterious by leaving out of it the vastly important factor of American actions in Asia.[73] It is much more revealing to bring the conditions under which cultural comparison occurs into the comparison itself than to let those conditions appear again and again in the guise of properties ascribed to the object.

From Jullien's demonstration we draw, once more, the lesson that a scheme for cosmopolitan, "cotemporal" thinking is only as good as its milieu is rich. The great danger is that of articulating the relations of East and West in a "phonological" way, as an inventory of distinctive traits in systematic opposition.[74] That only sets up an infinite repetition of reversed images, as in two mirrors set face to face. How do we make cotemporality real, that is, dense with consequences? A similarity emerges between Jullien's contrastive reading of philosophy and Ferrari's world history: both are active only at their poles, China and Europe. The place where the transmission of arms and ideas must have taken place (the "realm of effective understanding" for the one, the majority of the Eurasian continent for the other) is inhabited solely by a hypothesis.

What the Traffic Will Bear

Caesar plots against India,
Tigris and Euphrates shall, from now on, flow at his bidding,
Tibet shall be full of Roman policemen,
The Parthians shall get used to our statuary
    and acquire a Roman religion,
One raft on the veiled flood of Acheron,
    Marius and Jugurtha together.
                    —Pound, *Homage to Sextus Propertius*

The missing middle is the subject of a resolutely empirical study by Frederick Teggart, *Rome and China* (1938). Written without awareness of Ferrari's work, it leads to conclusions just as unsettling for imperial vanity.

Teggart began by compiling a chronological table of "all known events, wars, and disturbances" recorded for "each separate kingdom or region of the continent of Eurasia" (his definition of "events, wars, and disturbances" is not given, but presumably these categories emerge clearly enough from the sources) during the five hundred years of the Roman and Chinese empires' greatest extension. The labor involved in identifying and dating events, not to mention reconciling vague and conflicting ancient chronologies, geographies, and ethnographies must have been immense, but the volume confines itself to presenting results. Teggart determines that

between 58 BC and AD 107 barbarian uprisings in Europe were preceded invariably by the outbreak of war either on the eastern frontiers of the Roman empire or in the 'Western regions' of the Chinese. Also it has been found that the invasions which followed disturbances in the Roman East occurred both on the lower Danube and on the Rhine, whereas the uprisings which followed disturbances in the Tian Shan 天山 affected only the upper Danube. Further, there were no uprisings in Europe which were not preceded by the respective disturbances in the Near or Far East, and there were no wars in the Roman East or the Tian Shan which were not followed by the respective outbreaks in Europe.

"These two-way correspondences," announces Teggart with understand-able pride, "represent Correlations in Historical Events"—"a matter of signal importance, for it demonstrates the existence of a type or order of historical facts which has not hitherto received attention, and . . . enlarges the scope of historical inquiry."[75] Comparative analysis reveals that "if the history of Eurasia in general and of Europe in particular is to be understood, the his-tory of China must be placed in the foreground."[76] To take one example:

In AD 102 the great administrator Ban Chao 班超, who had maintained Chinese power and prestige in the Tarim basin for thirty years, was permitted to retire, and his departure was soon followed by the outbreak of disturbances all the way from Gansu to the Pamirs. As a consequence, in the years 105–107 the Chinese were forced to withdraw from the "Western Regions." Also, in the Near East, in 105–106 Pacorus, king of Parthia, was overthrown, while contemporaneously Cornelius Palma [the Roman governor of Syria] took possession of Petra and annexed Arabia. Again, in Europe, in 106 Trajan invaded Dacia, and in 107 annexed it. More re-motely, in or about 106–108 the Romans were forced to evacuate Scotland. In the same period, moreover, the Xiongnu (Huns) took Guchen and Turfan from the Chinese (in 105), and, in correspondence with this event, the barbarians invaded Pannonia (i.e., Hungary west of the Danube).[77]

To make the connections somewhat more explicit: Ban Chao's resigna-tion left the Chinese West in uncertain hands, and shortly thereafter the Latter Han were no longer able to continue protecting the trade routes, so that the Xiongnu took advantage of the resulting power vacuum in the Tarim. Farther to the west, the king of Parthia, who in more tranquil times could count on a profitable intermediary position in the East-West trade, now had to confront attacks by the Alani, by the Armenians, and by internal rivals (including the ultimately successful contender, Osroes). In order to forestall a possible break in relations by the Nabataean rulers of Petra, now no longer reliable Roman allies, Trajan ordered his legate, Cornelius Palma, to occupy that part of Arabia and make it a province. Similar reasons prompted Trajan to mount a pre-emptive campaign against his old enemy

Decebalus, king of Dacia. The need to strengthen the garrisons along the Danube or in the East probably accounts for the Roman retreat from Scotland. In sum, the weakening of Chinese authority over the Western Regions fostered rivalry among groups eager to control the Central Asian trade routes; satellite governments that had been loyal to one or the other great power now saw their chance to break away; rather than lose the outer territories of an informal empire, the Romans moved to incorporate them behind a definite frontier. The story of the expansion of Roman provinces eastward and northward begins, not with decisions on the Capitoline Hill, but with the acceptance of a retirement petition in Luoyang.

Teggart is reluctant to theorize about his history, preferring the bare enumeration of events and dates, but a mechanism accounting for wars, revolts, and strategic retreats in terms of human interests does emerge. "The correspondence of wars in the East and invasions in the West was due to *interruptions of trade*." "War in the Tarim occasioned an interruption of traffic on the silk route, and this interruption aroused hostilities at points along the route as far west as the Euphrates."[78] The control of trade routes is the primary motivator of political events in Central Asia. The capitals at the two ends, each beset with its apparently unremitting "barbarian problem" and expending lives and treasure to bring it under control, see only the challenges to their authority and miss the "correlations" behind the events. Failure to understand the mechanism (and "mechanical" is the right word for something that produces such automatic and regular correlations) of struggle in the space between empires condemns imperial leaders, however powerful and able, to wasted effort and ever greater difficulties down the line.

Wars which were undertaken by the governments of China and Rome in pursuit of what were conceived to be important national aims led inevitably to conflicts among the peoples of northern Europe and to invasions of the Roman empire. . . . But the Chinese emperors and their advisers were unconscious of the fact that their decisions were the prelude to conflicts and devastations in regions of which they had never heard. The Romans were equally in the dark with respect to the consequences of their wars. . . . So Augustus persisted in his attempts to dominate Armenia, though the actual results on the Danube and the Rhine might have been unerringly predicted.

The conduct of affairs by Augustus is typical of statesmanship in every age.[79]

What appear to be border conflicts or raiding expeditions are actually, from Teggart's perspective, episodes in a world war lasting for generations and fed by every attempt to put it down. It is easy to think that Teggart's domino dynamics might have been suggested by the play of alliances in 1914 or the shouting for *Lebensraum* in the 1930s. His is a tightly interrelated world, one in which every stone thrown hits somebody. But major cultures do not experience it that way. For them, the barbarian attacks are a series of accidents, interruptions, repeated episodes of violence breaking in, like plagues, on normal time.[80] Teggart's correlations seek to correct this perception of randomness. China and Rome indubitably occupy "a single time" and act on each other, but the place where their synchronous relationship occurs is just beyond their ken. The imperial powers will figure in this new story of their mutual dealings as blind actors who create conditions for, but are never in control of, a network of causally related events. The powers write history (virtually all of Teggart's material comes from canonical histories) but are fated to misunderstand this history as being about themselves. It is not. (In an appendix, Teggart dismisses the dominant theories of barbarian migration since Caesar as based on guesswork, hypothetical population or climate trends, or simply rooted in crude accounts of barbarian psychology: their "love of plunder," "fearlessness," "warlike nature.")[81] That their respective states were not the initiators and protagonists of world history, that the global dimension of history is best revealed by the fates of the bandit kingdoms of Parthia, Armenia, Moesia, Sarmatia, and so forth, is a perspective hardly to be imagined by the classic historians of either Rome or China.

Of course I am using Teggart's work half for itself, half as a metaphor for the work that has not been done, and may be impossible to do, in comparative philosophy—work about historical connections and influences (supposing they existed) and work taking into consideration the "presentness" and interestedness of comparative reading. If the metaphor is at all informative, it teaches us about identities, appropriations, and media. In seeking the intellectual connection between China and Europe, those two vast textual and historical bodies, it is an error to be distracted by the similarities and differences, the things that make the other empire a mirror of one's own. Look for the bothersome people right on the borders of your own empire who keep getting in the Royal Way. They live on communication and have every interest in making sure it is not direct. In short, they are the consequential middle, the people who know where the road goes, and you had better try to understand what they are about.[82]

6

Postmodernism in China:
A Sketch and Some Queries

The various "posts" that have attracted so much attention in China lately—principally postmodernism (*houxiandai zhuyi* 後現代主義) and postcolonialism (*houzhimin zhuyi* 後殖民主義), and in an idiomatic sense poststructuralism (*houjiegou zhuyi* 後結構主義), or as the Chinese authors conveniently call them for short, post-learning (*houxue* 後學)—look like translations into modern Chinese idiom of terms and ideas pioneered elsewhere.[1] But I mean by that no more than "look like." The key to making sense of them, I think, is to discard the hope that understanding them and, above all, judging them can be accomplished by reference to a more familiar "original" postmodernism. What more uncomfortable paradox can be imagined than attempting to argue that one's own postmodernism is the real, the authentic, the historically originary, the ancestrally legitimate, brand? Rather than fall into the trap of saying that the Chinese post-ists have got it wrong and trying to put them right by a more heavily supported reading of Derrida or Foucault or Lyotard, let us ask what an appropriate frame of reference for understanding Chinese post-ism might be.

Not that anyone is quite ready to answer that question. It is still a time for making and testing hypotheses. Certainly part of the frame of reference we will require is the academic context of present-day Europe and America, in which the post-ideologies were first elaborated, distributed, and made part of the intellectual lives of scholars and readers (Chinese-speaking or not). And the availability, the relative transparence and familiarity of the words and gestures, not to mention the black-on-white footnotes, tempts us into think that post-ism amounts to an application to Chinese realities of something Jameson or Rorty has already said. But that would set us on precisely the path that a cursory reading of Chinese post-ist publications causes me to fear—that of taking for granted the correspondence of discursive universes to the nondiscursive, possibly unutterable, situations in which they are pronounced. Euro-American precedents are only part of the frame of reference and far from the most interesting part.

A first gesture toward derailing the Euro-American reader's confidence—the confidence that says: *if that's postmodernism, then I already know all about that (including whether I like it or not)*—would be to adopt the attitude of some scholars of traditional Chinese philosophy who like to say that Chinese thought was always postmodern because it never bothered to become modern.[2] I think this is a fallacy in its original setting, but it can be helpful here for its air of paradox. The original fallacy is that of supposing that two things are alike because they are different from a third thing.[3] That fallacy may, nonetheless, guard us from a second fallacy, that of assuming that there is only one right way to get to postmodernism, by taking the path that leads (etymologically enough) through and past modernism. Both accidental similarity and historical inevitability furnish disreputable grounds for argument. By mixing together a bit of each, we may discredit both.

One might say that philosophical modernism is an attempt to regulate the relationship of fact and value, and that postmodernism is the abandonment of such attempts—resulting in claims that knowledge can never be grounded, or that values are entirely arbitrary, or that trying to work out principles for either is just a thinly disguised policing of discourse. Then in traditional China one would not have the relevant illusions to discard, since generally speaking the project of Chinese thought has not been to propose transcendental guarantees for knowledge or exception-free prescriptions for conduct.[4] If this is true, postmodernism looks like an absurd detour in the Chinese context—the taking of medicine to cure ills one never suffered from. (Or an inoculation against modernity?) Is this the secret of the discursive vigor that has been shown in these recent debates—the fact that nothing very real is at stake? What kind of critique is it in which no one's ox is gored?

But no twentieth-century Chinese person, of whatever degree of literacy, has been able to live a purely traditional Chinese life, and therefore the imported oddities of modernity are live targets for critique. Indeed, how far back in history would we have to go to discover the inhabitants of so blissfully isolated a Peach Blossom Spring? The very ideals and models many people would distinguish from the enterprise of canonical Chinese thought have been active in the Chinese world for at least the past 150 years, furnishing one regime after another with challenges, forms of legitimacy, or aims of struggle. Their attraction survives much clumsiness in translation.[5] The idea that one can know the world as it is and that by knowing it one can transform it into the world as it should be has quite a pull, even for those who are not professional philosophers.

The postmodernist gesture that holds the most attractiveness for *houxue* is the rejection of modernist, cosmopolitan legitimation-devices. Are we called to submit our judgments to the court of science? To the norms of democratic constitutionalism? To the aesthetic canons of Sophocles and Phidias? If it's a norm, it's out of bounds. The fact that for most of this century the ruling standards, not to mention ideological currents and political influence, have been derived from international culture, commerce, and technology means that for mainland Chinese thinkers the rejection of modern modes of legitimation is doubled with the identification of these modes as specifically Western.[6] (I normally refuse to bow to the idol referred to by this term, but in some contexts "Western" is the accurately vague word, however many distinctions are sacrificed by pronouncing it.) As far back as living memory goes, indigenous Chinese standards have not had the backing needed to command belief and practice, save for a few exceptionally constituted domains such as family life, specific areas of scholarship, religion (where and when tolerated), and some forms of art. The ghostly local standards can therefore furnish a comfortably vague countermodel to the models derided as hegemonic yet obsolete. I see in several authors a mood that might be paraphrased as follows: "The European Enlightenment went bankrupt—we have only to follow the postmodernist argument to see it collapse. No matter for us! We still have something to fall back on—cultural goods that escaped the crash because nobody thought to bid them unrealistically high."

As received in China, the devices and authorities of postmodernism have produced not a uniform set of doctrines but a set of opportunities variously taken. It would be folly to try to summarize them all under one ideological or sociological heading. Nor do I have the space or the learning to describe the whole intellectual ecology of 1990s China.[7] But by exploring some of the niches in which argument grows, I may be able to describe the conditions under which these opportunities arise and guess about their likely consequences.

♦

While I was writing this essay, I made my first trip to Beijing in over ten years, on business for my university, and was predictably startled by all that was new and much that was not. Just as on an earlier trip, someone kindly took me to see the stone set up over the ashes of Edgar Snow, next to the lake on the campus of Peking University. "Edgar Snow—An American Friend of the Chinese People," reads the inscription. For Snow, of course, is the American journalist who "discovered" and loyally championed Mao Zedong and his Yan'an rebels, returning several times in the 1960s and 1970s to interview Mao and tell the world that collectivization, the Great Leap Forward, and the Cultural Revolution were splendid and beneficial transformations. Of course taking American visitors to see Snow's tomb is a gesture of solicitude, and it would have been poor manners to say what I thought of the definition of friendship the stone implied. "The American friend of *some* Chinese people," I said instead, and this was all right, because it led the conversation toward Mao's personal foibles, which is a permitted, indeed encouraged, subject.

Many of the *"houxue"* essays suppose that communication between China and foreigners interested in it should be held up to the ideal represented by Snow's truckling to Mao. It is no longer the charismatic leader but rather Chineseness to which the acceptable foreigner must pay respect. I am less concerned about the implicit xenophobia than about the effects of cultural nationalism on its domestic public. Whose interests are advanced by the circuits of identification that cause people to make much of "China's ability to say no," while many individual Chinese are unable to say no to each other?[8] Is not the cause of national unity supremely useful, in peacetime, for foreclosing both majority rule and minority protections? Is "cultural democracy" (a strategic term to be defined below) a barricade worth mounting while Chinese political economy, based on a mode of production that is both low-wage and increasingly high-tech, works its way toward constitutional guarantees of worker docility and efficiency? The "friend of *some* Chinese people" that I am worries about these things, because I worry about them at home, too.

The historian Xu Jilin 許紀霖 describes the conditions making for an eager reception of the anti-Enlightenment streak in postmodern thinking as in part intellectual, in part sociological:

To consider the factors internal to epistemology, [the "anti-Western" theorists of the 1990s] all had begun by accepting the mainstream discourse of the Western intellectual genealogy. They believed that Western modernist thought should and could contribute to China's modernization adequate intellectual resources and patterns for action. As a consequence, the deeper their previous commitment, the more they were able to discover that the supposed universals of modernist theory were really nothing more than particular products of Western history/culture and were separated by a great gulf from the discourse of China's contemporary culture and historical tradition. This gap between Western theory and Chinese discourse made it impossible for them not to shift their gaze from Western mainstream discourse and toward marginal discourses such as postcolonial cultural theory, analytical Marxism, and so forth. They hoped to find there inspiration for a pattern of modernization that would fit Chinese conditions. . . . Unlike previous cultural conservatives, these scholars' plan was not to "confront Western learning with native learning," but rather to "use the aliens to control the aliens," to use Western marginal discourses to resist Western mainstream discourse. . . .

From the external, sociological perspective, the anti-Western trend is closely connected to a series of changes in the environment at home and abroad. Following the sudden takeoff of the Chinese economy, the national strength of China grew enormously; and the first reaction of a disfavored people that is emerging from its disfavored status is always to say "no" to those privileged peoples it has long been attempting to overtake. In the 1980s, China's contacts with the West were limited, conflicts of interest were rare, and intellectuals had a flattering image of the West, so that Westernization had a suitable psychological support. But from the beginning of the 1990s China began to enter the international political-economic system, and conflicts between China and the West became more and more direct: the opposition of the Western countries, particularly the United States, to China's joining the WTO and hosting the Olympic Games, trade frictions, the *Yinhe* incident,[9] and a series of other events caused Chinese intellectuals to lose a great part of their faith in the West. Behind their beautiful Western discourse, they discovered ugly relationships of power, and an unequal power relationship that the Western countries were determined to force onto China. . . . Thus the nationalistic feeling of Chinese intellectuals was greatly awakened, so that anti-Westernism had a deep psychological foundation.[10]

One thing is missing from the chronology. If Xu's account accurately represents the thinking of Chinese intellectuals, then someone has perfected the art of spin control. Although the trade frictions and boycotts Xu lists surely harmonized with the self-interest of many of China's trade partners (though not all, and certainly not for long), the proclaimed reason for denying China such badges of international recognition as WTO membership and the hosting of the Olympic Games was to punish the government for its bloody repression of the popular movements of 1989. To have done otherwise would have been to display friendship for the wrong people. As "unequal power relationships" go, some are uglier than others. Better that some contracts be canceled and some international meetings be spoiled by an unwelcome speech or two than that the memory of the dead be too quickly swept under the rug. That June 1989 marked a turning point in recent Chinese intellectual life is undoubtedly a fact, but it would startle me to think that the main pivot of the turn was the discovery by Westernizing scholars that foreign countries have economies of their own, advantages to protect, and a weakness for self-serving policies, especially in election years. (In another essay, Xu contends that "the Tiananmen incident of 1989 not only brought an abrupt halt to the 'culture fever' [of the 1980s] but also caused mainland intellectuals to lose some of their passion for politics.")[11] Does no one remember the boycotts of Japanese goods during the 1930s and 1940s? Or was the short-lived, American-led cooling of trade relations with China such a propaganda failure that none of the people who, in China, had the best chance to learn of it could ever figure out what it was about? In any case, Xu's analysis of anti-Westernism assumes that the educated classes of China see the power aims of their present government as identical to their own aims or those of the Chinese people generally—which I should think needs to be shown, even without the killings of unarmed students to inspire reflection.[12] The critique of universalism seems to have skipped over some important steps. Or, it may be that Xu is using an advanced Aesopian technique, and counting on us to note the omission and therefore read the whole essay ironically.

♦

It takes a *xenos* like me to imagine that a Chinese intellectual movement is all about xenophobia or xenophilia. One ought to try to keep things in proportion, just as one ought not to assume that *houxiandai zhuyi* attempts to reproduce French or American discourses about "postmodernism." Where a Chinese writer seems to "get it wrong," to conjoin incompatible streams of thought, we need to ask if the story being told is different from the one we already know.

The poet, professor, and translator Zheng Min's 鄭敏 essay "Retrospect at Century's End: The Transformation of the Chinese Language and Modern Chinese Poetic Creation" is confusing—and therefore, I will argue, in-spiring—on precisely these grounds. By attempting to correct its author's historical perspective or theoretical information, its readers overlook its most provocative aspect, its revision of the collective story about Chinese moder-nity (poetic and political). So let us try not to miss it this time.

Zheng's opening question seems calculated to address the national-interest theme: "Why is it that literature in [modern] Chinese, with thou-sands of years of poetic history behind it, has been unable to produce inter-nationally recognized great works or great authors?"[13] Zheng proposes to re-examine the history of the Chinese language and literature over the past hundred years as a way of tracing the inadequacies of modern poetry back to their social and linguistic sources. The May Fourth modernizers—leaders of the vernacular literature movement and the New Literature movement—erred by

cutting themselves off from classical literature . . . they forced literary creators to turn their backs on and abandon classical poetry, and they rejected the ideas of those scholars (Zhu Jingnong 朱經農, Ren Hongjun 任鴻雋, Qian Xuantong 錢玄同, and others) who advocated integrating classical poetry with the new literature. Moreover it was announced by Chen Duxiu 陳獨秀 [1880–1942; one of the leaders of the May Fourth Movement and cofounder, in 1921, of the Chinese Communist Party] that [on the adoption of vernacular language] "we must not allow our oppo-nents any room for discussion" (5).

Zheng sees as the cause of this dogmatism an overly simple understanding of language and meaning. Hu Shi 胡適 (1891–1962) and Chen Duxiu saw in language nothing more than a tool for exchanging information and therefore demanded a literal, immediately understandable, contemporary idiom (19). But for Zheng, following Saussure, "language is principally an *arbitrary, inher-ited* system of signs that *admits of no choice,* and its reform must be on the ba-sis of inheritance" (emphasis in original); moreover the reformers "were not aware of the gap between the signifier and the signified, a fissure that, ac-cording to the theory of J. Lacan, is never completely bridged, causing a part of every language to remain hidden from view" (10). By calling for writing to base itself on speech, rather than on previous examples of writing, Hu Shi and Chen Duxiu attempted to erase the "archi-writing" of cultural codes, of memorized literature, of the whole Chinese past. If by "language" we mean what Saussure, Heidegger, Lacan, or Derrida mean by language, then the May Fourth generation hated language. What they wanted from language,

Zheng suggests, simply could not be given within language. But rather than admit that they were engaged in a futile project, the modernizers went on the offensive against backsliders. Zheng sees in this radicalization of the modernizing movement a pattern that remained consistent in twentieth-century Chinese literary theory—

> the logic of the binary opposition: protecting this / overthrowing that. The result is that we turned the complex relations of culture, literature, and history into pairs of mutually exclusive binary oppositions: *vernacular writing / classical writing; proletarian culture / bourgeois culture; traditional literature / up-to-date literature; authentic literature / inauthentic literature; poetry for the masses / misty poetry; revolutionary poetry / decorative poetry about little grasses and flowers.* . . . This strategic logic seems to have been our normal logic ever since the May Fourth movement, and its authority has gone un-contested. (6)

In the early years of the vernacular movement, Zheng concedes, it must have been helpful to have an ideology that, by casting aside complexities and qualifications, split the world into good and bad camps. But the conse-quences have been a public psychosis. "From 1919 onward, every cultural movement in China has been marked by the same extraordinary tensions. The unprecedented Cultural Revolution of the 1960s went from literary skirmishes to actual battles, from the flourishing of pens to the flailing of whips, resulting in a bloody revolutionary drama" (7).[14] Zheng's reconsidera-tion of the May Fourth reformers, then, is meant to trace the radicalizing logic to its roots and to critique it, not only in its aftereffects but in its basic structure, which she calls "precisely a closed, metaphysical way of thinking that proceeds through symmetrical contradictions" (7).

Zheng's essay puts European literary theory to strategic use, invoking "recent linguistic science" to correct the instrumentalist views of Hu and Chen and benefiting from the general intellectual climate of the present to discredit the logic of binary oppositions. Some of her readers have been shocked by her tradition-minded reading of theory: it is surely idiomatic to join Derrida's reading of Freud's "scene of psychic writing" and Lacan's claim that "the unconscious is structured like a language," in order to reach the conclusion that the more traditional a language is, the more deeply it is con-nected with the unconscious, and therefore that language reform represents an attack by the conscious on the unconscious mind (18–19).[15] Her Saussure and Derrida sit on the same bench with the Eliot of *Notes Towards the Defini-tion of Culture* and Heidegger in *völkisch* mood. These and other applications of theory are bound to surprise readers more familiar with a canonical set of poststructuralist writers and positions.

Does Zheng's essay represent a postmodern understanding or is it a mishmash of postmodernistic citations in an old-fashioned argument? Is it, as Zhao Yiheng 趙毅衡 puts it, an example of "a neoconservative trend that uses postmodern theory as a base or corroboration"? "Surprised" to see that "the conservative judgment on the May Fourth movement current abroad has now found its way back to the Chinese mainland," Zhao is equally astonished to find that "although the topic is an old view on an old subject, the author uses new theories: Lacanian psychoanalysis and Derridean deconstruction."[16] He finds the essay evidence of "the neoconservative trend with, as one of its symptoms, the return to traditional culture. . . . Zheng Min blames modernistic poetry for 'cutting itself off from the ancients.'"[17] In a response, Zheng characterizes Zhao's objection as revealing his "orthodox [modern] traditional viewpoint: he seeks to defend the 'revolutionary character' of the May Fourth movement, without suspecting that my article was intended precisely to bring us out of this traditional position of reducing literature to politics. . . . To leave behind us this binary political theory of 'revolution' versus 'conservatism' is . . . the urgent task of the twenty-first century."[18] Zhao is, for Zheng, a part of the problem she seeks to diagnose (binarism, all-or-nothing-ism, linear history, the political immediacy of art).

Conversely, Zhao's puzzlement at Zheng's call for a return to tradition seems prompted by the perception that a postmodern premodernism is either nonsensical or uncomfortably ambiguous. But to call Zheng's arguments "neoconservative" underrates their revisionary force. I think that if some peculiar interpretations can be allowed it, the essay performs precisely the work of classical deconstruction on the territory of modern literature as studied in China. It describes a logic of airtight oppositions, for example, the polarizing of past and present in modern literary history, and tries to discover ways of subverting the distinctions, as in the claim that language is always and necessarily an "inheritance" from the past. Moreover, it returns to the root of a historical paradigm, partly in the mode of classical cause-seeking, but also with the aim of showing that what one history narrates as necessity and prescience becomes, in another history's telling, repression and bad faith. Zhao's response, then, shows why Zheng's article makes a difference. The disagreement between Zheng and Zhao amounts to a choice of narratives and confirms Zheng in the tacit argument that legitimacy (both literary-historical and political) grows from the barrel of a story. Zheng's critique of twentieth-century poetic language—a critique carried out almost totally without citation of poetic texts!—may seem the least consequential, most apolitical of essays, but if you want to displace a master narrative (*yuan xushu* 元敘述), the best way to start is to propose a rival master narrative. If the adventuresomeness and determination displayed in Zheng's essay were more common, there would be more excitement and less hack-work in Chinese literary criticism. Even in its shortcomings it shows the possibility of generating, within mainland literary history, positions corresponding to some of the histories proposed and debated in the less rigidly ordered circumstances of Taiwan and the overseas Chinese world. And that would break down some large, publicly held "binary oppositions" indeed.

✦

What the casual reader of Zheng's essay notices as an argumentative asymmetry—the absence of a general account of cultural constructedness—suggests that some forms of nativism pass without comment in contemporary China. After critiquing modernist vernacular literature for its artificiality, she can endorse premodern classical literature as the "house of being" proper to Chinese writers and readers, their "cultural unconscious," without having to mount an explicit case for its naturalness. It is surprising that that should not be surprising. But that has been a large part of the appeal in China of postmodern theories (especially postcolonialism): the fact that they seem to make room for Chineseness. If the postmodern impulse amounts to marginalizing the center and centralizing the margins, then Chinese intellectuals have nothing to lose from identifying their own central themes with some once-marginal, now-prominent values and cultures in postmodern Western discourse. Zhang Kuan 張寬 seeks to take Edward Said's *Orientalism* one step further, arguing that

Said has only critiqued a hollow "Orient" molded by the West, he has not sketched out what the real Orient ought to be like. If he is unable to supply a real Orient to replace the false Orient, then his castigations of "Orientalism" are without force. Moreover, Said's critiques of the West find their moral support in the very humanism championed by Westerners. He must have forgotten that the Renaissance, when the flag of humanism was brandished most boldly, was the bloodiest period of the West's colonial expansion, and that the understanding of "man" in Renaissance humanism as well as its concept of universal human nature were the moral anchors of colonialism.[19]

For Zhang, it's a package deal: if you want Montaigne, you have to take Cortez and the Inquisition; if you admire Matteo Ricci, you'll have to extend your appreciation to the Opium War. Said "must have forgotten" these details. Zhang is able to wrap up cultures so comprehensively because his view of the Chinese past is equally without differentiation. He does not, say, apologize for the Boxers and the Qing court, the better to praise the reformist statesmen of 1898. History for him no longer sorts out into thematic streams of "progressives" and "reactionaries" (or what have you) establishing their principles through internal and external struggle; rather, it is primarily a field of ethnic or culture-wide agency.[20] This fits with his view of the relevance of postcolonial theory to the present moment in world politics:

The international situation since the end of the Cold War shows an ever more obvious tendency toward reorganization on the basis of ethnic characteristics and cultural identity. Ideology correspondingly fades. Although the West continues to present itself as powerful, postcolonial criticism brings a bit of deconstruction to all the myths of the grandiose Western discourse—and for us this is surely a good thing. No doubt about it, Said and anticolonialism are not reasons for stopping China's processes of reform and openness in favor of closing the door and protectionism, but for the sake of strengthening the cultural self-image and ethnic solidarity of the Chinese people as we go forth to face the stirrings of a "clash of cultures," these are questions that no responsible Chinese intellectual can fail to take seriously.[21]

As with Zheng Min, the combination and linking of sources in Zhang's writings is surprising. For the American left-liberal reader, there is no great chasm separating Said's political commitments from Noam Chomsky's, and Chomsky's denunciation of the United States as "the leading violator of the three principles America claims to campaign for,"[22] cited by Zhang, is often echoed by Americans critical of their country's foreign policy. Where Zhang leaves the beaten track is his disavowal of humanistic principles as such. If Chomsky were simply interested in maximizing the power of the United States, he would doubtless still be critical of his country's foreign policy, but in different ways and with different standards. Cambridge, Massachusetts, is a small place, but to go from Chomsky's rights-based criticism to Samuel Huntington's theory of a coming "clash of cultures" based on ethnic and cultural power blocs is to travel quite a distance in terms of assumptions held and company kept.[23] (In the eyes of American liberals, Huntington's main accomplishment has been to discover a new excuse for maintaining our military budget at Cold War levels.) Zhang is able to make this transition because the language of human rights is to him only a dialect of the "language of the powerful" used by Western countries in coercing China. Talk of human rights has no substance; the only real story is ethnic. "Reform and openness" are good policies only insofar as they add to the national wealth and power.

Appropriations like Zhang's show how many surprises the "traveling theory" show can deliver. Foucault, Chomsky, and Said gain our attention by denouncing not just abuses but hypocrisy—the practice of claiming to be generous or objective when one is actually rather more small-minded. Their critique asks us to be as good as our word. In the most revisionary theories there may be a core of idealism. In Zhang's picture of history there is no room for hypocrisy or its critique.[24] Is this a consequence of Foucault's having passed through an American filter of presentation and translation (emphasizing the critique of liberal institutions) on his way to China? In his Chinese version, Foucault is the person who described democratic society as a prison, the demolisher of Enlightenment folklore about the free individual conscience—certainly not the activist familiar on the French scene of the 1960s through 1980s, who sought "the point of linkage between ethical preoccupation and the political struggle for the respect of rights, the connection between critical reflection against abusive governmental techniques, and the search for an ethics on which individual freedom may be based."[25]

It is always a failure of critical sense to "absolve a certain political regime of its responsibilities in the name of the 'principles' that inspire it"[26] (that splendid Cold War maneuver), but there is a difference between the critique of Enlightenment theories or practices by people who think enlightenment is a good thing and its critique *qua* enlightenment by people who think other objectives are more worthy. In the United States, postmodern idiom has provided a big tent for both sorts of critique, and some prominent figures (Stanley Fish, for example) are hard to pin down as definitively belonging to one side or the other. But this coexistence is possible because the postmodern critique has yet to affect the comforts and liberties of daily life in any tangible way. If there were something more important than professional standing to be gained or lost, presumably the temporary community of those who dissent from the Cartesian-Kantian model of the subject would begin to dissent from one another more vigorously. What is the purpose of dissolving the consensus surrounding liberal society? To create more truly autonomous individuals or to strengthen the collectivity? Without making the cultural argument that communitarianism is natural to China (that habit will come in for examination later), one can see why, under present conditions, the Foucault who comes across most easily in translation is a fragment.

◆

One evening, I went out to Dachengfang Street to browse the used-book carts. Among the software manuals and tales of derring-do, I uncovered *Gaige qianhou lüewang lu—julong fusu* 改革前後略忘錄—巨龍復蘇 (A chronicle of the reform process—the giant dragon revives; 1993) by the apparently pseudonymous Wei Da 威達.[27] The next night's insomnia found me reading its chapters on the Democracy Wall movement of March 1979, especially "Shou che" 收車 (The towtrucks are coming) on its aftermath. Wei Da is surprisingly fierce in describing the sloppiness of the trial that convicted Wei Jingsheng 魏京生 of "selling state secrets."[28] Wei Da underlines the vagueness of the charges, the predetermined outcome, the flimsiness of the evidence. What I find most useful in Wei Da's account is the fact that although he or she is able to cite foreign scholars and newspapers—Roderick MacFarquhar, the *Manchester Guardian*, *Le Monde*, the *Bangkok Post*—the case against Wei Jingsheng's accusers is not made by appealing to some international standard of human rights. Rather, Chinese notions of consistency, proportion, and due process are adequate to revealing the show trial as a scandal; and that is encouraging, although not yet a bill of rights. It is good to be reminded that this is possible and also that the protection of powerful outsiders is not always the protester's only guarantee of safety. The notion that human rights are a gospel that the Chinese are only reluctantly coming to accept suits the needs of certain international organizations, along with the Chinese and American governments—it gives all of them a space in which to exhibit "determination," "flexibility," and "understanding" and score "victories" and make "concessions," but it is probably worse than useless to citizens in a tight spot.[29] Without universalistic or particularistic fanfare, counting on pedestrian, everyday reactions to unfairness, this obscure Wei Da shows how to make native rights talk work.

I carry these thoughts to dinner with a group of professors and administrators whose specialty is the teaching of Chinese to foreigners. In a discussion of the international reach of Chinese cultural figures, someone brings it up as an article of praise that "no matter how bitterly Hu Shi railed against his opponents in China, whenever he went abroad he had nothing but nice things to say about Chinese culture." In other words, Napoleon's rule about dirty linen—it's to be washed *en famille*. That the mere mention of Amnesty International or the concern of external organizations in relation to a case like Wei Jingsheng's is usually sufficient to cloud matters is made plain by the following selection from Wei Da's treasury of press clippings:

How can it be that foreigners aim to bestow on the Chinese [concepts of] "human rights" and "democracy"? Impossible! . . . Before Liberation, the whips, knives, and guns of imperialism never breathed a word about "human rights" and "democracy." In certain parks there were signs reading: "No Dogs or Chinese Allowed."

What business does a millionaire who has stuffed his paunch with the blood and sweat of laboring people have preaching "human rights"?[30]

Conveniently, through such feints, all foreigners collapse into one, the writers of Amnesty letters are as one with the empire builders and union busters, the better to mold the home population into a matching ideal unity. These quotations date from 1979, but the technique, the use of alleged ethnic and national interests to discredit anything said by foreigners or through foreign channels, is very much in force twenty years later. Its renewed persuasiveness may show that some of the themes of the Chinese postmodernists—their communitarianism, their refusal of universal ideals or narratives, their self-depiction as "decolonizers of the mind"—mirror a consensus, or a deadlock, of the moment.[31] Is the appeal of postmodernism a fortuitous epicycle upon untheorized social grounds? To answer this question, one would need to see into the future of China—farther than I can, at any rate.

◆

The reader will have divined that I see in the postliberal, Huntingtonian theory of history a resource for governments that like to speak for the collectivity and show their "strength" by "standing up" to the meddling of other peoples in their "internal affairs." If a pattern of increasing tension with the United States indicates that China is now big enough to be taken seriously, it is in this calculus a plus for the regime, even when the cause of the tension is the regime's ill-treatment of its subjects. ("A great deal for China, a bad deal for the Chinese"—such formulations are unfortunately neither absurd nor impossible in any country.) The potential bifurcation of interests has not escaped the critics of *houxue*, who often raise the question of which kinds of argument harmonize with the "official line." Liu Kang 劉康 finds that "authoritarian capitalist modernization, spread by the global cultural imaginary, has become the mainstream school of thought among Chinese intellectual and cultural figures, filling in the ideological gaps left by the declining hegemony of the Communist Party."[32] For Zhao Yiheng, the situation sketched by Liu amounts to "neoconservatism under the slogan of exceptionalism, with theoretical support from the various 'post-discourses' of the West and a background of cultural nationalism," and calls into question the project of modernization.[33] Xu Ben's 徐賁 analysis faults the postmodernists for staying well within the zone of "permitted discourse" and even chiming in with "the official discourse that says that 'the meaning of human rights is just the right to survival, food, and clothing.'"[34]

Under contemporary Chinese conditions, postmodernity's antipathy to universals together with its inability to formulate a principled pluralism gives it the specific contours of an official-thought-in-waiting. For many post-ists, the specificity of their moment in history—the "post-new period"—is best defined through a contrast to the enthusiasm for civil society and liberal regimes that marked the 1980s. The 1980s were a period of "Western studies"; the 1990s, of "national studies" (*guoxue* 國學).[35] "National" is taken in a special and rather defensive sense. Zhang Kuan: "Freedom, democracy, pluralism, the independence of authors—these have been discussed for years, but the key issue is that distinctions must be made under differing historical conditions, and we cannot embrace unconditionally this chain of capitalist concepts. . . . Our thinking on these problems today cannot stop at the 1980s, we must take a step forward."[36] Zhang Yiwu 張頤武: "The split between the 'new period' and the 'post-new period' has already become obvious. The old style of discourse used to interpret mainland Chinese culture has been rejected by the new cultural practices of the present."[37] Elsewhere Zhang defines the "post-new period" of the 1990s "as a total surpassing of the 'modernity' sought by 'new period' culture from the late 1970s onward; it gives the general outline and description of the contemporary Chinese cultural situation in the global post–Cold War cultural context. It is a new period led by consumption, dominated by the mass media, structured by pluralist cultural discourse, and strongly utilitarian."[38] So much for critique: by declaring a "post-new period" that "totally surpasses" what went before and consecrating the intellectual attitudes appropriate to it, one has gone over the heads of one's potential opponents.

It is perhaps too much to expect anyone to adopt willingly the label of *guanfang* 官方, "official," thinker, although the post-ists seem unable to avoid positions that echo, resemble, or are convenient to the policies of China's rulers.[39] The citation-history of Zheng Min's essay on modernist poetics is instructive. That essay's redescription of the institutionalization of modern vernacular literature as a process not of creation but of elimination might be read as pointing the way to a more truly pluralistic politics in the literary world—pluralistic in the sense of putting forward more than one legitimation-story for the community to consider. But the criticism of the May Fourth movement in that essay has also been used as a cat's paw for the critique of all "Westernization" movements, including the 1980s influx of liberal-democratic ideas. Zhang Yiwu appropriates Zheng Min's second thoughts about the modernist movement to denounce the whole project of enlightenment: for him, "May Fourth" is simply "the completion of a process begun in the Opium Wars" whereby Chinese intellectuals "internalized the point of view of the Western subject." Even Chinese nationalism is stained by its relation to Western nation-state thinking. "This process of 'othering' one's own culture is the most important mark of modernity in China."[40] So the sooner an end to modernity is proclaimed, the better for all Chinese, goes the story. When Zhao Yiheng, descrying a conservative agenda in Zheng's essay, recited the more conventional foundation-story of modern Chinese literature, he was spurred to do so by a dread of this set of implications. What meaning does the term "conservative" have in this context? Appealing to a longer, more complex account of the Chinese past may suggest the legitimacy of rival versions of modern history, thereby breaking the monopoly of textbook triumphalism, but if a more searching discussion is impossible, it may only bring grist to the mill of national-interest theoreticians who see in it a chance to discredit cosmopolitan ideals. The opening represented by some aspects of Zheng Min's essay closes down all too soon. Perhaps it is simply intolerable—intolerable because undecidable?

♦

The question of pluralism is, like the label "conservative," ambiguously dependent on the contexts of its use. The theory of "cultural democracy" developed as an annex to Chinese postcolonialism provides a case in point. According to Zhang Yiwu, it is "thanks to postmodernism [that] the basis of a powerful cultural practice, a pluralist culture, a new cultural democracy, and limitless options have all sprung up overnight."[41] Zhang's optimism is interestingly interwoven with the idea of "resistance."

At the beginning of the 1990s, quite a few overseas scholars painted a dark and gloomy picture of mainland Chinese culture, but the vitality and richness of that culture has proved them wrong. The irony of history as it comes sharply into view at present is that the process of Chinese politics, culture, and economics has completely escaped the control of those discourse-centered "intellectuals"; it has also completely escaped the grasp of the ready-made discourses and interpretative models produced abroad or at home. China seems to have become an uncontrollable "Other."[42]

Like Zhang Kuan, Zhang Yiwu takes his cues from Edward Said, but reads many of Said's gestures as in a mirror. Said argued that the West built a scholarly discourse around the East in order to dominate it. Zhang Yiwu's conclusion is that China must be incomprehensible if it is to shake off outside domination. Against "Orientalism"—which he defines broadly enough to include any opinion about China that foreigners may express—Zhang Yiwu insists on "Chinese cultural specificities." The point is not to form a theory or description of Chineseness but to "resist," in any way possible, foreign (or foreign-tainted) discourses about China. Sneering is a favorite method:

These two essays [Xu Ben's "Disanshijie piping zai dangjin Zhongguo de chujing" (The place of Third World criticism in contemporary China) and Zhao Yiheng's "'Houxue' yu Zhongguo xin baoshou zhuyi" ("Post-ism" and Chinese neoconservatism)] have one extremely obvious common feature, a strong degree of what Homi K. Bhabha calls the "pedagogical" style. This "pedagogy" does not just take the form of ideas, it is also a rhetorical strategy. It shows a lofty condescension, a sympathetic, nay tragic understanding, as if the writer were a prophet holding the blueprint of history and surveying from a high tower the native critic in his troubled realm; it is the style of a writer in the "observer" position, taking note of the struggles and pursuits of the "observed."[43]

Moreover, persuaded that the observations or analyses of foreigners (or of Chinese-born people living abroad) are "regulated by Western cultural hegemony" and aimed at "making China an obedient 'Other'" to the West, he refuses to grant them the status of knowledge and marks this by surrounding the words "knowledge" and "China" with quotation marks. This is a wonderful application of postmodern theory—to write off other people's claims to knowledge as social constructions and leave one's own unquestioned![44] This passive-aggressive style—casting every dialogue or critique as an unequal contest—is in itself such a heavy verdict on the discourse in which it appears that I marvel at Zhang Yiwu's appetite for controversy. But it is not simply a mannerism. It mirrors the substance of what he has to say and models, by establishing a set of language games and structuring individual behavior, a certain relationship between "China" and "the West." The language games deserve attention, however trivial their content.

Zhang's recommendations for criticism at the present time are not bold.

This exploration tries, first, to find a new position: "the Other of the Other." While seeking to transcend the old condition of "Otherness" and refusing to take either side of the oppositions of universal/particular, classic/modern, it reflects on both in the context of contemporary culture and offers new insights. Second, it implies participation in contemporary culture—it implies the Gramscian role of the "organic intellectual." It neither stands apart from culture, nor tries to transcend culture, but seeks theoretical advances from within the dialectical thought of transformations in society and culture. It maintains a critique of Western cultural hegemony, but this critique does not imply a decisively nativistic conservative perspective. This new perspective allows a new grasp on the "condition" of hybridity in contemporary China. This grasp was made possible by the appropriation of Western theories, but this appropriation does not imply the use of theory to advance interpretations of the Chinese context; rather, it recognizes that the transcendence of theoretical hegemony is dependent on reflection about and critique of theory. This requires the use of theory to critique theory, using contemporary Chinese conditions to reflect on theory, and using theory to match contemporary Chinese conditions, so as to produce a two-sided hermeneutic and gain a new cultural imagination and creativity.[45]

There is a determined defensiveness in this program. It is as if Zhang has compiled a list of the current terms of abuse—"conservatism," "nativism," "hegemony," "elitism," "commercialism," "radicalism"—and devised postmodern-sounding formulas that steer clear of all of them. Committed to nothing but also standing apart from nothing, and without a specific *modus operandi*, it is a very safe place to be. It resembles what Roland Barthes, reporting from the bourgeois world, called "Neither-Nor criticism."[46]

A criticism without thorns or horns, seemingly—but in practice things can be quite different. After repeating some points of this program in another essay, Zhang mentions two styles of play that he finds "unhelpful": "the desire for a discourse that privileges politics" and "the desire for a discourse that privileges values." In response to a reader's objection that his resistance to human rights talk makes him sound like "the [Chinese] Foreign Ministry's official spokesman," Zhang Yiwu retorts that this amounts to "calling any 'Other' whose choices are different from one's own, whose scholarly opinions go in a different direction, a 'spokesman for the Foreign Ministry'—and the implications are so obvious that they do not need to be stated. . . . It all turns into a dramatic 007-style combat between the angel of freedom and the devil's advocate." Likewise, when fellow scholars argue that the attack on modernity is indiscriminate and fails to recognize the better purposes to which modernization has sometimes been put, Zhang Yiwu complains that he has been "picked out as a person with evil motives."[47] People who attack *houxue* show that they cling to "absolute values beyond experience," which clearly renders them unfit for the job.[48] If politics and values are both out of bounds, and if the role of "theoretical reflection on theory" is to shift discussion from substantive issues to one's displeasure at being criticized—if, in short, no "privileged discourse" is permitted—then a kind of perfection of mere pluralism (or plurality) has been achieved, and the power of debate to change minds and worlds is at a standstill.

Zhang Yiwu shares with all the "post-ists" an unfavorable verdict on the May Fourth movement with its enthusiasms for John Dewey, Bertrand Russell, and Lev Tolstoy. Like Zhang Kuan, he describes modernity as "a set of knowledge/power discourses centered on Western Enlightenment values. As far as non-Western societies and peoples are concerned, 'modernity' is a concept bound up with the colonizing process."[49] A historical coincidence perhaps? "In the Chinese context, 'modernity' meant the construction of 'enlightenment' and 'salvation' as measured by Western discourse. . . . 'Modernity' in China . . . gave rise to a body of 'knowledge' about China / the West, with the purpose of deciding China's place in the world by the application of this 'knowledge.'" As we have already seen, Zhang considers the May Fourth movement to have marked the definitive self-colonization of Chinese intellectuals by their imagination of the West. "'Modernity' is a set of important 'knowledges,' the contours of which cannot be separated from the function of intellectuals. 'Modernity' and its 'knowledge' produced intellectuals who received and expressed them, and the 'intellectuals' reinforced the indubitable authority of the 'knowledge' of the discourse of 'modernity.'"[50] The new-style intellectual was "named and scripted by Western discourse. . . . This 'othering' was involved in the whole process of producing 'modernity' and 'knowledge.' The classical form of this production was the making, through Chinese-Western comparisons, of a discourse of 'otherness' concerning the specificities of Chinese culture and a way of knowing in reference to China."[51] But the promulgation of ethnic stereotypes, however unflattering, could not have undermined ethnic consciousness to the degree desired by the modernizers. That job fell to the concept of the "human," the universal Enlightenment subject: "from Lu Xun's 魯迅 call for 'authentic people' [*zhende ren* 真的人] to the 1980s theoretical thinking about 'the objectification of the intrinsic powers of the person' and 'subject formation,' an unconditional identification with the values of universal human nature prevailed."[52] Now, says Zhang, that is all over. "Modernity" has been shown to be an effect of "othering," all its goals are discredited as side effects of colonial false consciousness, and as a result "reflecting on and critiquing 'modernity' are the basic tasks of contemporary culture."[53] "The old-time 'pathfinders,' the traditional Enlightenment intellectuals" find themselves on the wrong side of an "Althusserian epistemological break"; a new species, the "post-intellectual," has already come forth to replace them.[54] "Thanks to pluralist culture and its multiple strategies of progress, the phase [of modernity] is on its way out."[55]

"Pluralism" and "hybridity" are occasional synonyms for the "cultural democracy" Zhang Yiwu advocates. But when actual hybrid cultures—such as May Fourth modernity—come into view, he faults them for their "surrender" to foreign notions. In a proper "cultural democracy," no one would presumably compare Chinese values to Western Enlightenment values—at least, never unfavorably—and there would be no forcing of universals of any kind down the throats of autonomous peoples.[56] "Cultural democracy" is meant to be an extension to cultures of the processes of democracy—one culture, one vote. But what is a culture? What rights do cultures claim? Zhang does not give a substantive account of "Chinese culture" or tell us what is precious about it. He defends it on principle. One need only know that in the twentieth century it has been the subject of a "subaltern discourse" and the whipping boy of indigenous reforming intellectuals. If Lu Xun and Chen Duxiu were degraded, foreign-devil-worshipping Chinamen, then how pure indeed must the true, non-Othered China be! In the present, Zhang finds much to correct in

the "knowledge" about "China" created by global cultural interests. Major cultural products about the special political circumstances of China have already become an indispensable resource for international investment. From the discourse of "human rights" advanced by Western governments to the striking use of Chinese politics in the films of Zhang Yimou 張藝謀 and Chen Kaige 陳凱歌, Chinese politics has become a precious cultural bit of recycled goods. "Human rights" has long been a bargaining chip in the effort to take control of the Chinese market and mastermind commerce; it is the last illusory shadow determining the Otherness of "China." As Rey Chow has shown, the democracy represented by the [statue of] the Goddess of Democracy [in Tiananmen Square, May 1989] was "a naïve, idealistic clamor for democracy 'American style,'. . . converg[ing] on the symbolism of the white-woman-as-liberty."[57] And the major symbolic products about the oppressiveness of the Chinese government, just now wildly popular, . . . turn this "clamor" into marketable commodities . . . that display the "Otherness" of China.[58]

If foreigners who address problems in China can be shown (or suspected) to have selfish motives—including that pleasurable frisson of horror at the "oppressiveness of the Chinese government"—then the problems, magically, no longer exist. Chinese objectors may, surely, be characterized as having "othered" themselves, with or without the rewards of participation in the discourse of authority. Knowledge (well-founded or not) about China becomes "knowledge" about "China," projections of a false consciousness. In his triumph, Zhang has confused autonomy with autism.

This style of argument capitalizes on long-held, and partially justified, resentments. But the fact that rascals and thieves glorify something does not make it bad. Nor does the fact that something is odious make its opposite (or supposed opposite) automatically good. One must make appropriate distinctions; otherwise it would be enough to look no further than slogans. Postmodernism, it is good to remember, began as literary criticism, and all along it has excelled in showing strange relations of mutual influence between the content of cultural products and their ways of being in the world.[59] But when the story disappears and cultural critique exclusively addresses the story about the story, or the story about the story about the story, perhaps another type of questioning better deserves the name of critique.

♦

The strategic role of the term "culture" varies—consider the British study of "working-class culture" in the second-tier universities of the 1950s and 1960s, in which establishing that the working class had a culture was the main task, as contrasted with the easy accreditation of "cultures" in the American system of competing interest groups (the culture of poverty, youth culture, biker culture, Winn-Dixie's corporate culture).[60] In China, "culture" (*wenhua* 文化, with or without its newly acquired epithet of opprobrium, "elitist": *jingying wenhua* 精英文化), is the category through which the intellectual vanguard (carefully distanced from direct political power since 1949, but still

the primary audience for state speech) can think of itself as "China." Zhang
Yiwu does have some things right. He sees, for example, that modernization
conferred on the educated few the right to speak for the masses, to speak as
China (a dynamic considered more ripely by Partha Chatterjee and Prasenjit
Duara).[61] A shift of the definition of progress lays bare the systematic ambiguity about the relation of the cultural vanguard, the onetime organic intellectuals, to the rest of China (were they organic in respect to party, state,
masses, sociological minority, information network, culture, or what?). Like
other post-ists, Zhang sees the reorientation of Chinese society toward consumption and production for the outside market as the twilight of the intellectuals.[62] I think this last point is accurate. "Culture" is a term of power in
China. Although "cultural democracy" in its foreign-relations mode contends that a "culture" is a law unto itself (no longer subject to evaluation in
an "Enlightenment" or other framework), in its domestic mode the term announces the destitution of intellectuals' authority: it will be a pluralism, thus
an absence of guiding role, carried to the one province where the educated
classes might still claim leadership. If the power of culture was first har-
nessed by the scholar-official class and then passed (with changes in the content of "culture") to the reforming intellectuals of the twentieth century, it
has always furnished a means of rule for a state that needed educated people
as its managerial-political class. The one-party consumer state no longer
needs intellectuals, except as specialists in technology, management, enter-
tainment, and advertising. The new "organic intellectuals" will be employees.
Disruptions like those of 1919, 1956–57, 1976, 1979, and 1989 will no longer be
their affair.[63] Thus the vanishing of culture as power means the end of that
traditional source of dissent.

The new-fashioned cultural chauvinism of the post-ists has not yet had
the pragmatic effects on people's lives that the old Orientalism had as a sub-
division of colonialism, but it has all the potential to do so by making "Ori-
entals" of its own people—fellaheen who must bow to the decisions of their
betters, whether these are mandarins, warlords, Central Committee chair-
men, or tycoons. The message of both is the same: culture is destiny. But the
"Oriental" culture in which these state intellectuals seek the pattern of
China's political and social future is all the more insubstantial for being a reversed caricature of an exoticized "West."[64] It was shortsighted to speak as if
"Orientalism" were adequately defined by *negative* perceptions of the "Orient" and as if it could be countered by proclaiming *positive* judgments; you

can reverse the polarities, keep the wiring intact, and the machine will run as before. The root of the error is just what is presented as the decisive step beyond Said, that of perceiving "the Orient" as a substantial thing rather than an intercultural fiction with real consequences.

◆

Eight months after the main part of this essay was written, confirmation of the post-intellectuals' worldview, or at least a genuine shot in the arm for their reputations, was unexpectedly provided by the three NATO missiles that struck the Chinese Embassy in Belgrade, killing three Chinese citizens, on the morning of May 7, 1999. No one in China thinks much of the American explanation that it was an error caused by faulty reconnaissance and an out-of-date map.[65] The general assumption has been that the attack was intentional, and the only question is how to assess the bombers' motives. On May 20, the *People's Daily* sponsored a World Wide Web interview with Wang Yizhou 王逸舟, the vice-director of the Institute for World Politics and Economics of the Chinese Academy of Social Sciences. Wang's interpretation of the crisis falls in perfectly with the geopolitical and ideological frameworks of the "post-intellectuals." In response to the question, "What is NATO's strategy?" Wang elaborated:

First, from a defensive military organization it is becoming a tool for expansion, first to all of Europe, then to the whole globe. . . . Second, NATO's new concept demands that NATO no longer stay within its traditional geographical bounds: it will expand to wherever it is needed. For example, the first step was a peaceful eastward expansion with the entry of Poland, Hungary, and the Czech Republic; the next step is to press on toward the Mediterranean and North Africa; it may be that step three is to expand to the other nations of the world in order to realize NATO's goal of replacing the U.N.

Third, in the past NATO was a strictly military alliance, and now it is moving in the direction of military government, so that, for example, it will no longer be concerned with security alone but will take on human rights issues, refugee issues, drug issues, criminal issues, etc. This is NATO's ambition of global expansion.[66]

If the United States has acted in such a way as to make this scenario imaginable—and indeed it has—that it would undertake a series of wars radiating eastward from the Balkans is nonetheless implausible. Appetite for territory no longer suffices to justify the massive expenditures of modern warfare. But not all conflicts have to be territorial, as Wang Yizhou asserts:

The speed of China's modernization is sure to disturb the present international political and economic order and insensibly threatens U.S. and Western leadership. So we will certainly become the object of more and more attacks. The rest of the world will come forth with all kinds of excuses and pretexts for limiting or cornering China—human rights, the environment, non-proliferation, guided missile technology, trade deficits, etc. By setting impossible requirements, they hope to limit China's development, confine China to a frame set by themselves. . . .

About the "anatomy of U.S. hegemony" and "the United States's use of theory to shore up their hegemony": . . . American hegemony, apart from its military and political aspects, is a cultural or conceptual hegemony. This is a much more complex, much craftier form of hegemony. Think of Hollywood movies or the global position of the English language, or American inventiveness in the field of ideas.

We can point to any number of examples to show how U.S. hegemony gets various kinds of theoretical support. The first and most famous is the "clash of cultures" theory, which is a plan to give the United States the dominant role in determining the value of every people, every culture, every civilization. . . . Another aspect is what is called "peace and democracy." Here the plan is to tell every country in the world: if you follow the pattern of the Western "democracies," you'll have peace and security, but if you refuse Western "democracy," you'll meet the same fate as Yugoslavia. . . . Another means is the famous principle that "human rights take precedence over national sovereignty."[67]

Perhaps the post-ists are not so marginal after all. You only need to replace "Enlightenment" with "America" to get a wider and angrier audience. At a time of tension, the "universal subject" has left town, and the rejection of human rights, democracy, and open discussion as another dose of the "sugared bullets of capitalism" finds considerable acceptance among the Chinese public. The mechanical pseudo-dialectics of East and West—"there are the values and ideologies characteristic of the West, and there are those of the Orient, which are the contrary to the former"[68]—may be absurd, but they make up a piece of the lived reality of many Chinese people, including directors of institutes and think tanks, holders of degrees earned abroad, beneficiaries of that "ladder of success" which is the best approximation in contemporary China to a civil society with space for debate. It is not certain that many people will march off to die for cultural nationalism, but if enough people can be persuaded to accept it as their final horizon of political aspiration, it will have done enough damage. And the blame will not lie entirely with the Chinese government. As we have seen countless times in the century just past, the United States at war is not the best teacher of democracy.[69]

If Chinese observers seem to fall into an unreflective nationalism in rejecting the human-rights agenda, it is because they have come to parse talk of human rights as an American nationalism. And this is not entirely inaccurate, as on this side of the Pacific the ideology of rights passes from being an oppositional to a "mainstream" mode of thought and becomes available for various indiscriminate uses, some thoroughly self-serving. Chinese observers force us to recognize the hypocrisy lurking in state adoption of rights talk.[70] But asserting the right of states to do with their populations what they will is not a good way out of the difficulty either; it makes sense to take that stand only if you think you are isolated from any harm the state might be in a position to inflict. If it is uncomfortable to consider the ways in which the philosophy of rights can be exploited, consider the many theories of government that can hardly be accused of hypocrisy or universalism. For better or worse (and often very much for the worse), the "worldliness" of the idea of human rights is long since launched: the job of those for whom it is a final good is to keep it from becoming a merely instrumental good or pretext.

◆

Is there any truth to the consensus of journalists and diplomats that the economic liberalization of China is preparing the way for a stronger conception of personal rights?[71] Or is that theory a product of inappropriate universal humanism? One reason for confusion in the discussion of democratic culture and its spread is that there is almost no way to know whether people want more democracy than they have, in the very places where it would be most important to find out. The spokesmen, self-appointed or not, are always unreliable (although the "they don't have it and they don't want it" argument is, I think, intrinsically suspect). Satellite television, often described as the inevitable herald of democracy, teaches more about consumption and celebrities than about autonomy. It is after all imaginable that the majority of Chinese people (or for that matter, American people) are persuaded that economic growth, international prestige, social order, and a thriving culture are best achieved without the distractions of democracy and rights talk; and in that case, it will be futile to tell them otherwise—although no one has asked them yet in any way that counts. The very thought of asking them would be a tremendous departure from the history of Chinese modernization, not to mention postmodernization.

Some years ago Tang Xiaobing, looking into China's future, stated that "between political unfreedom and market indifference, there is no real choice for the better."[72] This balanced assessment of pseudo-alternatives shows how much harm a lingering Cold War pattern of thought can do. The labels of "new Left" and "neoliberal" (*xinzuoyi* 新左翼, *ziyou pai* 自由派), as they are applied in shorthand fashion to contemporary Chinese debates on culture and politics, seem to beg exactly the same set of questions.[73] History in the guise of the vanguard party now seems bent on showing that it is no longer a matter of choice: you can have *both* "political unfreedom" and "market indifference." The passing of the Cold War paradigm should allow us to see that "capitalism" and "democracy" are contingently, not essentially, related; you cannot expect that one will always bring the other, and maintaining what is known as a "favorable investment climate" under conditions of economic oligopoly and political monopoly hardly encourages the fashioning of new pluralistic institutions.[74]

♦

The question about democracy comes down, in any case, not to a matter of concepts or culture but to a matter of speech in the most pragmatic sense. Who has the floor? Can the floor be shared? Can it be yielded? The greatest cause of distortion in the *houxue* democratization debate is that the conversation takes the form of intellectuals asking each other what they think about concepts and principles. It is not as a concept that democracy is valuable but as a practice. In 1989 students, teachers, office personnel, factory workers, small merchants, casual laborers, and others took to the streets to ask for a broadening of reform. These innovations in social action have not been repeated since, however often issues of "elitism," "popular culture," "market values," and intellectuals' "participation in contemporary culture" have been invoked in the 1990s debate. The term "culture" has expanded so relentlessly in its passage from Euro-American literary theory to Chinese "post-studies" precisely because it allows the issues to be handled as matters of verbal discrimination, not of things done in shops, buses, prisons, and streets. Intellectuals are at home with verbal discriminations, even as new forms of relation underpinned by economics, for example, escape their guidance.

What people need, if modernity—and postmodernity, for that matter—is to make good on its promises, is more narratives, more debate about what goes on and why; which is to say that unlicensed citizens need to speak and be heard. Of course, debate is a form of practical action, and it emerges on the basis of other practices. The most oppressive thing about Zhang Yiwu's "cultural democracy" is that it is conducted in a sort of last-round international chess tournament space, where his tales of postcolonial resistance are all alone with the Fukuyama-CNN-IMF modernization narrative. Zhang is only one case; the same narrowing of options ("the West, and its Other") appears throughout contemporary discussion, producing a simulacrum of dialogue from which the people with the greatest need to speak are excluded. Where are the veterans of China's border conflicts? The soldiers and demonstrators of June 1989? The people who produce export goods of higher and lower added value? Urban migrants? No one but fellow intellectuals who share a great deal of background with the contenders has so much as a supporting role. That is more discouraging practically than theoretically. The historiography of the Taiwan nativist movement, for example, is deeply flawed—irresponsible and transparently self-serving on many counts—but in the event of reunification the independence movement's narratives are not going to be debated, merely suppressed (along with their authors, no doubt) as contrary to public order. Authentic pluralism would protect from punishment the fashioners of these and many more sorts of narrative. But this is not what the emitters or the receivers of human rights and democracy talk are bargaining about, as the transcript of President Bill Clinton's 1998 speeches in China shows.[75]

Reform under tightly controlled conditions—that could summarize not only the past twenty years of Chinese internal politics but the ambitions for the future expressed by Chinese "post-studies." The capitalization of "Chinese political cruelty" denounced by Zhang Yiwu is a predictable consequence of Chinese governmental decisions, at the beginning of the economic reform process, to open up some areas of history for reconsideration (the Hundred Flowers, the Gang of Four, the cult of Mao Zedong) while keeping the rest under lock and key. It was a strategic move—redirecting criticism toward safe targets. Postmodernism with its particular pluralisms offers a similarly limited critique. But pluralism with a checklist is plural only in the barest numerical sense. It is still answerable to and defined by the grantors. A pluralism more deserving of the name would be open-ended. If the people of China were sure of their ability to form peaceful assemblies, petition for redress, and coordinate labor actions, the result would be a pluralism worth listening to and ample compensation, if it came to that, for the fading away of the leadership of the educated class.

The opposition, beloved of comparatist scholars in a hurry, between Western individualism and Chinese communitarianism reposes on silences of long standing. In principle, every community with a grievance is capable of producing its "organic intellectuals." And every community has a grievance—for that is what spawns narratives and maintains communities. At present, however, China, like its postmodernists, only recognizes one community. So what we should be talking about, if the consensus of modernity really is at an end in China, is forming the preconditions for the practices the Western countries, with their curious theologies and ethical assumptions, describe as the exercise of individual rights. But none of this will come to pass so long as Chinese nationhood is so nearly successful in holding the local franchise on requests for representation and "cultural identity" in the global information order.

7

Outside the Parenthesis
(Those People Were a Kind
of Solution)

And some people have just come from the borderlands,
And they say there are no Chinese any more.
And now what will we do without Chinese?
    —C. P. Cavafy, "Waiting for the Chinese"

Do we know the difference between structuralism and poststructuralism? Although we may be hard put to define the difference, we can usually describe it by referring to an insurgent sensibility (although structuralism had its wild men: see Barthes's *Mythologies*), points of doctrine (the asymmetry of oppositions, the impossibility of a "transcendental signified," the absence of metalanguage), or an exemplary incident where the paths forked (for most Americans that would be Jacques Derrida's contribution to the great Structuralist Clambake of October 1966, "Structure, Sign and Play" with its critical examination of Lévi-Straussian "nostalgia").[1] I here propose an additional marker with some diagnostic value, both for figuring out what distinguishes poststructuralism and for separating impulses within it: the resort to Asia.

From the outset, poststructuralism and deconstruction have thought about China and the cultures influenced by China. It is unclear to me, as I look over the record, whether the intersection is that of a *method* coming to affect an *area* or whether the area was always somehow part of the method, so that deconstruction is unable, for historical reasons, to think about anything without to some extent thinking or dreaming about "China."[2] This thinking or dreaming occurs under the two broad headings of *grammatology* and *the end of humanism*. (If, indeed, these are two: as we shall see, the one tends to shade into the other.) I begin with some representations of Chinese writing that invoke the arguments about writing, speech, time, and presence—about the "logocentrism" of classical Western philosophy—familiar to us all through the early writings of Jacques Derrida. The first is from Michel Foucault, the second from Philippe Sollers:

Is not China, in our dreams, the privileged home of space? For our imaginary system, Chinese culture is the most meticulous culture, the most hierarchical, the most impervious to occurrences in time, the one most attached to the pure unfolding of distance. We imagine China as a civilization of dikes and dams under the eternal face of Heaven, spread and immobilized across the whole extent of a wall-encircled continent. Even Chinese writing does not reproduce in horizontal lines the fleeting passage of the voice, but arranges in columns the motionless and still recognizable image of things themselves.[3]

In classical China, just as the orientation of a map is established from within the map—north at the bottom of the frame, east at the left for a virtual observer, that is, as if the unfolding of the represented space came *from behind the map*, from a potential point both *in front of* and *within* the representation (and not like a specular projection)—so the vertical columns of writing would function, in our view, backwards, going from right to left, as if they were parallel rings in which air circulates and resounds. A Chinese classical book was not a "book" but rather, by its framing and even by its binding, a series of perspectives, a striation of fields, of cascades, with subfields and sliding transitions in anticipation of an always deferred return. Here, the verso is the recto [projected] as depth, while, for us, it is by excluding the verso that the recto becomes possible. Let us take a better look.

Writing *wells up* [*sourd*, with a pun on 'sourd,' deaf] from the inscriptional perspective because it occurs at an invisible distance and temporal remove (not in a face-to-face encounter): it invites not a seeing but a tracing, whereby the physical support is split into corridors, as if to recall the plural void where writing takes place. Writing is merely detached onto the surface; it weaves itself onto the surface, mandated by a source which is not a source toward a surface which is no longer a surface but a fiber written by its lower part held perpendicularly from its upper part (the brush is held straight up in the palm). So the ideogram takes its place in the column—tube or ladder—and fits there like a complex bar released by the monosyllable in the field of speech.[4]

These two passages, both from the late 1960s, represent Chinese writing as an antitype to the horizontal, vocal, temporally linear, and unidirectional writing of alphabetic cultures. Both assume that the definition of writing as the visual representation of speech is not exhaustive; they look for that whereby Chinese writing exceeds speech, any speech, even Chinese speech. Foucault sees Chinese writing as taking on the functions of a written work, an encyclopedia, prior to the participation of any encyclopedist or author. It is a kind of automatic archive. Whereas Western writing is always a track to be pursued by the relentless sequence of Nows marked by the voice in its articulation of letter after letter and so must be articulated anew for every act of writing or reading, Chinese writing stores the images of things in vertical rows, "puts them up" as we say of summer vegetables, in those durable and translucent jars furnished by a nonphonetic writing system. Chinese writing exhibits "verticality" not simply in the visual sense; Foucault plays on the designation of the vertical dimension as the *paradigmatic* axis, the axis of selection, in Jacques Lacan's analysis of poetry (which in turn stems from Roman Jakobson's essay on the two operations of language and two types of aphasia).[5] Foucault's imaginary spatialization of Chinese writing weakens the syntagmatic connections and reinforces the paradigmatic connections in such a way that sequence and subject-predicate relations cease to matter: thus, Chinese writing does not fashion sentences but "arranges [signs] in columns." Just as all kinds of objects coexist in space, so the terms of Chinese utterance are piled alongside or on top of each other in a storehouse the size of a continent. Contemplation of such an antitype is, for Foucault, a shock treatment for ethnocentrism. It is meant to remind us of the specific history that lies behind the categories we use in the Western world for making sense of things—a history his *Les Mots et les choses* attempts to narrate not as the only possible history but as a constrained yet internally tight set of logical choices. The Chinese antitype takes us out of this specific history and perhaps out of history in general, by making it possible to imagine a *tabula rasa* on which no categories would be set down in advance. The Chinese allusion can exercise this enabling function regardless of its factual accuracy—it is enough for Foucault's purposes to have granted us a glimpse of an ontology and a writing so capacious and so underdetermined.

Foucault was cautious: he delimits this China as occurring "in our dreams" and "for our imaginary system," much as Derrida refers to the "European hallucination" produced by early reports of Chinese writing.[6] The second passage, invokes Derrida's analysis of writing and the book to more pointed—more "realistic"—effect.

In *De la grammatologie* Derrida foretold "the end of the book and the beginning of writing": "The idea of the book, which always refers to a natural totality, is profoundly foreign to the meaning of writing. The idea of the book is the encyclopedic protection of theology and logocentrism against the disruption of writing . . . [and] against difference in general."[7] For a vision of "the idea of the book," no author can match Dante at the end of his *Comedy*: "In its depth I saw ingathered, bound by love in one single volume, that which is dispersed in leaves throughout the universe: substances and accidents and their relations, as though fused together in such a way that what I tell is a simple light."[8]

Sollers, however, makes the Chinese book evidence of a completely contrary metaphysic, somewhat Deleuzian in character: its operation on the mind is not to ingather but to disperse and multiply.[9] Anyone who has tried will know how bootless it is to force a classical Chinese philosophical book, often a compilation of fragments and anecdotes, into a systematic unity. It is quite accurate, and good advice for readers, to describe the *Analects* or the *Han Feizi* as "a series of perspectives, a striation of fields, of cascades, with subfields and sliding transitions." Yes, but observe the logic of the antitype: for Sollers, the Chinese book is specifically and determinately *what our books are not*. To the "end of the book" symptomatized by an appreciation of writerly dispersal, Sollers conjoins a "beginning of writing" that coincides with some points of Foucault's account of Chinese script. Differences between source and surface, between the writer and the process of writing, are attenuated almost to the point of disappearing. Writing is not scratched or incised (permanently, unidirectionally) but "detached onto a surface," released from one area of a "fiber" (the brush) onto another (the paper). The ideogram inhabits "its place in the column—tube or ladder—and fits there like a complex bar" in a page "split into corridors," a notable reversal of the reduction of the book to the authorial voice. This writing happens as a process of differentiation between like things (or even between parts of the same thing, if we call that thing "fiber"), and there is no necessary or anticipated end to the process, no opening and calling of the names from the Book of Life.

As images of a possible other world, these constructions of China lend support to a deconstructive project. To put it quite simply, China is deconstruction; or perhaps, China is what deconstruction will turn the world into or reveal the world as always already having been. Staging the surprise-effect of news from far away, the writers calculate (more or less transparently) a demystifying outcome. The distinctiveness of Chinese writing evokes a vision of logical relations, subjectivity, ontology, temporality, and eschatology that counters the models associated, in the West, with phonetic writing. A certain way of doing things is not the only way; history could have a different set of givens and a different plot structure; the end of civilization as we know it would just be the end of civilization *as we know it*. Neither author has to be a China specialist to say this or listen to the complaints of those of us who are. It is not very useful for the discussion of method, however true, to point out that Sollers, Foucault, and the rest did not speak Chinese or know a lot about China. You cannot fault a method for the richness or poverty of its objects. A method is there to suggest ways of proceeding with whatever objects you do have.

As for the project of overcoming metaphysical history, however, it is reasonable to point out that it did not happen in China. Even if Maoism exhibited the properties of material writing that made it a seductive analogue of the literary revolution after the New Novel, the combat for the reversal of phonocentric idealism in which Sollers sees himself as engaged happens at home, where it is needed; China works chiefly as an example of what life might be like after the passing of the civilization of the book and the voice.[10] A searching yet sympathetic reading needs to recognize this particularity of audience and moment. To talk about China in deconstructive vocabulary is to take that vocabulary out on a bold and provocative expansion, but not yet to do the work that that vocabulary was assembled to do. It is illustrative, analogical, or allegorical—in relation not to a real China but to deconstruction's own project.[11]

Zhang Longxi has recently called for a humbler reconsideration of "Western theory" about China in light of "Chinese reality."[12] There is room, however, to perform a chiasmus on the predicates. If we take these passages (and so many others from people of that same generation) as being about China, they do look like immodest generalizations from a weak empirical base.[13] They are not about China, or not exactly, although they have to seem to be so in order to do the critical work they do. The power and urgency invested in these representations is exactly the sign that they are *not* about China: for China here appears as the symmetrical opposite to what the reader already knows in the West.[14] And from the perspective of that "West," with its limited and limiting ideological commitments, the horizontality, the spatiality, the undifferentiatedness, of the Chinese written world appears as a truer reality. "Philosophers have only interpreted the world, in various ways; the point is to change it."[15] Marx proposed to begin the transformation by turning Hegel upside down and putting him on his feet. Sollers and Foucault, more sparing by 90 degrees, will turn world history on its side, so that, when its meaning ceases to circulate from top to bottom and starts to seep from right to left, "we" will have become "they." A "Chinese" theory modifies Western "reality."

The point of method that needs to be raised has to do with the idea of an "alternative." What kind of alterity comes to presence here? The "Chineseness" of the fables about Eastern writing emerges from a contrastive process of perception that selects from the pool of possible details those that correlate antithetically with some picture of the familiar way of doing things. Given Dante's or Derrida's conceptions of the book, Chinese books are antibooks and their authors perhaps antiauthors. That is enough for a discussion of the (European) concept of the book, but it tells us nothing about China: we would not be justified in imagining that just because a book is aphoristic and loosely organized, no stern orthodoxies could have proceeded from it, and that China has therefore never experienced the grasp on thinking and practice that a powerful book or doctrine can exercise. To say so would be to contend that there was no point in going to see how things play out in China, beyond our perception of the Chinese way as different from ours.

The analyst of contrastive mental space remains Ferdinand de Saussure, who described "the mechanism of language" as "turning entirely on identities and differences, the former being merely the counterparts of the latter." Terms are defined not positively—that would be a *Ding an sich*, and like the dog chasing cars, we don't know what we would do if we caught one—but negatively: "their most exact characteristic is that of being what the others are not." "The idea or the phonic substance contained in a sign matters less than what is going on in the other signs around it. The proof is that the value of one term can be modified without any change occurring in its sound or its meaning, simply because of a modification in some neighboring term."[16] What makes it possible for there to be such a determining relation among the properties of neighboring signs is, in Saussure's account, the fact that they all inhabit the same linguistic space and vie for existence like adjacent bubbles in a fluid; their relations cannot but be systematic.

When our comparative thinking treats our objects of thought—say, those huge objects, "China" and "the West"—as "oppositive, relative, and negative entities," tacitly fashioning a system of relevant differences, our language, in the strict Saussurian sense of that term, has run on ahead of us. "In every case we uncover, not *ideas* given in advance, but *values* emanating from the system." That "the [distinctive] characteristics of the entity are none other than the entity itself"[17] is an axiom of language but not of China studies, at least not until the latter has been refined into a closed linguistic system. Symptoms of such a closed system appear in the short texts we have examined: in particular their common motif of verticality. By it Foucault and Sollers are trying to articulate a difference. But the difference between vertical and horizontal is highly determinate; it refers back to a point of sameness, to the origin point of an x–y axis. As long as there is a difference between vertical and horizontal, we are not lost in space with no up or down. The alterity operates within a common category (that of dimension or directionality). Chinese writing is not, to sum up, *necessarily* vertical or timeless; it is vertical and timeless *insofar as* we think of ours as horizontal and time-bound.[18] Otherness resolves into antithesis—a figure of speech, not a logical operator or category of being.

When a text is generated by a trope or, better, a grammar of tropes (for there are many varieties of antithesis) and yet presents itself as description and reference, we confront precisely the form of allegory that readers of Paul de Man are trained to deal with.[19] In the figure of antithesis, we need to recognize language talking. When language talks, we are in the presence, however moderated, of glossolalia—and Jakobson showed that glossolalia can do without sense but cannot long abide randomness.[20] One good place to begin the work of deconstruction—following distinctions to their point of identity and identities to the point of their bifurcation; showing the incompatibility between statements and the language in which they are formulated; setting language and reference at odds—is in observing the confusion of the observer's relation to China with China's relation to itself.

The question rhetorical readings of "sinography"[21] must ask, at the risk of annoying by repetition, is Can the China in this text be constructed by projection from European starting points? No one will ever, I think, be able to answer conclusively "no": establishing and exalting a category of raw perception is neither useful nor honest. But if the effort to say something about China establishes a relation, opens an inventory of objects in Saussurian mental space, then the prizes for inventiveness should go to those whose constructions are most detailed, come closest to escaping the magnetic pull of antithetical thinking, delay as long as possible the snapping shut of the jaws of tautology.

The examples just given present writings that attempt—by adopting an alien point of view—to contribute to the dismantling of classical Western philosophy and its idols and yet the differences they construct must be traced back to a single origin (the asserted differences amount not to radical otherness but to twin aspects of contrastive identity). The methodological lesson that I would like to draw from this is that deconstruction cannot be a list of authors, a belief system, or a set of themes. It may articulate themes and present pictures of reality, as we see Derrida and Sollers do with their handling of the image of the book, but for the work of deconstruction to go forward these representations must be dispensable. It is proverbial that generals are always preparing to fight the last war. That's how method works; the last war is, after all, the one we know how to fight. But it is entirely likely that the next things worth questioning with the methods of Derrida and de Man will prove to have nothing in common with those on which junior deconstructors cut their teeth. At stake is the definition of deconstruction: is it a method, or is it just a peculiar genre of writing with a finite, enumerable set of thematic and formal markers?[22]

◆

The language of the texts I have been citing, from 1966 and 1969, testifies to an exceptional moment in French intellectual life, the high noon of *Tel Quel*, at which it seemed that the combined resources of Derrida's and Lacan's questionings (accompanied by Barthes, Foucault, Kristeva, Sollers, and many others) were about to open an entirely new era in the human sciences; the later rifts among the principal personages could not be anticipated.[23] That moment, that alignment of the star thinkers, would not last. But the texts that make of the East a conceptual bridge between grammatology and the end of humanism pose questions of structure and deconstructure that remain with us, although not, I will argue, so much as a set of questions as a soft consensus. To reread the texts may lead us to reopen the questions.

Chinese writing furnishes Julia Kristeva the vehicle for another exploration of a differently organized world. She remarks on the difficulty of early missionaries and translators who could render only haltingly, in Aristotelian or Cartesian language, the Chinese vision of the mutual

immanence of "reason" within "matter," so complete that no "reason" or "matter" could be said to exist outside their interdependence. . . . Their unrepresentable, heterogeneous scission takes form, derivatively, only through a combinatorium of opposite marks (+ and –, heaven and earth, etc.) with no hierarchy among them. In other terms: there is no symbolic principle that may be isolated *per se*, in front of us, as a transcendent law. . . .

Chinese writing, destined for a tonal language, is the other essential characteristic of the Chinese world to which we should direct our attention—and doubtless the first to strike our eyes and ears. Linguists know that Chinese functions just as all other languages do, and that it can transmit any message without ambiguity; present-day theoreticians of generative grammar have achieved a certain success in formulating rules for Chinese grammar that obey rules of universal reason. Let us not consider classical Chinese and the various poetic genres that disturb the transmission of messages by their many ellipses and condensations. In the ordinary spoken language of today (*bai hua* or "white speech"), the role of tones is obvious: they distinguish among different meanings. This differentiating role, common to all tonal languages, reveals what certain psycho-linguists have already surmised: tonal variations and intonations are the first distinctions in the flow of sound that children are able to apprehend and imitate. However quickly these intonations are lost in a milieu where tones are not a functional part of language, children surrounded by tonal speech begin to retain them quite early: for this reason, little Chinese enter into the linguistic code of social communication before other children do, as early as the fifth or sixth month, since they begin very early to distinguish tones as basic features of their language. And since, at this young age, the child's dependence on the body of his/her mother is enormous, the psycho-corporeal imprint of the mother will shape the tonal flow of sound; and this imprint will be transmitted, not obliterated, as a subjacent but active layer of communication after the child has acquired the grammatical system—this system being more or less secondary, more "socializing" since it conveys a message with a meaning (not just a tonal impulse) to other recipients, not just the mother. Can it be that the Chinese language preserves, thanks to its tones, a presyntactic, presymbolic register (for sign and syntax are concomitant), a pre-Oedipal register (even if it is clear that the full realization of the tonal system must await syntax, just as with the phonological system of French)?

The same question arises regarding writing. Originally at least partly imagistic, but more and more stylized, abstract, and ideogrammatic, writing retains its evocative visual character (by resemblance with the object or the objects that underlie an idea) and its gestural character (to write in Chinese one must have not only memory for meanings but also a memory of movements). Can these visual and gestural components be considered as deriving from more archaic layers than those of meaning and signification (inasmuch as these latter are logical and syntactic abstractions)—as relics from unconscious deposits that the subject would thus never have definitively left behind? . . . The logic of writing (visual representation, marks drawn from gesture, a signifying combinatorium subtending sign, logic, and a certain syntax) implies, at its base, a speaking/writing subject for whom what appears to us today as a

pre-Oedipal phase (dependency on the maternal and socio-natural continuum, absence of sharp distinctions between the order of things and the order of symbols,
predominance of unconscious impulses) would have had major importance. Ideographic or ideogrammatic writing uses [this phase] for the purposes of state power,
politics, and symbolism, but without censuring it. A despotic power that remembers
its debts to the mother and to its historical precursor, the matrilineal family: Hypothesis? Phantasm?—These reconstructions would at least help to explain the de-
struction of the great civilizations of writing after the rise of monotheism (or due to
its assaults). Now Egypt, Babylonia, and the Maya are gone, and only China (with
its followers in Japan or Southeast Asia) continues to "write."[24]

Like Fenollosa in *The Chinese Written Character as a Medium for Poetry*,
Kristeva sees Chinese writing as operating a "transference of power" from
nature to paper or silk and thence to the reader. "The naming function, the
symbolic function, is not isolated as such [in Chinese writing]: it is immanent and makes itself noticed in the rigor of gesture and brushstroke, in the
precision of the spaces articulating them, in the concision of the document
that does not express but transfers (*n'exprime pas mais translate*) an utterance
into a body and into a social, historical, natural space."[25] Chinese language
and writing, like music, suspend or, more precisely, overwhelm the linear
discourse of the symbolic.

For Kristeva, the immanence of Chinese logic and the concreteness of
Chinese writing contrast with the tense, hysterical, metaphysical excesses of
Western monotheism and alphabetism, both forms of a "law of the Father"
that makes meaning through the exclusion, the definition as nonmeaning
and nonbeing, of the presymbolic or pre-Oedipal "semiotic" register. In
China, owing chiefly to the survival of matrilineal patterns in family life, the
exercise of authority "uses but does not censor" those archaic energies. Chinese authority resembles the psychological agent, half censor and half poet,
who sits at the gates of dream and "translates" repressed thoughts into "representable" content, preserving yet disguising them.[26] And so the telling of
history takes the shape of dreamwork or lay analysis:

Instead of embarking on an explanation that seeks causes, makes deductions, and
specifies determinations, appearances, and essences while forecasting the consequences of an event—the only logical form of explanation for us, that which derives
from the principle of a logical and metaphysical causality—the Chinese present a
tableau of a "structuralist" or "strategic" type. Behind the event appears an association (or a combinatorium) that schemes for the reversal of the previous order; a
combat between forces of good and evil; two-faced personages; persecutions, sur-

prising reversals, conspiracies. As if metaphysical, causal, deterministic logic had collapsed in the face of the (traumatic) event whose origins we now seek; but without losing the symbolic level, the Chinese speaking subject articulates the event as a game, a war, a combinatorium. . . . Such an aesthetic style of reasoning, disconcerting though it may be to us, has a sure symbolic efficacy: by eliminating from the outset the problem of an "objective truth," impossible in a political world saturated with power relations, it relocates people into symbolic situations from the past or from literature, chosen for their historical power in the present. And in this archetypal symbolic situation are played out and revealed, as in a show, in a staged return of the repressed, a happening like those of antipsychiatry, the theater that Sade first created for the benefit of the inmates of Charenton—the emotional, ideological, and political dramas underlying the present traumatic event that concerns us and that we, on our side, wish to "understand."[27]

Where metaphysical logic demands truth, immanent logic seeks therapy, acting out, the confirmation (through performance) of screen memories—or *efficacy*, as Jullien will later put it.[28] This (psychoanalytically and historically) "archaic" way of thinking connects ancient China to the present of the Cultural Revolution and separates the Chinese from their Western interlocutors.[29] But it raises a further problem of historiography—appropriately, since that is where the impulse to look to China began. How is the predominance of the "archaic" in China to fit into a historical narration? Is this another "fact" about China that no completely "Chinese" observer could ever understand? The *absence* of difference in their minds, history, language, and so on signifies their difference from "Occidentals." If history seeks causes and specifies agency, then Chinese "structuralist tableaux" will never address history; they may occasionally hit upon a representation like those of history, but in obedience to a different dynamic. History then goes over, along with the symbolic, logic, and the Law in general, to the "West," perhaps a worrisome incorporation.

The question of difference and its others goes to the root of *Tel Quel* sinophilia and its motives. Like Sollers, Kristeva is attempting to find in China another form of historical time, a way around the teleological version of world history, in which non-Western societies are either precursors of modern freedom and reason or dead ends.[30] Sollers's *Sur le matérialisme* worked around Hegel's narrative by weaving Greco-Roman atomism, the materialism of the eighteenth and nineteenth centuries, Chinese physicalism, and Mao's "On Contradiction" into a continuous discourse: by turning metaphysics from Plato to Hegel into a finite series and embedding it in a larger, antithetical, milieu as nothing but "the long history of the repression, by idealism, of materialism and dialectics."[31] As the symbolic floats (and tosses) on the semiotic, as rationality opens a tentative parenthesis in the unconscious, as capitalism sinks its foundations in the exploitation of laborers who will eventually revolt, so metaphysics owes its appearance of completeness and system to a dependency that it cannot avow. "The exclusion of materialism, of sexuality, of history, of the multiplication of language, this is the surplus-value *gesture* of idealism."[32] And as a defiant answer to this gesture, Sollers unveils the description of Chinese maps, books, and calligraphy cited above. "This is where China *comes from*," he concludes. "And us?" The non-differentiation that China "comes from"—the space in which paper and brush, image and word, semiotic and symbolic, mother and child, reason and form, present and past, self and other, all intermingle and imply one another—is the space from which to expect transformation.

In that sense, China is ahead of Europe:

Why is it that the Great Proletarian Cultural Revolution *initiates* a new, multilateral, noncentered, conception of the historical process, a different global ratio of forces with multiple contradictions occupying different levels, which most people, stamped with their primary black-and-white symbolism, are unable to understand? Why is it that the Cultural Revolution finally initiates a nonreligious conception of history, in other words the concrete, daylit, manifestation in history of a unified *pluralization* of contradiction?[33]

Kristeva stages the contrast of nondifference versus difference by telling the story of a double volleyball game: the Chinese men's and women's teams versus the Iranian. The Iranians' bodies bulge with the signs of sexual difference: the women are "corpulent, their hair floating in the wind, passionate, exalted, hugging feverishly after every goal, and piercing the air with strident cries"; the men are "real machos, patriarchs of the soil." On the Chinese side, the women are "like slender boys," and the men "frail, more adolescent."[34] If to be Indo-European is to rush loudly and violently toward the two extremes of the sexual spectrum, to be Chinese is to inhabit a middle zone in which male and female characteristics overlap. Chineseness is the antithesis of antithesis itself, and if the Chinese women's team wins the volleyball game, it is (as the Marxists like to say) no accident.

With contrasts so faintly marked and no Text visible but the universally repeated slogans and exhortations of the Cultural Revolution's late phases, semiotic China is not a space of tension but of peace, of the neutralization of opposition. It is the antithesis of the antithetical: China is a place "without theater, without noise, without posturing, without hysteria." It reduced Roland Barthes to despair, often for the very features that so enchanted Julia Kristeva:

China seems to withhold the meaning [sought by the visitor], not because China has something to hide but, more subversively, because (in very un-Confucian style) China dismantles the constitution of concepts, themes, and names. . . . It is the end of hermeneutics. . . .

Leaving aside its ancient palaces, its posters, its child ballets, and its May Day parade, China is not *colorful*. The countryside is flat . . . no historical object interrupts it (no steeples, no manor houses). . . . No exoticism . . . .

Finally, this so apparently coded discourse [of politics] does not exclude invention, and I would even go so far as to say, a certain playfulness; take the current campaign against Confucius and Lin Biao; it extends everywhere, and takes a thousand forms; even its name (in Chinese: *Pilin-Pikong*) jingles like a joyous bell, and the countryside is covered with invented games. . . . The political Text (and it alone) engenders these miniature "happenings."[35]

◆

Kristeva saw in the China of 1974 the project

of constructing a society in which power, as it acts, is not represented by anyone: no one can appropriate it so long as no one is excluded from it—and this means women as well, those ultimate slaves, necessary supports to the power of the masters, who by being held at one remove from power make it possible to represent power, indeed make it something that must be represented (by fathers, by lawmakers).

A power, then, that is represented by no one, woman or man. But which is recognized by and for everyone, assumed and exercised by and for everyone: men and women; men and women exercising power only to critique it, to keep it in play, to make it move. This must be why the "law court" (*tribunal*) in China is replaced by "popular meetings": there would be no more instance of the Law per se, if every subject, man and woman, took it on him or herself and refashioned it in a permanent confrontation of his/her practice and discourse with those of others—in every act, at every moment? A utopia? A possibility to be dreamed of for the future, while in the present nothing has been able to overcome the rational rigor of bourgeois law and its associated ethics?[36]

Michel Foucault likewise found an opportunity of giving the Maoists a lesson in concretizing their own praxis, which he found dismally compromised with the relics of bourgeois idealism.

Foucault: We have to ask if these acts of popular justice can or cannot take the ordered form of a tribunal. My hypothesis is that the tribunal is not the natural expression of popular justice, but that it has rather the historical function of taking hold of it, mastering it, strangling it, while reinscribing it within institutions that are characteristic of State apparatus. . . . Is the establishing of a neutral instance between the people and its enemies, one that might separate true from false, the guilty from the innocent, justice and injustice, not a way of opposing popular justice? . . . What is the organization [of a tribunal]? A table; behind this table, which sets them apart from the plaintiffs, a group of third parties who are the judges. Their position indicates, first, that they are neutral as regards either party; second, that implies that their judgment is not determined ahead of time, that it will take shape after both parties have had their say, in keeping with a certain norm of truth and a certain number of ideas about justice and injustice, and third, that their decision will have the force of authority behind it. . . . Now this idea that you can have people who are neutral in regard to both parties, that they can judge them in relation to ideas of justice that are absolutely valid, and that their decisions must be obeyed, I think this all goes very far and seems quite foreign to the idea of popular justice. In popular justice, you don't have three sides, you have the masses and their enemies. And then, when the masses see someone as the enemy, when they decide to chastise or re-educate this enemy, they don't refer back to some abstract universal idea of justice, they simply refer to their own experience, the experience of the harm they have suffered and the ways they have been wronged and oppressed; and finally, their decision is not a decision of authority, that is, they don't go through a State apparatus to validate their decisions, they purely and simply execute that decision.[37]

Foucault urges the masses to stop interpreting their actions in terms of a law that does not belong to them and to show what they are doing by doing it and becoming a law unto themselves; Kristeva dreams of social action, "a permanent confrontation of [everyone's] practice and discourse with those of others," being sufficient unto itself, with "no instance of the Law per se." This is somewhat different from the chiaroscuro melding of polar qualities (masculine and feminine, heaven and earth, + and –). China erases the difference—or removes the table—that subjects ordinary practice and discourse to the eyes of the law, truth, a transcendental signified. China shows us how it is possible to live without the Law as such, without the Symbolic.

But what precisely is taking the place of the Law? The Despot? The People? Or is it that artifact of oriental ethnography, the Absence of the Law?

♦

It is not for their attempts to seize the movement of history that we remember the rebellious ex-structuralists (and it is not a bow to the post-1989 consensus about Marxism to say so). Like their appropriation of psychoanalysis, their historiography was a means of making claims about art; their relation to East Asia, which interwove Freudian, Marxian, and feminist themes, was perhaps most of all the articulation of an aesthetic. (I do not mean to say that it was therefore trivial, only that the language of art corresponded more nearly to their vision and abilities.)

Roland Barthes's short illustrated account of a visit to Japan, *Empire of Signs*, has greatly annoyed specialists of Japan because of its cheerful irresponsibility—in the words of one critic, its "narcissistic japoniaiserie" and "provincial anachronism."[38]

If I want to imagine a fictive nation, I can give it an invented name, treat it declaratively as a novelistic object, create a new Garabagne. . . . I can also—though in no way claiming to represent or to analyze reality itself (these being the major gestures of Western discourse)—isolate somewhere in the world (*faraway*) a certain number of features (a term employed in linguistics) (*un certain nombre de traits [mot graphique et linguistique]*), and out of these features deliberately form a system. It is this system which I shall call: Japan. . . .

To me the Orient is a matter of indifference, merely providing a reserve of features whose manipulation—whose invented interplay—allows me to "entertain" the idea of an unheard-of symbolic system, one altogether detached from our own.[39]

This is, of course, exactly what I have argued is a persistent source of error in studies of "the East": the antithetical nomenclature that frames "the other" as "our other," the very thing that "we" are *not*. When done straightforwardly and presented as the results of knowledge, such writing produces inverted tautologies ("heterologies" not "allologies"), negative portraits of what we think of ourselves. But Barthes is not interested in knowledge. He is "indifferent" to the reality of Japan (perhaps this hurts the specialists more than the clichés and blanket judgments they denounce).[40] He is "deliberate" in his plan of using contrastive rhetoric as a sensory mechanism, a "reserve of *traits*" (distinctive features, as in phonology; strokes, as in calligraphy). For the animal in the bush to survive, the perception of movement needs to trigger an instantaneous response; for the semiologist, the perception of contrast automatically creates entities, oppositions, series, grammars. Neither creature could thrive for long without its sensorium.

And so Barthes takes the reader into a reality perceived through such a sensorium, explicating everything in Japan as the contrary of its French counterpart. The fork stabs, the chopstick disentangles; tempura, light, airy, constellated with holes, is worlds away from the heavy lumpiness of French *friture*; we prize the gift, a Japanese prizes the wrapping; the Western actor strives for authentic expression, the Eastern actor for perfect adherence to convention; the one-armed bandit coughs up a flood of silver dollars, the pachinko machine, less vulgar and more self-referential, releases as its payout nonnegotiable pellets good for yet more games of pachinko. Each perception invokes a counterperception (the implicit contrast with our ways of doing), and the "system" to which these features add up, the common axis around which the perceptions revolve, is that Japan is a country of strong signs, self-sufficient signs, signifiers that are not slaves of any meaning, intention, or referent.[41] The name Barthes gives to these semiotic practices—these performances of, by, and for the sign—is again and again "writing." Almost any episode of Barthes's essay could serve as the example of examples—such a hall-of-mirrors effect is indeed one of the essay's main strategies—so I will seize on one with strong cultural connotations: the art of flower arrangement.

In a Japanese bouquet . . . what is produced is the circulation of air, to which the flowers, leaves, and branches . . . are merely partitions, corridors, or hurdles . . . one can insert one's body into the gaps between the branches, in the apertures of its stance, not so as to *read* it (to read its symbolism) but to retrace the path of the hand that wrote it: truly a writing, since it produces a volume, and since, while denying to reading the possibility of simply deciphering a message (however deeply symbolic), it allows reading to re-create the outlines of its work.[42]

That is how to read Barthes's book, too: not to decipher its message, not to gain information about Japan (it contains none, or so the author tells us), but to insert one's body into the gaps, to observe the writer's hand gracefully engaging with and disengaging from the phenomena of a visit to Japan. Otherwise one misses the book's experiment, its constant narrative present. (This observational present tense distinguishes Barthes's writing from that of a Kristeva always hurtling toward the archaic stratum in her most everyday exchanges with modern Chinese.) At its riskiest moments, the experiment has to tackle extreme cases, in which it seems that semiology is out of its depth and can never achieve an adequate description of the things being discussed:

The violence of the Zengakuren [the militant All-Japan Federation of Students, just then protesting against the U.S.-Japan Mutual Security Treaty and the Vietnam War] . . . is immediately semiotic: because it is not an expression of something else (of hatred, indignation, or some moral idea), it comes to rest in some transitive aim (occupying a city hall, breaking down a barbed wire fence). . . . All this contributes to the production of a mass writing, not a group writing (the gestures are carried out to their end, no one finishes anyone else's action); and finally, in an extreme of semiotic audacity, it is sometimes permitted that the demonstrators' rhythmic chants evoke, not the Cause or the Subject of the action . . . but simply the action itself (*"The Zengakuren are going to fight"*). This action is, then, no longer crowned, directed, justified, purified by language—a divinity above and apart from the combat, like a Marseillaise personified with her Phrygian bonnet—but doubled by a pure vocal exercise, adding simply one more gesture, one more muscle, to the volume of violence.[43]

In other words, the formula for the student demonstration is the same as that for the flower arrangement: gestures that are there not to be decoded but to be retraced. It took a stunning reticence not to report on such events "journalistically," by assigning motives and enlisting the reader's sympathy or condemnation. That reticence is Barthes' own "semiotic audacity."

The series of examples takes us once more from the theory of writing to the end of humanism, on a path that leads eastward. (A parallel argument is Alexandre Kojève's claim to have found in postwar Japan a society beyond history, where war and the motives for war had been replaced by the formalisms of aesthetic competition and "snobbism.")[44] Barthes is writing about writing with no humanistic corruption in sight. The many points of contrast (fork/chopstick, ritual bowing/uneasy sincerity, etc.) are incidents, prompts, pretexts for exploration, not signals to be interpreted. As a whole, the project recapitulates, but in a different mode, the ruthless analyses of popular culture in Barthes's early work. "Certain pages of *The Empire of Signs* recall the 'realism' of your texts in *Mythologies*," commented Jean Thibaudeau: "satire in 1957, utopia today." Barthes's response:

The little tableaux of *The Empire of Signs* are happy Mythologies: apart from certain personal reasons, this may be because my quite artificial position as a tourist in Japan—but a wayward tourist, really an ethnographer—enabled me to "forget about" the Japanese petty bourgeoisie, its domination over social behavior, the art of living, the style of objects, etc.: I was spared the nausea of mythology. One of my projects would be, precisely, to *forget* the French petty bourgeoisie (this will take a far greater effort on my part), and to catalogue those "pleasures" I enjoy by living in France.[45]

It is not just a matter of being new to Japan and illiterate in Japanese; it has to do with the morality of the sign, a reforming perspective that Barthes has abandoned. The example of the Zengakuren, whose language merely heightens the combat without appealing to a principle that lies beyond it, suggested to one interviewer that Barthes was no longer interested in historical or political engagement. Queried about the imperative "to enter completely into the signifier," Barthes maintained that

If I have changed on this point, it's a displacement, not a renunciation. . . . Now we need to move the combat forward and try to break down not just signs (signifiers over here, signifieds over there) but the very idea of the sign. . . . What we have to try to break down today is Western discourse as a whole, down to its bases and elementary forms. . . . In our Occident, in our culture, in our language(s), we must engage a duel to the death, a historical struggle with the signified.[46]

Barthes accepted the description of this task, and specifically of his *Empire of Signs*, as "deconstruction," "grammatology," "nihilism."[47] It is a different combat from that against hypocrisy. It involves opting for a field of signs from which the very possibility of hypocrisy is absent. "The nausea of mythology" is provoked by the recognition of dishonesty, and that is excluded (or useless) in a world of "strong signs." Let us suppose that two mortal enemies are observed bowing to one another: in Japan as Barthes imagines it, they cannot be accused of duplicity, for bowing does not have the function of symbolizing an inward friendliness. Bowing is bowing to the code of good manners in general. If you tried to denounce Japanese performances as hypocrisies, as Barthes had done in *Mythologies* for the sad spectacles of the French bourgeoisie, you would be going up the wrong alley, for a society of pure spectacle has nothing to fear from an unmasking. Barthes's Japan is a stage for the performance of Brechtian "epic theater": not poorly executed Aristotelian theater, but a realm in which illusion is superfluous.[48] Hence Barthes's fascination for the Bunraku puppet theater and for male actors playing women's roles.

Take the Western theater of the last few centuries: its function is essentially to manifest what is supposed to be secret ("feelings," "situations," "conflicts") while concealing the very artifice of such manifestation. . . . The stage since the Renaissance is the space of this lie. . . . With Bunraku, the sources of the theater are exposed in their emptiness. What is expelled from the stage is hysteria, i.e., theater itself. . . . Bunraku practices neither the occultation nor the emphatic manifestation of its means; hence it rids the actor's manifestation of any whiff of the sacred and abolishes the metaphysical link the West cannot help establishing between body and soul, cause and effect, motor and machine, agent and actor, Destiny and man, God and creature: if the manipulator is not hidden, why—and how—would you make him into a God?[49]

What is most precious about Japan, its power to strike the foreign observer with the self-evidence of *satori*, is its "exemption from meaning."[50] Exemption, as of a tax or a debt. Without constantly being held to its debt to meaning, then, Japanese signifying behavior operates through a single articulation of its constituents (rather than a double articulation: the laws of form plus the laws of meaning): it is a form of music more than of language, "un système sémiotique exempt du signifié et qui ne transpose qu'un jeu de différences où seul apparaît, privé d'idéologie, le procès défrayant les clôtures" (a semiotic system exempt from the signified, merely transposing a play of differences wherein appears alone, shorn of ideology, the process piercing the barriers [of identity]), to borrow a description from Kristeva.[51] In the paradise of signs, life in general (cooking, wrapping things, conversation) becomes synonymous with writing, which becomes identical with music, an *absolute* representation as opposed to *programmatic* or mimetic representation (a show in the service of some message outside it).[52] Whether a self-sufficient order of signs bears or needs criticism (in the name of what would one critique it?) is a question left unasked. The "case against and utopia for" Occidental signification has oddly reprised the late-romantic aesthetic of the total work of art.

◆

That so peculiar a union should take place (and in Japan, or "Japan," no less) must come down to some unusual historical givens.

On March 12, 1935, the director, playwright, and actor Mei Lanfang 梅蘭芳 arrived in Moscow with his "New Theater of Ancient Forms." He gave six weeks of performances in Moscow and Leningrad and held discussions with local theater people (among them Stanislavsky, Meyerhold, Tretiakov, Eisenstein, and Brecht, then an exile from Germany).[53]

Brecht's impressions of Mei's acting are recorded in his 1936 essay "Verfremdungseffekte in der chinesischen Schauspielkunst" (Alienation effects in Chinese acting).[54]

The alienation effect is achieved in the Chinese theatre in the following way. Above all, the Chinese artist never acts as if there were a fourth wall besides the three sur-rounding him. He expresses his awareness of being watched. This immediately re-moves one of the European stage's characteristic illusions. . . . The actors openly choose those positions which will best show them off to the audience, just as if they were acrobats. A further means is that the artist observes himself. . . . The audience identifies itself with the actor as being an observer, and accordingly develops his atti-tude of observing or looking on. . . . The performer portrays incidents of utmost passion, but without his delivery becoming heated. At those points where the char-acter portrayed is deeply excited the performer takes a lock [*sic*; more likely a braid] of hair between his lips and chews it. But this is like a ritual, there is nothing erup-tive about it. It is quite clearly somebody else's repetition of the incident: a represen-tation, even though an artistic one. . . . And so lack of control is decorously ex-pressed. . . . [The actor] is careful not to make [the character's] sensations into those of the spectator. Nobody gets raped [*vergewaltigt*, overpowered] by the individual he portrays. . . .

When Mei Lan-fang was playing a death scene a spectator sitting next to me ex-claimed with astonishment at one of his gestures. One or two people sitting in front of us turned round indignantly and sshhh'd. They behaved as if they were present at the real death of a real girl. Possibly their attitude would have been all right for a European production, but for a Chinese it was unspeakably ridiculous.[55]

The Chinese actor "limits himself from the start to simply quoting the character played."[56] Brecht's break with an "empathic" theater was spurred by a desire to introduce critique into stage performance, to interrupt the ac-tion and oblige the audience to consider their own interpretation of the events. In Mei Lanfang's acting, he saw a confirmation of his own work of the previous twenty years. This is the way Mei's legacy (if not his name) has been passed down to present-day Occidental theater practice, as an activat-ing element of socially critical theater, a means of disrupting the "false con-sciousness" that leads us to assume that our culture is the same as eternal na-ture. It is thus involved with the topic of "constructedness" in literary and social study (as most commonly practiced). Mei Lanfang exemplifies the person who gets out ahead of artificiality, who, rather than clinging stub-bornly to the naturalness of his categories, turns the wheel in the direction of the skid. A theater without deception, of self-recognizing artifice, in which nobody gets "raped" or "overpowered," is the result.

Brecht's response to Mei's acting naturally emphasized its critical, revi-sionary force for the bourgeois societies of what were soon to style themselves the nations of the "West." But there is more to the story than an exchange of techniques and attitudes between "East" and "West." The geographical terminology is something of an embarrassment, for precisely datable reasons. There are several "Easts" in play here: the cultural East, China and Japan, and what will become, after 1945, the political East, the Soviet sphere of influence. The "West" is another shifting category: the nations of the geopolitical West may have tried to consider themselves synonymous with the cultural West ("Plato to NATO," as the undergraduate shorthand goes), but nobody could concoct a single cultural category adequate to subsume the various non-Wests into one.[57] To continue anticipating the post-1945 terminology, Brecht in 1935, an exile from the "West," was sitting in the "East" watching a traditional artist from the "Far East," and the Soviet ("Eastern") audience's enthusiastic reception of Mei's work ran along somewhat different lines from his. The Easterners noticed above all

the peculiar and original rhythmical and musical structure and its interaction with the movement and the speech of the actors. There are no arbitrary sounds or movements without a purpose. Lanfang's hands: his ten fingers are like ten other characters on the stage, not in the program. One can fail to understand the music or to appreciate the elegance of the costume, or lose the thread of the subject, but it is impossible to distract the attention from these hands, always in movement, from the dance of the fingers, now meaningful, now decorative, now similar to the subtle decoration of clouds, leaves and grass in the old miniatures. (Tretiakov)[58]

When on Mei Lanfang's stage the gesture becomes dance, the dance becomes a word, the word becomes an aria (an aria that is extremely complex from the musical and vocal point of view, not to mention its execution), then we see this theater's organic integrity. . . . What we call conventional elements of representation are only the necessary form of its organic lawfulness and the expedient revelation of the inner structure of the whole representation. (Tairov)[59]

Eisenstein's praise of Chinese theater likewise emphasizes the economy and richness attainable by traditional means:

We see how he carries out an entire series of devices, of movements that are obligatory in an almost hieroglyphic way, and we understand that there is here a perfectly determinate expression, both well thought out and complete. There is an entire series of obligatory positions for the reflection of certain vital traditions. . . .

We all know the definition of realism that books give. We all know that plurality must be visible through singularity, as well as that the general must be visible through the particular, and that realism is built on this reciprocal penetration.

If we look at the artistry of Mei Lanfang from this point of view, it is then possible to observe a very curious feature: in Mei's theatre both opposite elements are pushed to the limits. This generalization reaches the symbolic and emblematic, while the partial representation becomes the individuality of the performer. In this way we have remarkable emblems, executed by the original individuality of the actor. In other words, it is as if the boundaries of these opposites were moved farther apart. . . . Our [Soviet] art is now almost completely reduced to one of its elements, that is, the representation. And this is being done to the enormous detriment of the image. We have witnessed the disappearance of the culture of the image, i.e., the culture of the high poetical form, almost completely not only from our theatre but also from our cinema. We can point at our time, the time of silent cinema, when pure figurative construction played a huge role, and not only the [naturalistic] representation of people.[60]

Mei Lanfang left several kinds of impression. Combining them is something of a constructivist project, in the Russian sense of the word. Unlike that of Brecht and Barthes, the Russians' appreciation of Mei Lanfang is built not around the axis "illusion/nonillusion" but around the idea of a self-generating artistic language, a complex "artifice" with an internal "lawfulness" visible in every detail—an "absolute," "organic" stage action. The eager discussion of Mei's performances in Moscow (recorded by twelve articles in *Pravda* during his short stay, an enthusiasm spilling over into symposia, master classes, and letters to the editor) is attributable, according to Georges Banu, to the opportunity Mei's undeniable success brought of opening up once more the question of formalism.[61] In 1935, the doctrine of "socialist realism" had been pronounced but not yet enforced as it would be, starting the next year, with purges and prison terms for any lingering "formalists." (Tretiakov, one of the founders of agitprop theater, would be arrested and shot for intellectual crimes in 1939; Meyerhold died in 1940 after several years in a labor camp; socialist realism effectively muffled Eisenstein, although it did not eliminate him.)[62] Discussions of Mei Lanfang were the last round for formalism and constructivism until the 1960s. The nonmimetic traditions of Mei's theater, the organic integrity of its "rhythm" and "music" (both terms taken in a literal and an extended sense), were object lessons in favor of the autonomy of artistic genres and the symbolic character of art—two often contradictory romantic principles here combined in an unusual alliance—and against the primacy of politically led "realism." (Mei's success in Moscow also blunted the critiques of Chinese leftist critics such as Tian Han 田漢, whose 1934 articles on Mei's theater had asked whether the genre was not an elitist feudal relic. Mei invited Tian to help choose the plays to be performed in the USSR.)[63]

The "Chinese actor"—that is, Mei Lanfang, multiply translated—is a variously exemplary figure. For Brecht, he represents a "citational," interrogative stance toward illegitimate social consensus; for Eisenstein, he represents the poetics of the imagination in its freedom from crude canons of "representation"; for Barthes, he grows to the dimensions of a population— all the Japanese together are actors "citing" the roles they inhabit and living lives of "happy mythology." Each out of his own need, and all for different reasons, they recognized Mei's minimally naturalistic acting as a "music." Under all these regimes and all these self-interested interpretations, one core of meaning: the adequacy of art. It is possible to be "indifferent" toward the East that Mei Lanfang represents, but only because he substitutes for it so completely.

What makes Barthes's "Oriental actor" exemplary is his performance of pure signification—a performance staged, necessarily, against a background of competing opposite terms (naturalness, "Western" models of meaning, inborn sexuality, the eschatology of the soul). Once we see Barthes's typological figure as a recollection of another staged performance—Mei Lanfang's in 1935—it becomes possible to understand Barthes's network of oppositional meanings as a permutation of the earlier performance, a rotation of one figure through two semantic universes (roughly speaking, the quite different universes of the expiring 1930s Russian avant-garde and of the postwar French avant-garde). Two contexts are far short of the infinite number of situations in which the "Oriental actor" may figure, but the thing is to think our way through to more than one: with that, the static oppositions of Barthes's Orient begin to reveal themselves as phases of a movement through time.

◆

Les structures ne descendent pas dans la rue.
—May '68 graffiti

There are two ends of humanism in poststructuralist writing, China and Japan: the disappearance of distinctions in the one and the disappearance of everything but distinction, of everything that might underlie a distinction, in the other. One results in archaeology (the hypothetical pre-Oedipal language, the link through the maternal to a society with antagonism but no

"Law"), the other in grammatology (the multiplication and citation through everyday writing of previously cited traits). No wonder that Barthes is so unhappy in Kristeva's China. It is the wrong end. But the meaning of the East, for these observers, is in one respect stable. It affords the opportunity of watching the dissolution of the West, of a specifically Western subject, the imagined person on whose behalf civil society, humanism, and the religion of inwardness all claimed legitimacy.

Much deconstructively tinged writing on Asia anticipates a future: that the world after the collapse of Western metaphysics will look a lot like the East. That is a good reason for being interested in Asia (although there are better ones). What does it say to people who are already engaged with Asia, the people who live there or study it? One reason for my reluctance to identify deconstruction with a set of literary themes, a thesis, or a belief system is the wish to keep it interesting. If you think that the purpose of deconstruction is to show that writing comes before speech, or that the subject is constituted by language, or that meaning is posited through political power, or that the limits of your language are the limits of your thought, or any of a variety of claims that have been made in an ambience of posthumanist arguments, you are in for a big surprise when you take your show to China and find that this is just what everyone already thinks, although they may not think it in quite the way you do. For what are no doubt profound historical reasons, educated people in China tend to overrate the importance of the written language (to pronounce a word is, as one usually says, to "read" it, *du* 讀, *nian* 念, even when there are no books in view).[64] For similar and related reasons, a top-down or outwards-inwards model of the transmission of ideas and meanings, privileging governmental agency over personal conscience, often goes unchallenged among book-reading people, because most of the books that are written present things thus. (This is not a fact about "Asianness," but a result of specific historical events: the formation of the scholar-official class, the coexistence of regional dialects with a single national written language, the professional role of historians, the place of outcome-oriented education in popular understandings of "success.") The result of bringing the good news to new shores is always unpredictable, sometimes mortifying. A position that spurs interrogation in one place may keep it from starting in another. If the question that starts all the other questions is "Are things necessarily the way we think they are?," then even to ask it requires that we stop to consider our starting point.

Angus Graham thought that the aim of Derrida's work was to unseat the hierarchical oppositions of Western thinking: presence/absence, male/female, good/evil, and so forth. "Derrida explains the Western aspiration to abolish B in favour of A by a logocentric, ultimately phonocentric orientation which starts its chains of oppositions from the pair 'signified/signifier.' . . . The Chinese tradition however is not logocentric in Derrida's sense, centred on living speech and the full presence of the signified."[65] Since the oppositions of Chinese thought are in Graham's view complementary, not antithetical—the stock example here is that of *yin* 陰 and *yang* 陽, neither of which is thinkable in isolation from the other—a deconstructor will find it hard to get steady work in China. Here I think a very great scholar has been led astray by an inadequate comparative method; there are certainly plenty of hierarchies in Chinese thought, you have only to look for them in the right places, and if you like unseating hierarchies, a good look around may tell you which ones to start with.

But the idea that binary oppositions and the evils associated with them are specific to the West dovetails, in many imaginations, with the idea of a "closure" of metaphysics.[66] If the history of philosophy since Plato has been a "forgetting of being" now superseded, either by a wholesale commitment to technology or by a return to pre-Socratic "thinking," then by being outside the parenthesis Chinese classical thought must be an "other" to philosophy—before or after philosophy, depending on whom you ask, but in any case beside it.[67] And if we are defining that thought negatively by reference to a certain profile of "Western metaphysics"—if we are defining Chinese ideas by what they, determinately, are *not*—then there is little relevant difference between the postmetaphysical and the nonmetaphysical. As in texts starting from grammatological suppositions, China becomes legible for postmodernity as a figure of its own future self. Contemporaneity makes possible a mutual appropriation. Thus we get "Zhuangzi and Nietzsche," "Confucius and Dewey," "Mencius and Heidegger," and many another project articulated on the similarity/difference axis, with the smart money betting on similarity.

What disappears, however, in this identification is deconstruction as an act or process—the practices of reading that enabled Derrida and de Man to hold philosophy as a hostage to its material, inscriptional base. Grammatology, the starting point of historical deconstruction, no longer leads into and frames the end of humanism. The consequences of this are grave. Without deconstructive reading, the themes of postmodernism become just another set of ideological options—and worse yet, they fit into a purported philosophy of history.

Although the author of the *Daode jing* 道德經 did not have Platonism before him, "perhaps Lao-tzu's Way is how the Trace will look to us when we are no longer haunted by the ghost of . . . transcendent Reality," says Graham.[68] Chinese thinking does not appeal to anything beyond the immediate. David Hall and Roger Ames, adopting this tack, announce that Chinese classical argumentation is "strictly speaking, 'groundless.' There is nothing ontologically final that serves either as the capstone of synthetic dialectics or as the analysandum open to no further analysis." The lack of moral absolutes, the looseness of explicit ontology, the pragmatic leaning of Chinese thought, now appear as its strong points. We can now understand sympathetically "the general rejection of the cultural requisites for a concept of a theory of truth."[69] A theory of truth is not something you have to have; you're even better off without it. "'Knowing,' then, in classical China is not a knowing *what* that provides some understanding of the environing conditions of the natural world, but is rather a knowing *how* to be adept in relationships. . . . The cluster of terms that define knowing are thus programmatic and exhortatory [rather than epistemological in import]."[70] In a very real sense, it is not what you know but whom you know. As for these relationships, the form in which they are encoded is known as ritual or *li* 禮, a total body of interrelated roles. People do not inhabit roles; rather, they are their roles, their roles are what constitutes them as human. (What to make of a person with no relationships, such as an orphan, is not a question for Hall and Ames, but contemporary anecdotal evidence may suggest an answer.) Travelers who have experienced the Japan of Roland Barthes will find this territory familiar. As in Barthes, an implied contrast between "shame" cultures (based on "face," publicly acknowledged respect, and role playing) and "guilt" cultures (based on absolute standards, the conscience one carries through eternity, and autonomous moral decision) here tilts in favor of the former.[71] The Chinese sense of self, Hall and Ames insist, is a product of the "ritually constituted society."[72] The Confucian community as Hall and Ames describe it is not a group of Truth-seekers, but of Way-seekers, and Confucians define the Way they seek interpersonally, through performances modeling in bodily action the dispositions of consensus and deference.

The Chinese penchant for achieving harmony involves a person in a set of associations that provides an aesthetic ground for what otherwise might be considered moral or ethical relations. . . . Persons are not perceived as agents independent of their actions, but are rather ongoing events defined functionally by constitutive roles and relationships. . . . The classical Confucian position suggests that, because self-realization is fundamentally a social undertaking, selfish concerns are to be rejected as an impediment to one's own growth and self-realization.[73]

In sum, then, no theory of Truth, just social dispositions, and no theory of Self, since the I is created in interchange with the ritual community. The conceptions of Truth and Self are conspicuously linked, for people in many Western countries, through the idea of "rights"; a just society, we are apt to think, is woven out of the recognition of the rights of others, freely deciding selves whose capacity to seek out what the truth is cannot be controlled, and should not be the objects of attempted control, by their fellows.[74] But "Chinese society cannot be interpreted as a complex of distinct and autonomous individuals who hold sovereignty over their own interiority, and whose togetherness is most significantly regulated by codes of law."[75] The role that rights play in some polities—as basic category of law and milieu of social interaction—is taken in a Confucian state, according to Hall and Ames, by "ritual" or *li*.

Li is not passive deference to external patterns or norms: it is a "making" of society that requires the investment of oneself, one's judgment, and one's own sense of cultural importances. . . . Beyond any formal social patterning is an open texture of ritual that is personalized and reformulated to accommodate the uniqueness and the quality of each participant. . . . There are variable degrees of personalization in ritual practices, and as a consequence, the roles they establish are hierarchical. These roles form a kind of social syntax that generates meaning through coordinating patterns of deference. . . . It follows, then, that individuality in the liberal democratic sense of autonomy and independence is anathema to ritually constituted society, suggesting even idiocy and immorality.[76]

Ritual-based order seeks to guarantee tolerance, for it is the basic nature of harmony, the aspiration of ritual practice, that it is enhanced by a coordinated diversity among its elements.[77]

The optimism of this account is obvious. One difficulty, however, is to figure out whether this "ritual-based order" existed in the fifth century B.C., the twelfth century A.D., the eighteenth century, or the present, or in all and none of these as an "ideal type." The China that is currently (as some would put it) withstanding an assault of rights language from outside is, in any case, a late-twentieth-century collection of strongly interdependent areas of Chinese language and culture, and it would be useful to know what rites obtain in any or all of them and whether the rites do produce order for all and protection for those in need of it. Hall and Ames sketch a present-tense realm of communitarian ritual creativity in which one might detect a version of the modern People's Republic:

> Contemporary China remains, even under socialism, a ritually constituted society, without even a rhetorical appeal to the belief in objective principles associated with Reason or Natural Law. This does not mean, however, that the Chinese are left with a mechanical society of external relationships. . . . The order of contemporary Chinese society is defined by the sagely exemplars resident in its historical tradition. The members of the society are themselves possessed of their humanity neither as a gift from God nor by virtue of a common genetic inheritance, but as created by ritual enactment.[78]

> In China, political directives appear to take the form of broad and abstract slogans promulgated in the public institutions and the press. What is not apparent is the degree to which such directives require interpretation and application as they ramify back down through society. Communication and consensus is, in fact, arrived at by a much less abstract mechanism than would be characteristic of a society constituted of strictly autonomous individuals. This is true in a large measure because the Chinese conception of humanness does not presuppose any notion of a moral order transcending the consensual order that could justify either demagogic appeals or appeals to individual conscience, and that might disrupt the consensus.[79]

Very nice. But as soon as one begins to think about the things that could go wrong, the language of Hall and Ames takes on the ring of philosophy by euphemism. What exactly is a "social syntax that generates meaning through coordinating patterns of deference"? What is "coordinated diversity"? What is entailed by the impossibility of "transcending the consensual order"? "Ritual" is after all a large category, containing both dances round the Maypole and human sacrifice. If the ritual order is indeed self-legitimating and "persons are . . . ongoing events defined functionally by constitutive roles and relationships," it is good but inadequate to know that "ritual-based order seeks to guarantee tolerance." A self-legitimating order does not necessarily provide avenues for antisystematic protest; it might be perfectly "harmonious" to jail or execute people, in the accepted ritual way of course, for presuming to break with the pattern. My failure to fulfill my "constitutive role" may entail the ending of my "ongoing event," and I would be hard-pressed to name a reason within the "social syntax" for delaying my extinction. "Not just role playing, but *appropriate* role playing, creates a self."[80] It should be structurally impossible for a self so created to challenge the parameters of its role, if the borders of its world are those of the "felicity" of the language game it inhabits.[81] Like Barthes's Zengakuren, whose speech amounts to saying "We are the We who do X," the Chinese of Hall and Ames do without transcendent justification and Phrygian bonnets. Their language has, and needs, no register more comprehensive than self-reference.

Hall and Ames take as acquired a certain winding down of both the truth out there and the self in here: these items no longer hold much magic for postmodern Westerners, and the Chinese have not lived with them long enough to believe in them. These themes come to a head (predictably) in the discussion of human rights. For the bearer of innate individual rights is necessarily, according to Hall and Ames, the historical Western self. A person whose prehistory does not include the same presuppositions cannot and should not be expected to behave the way a rights bearer does. Indeed, Hall and Ames name "the tacit or explicit belief in universals—Reason, Science, Human Rights—[as] the mask worn by ethnocentrism in the classical West."[82] If it is to survive and preserve its cultural particularities, China needs to capitalize on its idea of rites, of rituals, and hold at bay the idea of rights, of inalienable personal entitlements. China has its own definition of the "human" (a matter of "role," not intrinsic property), and the introduction of an incompatible definition would crack the whole structure. What we nonnative observers need to realize is that the Chinese ritual community functions perfectly well, *on its own terms.* By imposing our terms on it, we would only wreck the existing harmony and do so, moreover, in the name of inherently untenable principles. The students of 1989, I hear Hall and Ames not quite daring to say, fell victims to this error: they failed to recognize whose world they were in.[83]

At any rate, Truth-seekers and Way-seekers are engaged in separate pursuits. For Hall and Ames, however, the Truth-seekers are engaged in a delusive pursuit, and it will be better for the Chinese if they never embark on it.

Let us leave both the Truth-seekers and the Way-seekers and join the company of the Deal-seekers. You find philosophy in funny places. Socrates, famously, spent much of his time arguing with strangers in the marketplace. In principle the chances of doing philosophical work are as good in one setting as in another, and we all know how ossified things can get in a highly professionalized context. The following is a description of one of the rooms—definitely not a seminar room—in which the natures of truth and justice are, perhaps, being decided:

[The room has] no central table. Instead there are a number of couches down both sides and at the end. . . . While they negotiate, [the natives] eat fruit, probably smoke heavily and talk among themselves. If they are representing different groups, the members of each group will cluster around their own couch and table. [You may] feel a lack of control in these surroundings, because there are so many people and they all talk together without any regard for the discussion. . . . People wander in and out of the room without any introduction or explanation of who they are and what they are doing there. . . .

When the final version of the contract is presented for signing, the Chinese may well have changed some terms already agreed to, or added some of their own—without consultation, and without pointing them out. . . .

After signing the contract, the Chinese will request "clarification meetings" at which they will demand more than is stated in the contract and, often, ask for something they had to sacrifice earlier on to secure the contract. . . . The Chinese are not at all embarrassed about asking for more, at any stage. . . .

In the opening phase, the Chinese insist on principles they claim are not negotiable. . . . These principles are actually no more than demands which have been agreed upon by the team, and which serve to structure the negotiation so that one side gets its needs met without having to take into account the needs of the other side.[84]

This is a quotation from Carolyn Blackman's handbook *Negotiating China*, a manual for business people. You might take Blackman's smoke-filled conference room as a scene of nonclassical philosophy (in the sense that there is nonclassical physics), where argument proceeds without rules set down in advance, we are not sure what we are talking about, who we are, or whether we want to come to an agreement. The realm of nonclassical philosophy is similarly larger than that of classical philosophy, the latter being perhaps a subset of the former. The scenes here are, in some sense, about writing and difference, or rather the lack of stable writing and the uncertainty of difference. Without any pretensions to philosophical seriousness they align, somewhat as the Rosetta Stone did for hieroglyphic, demotic, and Greek, some claims about the relations of deconstruction and Cartesianism, Chinese philosophy and Western philosophy, poststructuralism and prepoststructuralism; and they help us question the logic of antithesis that presides over all these contrasts. (The Rosetta Stone was not a literary masterpiece; it just gave interpreters somewhere to start.)

Blackman's book contains many memorable vignettes and bits of advice. For example, she points out the importance of attending banquets with powerful people who, even though they may have nothing directly to do with one's negotiation, are in a position to impede it if they are not made to feel benevolent; she tells the reader not to be shocked by demands for money, automobiles, fictional salaries, and college scholarships for relatives of business partners or supervising cadres, since favors are the cement of business relationships; if a finance official armed with a Mercedes drives in such a way as to knock cyclists into the ditches, this merely "illustrates the power of official position in China. Ordinary people accept this kind of behaviour."[85] It is reasonable to change the terms of a contract after signing it because you need only consider the consequences for your side, and there is no impartial judiciary to enforce both parties' promises. This is life in a community ordered by ritual. Blackman is no more concerned to protest against its order than are Hall and Ames. But the difference she is expounding is not between people who believe in eternal truths and universal values and other people (postmodernists or Confucian communitarians) who do not; rather, it is between people relying on different kinds of institutions to mediate among themselves.[86]

I think it is possible to have a pragmatic (nonmetaphysical) characterization of both sorts of institution. In fact that is what we must have if we are to escape Hall and Ames's false antithesis between a society of rites and a society of rights. Rights are simply a curious formulation of the ritual system of modern Europe and America, and the proof of their pragmatic effectiveness is that they fashion the sorts of subject, and the sorts of interaction, that they do, even to the point of inspiring the touching fiction that the rights-holding subject is the natural, prepolitical subject. (Remember that Rousseau had to begin the discussion of inborn rights by "rejecting all the facts.") Whether people actually have inalienable rights, and what they are, is immaterial, if what matters is whether they treat each other as if they did. Although its metaphysical background is dodgy, the concept of universal, natural, or inborn rights has the practical, the argumentative, advantage of favoring the subject claiming a right at the moment of justification.[87] Would you rather have your liberties as an assumption, whose limitation is an exception needing to be justified, or as a privilege to be sought on every occasion of their use? To say this is not to put the idea of rights beyond discusion, only to make the suggestions that the idea does a good job of justifying itself pragmatically, quite apart from a transcendental claim about its origin, and that nobody has a monopoly on pragmatism.

♦

Non des Lois, mais des Modèles.
—Marcel Granet

When grammatology recedes, leaving behind the memory of some of its interventions, the new organization of what was supposed to be a posthumanist world is, oddly perhaps, a recapitulation of structuralism. A good structuralist interprets a fragment of myth or ritual not by likening it to another thing of the same kind but by observing its syntactic relations with the other elements of its own cultural field. Within the field we have the possibility of ordered relations; outside it, arbitrariness. The relational, patterned, well-rounded ritual action in which Hall and Ames see both the Confucian Way and the felicitous outcome of postmodernism recalls the balanced graphs and regulated transformations of Lévi-Strauss.[88] Structuralism is a dream of harmony both social and hermeneutic. It is a "happy mythology."

It is also, for historical reasons, a *Chinese* dream of harmony, a ritual idealization. If Claude Lévi-Strauss is the father of structuralism, its grandfather is Marcel Granet, author of several impressive and beautiful syntheses of Chinese civilization. (*Tel Quel*'s interest in Chinese thought led to the journal's republishing long extracts from Granet.) These works, centering on what we now call "correlative cosmology," build a picture of China that owes a great deal to the examples of the *Records of Ritual* (*Li ji* 禮記), the *Book of Changes* (*Yi jing* 易經), and Dong Zhongshu 董仲舒, the synthesizer of Han court ritual and natural philosophy. (It also owes a debt to Durkheim and Mauss, whose work on systems of classification Granet knew intimately.) With their cycles of interaction among qualitatively defined elements (and parallel series of homologous elements), regulated periods of dominance and dormancy, and a musical sense of proportion, these cosmologies seek to work out the greatest number of transformations from a small vocabulary: theirs is the beauty of the self-sufficient and symmetrical. Granet's weak point, as has been observed for some seventy years now, is his habit of treating sources separated by hundreds or even thousands of years of history as complementary pieces in the great pattern of Chinese civilization: but from the ritual point of view, this is a triumph, not a failing.[89] The very purpose of sinology for Granet may have been to reconstruct and preserve that pattern. Within these limitations of aim and method, the work is admirable.

In the late 1930s Granet was engaged in the most formally challenging of all his works, a massively detailed work of reconstruction and inference full of charts demonstrating patterns of wife exchange. This book is called *Catégories matrimoniales et relations de proximité dans la Chine ancienne,* and its content explains why Granet was the only ethnologist in the Paris of the 1930s willing to talk about mathematics and kinship with a student named Claude Lévi-Strauss. Lévi-Strauss's debt to Granet is manifest in his first two books, *La Vie familiale et sociale chez les indiens Nambikwara* and *Les Structures élémentaires de la parenté.*[90] In Granet, said Lévi-Strauss many years later, "I discovered an objective reflection applied to social facts, but at the same time I was irritated to see that, to account for very complex systems, Granet let himself imagine explanatory solutions that were even more complicated. . . . At the time I was a sort of naïve structuralist, doing structuralism without knowing it."[91] Granet was, in a sense, what Lévi-Strauss would have been had he not met Jakobson: a gifted decoder of patterns—but ready to recognize them only when they presented themselves in the form of co-present systems of meaning. The encounter with Jakobson gave Lévi-Strauss the idea of latent patterns, or phonological sets in which the elements might not be meaningful or in evidence at the same time: that is to say, the idea of phonological structure as opposed to thematic, intellectual, or otherwise conscious structure.[92]

The genealogy leading from the *Li ji* through Granet to Lévi-Strauss suggests lurking paradoxes in the appeal to China as the land where *post*structuralism can come into its own. If, as I think is true, the ritual communitarians who see themselves as poststructuralists are really structuralists in the original, Chinese form of that persuasion, then it is hardly surprising that they should find those two "radically divergent cultures" (as is so often said), "China" and "the West," speaking the same language about a society without transcendence. It is not a matter of providence, a universal movement of thought, or a "fusion of horizons," but simply a reflection of the fact that the students of ritual are reading Chinese culture with an originally Chinese model. But this is not *the* Chinese model. It is a model with specific biases and interests (such as the definition of "Chineseness" through ritual observances, the convergence of all patterns and values on a regulating sovereign, the limitation of language—what can be spoken—to what can be spoken with propriety, and so forth). The model grew up slowly through the ten or so centuries of the maturation of the Chinese imperial state, from Shang to Han. It developed through successive reinterpretations (some willful, some mutually conflicting) of its own textual heritage (the heritage we know under the inadequately precise name of "Confucianism"). Through a long and contorted history, this model has now emerged as a useful model for a state that wants to liberalize economic exchange but monopolize symbolic exchange, that is, authority. "Confucianism" is not *simply* a philosophical option, as any Confucian of the last twenty-four centuries could tell you.

The multiple avatars of structuralism lead us back to the opportunities for deconstruction. Does a self-contained system admit of critique? Or does its structure allow only judgments of inside ("appropriate") and outside ("inappropriate")? The readings of structuralist linguistics and anthropology by which Derrida attempted to demonstrate that there can be no self-contained systems of this sort, that the founding postulates of such a system tend to undermine both themselves and their consequences, are both "internalist" and "externalist": they use evidence given from within the structure to breach the boundaries of that structure.[93] When postmodern keywords become an apologia for cultural relativism, the notion of totality has reclaimed, it seems to me, its old privileges. Then the task of deconstructive reading will be, as usual, one of finding opportunities for dislodging the perfect fit of the parts of those systems that make China "work" for us, cognitively and otherwise. The specific applications remain to be discovered. It may be that establishing a local form of the metaphysics of presence, the Enlightenment subject, or what you will, is the way of initiating deconstructive work in the China field; deconstruction should be just such a relative term, with no permanent components. The thing that most needs deconstructing is the claim that deconstruction has already occurred—in Paris, in New Haven, in ancient China, anywhere.

◆

One final contrast, to mime the expulsion of geopolitics from the imaginative resources of deconstruction. In "Le Puits et la pyramide: introduction à la sémiologie de Hegel" (The pit and the pyramid: introduction to the semiology of Hegel), Derrida explores Hegel's relationship to different kinds of writing and finds him unable to take seriously the nonalphabetic scripts of Egypt and China. "Alphabetic writing is in and for itself the most intelligent," says Hegel, and the reason for saying so is a matter of teleology. "History—which is always the history of Spirit, for Hegel—the unfolding of the concept as *logos*, the onto-theological deployment of presence—none of these are hindered by alphabetical writing. On the contrary, because the alphabet makes disappear, more effectively than any other writing, its own spatialization, it is the highest and most relevant mediation."[94] So Egyptian and Chinese writing, which provide more than a score for the voice to execute, are to be understood as hindrances: they clutter the mind with useless memory-details, they distract thinking with irrelevant pictures, and so on. The influence does not stop there. The flaws of Chinese writing appear to dictate the main properties of Chinese history: "immobilism" (the most ancient empire in the world is also the slowest to change), "exteriority" (the people of China, rather than consulting their own minds, follow slavishly their sovereigns who prescribe all sorts of infantile rites and punishments to keep them under control), and "naturality" (since the Chinese are unable to think beyond the images given them immediately in nature, their utterances are few, simple, and picture-like). But in following Hegel's argument, Derrida notes a number of contradictions, impossible to channel into the dialectical movement of contraries. They reveal above all Hegel's antipathy to writing and his determination to exclude the civilizations that he has identified with ideographic writing from the advance of Spirit. Derrida, who does not accept Hegel's major argument, drives home the lesser premise that the inability of the Egyptians, Chinese, and others to "think" really only reflects the inability of Hegel to admit that "thinking" could take the form of their writing, a writing independent of the voice. The challenge to raise would then be this: "What would be a 'negative' that could never be sublated?" (since Hegel has accepted that writing is a necessary "negative" passage of thought from its inward home to the outside, acceptable only so long as it is to be "sublated" and returned to interiority by a reader). A negative that would no longer be answerable to Spirit would be, according to Derrida,

a machine, perhaps, a functioning machine. A machine defined by its pure functioning and not by its final utility, its meaning, its efficacy, its work. . . . The thing that Hegel, the interpreter with the whole history of philosophy behind him, was never able to think, was a functioning machine. . . . [Such a functioning] would be unthinkable, as the nonthinking that no thinking could redeem by constituting it as its own opposite, as its *own* other. Philosophy would see in this a nonfunctioning, the absence of work, and would thereby overlook just what, nonetheless, in such a machine, works. By itself. Outside.[95]

For the reader attentive to the Far Eastern subplot of Derrida's reading of Hegel, the place of China and Egypt in this essay is that of the machine, which merely by functioning and being "By itself. Outside," stands as a reproof to the Hegelian ambition to comprehend everything in a single narrative of world history. The East must, then, be irreducible to reappropriation. Its place "outside" means that the history of Spirit is incomplete. It stands as an other and as a reproach to that history, like the Orients of Sollers, Kristeva, and Barthes.

Paul de Man, in a reading of some paragraphs of Hegel on language, forms a different account of contradiction. Hegel has just said that thought occurs in the thinking subject, the "I." But "since language states only what is general, I cannot say what is only my opinion (*so kann ich nicht sagen, was ich nur meine*)." Because *Meinung* (opinion) contains and etymologically refers to the signifier *mein* (my, mine), de Man sees the relation of language's generality and the self's singularity as self-undermining:

> What the sentence ["ich kann nicht sagen, was ich nur meine"] actually says is "I cannot say I"—a disturbing proposition in Hegel's own terms since the very possibility of thought depends on the possibility of saying "I." . . . Thus, at the very onset of the entire system, in the preliminary consideration of the science of logic, an inescapable logic threatens the entire construction that follows. . . . The very enterprise of thought seems to be paralyzed from the start. It can only get under way if the knowledge that renders it impossible . . . is itself forgotten.[96]

De Man says that the impossibility of the I's saying "I" has to be forgotten; Hegel actually goes him one better, by stating that thoughtful people (people who can think) will be able to think through the problem he has just raised, about whether thinking is possible. "Thought is proleptic," observes de Man, "it projects the hypothesis of its possibility into a future, in the hyperbolic expectation that the process that made thought possible will eventually catch up with this projection."[97] Rather than halting the business of thinking, contradiction makes it, if not possible, at least necessary. It is not exaggerating de Man's position to say that the vast flowering of the Hegelian system is an attempt to run ahead of, or forestall, the becoming-true of the original contradiction. The inability of subjectivity to account for itself becomes (in words that de Man applies to allegory as a disprized moment of the *Aesthetics*) "the defective cornerstone of the entire system."[98] Meaning (*das Gemeinte*) did not occur (although it was meant to occur); what occurred was grammar, the rule-bound generation of signifiers.

For de Man the contradiction, the inability of an I to say "I," is anywhere but "outside"—it is just what makes the Hegelian system happen, rather than a challenge puffing away in a field adjacent to it. Rather than reading "the West" as a previously constituted self, viable, but limited in ways that it cannot itself know (the option answered by Derrida's "machine," which refutes the West's claim to represent the universal self, the self everyone can become), de Man's example suggests reading "the West" as a substitute for itself, a "grammatical subject," a self produced proleptically in and through grammar rather than through meaning. "Outside" is where the non-self is *supposed* to be; by locating the East, the machine, and writing there, Derrida has missed a point worth disputing. For de Man, otherness or the machine is not outside us, it is within us, it makes our saying of ourselves happen. Or it will, not because it can, but because it must.

The grammatical projections, the obligatory antitheses between East and West, that we have seen—all of them necessary, under one or another semiotic law; none of them, doubtless, possible—bear up de Man's view. Reflections on Asian culture too often present us with an antithesis (nondifferentiation or antagonism, popular justice or the authority of law, rites or rights, ritually constituted actors versus autonomously knowing and willing subjects) when what we need is a transition. The proponents of Asian cultural uniqueness never explain how "we" got to be the subjects of rights. Were we always such subjects? Is it a matter of training? Is it a dream? Does it require massive social coordination? Is the experiment repeatable? By leaving the processes of becoming in the dark, they contribute to a mythology of "the West and the rest." None of us is a subject—the I cannot actually say "I"— but under the right conditions we can for a time "forget that knowledge."

8

Conclusion:
The Difficult Inch

On the bathing-tub of T'ang, the following words were engraved:—"If you can one day renovate yourself, do so from day to day. Yea, let there be daily renovation."[1]

> Tching prayed on the mountain and
>   wrote MAKE IT NEW   新, hsin[1]
> on his bathtub   日 jih[4]
>   Day by day make it new   日 jih[4]
> cut underbrush,   新, hsin[1]
> pile the logs,
> keep it growing.[2]

In the "Great Learning" (*Daxue*) chapter of the *Li ji* there is mention of a *pan* basin that it was believed had belonged to Tang, the founding father of the Shang dynasty (c. 1500–1045 BC). This basin is said to have been inscribed with the words *gou ri xin, ri ri xin, you ri xin* 苟日新日日新又日新. Although the composer of the "Great Learning" interpreted this inscription to be an exhortation to "renew" the people every day, Guo Moruo 郭沫若 (1892–1978) has shown that the text is probably nothing more than a composite of ancestor dedications on Shang dynasty bronze vessels. He suggests that the words transcribed as *ri xin* 日新 (daily renew) must originally have read *ri xin* 日辛, in which xin is one of the ten "heavenly stems" (*tian-gan* 天干) routinely used in the temple names of Shang ancestors. . . . Thus, the phrase would seem to reflect three different ancestor dedications, one to an "Elder Brother Day Xin," one to a "Grandfather Day Xin," and one to a "Father Day Xin."[3]

We think we are undergoing daily renewal, when in fact we are only sacrificing to forgotten ancestors. Nicholas Slonimsky, when he compiled his *Lexicon of Musical Invective*, discovered a similar misapprehension: from the beginnings of music criticism, new music was always unlike the music that had gone before, but to audiences it always sounded exactly the same. The same tropes and metaphors of "howling cats," "psychosis," "stomach-aches," "explosions," "lectures on mathematics in Chinese," and "hours in the dentist's chair" recur in the bad reviews of composers from Haydn to Stockhausen. The stimuli could not be predicted, but the reactions to them could.

In China studies, too, perpetually new situations and different subjects provoke a regular, nearly monotonous response. The problem has partly to do with the fact that studies of China (even the most China-centered and China-bounded) have always been studies of contact across ill-defined boundaries (boundaries that then become the main issue of the contact). Like any language or nation, China functions not as a universe of signification unto itself but as a domain within a universe. "Traditional China," however, is one domain that speaks of itself as the universe, much as historians speak of "history" without being able to include it all, or scientists speak of "science" without knowing all the relevant sciences. The name of the domain becomes a classifying operator—at times a normative idea. Talking about China involves bumping into, acknowledging or refusing to acknowledge, sometimes also reformulating, the bounds of the domain.

The conditions of European history over the past three or four centuries affect, obviously and unavoidably, the ways in which people relate to the boundedness of China, whether they encounter the limits from inside or outside. The odd thing is that the undeniable changes over the course of that history have not done much to change the way the boundary (or the realm beyond it) is experienced. The details change, but the outlines of the topic remain as they were. The boundary frequently functions as a narrative marker: crossing into China, for Matteo Ricci as for Angus Graham, signals the entry into a new ontological space. "Both nature and policy have so ordered [China] that it seems almost to stand apart from the rest of the world and to constitute an absolute microcosm, dependent on no other."[4] This space is usually defined privatively: it is the place (no desert, but a densely populated space) where metaphysics, the soul, logic, freedom, the Law, the Symbolic, grammar, and so forth no longer obtain. (Whether this is a good or a bad thing varies with the narrator.) Crossing the border thus provides a means of rehearsing a set of interrelated (though not identical) crises: the end of humanism, the disappearance of the subject, the end of history, the end of hermeneutics, the end of sexual difference. For those who begin their tour in China, discovering China as a specific place involves a set of demarcations no less tricky, although these may be cast in temporal terms rather than spatial (for the modernizers early in the twentieth century, China was "not yet" on the same footing as the "West"; for the postmodernizers at its conclusion, the "end of humanism" involved canceling the appointment).

The composite of these boundaries means that China most often enters discourse as the countercase to an essentialized West, the West being the one possible source of those magnificent burdens or crippling illusions to which the vision of China puts an end. (For "the West," we may read "modernity"—and deal with the essentialism all over again.) If this is so, it may not be the least of the "legacies of China" to have fashioned the modern West, as perhaps the Arab world encountered through the Crusades fashioned the medieval West, as the Soviet sphere did the postwar West, and as the "Third World" is now doing for the post-Soviet West. Naturally, China is not the only non-West; the West has a variety of antitheses; nor is the "West" the only "we" that needs a "they" in order to think through its own self-definition.[5] But the degree of anxiety that usually attends this particular comparison, the thematics of asymmetry evoked by the combination of "China" and the "West," are exceptional.[6] Dialogues and engagements on this basis are often defensive, and for good (semantic) reason: whether one's concept of the "we" is derived strictly as a projection from the properties of the "they," or whether it is a traditional normative ideal refurbished for the new context, it is sure to lead to the exaggerated, unyielding conclusions of a polar logic. We could call this "differentialism," a multi-player species of essentialism.

Observe that the logic of asymmetrical opposition rarely stops at one item: if the Chinese lack, for example, law, then it is because they also lack freedom, the soul, genuine religion, an achieved civil society, and so forth. The point looks beyond itself: it is there to aid in drawing a line. And a line is precisely what benefits the reductive intellectual politics of one-party rule: each new segment added to the line, each new "Chinese characteristic" added to the pile, confirms the notion that there is a core Chineseness that accounts for every feature and supersedes any internal difference among the parts. (For a view of the same process played out in reverse, see Yang Tingyun's imaginary Europe, gathered as tight as a diamond around its religious, political, and intellectual unifier.) Although I concede that concepts come "not single spies, but whole battalions," and agree that the way to deal with them is not singly but as interrelated sets, I think the persistent habit of drawing lines needs to become a question, not an answer, if we want to be thoughtful students of China. Correlation is not causation; there are many kinds of imbrication, many test cases for feeling one's way around the contours of an "episteme." What is tight, smooth, and self-evident as ideology must face point-for-point questioning and translation into inhospitable idioms. Rights/rites, law/power, grammar/imitation, phonetic writing/ ideogrammatic gesture, unhappy mythologies/happy mythologies, the West/the rest, China/the world—How would one's best effort to argue the purported distinctions, rather than merely asserting them, hold up? How can we acknowledge the logic of communication or translation that precedes statements of difference? How best to give one's understanding of "China," no less than of the "West," a many-centered internal dynamic?

In this book, I have tried to put the automatic assertions to the test of an unaccommodating reading. And it is not enough simply to deny: the prevalence of polar schemes should always lead us to try to reconstruct the historical emergence of the antithesis and find the common basis on which it tacitly rests.[7] (The more specifically the basis is defined, the better: "human nature" and "economic rationality," just to take two much-honored examples, are so broad as to exclude useful fashioning of differences.) On that footing, then, it becomes possible to redescribe the differences and recount their history: the poles were not always polar; they had to be polarized at some point. It is important to look for third parties, to try to neutralize oppositions by dissolving them in a larger framework, to trace their emergence or to show how artificial their symmetries are, because our previous equipment for thinking about China blinds us to such possibilities. One can, for example, find the single substance in which the opposed adjectives are rooted (thus Barthes's visions of "Europe" and "Japan" as bad and good theater, respectively, both derive from a transmitted memory of Mei Lanfang), hunt for the occasion that prompted an asserted difference to become salient (June 1989, for the "new conservatives" abruptly won over to Huntington's culturalist account of "East" versus "West"), detect the third parties who shape the alternatives of a duality (Sanskrit, the absent term presiding over the early comparative philologists' classification of Chinese), or specify the observer for whom a difference becomes real (the pidgin translator, not the native speaker or the elegant translator).

Antitheses are often false, but they can be instructive once reframed as historical events of category splitting. How exactly did rights become the symmetrical opposite of rites? When and on what conditions did "ideographic" and "phonetic" part company? Making sense of these assertions, as distinct from rehearsing them, is usually a matter of replacing antithesis with reciprocity, of seeing on what basis of understanding (or misunderstanding) the polar qualities make each other possible.

We also need to be vigilant in scrutinizing the comparative or parallel narrations that underlie polar thinking. What passes for an explanation of a difference often amounts merely to a restatement of the difference (the novelty of a concept of universal human rights may be "explained" as a consequence of the Christian idea of the immortal soul, which in turn may be "explained" by the Platonic concept of a timeless Form, which in turn may be "explained" by the peculiarities of Indo-European grammar, and so on and so on: each of these "explanations" serves mainly to transpose the same assertion from one time or domain to another and defer the recognition of tautology). These chains of difference run to a dispiriting sameness; to interrupt them one must find counterparts that differ from *that* way of differing. I have found it useful to keep in mind the Saussurean picture of an infinite web of nonhierarchical distinctions to which any node (or particular signifier) provides an entry. What are the kindred concepts that surround and frame a term, and what needs might have been answered by that term's coming to articulation? How might alterations in one term's value affect that of its neighbors?

Antithetical language has as one of its immemorial functions to exclude the middle. But the middle is where the action is: the action of carving out a place for German alongside Sanskrit and as far as possible from Chinese; the action of trade and communication as it escapes the notice of imperial scribes seeking to plot their history as the history of humanity; Ricci's brokering of intellectual and political alliances and swiveling between the roles of beneficiary and adversary of Chinese unregulated printing; the action of establishing laws to secure property and contract while leaving the law of persons unarticulated; most pervasively, the action of interpretation going on in several middles (between reader and text, to be sure, but among readers and texts as well). There are even cases where mediation supersedes itself, as when the *Li ji* is discovered to be the ultimate source of the interpretive models used to clarify . . . the *Li ji*. Each of these middles clears the space for a polarity, giving rise to a new game played on dualistic rules (grammar *vs.* semantics; Confucian Christianity, with a role for the sciences and a clear link to authority, *vs.* superstition; the rule of law *vs.* the whim of Party bosses; and so forth). If the purpose of antithetical argument is to foreclose alternatives (it is always a matter of "this or that," leaving out the myriad things that are neither this nor that), it seems obvious what the first line of response should be: to recover them. Obviously not every middle is good just because it is a middle; the point is to go against the rhetorical grain and frustrate automatic thinking.

It is not enough to denounce a specious polarity, as if a mental structure could not be simultaneously false (or factitious) and real. As several of the chapters in this book argue, collective boundaries do exist; they take on social flesh; they become as hard to walk through as other kinds of walls. The reality of the Great Wall of China is physically debatable but historically ponderous (there was, as Arthur Waldron's recent book teaches, never one uninterrupted Great Wall, fashioned in one continuous process for one intended purpose; thus no object answers to that traditional description).[8] In a certain sense and to a certain degree (a degree and sense that we must always try to capture more precisely), mythic objects such as the Great Wall or Confucius exist because someone wants them to exist. One has to engage with the Great Wall as event, retrace its formation, observe its cognitive weight on the minds and actions of people who deal with the geography of Northern China, take it nominalistically or normatively; what we should not do is restrict the Great Wall's field of operation to the evidence of the senses.

The power of antithesis stems from its fusing of observation with rhetorical articulation. Rhetoric builds the probable into the inevitable, turns a contrast into a choice; rhetorical analysis restores our freedom by dismantling the seeming necessity. "It ain't necessarily so." By shifting existing arguments from their axis, we can hope to recover positions or relations inaccessible via the standard paths. Why this axis rather than another? What peripheral pressures pushed an indeterminate translation-situation this way rather than that? This may sound very much like deconstruction, and rightly so (that is where I learned the power of such techniques), but the pursuit of such methods has led me to take on the rare "positivistic" moments (which are also, systematically, exotic moments) in historical deconstruction.

I, too, am fond of distinctions and admit to having constructed them as I needed them: the differences between structuralism and poststructuralism, or the "semantic" and the "syntactic" views of the Chinese sign, or between linear and plural histories are just a few. One makes distinctions in order to get a bit of work done, and the antitheses I reject I find bad, not as antitheses, but chiefly because of their invidious consequences. In mitigation for my own indulgences, I plead that each chapter has been written with a built-in record of its own process of construction, in the belief that an artefact duly signed and dated has nothing to apologize for. (I follow astronomers in using "artefact" to mean a distortion of representation caused by the means of representation.) The sort of reading I most hope to stimulate will take the antitheses I formulate as starting points and try to work back to their logical springs.

It is strange to end with such formalistic bits of advice (seek middles, trace emergences, question asserted dependencies). But the very ease with which so much of the argumentative matter of our discipline lends itself to formalistic accounting should be a warning in itself, like Slonimsky's observation about the hearing abilities of concert audiences over the years. The point of formalism is to encapsulate, and thus predict, a closed set of variants. Historically it has readily accompanied an avant-garde practice seeking the unpredictable, just as code breakers and code makers engage in the same trade.[9] This book began with a plea for attention to collective thinking processes—the networks of assumption and consensus that make communication possible within a discipline. It should not have to stop there, as if the moral were that we are creatures of our generation and our mentality, no matter what we do. Once we have ascertained the movements of a "universe" (say, that of Chinese studies, described over a longish stretch of time and space), it becomes possible to chart the displacements of individual thinkers within the same volume and even to plot courses that may lead one's own particle in directions that depart from the larger Brownian motion.

♦

Proclus described Euclid's *Elements* as "a cathartic and a gymnastic book."[10] Those goals—purging and exercise—make for an interesting departure from the language customarily used, since the seventeenth century at least, of Euclid: for we routinely speak of geometry as the domain of foundations, certainty, and clear and distinct ideas. Have we been missing something all these centuries, so that we take a work of critique to be the archetypal project of logical construction? Or is the difference (between philosophy as foundation and philosophy as therapy) illusory?[11] Without Euclid's elegance or simplicity, I have tried to provide antidotes to some of the enticing clarities that serve as intellectual bases for China studies. In closing, I think it only honest to say that hardly an error figures here that has not at some time been my own.

Reference Matter

Notes

For complete author names, titles, and publication data for the works cited here in short form, see the Works Cited, pp. 251–79.

Chapter 1

1. On peripheral knowledge, communities of practice, and reciprocity, see Brown and Duguid, *The Social Life of Information*.

2. Montesquieu, *Lettres persanes*, in *Œuvres complètes*, p. 78.

3. Quine, *Ontological Relativity*, pp. 2–3, 25; on "observation sentences," see pp. 102–3. In answer to Quine's questioning of the interpreter's "conceptual frame" and the likelihood that it "imposes" the interpreter's meanings on the things interpreted, Davidson has argued that there are no such things as conceptual frames, or if there are such things, they are only local patternings within a larger field of shared (if indefinite) meaning, a field that we invoke even as we define differences: "We improve the clarity and bite of declarations of difference, whether of scheme or opinion, by enlarging the basis of shared (translatable) language or of shared opinion" ("On the Very Idea of a Conceptual Scheme," in *Inquiries into Truth and Interpretation*, p. 197). The sense that linguistic differences are predicated on a basis of agreement leads Davidson to propose an interpretive principle of charity: read the other *as if* it were certain that he is mostly in the right (see "Thought and Talk," in ibid., pp. 168–69). Davidson's further proposal, that the investigation of meaning should proceed via an investigation of the norms of speech communities, is one I readily endorse.

4. For a critical examination of ethnography from a Quinean perspective, see Hallen and Sodipo, *Knowledge, Belief and Witchcraft*.

5. Said, *Culture and Imperialism*, p. 151 (summarizing Edwardes's *The Sahibs and the Lotus*); see also Said, *Orientalism*. For a pioneering discussion of themes that Said would later develop, see Abdel-Malek, "Orientalism in Crisis."

6. On the "guild tradition," see, e.g., Said, *Orientalism*, pp. 5, 43–46, 129–30, 208–9.

7. The formulation stems from Benedetto Croce. See Collingwood, *The Idea of History*, pp. 201–4.

8. As is well known, this is one of the points on which Freud fails to persuade many readers today. Masson and others have accused Freud of censoring the truth of his patients' accounts of childhood sexual abuse through this very methodological self-consciousness. On the other hand, therapists who claim to restore suppressed truth through "recovered memories" have not exactly distinguished themselves by moderation and critical sense; their advocacy writes off the power of suggestion that Freud's account of transference effects is meant to circumscribe. Unless one is content to conduct the whole discussion on the plane of Freud's personal life and character, it seems unwise to manipulate a particular set of events, however scandalous, into an overall rejection of methodological scruple.

9. Freud, "The Disposition to Obsessional Neurosis," *Standard Edition*, 12: 320. On related topics, see "Remembering, Repeating, and Working-Through" and "Observations on Transference-Love" (*Standard Edition*, 12: 147–56 and 159–71, respectively).

10. Wiener, *Cybernetics*, pp. 189–91.

11. Devereux, *From Anxiety to Method*, p. 270.

12. Ibid., p. xvi.

13. "Every rat experiment is also an experiment performed on the observer, whose anxieties and warding off maneuvers, quite as much as his research strategy, perception of data and decision making (interpretation of data) can shed more light upon the nature of behavior in general than the observation of rats—or even of other human beings—can" (ibid., pp. xviii–xix).

14. Ibid., p. xvii.

15. Tu Weiming, "Cultural China: The Periphery as the Center," in idem, *The Living Tree*, pp. 1–34; here, see esp. pp. 13–15.

Chapter 2

1. Luhmann, "World Society as a Social System," in idem, *Essays on Self-Reference*, p. 178.

2. For a compressed account of these relations, see Appadurai, "Disjuncture and Difference in the Global Cultural Economy"; Castells, *End of Millennium*; and Albrow, *The Global Age*. On "culture" mediated by print (which fixes a national language, collects its canons, and shapes its public) as the historic core of the national idea, see B. Anderson, *Imagined Communities*.

3. For an account of the recent evacuation of "space" as the link between peoples and sovereignty, see Guéhenno, *La Fin de la démocratie*.

4. On the relations between globalization, eschatology, and missionary aims in the early modern period, see Kadir, *Columbus and the Ends of the Earth*.

5. On this expression, see below, p. 28. "Ears and eyes" is a long-consecrated expression for the investigating officials of the imperial censorate: *ermu guan, tianzi ermu* 耳目官, 天子耳目. See Morohashi, *Dai Kanwa jiten*, 9: 185. The tasks of the censorate (*yushi tai, ducha yuan* 御史臺, 都察院) were not primarily those we designate as "censorship" but the review, criticism, and impeachment of officeholders. On the workings of this bureau, see Hucker, *The Censorial System of Ming China*.

6. Yang Tingyun, *Dai yi pian* (preface dated 1621), 2.20a–22b, in Wu Xiangxiang, ed., *Tianzhujiao dongchuan wenxian*, pp. 541–46. Yang Tingyun won the *jinshi* 進士 or highest degree in 1592 and held a series of important governmental posts. He was baptized in 1611 with the name of Michael; thus his apologetic works are sometimes signed "Yang Mige zi" 楊彌格子. For a biography, see Standaert, *Yang Tingyun*. For shorter notices, see d'Elia, ed., *Fonti Ricciane*, 3: 13; Hummel, *Eminent Chinese of the Ch'ing Period*, 2: 894–95; and Yang Zhen'e, *Yang Qiyuan xiansheng nianpu*. Apart from his numerous works on Christianity, Yang compiled a set of treatises on the *Yi jing* (*Wan Yi weiyan zhaichao* 玩易微言摘抄; A copybook for appreciating the subtle sayings of the *Changes*), cited in *Siku quanshu zongmu tiyao*, 1: 189. For the flavor of late Ming interest in the *Changes*, see Goodman and Grafton, "Ricci, the Chinese, and the Toolkits of Textualists," pp. 127–38. On the *Dai yi pian* in the context of the Rites Controversy, see Li Tiangang, *Zhongguo liyi zhi zheng*, pp. 126–28.

7. For details on printing techniques, see Twitchett, *Printing and Publishing in Medieval China*, pp. 68–86; on the economics of publishing, see Elvin, *The Pattern of the Chinese Past*, pp. 179–84. An authoritative general survey is Tsien, *Paper and Printing*; for a scrutiny of regional practices, see Brokaw, "Commercial Publishing in Late Imperial China." Printing costs were exceptionally low in Ming times, especially in the southeast provinces: see Tsien, *Paper and Printing*, pp. 372–73.

8. "E vi è nel loro modo una grande commodità, che è stare le tavole sempre intiere, e potersene stampare puoco a puoco quanto se ne vuole. . . . Di qui viene la multitudine de' libri che in questo regno si stampa, ognuno in sua casa, per essere anco grandissimo il numero di quei che attendono a questa arte di intagliare. . . . come in nostra casa, di alcuni libri che habbiamo intagliati, i servitori di casa gli stampano quanti ne habbiamo bisogno" (The great convenience in their mode of printing is that the blocks remain in one piece, and that more copies can be printed from them as they are needed. . . . This is the reason for the multitude of books printed in this kingdom, printed by each in his own house, the number of those who devote themselves to this art of block-carving being also very great . . . as in our house, we have the domestic servants print off as many copies as we need from the books we have had carved onto blocks; d'Elia, ed., *Fonti Ricciane*, 1: 31; see also 2: 314; cf. the approximate translation in Gallagher, trans., *China in the Sixteenth Century*, pp. 20–21).

9. For a detailed study of censored works throughout the imperial period, see An Pingqiu and Zhang Peiheng, *Zhongguo jinshu daguan*. The majority of recorded bans date from the Qing dynasty: on this period, see Brook, "Censorship in Eighteenth-Century China"; Goodrich, *The Literary Inquisition of Ch'ien-lung*, pp. 3–4, 19–29; Twitchett, *Printing and Publishing in Medieval China*, pp. 60–64; and Guy, *The Emperor's Four Treasuries*.

10. As will be shown below, the freedom of publication conferred by Chinese printing methods was merely potential; the fact that publishing was accessible did not mean that it was risk free. Confiscation and repression of printed books was one aspect of the perpetual struggle among the ruler, the administration, and the administered. It is surely too simple to blame it all on the despot; the case of Li Zhi and Zhang Wenda, to be discussed below, involves factions vying, through book banning, for imperial attention and support. For the classic expression of the theory of Chinese imperial despotism, see Montesquieu, *De l'Esprit des lois*, 8: 21. Montesquieu's main informant, the returned missionary Foucquet, is vividly depicted by the Président de Brosses (*Lettres familières*, cited in Etiemble, *Les Jésuites en Chine*, pp. 179–89).

11. The Chinese phrase is *yi-li* 義理—"works treating of the rational organization (*li*) of morality (*yi*)." A more precise translation occurs in Ricci's journals: "scientia morale" (d'Elia, ed., *Fonti Ricciane*, 1: 42). But the conception of a "moral science" belongs to Ricci's age, not ours. For comparison's sake, the Buddhist *Tripitaka* contains approximately six thousand volumes.

12. On these issues, see E. Eisenstein, *The Printing Press as an Agent of Change*.

13. On the examination system, see Elman's comprehensive *A Cultural History of Civil Examinations in Late Imperial China*. On other aspects of scholarly culture relating to the examinations and their social dynamics, see Elman, *From Philosophy to Philology*; and idem, *Classicism, Politics, and Kinship*.

14. On evolving standards, struggles over interpretation, and the eventual delegitimation of the whole examination system, see Elman, *A Cultural History of Civil Examinations in Late Imperial China*, chaps. 3, 8, and 11.

15. For a short biography of Wang, see Huang Tsung-hsi 黃宗羲 (Huang Zongxi, 1610–95), *The Records of Ming Scholars*, pp. 102–7.

16. See Huang Zongxi's summary of the minor figures of the Taizhou 泰州 school of *xinxue*, in ibid., pp. 165–72. For "enlarging the Way," an echo of *Analects* 15.29, see ibid., p. 107. For reactions to the mingling of the canons in examination papers, see Elman, *A Cultural History of Civil Examinations in Late Imperial China*, pp. 411–15.

17. "Mad Zen" had been current earlier as a disparaging label within Buddhism: see Mote, *Imperial China*, p. 677.

18. On this period in general, see R. Huang, *1587*. For examples of specific conflicts between the palace faction and components of the bureaucracy, see Hucker, *The Censorial System of Ming China*, pp. 152–234. For the placement rates of late Ming examination candidates, see Ho, *The Ladder of Success in Imperial China*, pp. 32–34, 107–111, and 184.

19. Chapter 5 of Hucker's *Censorial System of Ming China* concentrates on the battle between eunuchs and "righteous elements" in 1620–27.

20. This is Ricci's description of the commission: "grande autorità e potere di fare questo assolutamente, senza dipendere da nessuno de' mandarini del governo" (d'Elia, ed., *Fonti Ricciane*, 2: 81–82). The tumult coincided with Ricci's move from the out-of-the-way town of Shaozhou 韶州 (near Canton) to the southern capital, Nanking. On Yang Tingyun's involvement, see Yang Zhen'e, *Yang Qiyuan xiansheng nianpu*, pp. 17–18.

21. The "Donglin Party" began in 1604 as a regional academy and quickly attracted to itself scholars who shared a desire for conservative political action. As its members won posts in the higher reaches of administration, the group was able to press for dismissal of high officials who disagreed with it and replace them with its allies. In 1625–26, however, the eunuch Wei Zhongxian 魏忠賢 was able to lead a purge of several hundred Donglin members and imprisoned or executed its leaders. On the Donglin movement and its adherents, see Chen Ding, *Donglin liezhuan*; Busch, "The Tung-lin Academy"; Mote, *Imperial China*, pp. 736–38, 778–80; Elman, *A Cultural History of Examinations in Late Imperial China*, pp. 208–11. For a study of moral debates involving the Donglin as well as many other groups, see Brokaw, *The Ledgers of Merit and Demerit*. Huang Zongxi's account (*Records of Ming Scholars*, pp. 223–53) bears the marks of a *defensio pro domo*: his father was a prominent Donglin figure. For further notes on Jesuit-Donglin links, see Gernet, *Chine et christianisme*, pp. 36–38; and Gernet, "Politique et religion lors des premiers contacts entre Chinois et missionnaires jésuites," in idem, *L'Intelligence de la Chine*, pp. 215–43. Yang Tingyun had ties to the Donglin academy (Busch, "The Tung-lin Academy," pp. 43, 156; Standaert, *Yang Tingyun*, pp. 34–37, 80–85), as did many scholars friendly to the Jesuits; to claim, however, that the Donglin group was of Christian inspiration (as did Henri Bernard, following the self-serving memoirs of Daniel Bartoli: see the discussion in Busch, "The Tung-lin Academy," pp. 156–63) is certainly excessive. At most, it seems that Yang and other converts hoped to broker the sort of alliance that Bernard and Bartoli report as having been achieved in fact.

22. Primary materials on Ricci's life and work are collected in d'Elia, ed., *Fonti Ricciane*, and presented in English in Gallagher, trans., *China in the Sixteenth Century*. On Ricci's life, see Goodrich and Fang, eds., *Dictionary of Ming Biography* 2: 1137–44; and Spence, *The Memory Palace of Matteo Ricci*. On Ricci's interpretative methods, see Goodman and Grafton, "Ricci, the Chinese, and the Toolkits of Textualists." Ricci

was not always "the Mandarin from the West." The fathers' adoption of the dress and manners of the literatus (i.e., aspirant official) was preceded by a twelve-year interlude during which they had presented themselves in the garb of Buddhist monks. On the Jesuits' "conversion to the order of the literati" and its many implications, see Jensen, *Manufacturing Confucianism*, chap. 2.

23. *Ming shi* 明史, chap. 326 ("Wai guo zhuan: Yidaliya" 外國傳, 意大利亞), in *Ershiwu shi*, 10: 929. The *yi* of *hao yi zhe*, meaning "different, strange," is also found in the compound *yiduan*, "heresy": see above, p. 27. By 1617, the Jesuit presence had begun to appear to be a threat to social order: in that year a memorial was submitted urging their expulsion, alleging, among other reasons, that "from Matteo Ricci's entrance into China, the number of Europeans here has not ceased to grow. A certain Wang Fengsu 王豐肅 [Alfonso Vagnoni], living in Nanjing, did nothing but stir up the populace with the religion of the Lord of Heaven. From gentlemen and officials down to the common people of the lanes and alleys, many were attracted to follow him. . . . Their religion is no different from the White Lotus and Non-Action sects" (*Ershiwu shi*, 10: 930). On the "Jesuit textual community" as a cult, see Jensen, *Manufacturing Confucianism*, chap. 3.

24. D'Elia, ed., *Fonti Ricciane*, 1: 368–69. For the text, see Li Zhizao, ed., *Tianxue chuhan*, 1: 299–320. The content was translated from classical and Christian writers. Some extracts: "When friendship is based more on pleasure than on righteousness, the friendship will not last. . . . Among the ancients, 'friend' was a title of honor, now it is for sale, like an article of commerce: alas! . . . The benefits of friendship to human life are great indeed: none loves money to the point of turning into money, but there are those whose love of friendship makes them into friends" (p. 306). Li Zhi liked *Jiaoyou lun* so much that he had his disciples carve blocks and print a new edition as a favor to its author (d'Elia, ed., *Fonti Ricciane*, 2: 68). On editions and variants, see Fang Hao, "Notes on Matteo Ricci's *De Amicitia*."

25. Busch, "The Tung-lin Academy," p. 81. As Gernet (*Chine et christianisme*, p. 160) observes, one obstacle to the acceptance of Christianity among the lettered classes was that it leveled social distinctions, just like the more extreme types of *xinxue*. For a probing study of the theme of friendship in traditional literati circles and its implications for family ties, disinterestedness, nepotism, religion, and "civil society," see McDermott, "Friendship and Its Friends in the Late Ming."

26. This was Jiao Hong 焦竑 (1541–1620), on whom see Ch'ien, *Chiao Hung and the Restructuring of Neo-Confucianism in the Late Ming*.

27. D'Elia, ed., *Fonti Ricciane*, 2: 65–68. *Zhuangyuan*, "primus," was the title given the top-ranked examination candidate in the Metropolitan examinations, which were held every third year; the honor remained with one for life. On the syncretism of the "three sects" (Confucianism, Buddhism, and Taoism) and its origins in the

"left-wing" tradition issuing from Wang Yangming, see Busch, "The Tung-lin Movement," pp. 83–84; and d'Elia, *Fonti Ricciane*, 1: 131–32, 2: 187. For biographical sketches of other of Ricci's friends, see, e.g., ibid., 1: 371–72, 2: 42–43, 46–47. On Li Zhi's life, see Goodrich and Fang, *Dictionary of Ming Biography*, 1: 807–8; on Li's impressions of Ricci, see Li Zhi, *Fen shu*, p. 247; and idem, *Xu fen shu*, p. 1 (the passage is translated by Gernet, *Chine et christianisme*, pp. 29–30). On these encounters, see Franke, "Li Tschi und Matteo Ricci." On Li Zhi's thought generally, see Billeter, *Li Zhi*. Li Zhi's probable Muslim background, a neglected topic, is discussed in Hong Mingshui, "Mingmo wenhua lieshi Li Zhuowu."

28. Ricci here follows closely the phrasing of Zhang Wenda's 張問達 memorial (on which see below). Zhang summarizes Li Zhi's career thus: "While in the strength of his youth, Li Zhi held official position, but in later years he shaved his head [and became a lay monk]. Recently he has printed *A Book to Be Concealed, A Book for Burning, Zhuowu's Book of Great Virtue*, and other such works that circulate throughout our empire. He perplexes and confuses the minds of the people by contending that Lü Buwei 呂不韋 and Li Yuan 李園 were wise counselors, that Li Si 李斯 was a genius, that Feng Dao 馮道 was a retiring and unrecognized public servant, that Zhuo Wenjun 卓文君 had the right way of selecting a mate, that Qin Shihuang 秦始皇 was the greatest ruler of all time, and that Confucius had insufficient grounds for issuing praise and blame—all mad, flagitious, aberrant and willful theses, which must be abolished" (cited in Gu Yanwu, "Li Zhi," in idem, *Rizhi lu*, 18/28b). Lü Buwei, the architect of the rise of the state of Qin in the third century B.C., was portrayed by the historian Sima Qian 司馬遷 as an unscrupulous profiteer; Li Yuan smuggled his sister into the harem of the king of Chu and thus exerted influence over the next king, his nephew. Li Si was the architect of the Qin dynasty's policy of "burning books and burying [uncooperative] scholars alive" and thus the object of centuries of literati hatred. Feng Dao's narrow ambition was proverbial: he served under ten different rulers and four dynastic houses despite the precept that "a scholar has but one master." Zhuo Wenjun, a young lady of good family, eloped with the penniless poet Sima Xiangru 司馬相如. Qin Shihuang, founder of the imperial system, was cast as a perverse and ruthless tyrant by the Han historians Sima Qian and Ban Gu. By praising these historic reprobates, Li Zhi hoped to scandalize readers and bring about a reconsideration of traditional values. The exact weighting of these two aims is one of the controversial points in Li Zhi scholarship.

29. The memorial (dated April 14, 1602) was the work of Zhang Wenda, whose son later became a convert (d'Elia, ed., *Fonti Ricciane*, 2: 183; see also Busch, "The Tung-lin Academy," p. 89). For the text, see Gu Yanwu, "Li Zhi" 李贄, in idem, *Rizhi lu*, 18/28b–29b. On the ties linking Zhang Wenda, Feng Qi, and the Donglin and Jesuit milieux, see Gernet, *L'Intelligence de la Chine*, pp. 236–37.

30. Mentioned in the text of Ricci's funeral inscription, where discussions with Ricci are said to have inspired Feng's censure of heterodoxy (d'Elia, ed., *Fonti Ricciane*, 3: 11).

31. D'Elia, ed., *Fonti Ricciane*, 2: 182–86; a translation of Feng Qi's request and its imperial rescript appears on 184–187. For the original texts, see Gu Yanwu, "Kechang jin yue" 科場禁約 (A prohibition in the examination halls), in idem, *Rizhi lu*, 18/21b–23a. Gu's comments on Feng's memorial pass on some examples of unorthodox (or in some cases, simply incompetent) interpretations that had been condoned by official examiners in the years before 1603.

32. In Cynthia Brokaw's (*Ledgers of Merit and Demerit*, p. 24) formulation: "Their enemies were those who threatened . . . traditional structures and values, be it corrupt and incompetent power-holders like Wei Zhongxian or Wen Tiren (d. 1638) or the wild and irresponsible scholars of the Taizhou persuasion. The former disrupted political order by selfishly refusing to share power; the latter overturned moral order by denying the authority of fixed standards of right and wrong."

33. In the end, the rebuilding of a Confucian orthodoxy by the Qing government after 1644 doomed Ricci's policy to failure by depriving it of a problem to which a Donglin-influenced Christianity could serve as a solution. The Qing put the examinations back on a *lixue* 理學 basis and discouraged the Jesuits from seeking converts among the people. A missionary group continued to reside in the imperial palace, providing mathematical and scientific instruction.

34. Locus classicus: "Zengzi wen," *Liji*, 18.19a. "Zengzi asked: 'When there are two chief mourners, or two principal name-tablets in a temple—is this according to the rites?' Confucius answered: 'There are not two suns in the heavens, nor two kings over the same territory (*tian wu er ri, tu wu er wang* 天無二日, 土無二王). [The Son of Heaven] performs the *chang* 嘗, *di* 禘, *jiao* 郊, and *she* 社 sacrifices [all with different formulas and addresses], but [among the spirits thus honored,] only one is supreme (*zun wu er shang* 尊無二上).'" Commentary (by Kong Yingda 孔穎達, 574–648): "If there were two suns in the sky, plants and trees would perish of drought. If there were two kings on the same territory, attacks and counterattacks would never cease. So Laozi says: 'Oneness is what makes heaven pure; through oneness earth can be led to peace.' Quite so" (ibid., 19b). Not only this passage but the whole "Zengzi wen" chapter is an interrogation on ritual precedence: when two ritual obligations conflict, which should be honored? Through the allusion, Yang Tingyun suggests the future quarrels over the possible coexistence of Christian rites and Chinese ceremonies in honor of Confucius and ancestors (the stuff of the "Rites Controversy" of 1700–1704). On the controversy, see Li Tiangang, *Zhongguo liyi zhi zheng*; Minamiki, *The Chinese Rites Controversy*; and Etiemble, *Les Jésuites en Chine*.

35. The language and arguments of Yang Tingyun's repudiation of Buddhism echo those attributed to Zhu Xi 朱熹, the twelfth-century definer of Confucian

orthodoxy, in the latter's *Conversations on Various Topics*; see *Zhuzi yulei* 朱子語類, 126.1a–8b.

36. The political leader of the Donglin group at this time was Yang Lian 楊漣, the instigator of many reviews and impeachments from within the Censorate. See Hucker, *The Ming Censorial System*, pp. 63–64, on Yang, and pp. 165–171, on the brief rise in Donglin power between 1620 and 1623.

37. For another case of global information used to suggest universal authority, see Saussy, "*China Illustrata*."

38. See Spence, *The Chan's Great Continent*; Billings, "Visible Cities"; Etiemble, *L'Europe chinoise*; Pinot, *La Chine et la formation de l'esprit philosophique*; and Batchelor, "The European Aristocratic Imaginary."

39. For example, the *sinophilie* described in Etiemble's massive *L'Europe chinoise* or the satirical orientalism of Montesquieu's *Lettres persanes*.

40. In *De Potestate summi ponteficis*, 1610. "Indirect power" means the right to excommunicate a disobedient ruler, whose subjects might then legitimately desert him. The Jesuits made things difficult for themselves by clinging to a strong version of the argument for papal authority in a country where the power to license all cults rested with the emperor (see d'Elia, ed., *Fonti Ricciane*, 1: 131). On the discovery of the conflict between the jurisdictional claims of the emperor and the pope and the use made of this conflict by anti-missionary writers, see Gernet, *Chine et christianisme*, pp. 143–89.

41. Thomas Hobbes, *Leviathan*, p. 428. In this chapter (III, 42) Hobbes offers a philosophical grounding for the thirty-seventh of the Church of England's "Articles of Religion" (1562), while answering Bellarmine. See also Philippe de Mornay, *The Mysterie of Iniquitie . . . Where is also defended the right of emperors, kings, and Christian princes against the assertions of the Cardinals Bellarmine and Baronius* (London, 1612).

42. See, e.g., Etiemble, *Les Jésuites en Chine*; idem, *L'Europe chinoise*; Mungello, *Leibniz and Neo-Confucianism*; idem, *Curious Land*; Gernet, *Chine et christianisme*; Spence, *The Memory Palace of Matteo Ricci*; Küng and Ching, *Christianity and Chinese Religions*; Cook and Rosemont, *Leibniz, Writings on China*; and Jensen, *Manufacturing Confucianism*.

43. Gernet, *Chine et christianisme*, p. 127; see also pp. 31, 49, 68–70, 123, 124, 134, 333.

44. The papal decree of 1704, condemning the Jesuits' accommodation of Christianity to Confucian practices, assumes just such a definition of translation. See the text in Etiemble, *Les Jésuites en Chine*, pp. 109–11.

45. Gernet, *Chine et christianisme*, p. 332. For a social interpretation of the reasons for claiming to find incommensurability between languages, discourses, or theories, see Biagioli, *Galileo, Courtier*, pp. 211–44. The equivalence theory of translation is theoretically aligned with the correspondence, or representational, theory of truth. I find it odd that Gernet's predilection for relativist conclusions should be based on

such criteria, unless it is the failure of those criteria to operate that triggers the relativism. For an argument that follows a similar path, see Rorty, *Philosophy and the Mirror of Nature*, esp. pp. 349–50. Rorty, however, embraces the conclusion Gernet implicitly rejects: where no representational equivalences are to be found, we might as well take practical consensus ("edifying") as our standard.

46. On translation from and into Chinese and its pragmatic consequences, see Roger Hart, "Translating the Incommensurable: From Copula to Incommensurable Worlds," in Lydia Liu, ed., *Tokens of Exchange*, pp. 45–73.

47. On pun as the nucleus of allegory, see Quilligan, *The Language of Allegory*.

48. I follow the *Oxford English Dictionary* in reconstructing this word's history. "Broadcast, *a., adv., sb.*: . . . 1. Of seed, etc.: Scattered abroad over the whole surface, instead of being sown in drills or rows. . . . *v.* 1. To scatter (seed, etc.) abroad with the hand. . . . 2. *fig.* To scatter or disseminate widely. 1829 Taylor *Enthus.* iv. 270: The doctrine of missionary zeal . . . has been broad-cast over Christendom. 1880 Ruskin *Lett. to Clergy* 369 Showing his detestation of the sale of indulgences by broadcasting these gratis from the pulpit" (*OED*, 1st ed., original publication 1888); "1921 *Discovery* Apr 92/1 The [wireless] station at Poldhu is used partly for broadcasting Press and other messages to ships, that is, sending out messages without receiving replies" (*Supplement*, 1987).

49. On "latinization" as one dimension of globalization, see Derrida, "Foi et savoir" (in Derrida and Vattimo, eds., *La religion*, pp. 9–86), pp. 41–43.

50. See Goodrich, *The Literary Inquisition of Ch'ien-lung*, pp. 50, 52–53, 57, 59. Qianlong's major censorship campaign (carried out in tandem with the compilation of the *Siku quanshu* 四庫全書 omnibus anthology) lasted from 1772 to 1788.

Chapter 3

1. For a comparative survey of the issue, see Zhang Longxi, "The Debasement of Writing," in idem, *The Tao and the Logos*, pp. 3–33. The question of the value of writing obtained its present prominence in critical theory through Derrida, *De la grammatologie*. For an excellent study of the leading questions in the history of the arts of writing (both literature and calligraphy) in China, see Nylan, "Calligraphy."

2. Matteo Ricci, writing in 1597–1609, remarked on the Chinese "characters, similar to the hieroglyphics of the Egyptians" ("caratteri, al modo degli hieroglifichi degli Egittij") and gave the earliest Western notices of a number of themes prominent in later discussions of the writing system: monosyllabism, lack of inflections, homophony, noncorrespondence between spoken syllables and written forms, use of the same character system among speakers of different dialects or languages. See d'Elia, *Fonti Ricciane*, 1: 36–38. On the meaning that "Egyptian hieroglyphics" would have had to Ricci and his contemporaries, see Iversen, *The Myth of Egypt*; and Wittkower,

"Hieroglyphics in the Early Renaissance," in idem, *Allegory and the Migration of Symbols*, pp. 113–28.

3. The reason for the scarequotes is the uneasiness in referring to a writing system as "native" in the sense that languages are native (mother-tongues). The artificiality of the Chinese script is a frequent theme in comparative grammatology: see, e.g., Vandermeersch, "Écriture et langue graphique en Chine," in which writing is defined as a "graphic language" learned secondarily by literate Chinese and not a mere representation of the Chinese spoken language in a visual medium.

4. Liu Xie, *Wenxin diaolong*, p. 1. *Ziran* can of course also be translated as "spontaneity" or "that which is self-generating": my choice of the term "nature" reflects the subsequent history of this and other kindred passages in Chinese poetics. "Establishing words" is one of the "three undying deeds" mentioned in the *Zuo zhuan*: it means uttering speech that forms a precedent or touchstone for later generations. For alternative translations of this passage, see Shih, *The Literary Mind and the Carving of Dragons*; and Owen, *Readings in Chinese Literary Thought*, pp. 183–298. For commentary, see also Owen, *Traditional Chinese Poetry*, pp. 18–62.

5. A full bibliography of the subject would be immense; here two English-language references will suffice: Chow Tse-tsung, "Ancient Chinese Views"; and Owen, *Traditional Chinese Poetry*.

6. Stephen Owen (*Readings in Chinese Literary Thought*, p. 606) notes that "it is an established ceremony of commentary on the *Wenxin diaolong* to explain the range of the reference of *wen*."

7. Hjelmslev, "Sur les rapports entre la phonétique et la linguistique" (1938), in idem, *Nouveaux essais*, pp. 149–63.

8. For a technical use of "syntax" in this broad sense, see Morris, "Foundations," pp. 84–85, 88–94.

9. The necessity for this disclaimer was brought home to me by the reactions of sinological colleagues who refereed an earlier version of this chapter.

10. Further citations from this work appear as page numbers within parentheses. On Fenollosa's career in Japan as professor of aesthetics and advisor on cultural policy, see Sullivan, *The Meeting of Eastern and Western Art*; and W. Cohen, *East Asian Art in American Collections*. Some valuable studies on the ideogrammatic method are Davie, *Articulate Energy*; Yip, *Ezra Pound's "Cathay"*; Kenner, *The Pound Era*; Welsh, *Roots of Lyric*; Qian, *Orientalism and Modernism*; and Kern, *Orientalism, Modernism and the American Poem*. For a brilliant reading of Fenollosa, Pound, and Imagism generally, see Riddel, "Decentering the Image." (The writing of this chapter, as I discovered at the very end of the process, was in many respects an unconscious response to Riddel's essay.)

11. See Kennedy, "Fenollosa, Pound and the Chinese Character." De Francis, *The Chinese Language*, examines the "ideographic myth" and the "universality myth" as

mistaken ways of thinking about Chinese. Cai Zong-qi ("Poundian and Chinese Aesthetics") objects, with some justice, that pictorial quality was less important to Fenollosa's ideas about Chinese poetry than what he saw as its symbolic expression of natural force. As I shall try to show below, the difference is not great.

12. Derrida, *De la grammatologie*, pp. 139–40.

13. On the inevitability of a "double reading" of Fenollosa's essay—as "organi-cism" and as "irreducibly graphic poetics"—see Riddel, "Decentering the Image," pp. 139–40.

14. The assimilation of "reading" to "watching" may distract us from one of Fenollosa's sleights-of-hand, namely the asserted identity of speech and writing—an identity that is nonetheless always open to question, even (or especially) in "pho-netic" writing systems. For another attempt to unite "the vividness of painting and the mobility of sounds" via cinema, with copious reference to Chinese writing, paint-ing, and theater performance, see S. Eisenstein, "The Music of Landscape and the Fate of Montage," in idem, *Nonindifferent Nature*, pp. 216–383. For a rapprochement of Pound and Eisenstein via the ideogram, see Kenner, *The Pound Era*, pp. 161–62.

15. According to the *Book of Changes*, the process of change "in the heavens, yields *images*, and on earth, yields *shapes*" (在天成象, 在地成形; *Yi jing*, "Xi ci," part 1, 7.2b). Hence *xiang* + *xing*. A later section of the same chapter narrates the creation of writ-ing as an imitation of naturally given "images" and "shapes," just as the design of the *Book of Changes* itself is meant to lay bare the workings of change in the world. In discussing the structure of Chinese characters, Xu Shen seems to have classed them in order of increasing difficulty (nonimmediacy) of understanding:

> [Of the] Six Techniques [of character formation], the first is *zhi shi* ["indica-tives"]: *shang* 上 and *xia* 下 ["up" and "down"] are examples. Such characters one understands at a single glance; mere examination reveals their meaning. Next come the *xiang xing* 象形 ["giving an image of the shape"], the outline of which forms an object. According to their shape one glosses and voices them: 日 and 月 ["sun" and "moon"] are examples [i.e., the reading of the character is the name of the thing it depicts]. . . . The third kind is *xingsheng* 形聲, the composite of shape-element [signific] and sound-element [phonetic]. . . . The fourth kind, *huiyi* 會意, combines different meaning-elements [to make a new meaning]. . . . In the fifth kind, *zhuanzhu* 轉注, a character is appropriated [exclusively] to indi-cate a meaning other than its original meaning. . . . The sixth kind, *jiajie* 假借, is the use of homophones: where there is no character for a certain word, one makes do with another character having a similar sound. (Xu Shen, *Shuowen jiezi*, 15.1/4a–7a)

For a magisterial account of Xu Shen's typology and a grammatology based on Xu's categories, see Qiu Xigui, *Chinese Writing*. On Xu's character-formation methods as examples of "modular production," a device at work in many domains of Chinese culture, see Ledderose, *Ten Thousand Things*, pp. 9–23, 139–61.

16. *Da Dai Li ji*, "Ben ming," 13.3a; see also *Huainan zi*, "Yao lüe," 21.2a.

17. For a typical recent version of the evolutionary narrative, see Xie Yunfei, *Zhongguo wenzixue tonglun*.

18. Hegel, *Enzyklopädie der philosophischen Wissenschaften*, in idem, *Werke*, 10: 273–76.

19. Davie, *Articulate Energy*, p. 34.

20. See also Fenollosa, *The Chinese Written Character*, p. 19: "In all languages, Chinese included, a noun is originally 'that which does something,' that which performs the verbal action."

21. The theme of "sap," blood, or liquid is oddly obsessive in the essay as published (see ibid., pp. 12, 17, 19, 24, 32)—but not in Fenollosa's own versions. The manuscripts show beyond a doubt that the obsession is Pound's, who was at the time translating and writing a postscript for Rémy de Gourmont's *Physique de l'amour*. Compare, for example, the "walking-stick" passage in the notebook titled "E. F. F. The Chinese Written Language as a Medium for Poetry. Oct 1909" (Yale University, Beinecke Library, Pound Archive, catalogue number 3400, p. 39; copyright © 1997 by Mary de Rachewiltz and Omar Pound, used by permission of New Directions Publishing Corporation), with its predecessor drafts "Synopsis of Lectures on Chinese and Japanese Poetry" and "Chinese and Japanese Poetry. Draft of Lecture I" (Pound Archive, catalogue number 3375), pp. 14, 24. In fact the "Chinese and Japanese Poetry" lecture draft includes three figures of speech close in tenor to the "sap" image ("words . . . full of their original juices," "the juices of our Norman-Saxon language," "poetry follows nature in making its speech a single organism with common sap flowing through every vein"), all deleted by Fenollosa himself (p. 31a, b). On Indo-European preoccupations with sap and its supposed human analogues, semen and brain-matter, see Nagy, *Comparative Studies*, pp. 244–56; and La Barre, *Muelos*.

22. "Aryan," a word no longer respectable, meant in Fenollosa's time roughly the same as "Indo-European"; it had not yet been hijacked to evoke a hypothetical primitive racial and linguistic community. (For clarification by an authority nearly contemporary with Fenollosa, see *Encyclopædia Britannica*, eleventh edition [1911], s.v. "Aryan.") And of course Fenollosa is not responsible for anything Pound may have done to promote *The Chinese Written Character* as a political propaedeutic.

The early eighteenth-century missionary Joachim Bouvet, S.J., argued that the Chinese "hieroglyphic" and "symbolic" characters were a residue of the original names given the animals by Adam in Paradise; see Collani, *Eine wissenschaftliche Akademie*, pp. 50–51.

23. See Lessing, *Laokoön* (1766). Later semiology (for example, Morris's theory of signs; see p. 203n8) would amend this distinction, for syntax can occur in space: viz. the sign language of the deaf, the coded placements of the parts of an equation, or the expected placement of the elements of a complex Chinese character (phonetic clue usually to the right, classifier usually to the left, with many standard types for differing arrangements).

24. For an report of "lightning script" (legible patterns left on walls and columns by lightning strikes) from thirteenth-century China, see Zhou Mi, "Lei shu" 雷書, in idem, *Qidong yeyu*, pp. 218–19.

25. Aestheticians and linguists of eighteenth-century Europe debated the question of whether the word order found in one language was more natural (and thus better) than that found in another. Although any conclusion would now seem unwarranted, the discussion did lead linguists to conceive of the specificity of individual languages as a matter of internally coherent rules and thus to make possible, some generations later, Humboldt's and Saussure's conventionalism in matters of syntax. (I beg leave to stop short of a full consideration of Chomsky's contention that a common core of syntactic ability is innate to the species.) For a magisterial presentation, see Scaglione, *The Classical Theory of Composition*, esp. pp. 222–82; and for an intensive examination of Diderot's and Rousseau's positions with constant reference to modern-day polemics, see Genette, "Blanc bonnet versus bonnet blanc," in idem, *Mimologiques*, pp. 183–226.

26. For two influential citations of this passage, see Derrida, "La mythologie blanche," in idem, *Marges*, p. 258; and de Man, "Rhetoric of Tropes (Nietzsche)," in idem, *Allegories of Reading*, pp. 103–18.

27. Nietzsche, "Über Wahrheit und Lüge im aussermoralischen Sinne," pt. I, in idem, *Sämtliche Werke*, 1: 880–81.

28. Not that Fenollosa necessarily knew Nietzsche at first hand (the essay on truth and lie, dating from 1873, was first published in 1903 as an appendix to the *Untimely Meditations*; see *Nietzsches Werke*, pp. 189–207). Both Nietzsche and Fenollosa have a near ancestor in Emerson, the impress of whose essays is particularly clear in Fenollosa's imaginative philology. "It does not need that a poem should be long. Every word was once a poem. Every new relation is a new word. . . . Language is fossil poetry. . . . But the poet names the thing because he sees it, or comes one step nearer to it than any other. This expression, or naming, is not art, but a second nature, grown out of the first, as a leaf out of a tree." "Words are signs of natural facts. . . . The same symbols are found to make the original elements of all languages. . . . A man's power to connect his thought with the proper symbol, and so to utter it, depends on the simplicity of his character, that is, upon his love of truth and his desire to communicate it without loss. The corruption of man is followed by the corruption of language." ("The Poet" and "Nature," in Emerson, *Essays and Lectures*,

pp. 455–457, 20–22.) Through Mori Ōgai 森鷗外 and Inoue Tetsujirō 井上哲次郎, the Meiji intellectual world was aware of Nietzsche, but chiefly as an anti-Christian moralist, often paired with Darwin and set against Tolstoy: see Becker, *Nietzsche-Rezeption in Japan.*

29.   "Begin, ephebe, by perceiving the idea
       Of this invention, this invented world,
       The inconceivable idea of the sun.

       You must become an ignorant man again
       And see the sun again with an ignorant eye
       And see it clearly in the idea of it.

       Never suppose an inventing mind as source
       Of this idea . . ."

Stevens, "Notes Toward a Supreme Fiction," I, in *Collected Poems,* p. 380. "To speak truly, few adult persons can see nature. Most persons do not see the sun" (Emerson, "Nature," in idem, *Essays and Lectures,* p. 10).

    30. "The term 'ideography' has become a real opprobrium in linguistic circles" (Gelb, *A Study of Writing,* p. 35). For energetic attacks on the notion, see Boodberg, *Selected Works,* pp. 363–429; Boltz, *Origin and Early Development of the Chinese Writing System;* and Unger, "The Very Idea." For a study of its influence as a cultural construct, see Porter, *Ideographia.* For a recent attempt to rehabilitate the ideogram by giving it a more adequate theoretical base, see Hansen, "Chinese Ideographs and Western Ideas." Hansen contends that the ordinary notion of ideogrammatic writing rests on a convenient misunderstanding: the "writing of ideas" would be impossible for a culture that had never adopted the Platonic theory of intellectual Forms subsisting above and apart from the objects that instantiate them. There would thus be, in China, no "idea" for an ideogram to represent. What Hansen sees Chinese characters as inscribing is, rather, the nontranscendent historicality of the act of naming. Despite these and many other suggestive points, the essay suffers from weaknesses in exposition: its sweeping generalizations about "Indo-European" and "Chinese" theories of language and of knowledge invite skepticism, as does Hansen's readiness to build both "theories" on assumptions that are sometimes historically ill-attested or subject to major counterexamples. One may also see a kind of opportunism in the essay's wavering between the mission of vindicating the latent ideas of "ordinary language" (pp. 378, 380, 381) and that of overcoming "common sense" with linguistic relativism (pp. 367, 397). One of its good points is to observe the neglect of syntax by theorists of writing (pp. 375, 393); another is to point out that signs, whether "ideograms" or speech signs, are connected to their referents not by some immediate relation but by history and convention (pp. 374, 393); best of all is the suggestion that *all* writing be considered under the broadened heading of ideography,

rather than that 'ideographic' writing be set aside as an unusual exception among alphabetic systems of speech transcription (p. 388). But these three points are put with far greater systematic cogency in a well-known scholarly tradition left uncited by Hansen (see Saussure, *Cours*, pp. 24, 32, 34, 104–5, 110–11; Derrida, *De la grammatologie*, pp. 12–13, 20, 110, 132, 161). Hansen's attack on a straw man called Plato also ignores those modern analyses that have done much to dispel the indefinite mythology of the "ideal world" and to reframe Plato's activity in this-worldly ways: see, e.g., Natorp, *Platos Ideenlehre*; and Gadamer, *Plato's Dialectical Ethics*. For another critique of Hansen, see Unger, "Rejoinder."

31. On linguists' discomfort with the idea of "pictographic writing" and for a plea for "an inclusive definition of writing," see Boone, "Introduction," in Boone and Mignolo, *Writing Without Words*.

32. The first author to cast serious doubt on the ideographic nature of Chinese script was the American lawyer and jurist Peter Du Ponceau (*Dissertation on the Nature and Character of the Chinese System of Writing*, 1838). See also De Francis, *The Chinese Language*; and Boltz, *Origin and Early Development of the Chinese Writing System*, for the view that Chinese characters primarily record "words." Both authors hold that words are necessarily realized in sound and only secondarily represented in writing. Du Ponceau, interestingly, once served as private secretary to the French antiquary Antoine Court de Gébelin, whose vast synthesis *Monde primitif* attempted to demonstrate that all alphabetic and other characters had evolved from a limited set of original pictograms. For Du Ponceau's biography, see "Peter S. Du Ponceau, LL.D," *Journal of the American Oriental Society* 1 (1849): 161–70; on Court de Gébelin, see Genette, *Mimologiques*, pp. 119–48.

33. On "interpretants" and "Thirdness," see Peirce, *Values in a Universe of Chance*, pp. 387–90. Richard Sproat, whose research has focused on machine recognition and transcription of speech, observes that the idea of "phonetic" writing is hardly clearer than that of "ideogrammatism." "Much of the literature on writing, both popular and professional, has been devoted to the question of whether writing systems like Chinese represent language in a fundamentally different way from obviously phonologically-based systems. Lost in this debate is the fact that the primary purpose of writing is not phonetic transcription, but the representation of words and morphemes; purely phonologically-based systems are arguably merely the most efficient way of achieving this goal" (Sproat, review of Daniels and Bright, *The World's Writing Systems*, p. 81).

34. Benedict Anderson (*Imagined Communities*, p. 13) contends: "If Maguindanao met Berbers in Mecca, knowing nothing of each other's languages, incapable of communicating orally, they nonetheless understood each other's ideographs, because the sacred texts they shared existed only in classical Arabic. In this sense, written Arabic functioned like Chinese characters to create a community out of signs,

not sounds." The formulation will make linguists wince, but it contains a useful insight. Obviously Arabic writing developed as a phonetic notation, but in the right situations a phrase of written Arabic can be used as a symbol of its meaning with scant regard for the sound values of its letters; "ideography" is a species of social use, not solely a technical description. The case adduced by Anderson could be compared to the recognition of flags. What they "express" is thin (few flags are genuinely pictorial, and their native cultural associations diminish in the international context of flag display), but their acquired meanings can be quite thick. One prominent class of characters in Chinese bronze inscriptions consists of clan or family symbols, no longer readable because their social referents have become extinct.

35. "L'écriture chinoise a fait un pas de plus [sur l'écriture égyptienne]: elle a rejeté les *images*, & n'a conservé que les *marques* abrégées, qu'elle a multiplié jusqu'à un nombre prodigieux" (Jaucourt, "Écriture chinoise," in Diderot and d'Alembert, *Encyclopédie*, 5: 360; italics added). The Chevalier de Jaucourt's history of writing is indebted to Warburton, *The Divine Legation of Moses*. For a reprint of the 1744 French adaptation of Warburton's work, followed by additional notes on Chinese writing by the translator, see Warburton, *Essai sur les hiéroglyphes*.

36. On these projectors, see Knowlson, *Universal Language Schemes*; M. Cohen, *Sensible Words*; Salmon, *The Study of Language*; Slaughter, *Universal Languages and Scientific Taxonomy*; Stillman, *The New Philosophy and Universal Languages*; and Eco, *The Search for the Perfect Language*.

37. Saussure, *Cours*, pp. 150–52; discussed by Derrida, *De la grammatologie*, p. 45. They are idealities only in the sense that their material realizations are not sufficient to constitute them; recognition makes them what they are.

38. Champollion, *Lettre*, pp. 1–3: "écriture . . . idéographique, c'est-à-dire peignant les idées et non les sons d'une langue . . . Les Chinois . . . se servent également d'une écriture idéographique." For the three classes of characters, see Champollion, *Grammaire égyptienne*, p. 22. The OED's earliest citations for "ideography" and related words (1822, 1823) are passages commenting on Champollion's discovery.

39. See Horapollo, *Hieroglyphics*. On the Renaissance neo-Platonic movement that gave this late classical work its "undeserved prestige," see Gombrich, *Symbolic Images*, pp. 145–60. On the fate of Chinese characters incorporated into manufactured objects and dispersed beyond the Chinese culture-area, with examples from ancient and recent times, see Falkenhausen, "Inconsequential Incomprehensions."

40. See Giehlow, *Die Hieroglyphenkunde des Humanismus*; Baudelaire, "L'Art philosophique," *Œuvres complètes*, 2: 598–605.

41. Bacon, *Advancement of Learning*, pp. 399–400. Compare Wilkins, *Essay Towards a Real Character*, p. 13: "a *Real universal Character*, that should not signifie words, but things and notions, and consequently might be legible by any Nation in their own Tongue . . . is possible, and hath been reckoned by Learned men amongst the

Desiderata . . . besides what is commonly reported of the men of *China*, who do now, and have for many Ages used such a general Character, by which the Inhabitants of that large Kingdom, many of them of different Tongues, do communicate with one another, every one understanding this common Character, and reading it in his own Language."

42. Aristotle, *De interpretatione* 16 a 2 – 3.

43. See Rossi, *Clavis Universalis*; Derrida, *De la grammatologie*, pp. 109–42; idem, *Marges*, pp. 113–34; Slaughter, *Universal Languages and Scientific Taxonomy*; and Eco, *The Search for the Perfect Language*. On universal language projects generally, see Albani and Buonarroti, *Dictionnaire des langues imaginaires*.

44. Duret, *Thrésor*, pp. 158–59: "Le tout dépendant . . . de la résolution des mots en syllabes et lettres, dont consiste la représentation de l'essence des choses qu'on veut exprimer par leurs droites appellations." On the translation and appropriation of kabbalah in non-Jewish circles, see Secret, *Les Kabbalistes chrétiens*.

45. Ezra Pound's footnotes to Fenollosa highlight this tendency: Pound (*ABC of Reading*, pp. 30–31) speaks of a sculptor friend of his who used to "read" the Chinese characters "almost at pleasure," though he had never studied the language. Trithemius, presaging Rousseau's *Essai sur l'origine des langues*, writes thus of the writing system invented by the first men on earth: "Fuerunt autem aliae literae tunc, ut referunt, ab his quas mundus hodie habet multum diverse, ad formam et similitudinem arborum, plantarum et animalium excogitatae, quae tamen cum tempore postea multipliciter sunt immutatae" (Letters were greatly different then, it is said, from those the world has today: originally devised in the shape and likeness of trees, plants and animals, they have since changed in many ways with the passage of time; *Polygraphia*, unpaginated).

46. Agrippa, *De occulta philosophia*, p. 140. "Dicunt . . . sive verbo sive nomine in iam suis articulis formato ipsam vim rei sub significationibus forma, quasi vitam aliquam latere." Agrippa's starting point may be a misunderstanding of the use of the word *dynamis* in Greek to denote the sound value of a letter, as opposed to its name: see Liddell, Scott, and Jones, *A Greek-English Lexicon*, s.v. δύναμις, par. iii b.

47. Agrippa, *De occulta philosophia*, p. 60: "sacras sive divinas litteras. . . . Suntque ubilibet nationum et linguarum eadem atque sibi consimiles permanentesque."

48. Nock, *Corpus Hermeticum*, 2: 231–32; translation from Copenhaver, *Hermetica*, p. 58. For "sound" (ἤχω, Nock's conjecture), Franz Cumont suggested "intonation" (τόνωσις), and Nicephorus Gregoras, citing the passage in the early fourteenth century, has "power" (δύναμις). The *Corpus* thus exhibits a striking lack of interest in the pictorial qualities of hieroglyphic writing. The real contrast between Greeks and Egyptians emerges further down: "For the Greeks, O my king, have empty discourses whose only effect is that of demonstration (ἀποδείξεων ἐνεργητικούς), and such is the philosophy of the Greeks, a hubbub of words. We Egyptians do not use

discursive language (λόγοις), but rather sounds saturated with action (φωναῖς μεσταῖς τῶν ἔργων)" (my translation). Thus a return to the sound symbols of the *Cratylus*. Of course, this diatribe against Greek dialectics was delivered in Greek to an audience of Greeks, rather like Fenollosa's praise of Chinese picture writing, formulated with scant reference to existing speakers of Chinese. For a less mysterious ancient Greek view of hieroglyphic writing, see Diodorus Siculus, *Bibliotheca historica* 3.4.1: "The [Ethiopians' and Egyptians'] art of writing does not transmit the underlying idea (λόγον) through the combination of syllables [i.e., linguistic sounds], but rather does so from the appearances of the things transcribed, and through metaphor assisted by memory."

49. Kircher, *China illustrata*, p. 226. Kircher held, following chapter 10 of *Genesis*, that the East was populated by descendants of Noah's son Ham (Cham). One son of Ham, Mizraim or Aegyptus, was the ancestor of the Egyptians, and Hermes Trismegistus or Thoth was a son of Mizraim.

50. Ibid., p. 278: "serpentes mirè intricatos, et in formas varias, pro diversitate rerum, quas illis significabant, transformatos."

51. Ibid., p. 234: "occultas operationes quas non tantum Sol materialis in hoc sensibili mundo, sed et archetypus in intelligibili mundo efficit. . . . Quae omnia in Sinensium characterum structura deficiunt: cum hi praecise solum ad vocum nominumque simplices conceptus indicandos, nullo alio sub iis latente mysterio instituti sint."

52. On Kircher's "decipherments" of Egyptian writing, see V.-David, *Le Débat sur les écritures*, p. 48; and Iversen, *The Myth of Egypt*, pp. 89–99. Kircher did, however, propose using Coptic as an avenue into the study of the Egyptian language, a line of inquiry that later bore fruit. The scope of this essay does not permit me to trace the contrasting, chiefly technological, line of development followed by the idea of the Chinese character in Europe. Its main figures are Bacon, Kircher (again! see his *Polygraphia nova et universalis*, 1663), Wilkins (*An Essay Towards a Real Character*, 1668), and Leibniz.

53. Kircher, *China illustrata*, pp. 226–30. Knud Lundbæk (*The Traditional History of the Chinese Script*, pp. 30, 45, 48–50, 53–55) has identified as the source of Kircher's "primitive characters" a popular miscellany entitled *Tianxia bianyong Wenlin miaojin wanbao quanshu*, preserved in the Vatican Library. Not all of Kircher's examples are found in this particular work, however. A likely model for the *Wanbao quanshu's* primitive characters is a well-known Ming edition of the *Diamond Sutra*, in which the sutra was rendered in a virtuosic display of thirty-two unusual variant styles (Kumarajiva, attr., *Sanshi'er zhuanti Jin'gang jing*). See Figures 3.1–4, pp. 51–54.

54. Creuzer, *Symbolik und Mythologie der alten Völker*, p. 26. For a discussion of the allegory/symbol distinction in European romanticism, see de Man, "The Rhetoric of Temporality," in idem, *Blindness and Insight*, pp. 187–228.

55. The humoral appreciation of languages as hot or cold, dry or wet, enters the European mind around 1750 through Rousseau standing on Montesquieu's shoulders (Rousseau, *Essai sur l'origine des langues*, pp. 118–43; Montesquieu, *Œuvres*, pp. 613–15). Fenollosa's rejection of the verb "to be" may be primarily artistic, but it also harmonizes with A. C. Graham's renovation of John Stuart Mill's case against the ambiguity of "to be," copulative and existential, for having "spread mysticism over the field of logic, and perverted its speculations into logomachies" (Mill, *A System of Logic*, 1: 85; Graham, "'Being' in Classical Chinese").

56. On thermodynamics as a source of literary metaphors and anxieties, see Donato, "The Museum's Furnace."

57. "Jamais [les animaux] ne pourroient user de paroles ni d'autres signes *en les composant* . . . pour répondre au sens de tout ce qui se dira en leur présence" ([Animals] could never use words or other signs *by joining them together* to respond to the meaning of whatever is said in their presence; Descartes, *Discours de la méthode*, part V, in *Œuvres philosophiques*, p. 629; italics added).

58. At the level of letters and phonemes, Mulder and Hervey (*The Strategy of Linguistics*, p. 83) call this principle "cenotactics." I refer to it as syntax in order to emphasize the common feature of ordered combination. "Magical" linguistic theories may derive their power from syntactical as well as semantic properties. Vigenère (*Traicté des chiffres*, p. 83) saw Hebrew as a model language because the order of its letters were as productive of meaning as the order of words in a sentence: "en un contexte d'escriture, si les lettres en sont transposées & jettées hors de leurs précédant ordre, assiette & disposition, le sens qui y estoit s'altère et change" (if the letters of a passage of writing [in Hebrew, minus vowels of course] are transposed and thrown out of their former order, standing and arrangement, their meaning changes into a different one). Vigenère glorifies Hebrew for being wholly meaning-generating, unlike other alphabetic languages in which it is highly probable that a random sequence of letters will be nonsense (intrusion of the cenematic upon the plerematic).

59. Hegel, *Enzyklopädie*, par. 459 *Zusatz* (Hegel, *Werke*, 10: 274), prominently featured as the third opening epigraph in Derrida, *De la grammatologie*.

60. Beck, *The Universal Character*, "To the Reader."

61. On the surprising importance of negative constructions to such arguments, see Saussy, *Problem*, pp. 34–35. For examples from another domain, see Sivin, "Why the Scientific Revolution Didn't Take Place in China—Or Didn't It?"

62. Owen, *Traditional Chinese Poetry*, pp. 15, 61, 57–59; cf. Jullien, *La Valeur allusive*, pp. 46–47.

63. Owen, *Traditional Chinese Poetry*, p. 7.

64. Yu, *The Reading of Imagery*, p. 35, with reference to Liu Xie. One premise of such assertions (voiced by Yu, as by Owen, Jullien, and others discussed here) is the

claim that Chinese cosmology had no room for the idea of "creation" or radical beginning. On "beginnings" as an intellectual and social problem common to many influential early Chinese thinkers, see Puett, "Nature and Artifice."

65. Fuller's discussion refers primarily to M. H. Abrams's *The Mirror and the Lamp.* I am supplying the Aristotelian links; Fuller is not responsible for them. On the correspondence theory of perception, see Aristotle, *On the Soul* 424 a 20 – 424 b 18. "Generally, about all perception, we can say that a sense is what has the power of receiving into itself the sensible forms of things without the matter, in the way in which a piece of wax takes on the impress of a signet-ring without the iron or gold" (trans. J. A. Smith, in *The Complete Works of Aristotle*, p. 674). For lapidary statements of the correspondence theory of truth, see *On Interpretation* 19 a 33; and *Metaphysics* 1051 b 1 – 1052 a 3. Not by chance, I would maintain, it is the "origins of poetry" section of the *Poetics*, with its enchainment of perception, mimesis, syllogism, and learning, that most economically brings these themes together (*Poetics* 1448 b 5 – 23). For a poetic exposition of Aristotle's cognitive theory, see Dante, *Purgatorio*, 18: 19–45.

66. Fuller, "Pursuing the Complete Bamboo," p. 21.

67. Allen, *In the Voice of Others*, p. 19.

68. For Jurij Tynjanov's idea of "the dominant," a notion I find more useful in discussing literary history than in discussing literary production, see Ehrlich, *Russian Formalism*, p. 171. Of course, the dominant position of *shi* poetry vis-à-vis genres considered artificial, unserious, or convention-ridden and the exaltation of certain *shi* poets above others for their sincerity and stylistic naturalism was the handiwork of several centuries of Chinese critics, and the scholars I mention acknowledge this inheritance. Here I merely wish to point out the shift of value that takes place when a distinction among Chinese poetic genres (*shi* versus *ci*, *yuefu*, *qu*, etc.) becomes the basis of a distinction between Chinese and European poetic assumptions.

69. For a chronological survey, see Yingjin Zhang, "Engaging Chinese Comparative Literature and Comparative Studies," in idem, ed., *China in a Polycentric World*, pp. 1–17.

70. Yourcenar's "Comment Wang-Fô fut sauvé" (in idem, *Nouvelles orientales*, pp. 11–27), at the end of which an artist sails away on the seascape he has just painted, recapitulates and typifies as "Chinese" the worlds-within-worlds logic, a form of hyperrealism first explored by Zhuang Zhou (*Zhuangzi*, chap. 25, "Zeyang" 則陽) in the fable of the warring kingdoms on the horns of a snail.

71. Pound, *ABC of Reading*, p. 22.

72. R. P. Blackmur (*Form and Value in Modern Poetry*, p. 111) pointed out, accurately I think, that "the Cantos are an anthology of such jewels and read as most people read anthologies."

73. Yip, "Wang Wei and Pure Experience," in idem, *Hiding the Universe*, pp. v–vii; italics in original.

74. See S. Eisenstein, *Nonindifferent Nature*, for many statements of an "ideographic" aesthetics of film montage. I am obliged to Pei-kai Cheng for pointing out this connection to me.

75. Yip, *Hiding the Universe*, pp. ix–xii. For strictures on this reading of Wang Wei and comments on Yip's translations, see Pauline Yu, "Wang Wei: Recent Studies and Translations," pp. 234–36.

76. Yip, *Hiding the Universe*, p. xiii. Yip's example comes from Bynner and Kiang, *The Jade Mountain*, p. 189. Eliot Weinberger (*Nineteen Ways of Looking at Wang Wei*, p. 27) observes that in a later rendition, Yip "clipped the first line to the almost pidgin *Empty mountain: no man.*"

77. For the essentials of this codification of taste, see Pound, "A Retrospect," in idem, *Literary Essays of Ezra Pound*, pp. 3–14. A. C. Graham ("The Translation of Chinese Poetry," in idem, *Poems of the Late T'ang*, pp. 13, 20) brings his customary judiciousness to bear in observing, on the one hand, that the "strength [of Classical Chinese] lies in its concreteness and conciseness" and that "the element in poetry which travels best is of course concrete imagery," but on the other that "the English reader continues to recognize Chinese poetry by the face which it turned towards the poetic revolutionaries of the second decade of the [twentieth] century, just as he knows Persian poets only as world-weary wine-bibbing Victorian aesthetes."

78. Wang Wei, *Wang Youcheng ji jianzhu*, p. 243 (the familiarity of the poem has lulled the typesetters of this edition into substituting *ru* 入 for *ren* 人 at the close of the first line!); Weinberger, *Nineteen Ways of Looking at Wang Wei*, pp. 10, 24, 42. On the unusual reading of *shang* in the last line to mean that the moss is located "above," Snyder states that the sun "is illuminating some moss *up in the trees*. (NOT ON ROCKS.) This is how my teacher Ch'en Shih-hsiang saw it, and my wife (Japanese), too, the first time she looked at the poem" (ibid., p. 43). Pauline Yu (*The Poetry of Wang Wei*, p. 202) translates:

> Deer Enclosure
> Empty mountain, no man is seen.
> Only heard are echoes of men's talk.
> Reflected light enters the deep wood
> And shines again on blue-green moss.

79. For better insights into the grammatical syntax of Chinese poetry, see, above all, Kao and Mei, "Syntax, Diction, and Imagery."

80. *Shuowen jiezi*, 9:1.20b. Similar language occurs in the "Appended Statements" ("Xi ci") section of the *Book of Changes*: *Wu xiang za, gu yue wen* 物相雜, 故曰文: "The 'objects' or 'bodies' [of *Yi jing* divination] are intermingled: this is called *wen*"

(*Yi jing*, 8.22b). The passage is glossed by Wang Bi 王弼 (226–249) thus: "The hard and the soft connect and cross; Azure and Yellow [i.e., heaven and earth] cross and intermingle." The special use of *wen* here is common to the *Yi jing* and *Kaogong ji*, and interwoven with the *Yi jing*'s particular theoretical project; yet on this point the *Kaogong ji* is the more explicit of the two works, as Wang Bi's commentary acknowledges by quoting from *Kaogong ji* to clarify the *Yi*. Liu Xie, in turn, seems to have adopted Wang Bi's commentary as a pattern-text for his own praise of *wen*. For a significantly different translation of the Wang Bi passage, see Chow Tse-tsung, "Ancient Chinese Views," p. 8.

81. *Shuo wen jie zi*, 9:1.20b. The story about reading animal tracks occurs in *Yi jing*, "Xi ci," part 2 (8.4b), and again in Xu Shen's postface to his *Shuo wen jie zi*, 15:1.1b–2b. Its canonical standing is borne out by such passages as the following from the *Hou Han shu*: "In remote antiquity, people lived in caves and desolate places, dressed in furs and skins, and lacked differentiation [of rank]. Later, the sages changed this. . . . They saw how birds and beasts had tufts, antlers, whiskers and dewlaps, all in order; and so they formed hats, caps, tassels and cap-pendants for the sake of ornament, and the nine types of decorations." Then follows a recitation of the *Yi jing* source passage (Fan Ye, *Hou Han shu*, 30.1a–b). The fact that this story could follow only a few pages after an argument about the derivation of vestimentary distinctions from social utility shows that the principle of contrast between nature and culture needs, at the very least, to be rethought (by which I do not mean rejected) by students of early Chinese semiology. See Greimas, "Conditions d'une sémiotique du monde naturel," in idem, *Du sens*, pp. 49–91.

82. "Dong guan: Kaogong ji" 冬官, 考工記, "Hua hui" 畫繪; *Zhou li*, 40.24b–26a. The *Kaogong ji* is the latest section of the *Zhou li*, reportedly added in middle Han times as a replacement for a lost chapter of the same name; the paragraph cited by Duan is a mix of elements from *Shang shu*, *Zuo zhuan*, *Li ji*, and *Lun yu* (this last cited in a suspiciously opportunistic way). Whatever its provenance, it would certainly have been a classic book in Liu's time.

83. Jones, *A Grammar of Ornament*.

84. *Zuo zhuan* (Duke Huan, second year), 5.7a–16a. *Wenwu* has since entered the language as a compound meaning "object of historical value."

85. See, e.g., Jullien, *La Valeur allusive*, pp. 24–28.

86. The emphasis on constitutive difference is one reason for music's prominence in ritual aesthetics. For numerous practical illustrations of the principle, see "Fang ji" 坊記, *Li ji*, 41.7a–27b.

87. "Yue ji" 樂記, *Li ji*, 37.4a, 38.10b–11a.

88. On the role of writing (in all its forms: Classics, imperial edicts, tallies, seals, memoranda, messages from the beyond, literary careers, and styles, etc.) in the formation of the Han empire, see Lewis, *Writing and Authority in Early China*.

89. B. Anderson, *Imagined Communities*, p. 36. See also the critical discussion in Duara, *Rescuing History from the Nation*, pp. 52–56.

90. See the humorous counterstatement and dialogue of Owen, *Traditional Chinese Poetry*, pp. 27–34.

91. For an exquisite rhetorical presentation of the idea that the king's role is to harmonize the diverse, see *Guo yu* 16, "Zheng yu," esp. 16.3b–5a, a speech in which occurs the striking formula: 聲一無聽, 物一無文 (when sound is all of one kind, nothing is heard; when objects are uniform, there is no pattern). See also the discussion of this and related passages in Feng Youlan, *Zhongguo zhexue shi*, p. 59 (Fung Yu-lan, *A History of Chinese Philosophy*, trans. Bodde, pp. 34–35). On kings as inventors, see Lévi, "Le mythe de l'âge d'or." The story of the goddess Nüwa "tempering blocks of five-colored stone" (once again that synecdochical five) to repair the cracks in heaven often serves poets as a myth of imperial creative mission.

92. According to Ding Wenjiang, writing in 1931, Granet's syntheses "completely disregard the element of time: customs and beliefs are described as if they had existed throughout the ages" (cited in Rémi Mathieu, "Postface," in Granet, *La Civilisation chinoise*, p. 566). On Granet's relationship to structuralism, see below, chapter 7, pp. 177–78.

93. Granet, *La Civilisation chinoise*, pp. 93–99.

94. In other words, rhythm suggests a pure form of syntax. Morse code also "provides an excellent example of a semiotic system with only a cenological ordering" (i.e., a syntax of nonmeaningful elements). "We can demonstrate that '∙ –' is an ordered cenological complex by the fact that it is distinguished purely on the basis of ordering . . . from a cenological complex '– ∙.' The Morse Code contains ordered cenological complexes, but no plerological complexes at all" (Mulder and Hervey, *The Strategy of Linguistics*, p. 79).

Chapter 4

1. On the commonplace, see Ramsey, *The Languages of China*, pp. 49–57. On the history of European ideas about Chinese grammar, see Egerod, "Typology"; and Harbsmeier, "John Webb and the Early History of the Study of the Classical Chinese Language in the West." As early as 1912, Morgan, in *Wenli Styles and Chinese Ideals*, protested that "language without grammar" was nonsense. I am not here presenting the whole history of Chinese linguistics as practiced in Europe and North America; rather, I am tracing the career of one influential misconception. Impressive early grammatical studies of the language were performed by Stanislas Julien (*Syntaxe nouvelle de la langue chinoise*, 1869–70) and Georg von der Gabelentz (*Chinesische Grammatik*, 1881). The first grammar of Chinese composed in Chinese, Ma Jianzhong's 馬建忠 *Ma shi wen tong* 馬氏文通 of 1898, was written, according to Victor Mair ("Ma Jianzhong"), to redeem the slight: it takes its place along other proposals

made by Ma for economic, diplomatic, and intellectual reform. Educated by Jesuit missionaries and sent abroad by Li Hongzhang 李鴻章 to study French political institutions, Ma is a representative figure of the 1898 Reform movement.

2. Eco, *Foucault's Pendulum*, pp. 74–75.

3. By "interaction" I have in mind a loose analogy to the ways in which physicists have learned to describe measurement since Einstein's relativization of space and time. For an intriguing set of papers on measurement, observers, and interaction, see DeWitt and Graham, *Many-Worlds Interpretation*. For a philosophical and literary study of such "general economies," see Plotnitsky, *Complementarity*.

4. On the tendency to give prominence to the sign rather than to the sentence, see Chapter 3.

5. For the history of this change, as well as the sources and their reception, see Etiemble, *L'Europe chinoise*.

6. Whitney, *Language and the Study of Language*, p. 331. Whitney takes his version of Mencius from Schleicher, *Die Sprachen Europas* (1850), pp. 50–52, and Schleicher has it from Stanislas Julien, *Meng Tseu vel Mencius* (Paris, 1824), p. 1. Schleicher translates: "König sprechen, Greis, nicht fern 1000 Meile und kommen, auch wollen haben zu Vortheil (ich) mein Reich (Fragepartikel)?"

7. Legge, *The Works of Mencius*, Book I, part 1, in idem, *The Chinese Classics*, 2: 125.

8. Jowett, *The Dialogues of Plato*.

9. Benjamin, "Die Aufgabe des Übersetzers," in idem, *Gesammelte Schriften*, 4.1: 20–22. Translation mine; for the complete text, see idem, *Illuminations*, pp. 80–82.

10. On the cosmopolitan-romantic ideal, see Berman, *L'Epreuve de l'étranger*.

11. On such processes, see Weinreich, *Languages in Contact*. On China Coast Pidgin particularly, see Bolton, "Language and Hybridization."

12. Whitney, *Language and the Study of Language*, pp. 330–34.

13. Ibid., p. 257. "Scanty and crippled" calls for comment. George Devereux (*From Anxiety to Method*, pp. 162–77) supplies a chapter's worth of stories which medical practitioners react to somatic features normal in ethnic groups other than their own as if they were deformations (sometimes by ignoring, sometimes by irrelevantly highlighting, the difference). The practitioners may even react to this factitious defect with anxiety, as if it threatened their own bodily integrity.

14. For similar statements, see Humboldt, *Sur l'origine des formes grammaticales*, pp. 102, 105, 147.

15. For examples, see Fingarette, "A Way Without a Crossroads," in idem, *Confucius*, pp. 18–36, on the claim that Confucius never conceived of moral choice; and Hansen, *Language and Logic*, who maintains that the Chinese language dictates an ontology of stuffs, not substances, individuals, or classes.

16. Schlegel, *Sprache und Weisheit der Indier*, p. 45. On Schlegel and his influence, see Davies, "Language Classification."

218 • Notes to Pages 83–90

17. August Wilhelm von Schlegel, *Observations sur la langue et la littérature provença-les* (Paris, 1818), cited in Benfey, *Geschichte der Sprachwissenschaft*, pp. 366–67.

18. Humboldt, *Über die Verschiedenheit des menschlichen Sprachbaues* (ca. 1830–35; first publication, 1836), in idem, *Gesammelte Schriften*, 7.1: 254.

19. Humboldt, "Lettre à monsieur Abel-Rémusat sur la nature des formes grammaticales en général et sur le génie de la langue chinoise en particulier" (1806), in idem, *Gesammelte Schriften*, 5: 254–308. Jean-Pierre Abel-Rémusat was the first professor of Chinese in the Collège de France (the chair was established in 1814). For a German translation of this letter with extensive commentary based on genuine si-nological knowledge, see Harbsmeier, *Wilhelm von Humboldts Brief an Abel-Rémusat*.

20. Humboldt, *Über die Verschiedenheit*, in idem, *Gesammelte Schriften*, 7.1: 271, 274.

21. Ibid., p. 253.

22. Schleicher, *Die Sprachen Europas*, pp. 7–9.

23. For the quotation, see Hegel, *Enzyklopädie der philosophischen Wissenschaften*, Pt. II, *Die Naturphilosophie*, §343, "Die vegetabilische Natur," in idem, *Werke*, 9: 371. Translation mine; for another rendition see Petry, *Hegel's Philosophy of Nature*, 3: 45.

24. Schleicher, *Die Sprachen Europas*, pp. 14–15.

25. "There is one language, the Chinese, in which no analysis of any kind is re-quired for the discovery of its component parts. It is a language in which no coales-cence of roots has taken place: every word is a root, and every root is a word. It is, in fact, the most primitive stage in which we can imagine human language to have ex-isted. . . . All languages must have started from this Chinese or monosyllabic stage" (Müller, *Lectures on the Science of Language*, p. 273). For Jespersen's views, see his "The History of Chinese and of Word Order," in idem, *Progress in Language*, pp. 80–111.

26. See Scaglione, *The Classical Theory of Composition*, pp. 337–49.

27. Schlegel, *Weisheit und Sprache der Indier*, pp. 61, 63. *Besonnenheit* (understanding, reflection) was the middle term by which Herder had threaded his way past the risky alternatives of the Berlin Academy's prize essay theme of 1770, "whether the origin of language was divine or human?"; see Herder, *Abhandlung über den Ursprung der Sprache*.

28. Schlegel, *Weisheit und Sprache der Indier*, p. 66.

29. Bopp, *Über das Conjugationssystem der Sanskrit-Sprache* (1816), p. 147. "Bopp ac-tually seems to have held that in the proto-language the primitive semantic elements were by and large expressed by separate morphemes. The morphology of a Proto-Indo-European word, Bopp believed, was a *representation* of the elements of its meaning. Obscured as this state of affairs was in the daughter languages, because of phonetic decay, it was nonetheless reconstructible by the comparative method" (Ki-parsky, "From Paleogrammarians to Neogrammarians," p. 332; italics added).

30. Whitney, *Language and the Study of Language*, pp. 230–32. A specific dimension of the "last and greatest era of Indo-European supremacy" would be the settling of

the Americas (the precondition, in so many ways, of Whitney's addressing the Smithsonian Institution on the subject) and the takeover by European merchants of trade networks previously dominated by Arab shipping. The existence of this earlier "world-system" of trade was no secret to participants in the mercantilist colonial enterprise: as Putnam Weale (*The Vanished Empire*, p. 157) puts it in retrospect, the result of the First Opium War of 1842 was that "the five ports from Canton to the Yangtsze, which for hundreds of years had been Arab anchorages, were thrown open to international trade." On the shifting patterns of global trade in the period 1400–1800, see Frank, *ReOrient*, pp. 52–130.

31. Hannah Arendt outlines the history of "Race-Thinking Before Racism" in idem, *The Origins of Totalitarianism*, pp. 158–84. She contends: "As for the philologists of the early nineteenth century, whose concept of 'Aryanism' has seduced almost every student of racism to count them among the propagandists or even inventors of race-thinking, they are as innocent as innocent can be. When they overstepped the limits of pure research it was because they wanted to include in the same cultural brotherhood as many nations as possible. . . . In other words, these men were still in the humanistic tradition of the eighteenth century and shared its enthusiasm about strange people and exotic cultures" (ibid., p. 160n6). I think that the line between eighteenth-century cosmopolitanism and later race classification passes through Schlegel's *Weisheit und Sprache* (it underlies the distinction between languages of imitation and languages of reason) and persists in the work of genuine philologists who followed him. For views that cast Schlegel as a proto-racial thinker, see Bernal, *Black Athena*, 1: 227–39; and Said, *Orientalism*, pp. 98–99. On a related linguistic controversy in which objections to racial ideology came to the fore, see Aarsleff, "Bréal vs. Schleicher: Reorientation in Linguistics During the Latter Half of the Nineteenth Century," in idem, *From Locke to Saussure*, pp. 293–334.

Chapter 5

EPIGRAPHS: Segalen, *Essai sur l'Exotisme*, p. 36 (these notes date from 1908); Emerson, *Essays and Lectures*, p. 259.

1. "Das Bekannte überhaupt ist darum, weil es *bekannt* ist, nicht *erkannt*"; Hegel, preface to the *Phänomenologie des Geistes* (in idem, *Werke*, 3: 35).

2. Examples of such deflationary arguments are legion. Said's *Orientalism* insists on the "created consistency, that regular constellation of ideas" about non-Western countries in a way that suggests that the more tightly knitted this body of knowledge can be shown to be, the less it presumably owes to observation. Is there something wrong with consistency and regularity (not, at first glance, reprehensible features of a scholarly field)? Two sorts of objection emerge from Said's investigation. As it became a self-confirming matter and manner of study, "Orientalism" failed to notice a great many new facts about its "objects." Second, its hidden purposes may

have had little to do with knowledge anyway: from around 1700 to around 1950, "European culture gained in strength and identity by setting itself off against the Orient," Said contends (pp. 5, 3), but the converse cannot be maintained. How to extend *Orientalism* into a methodological critique and recommendation for future practices is, to my mind, still an open question, although the twenty years since its initial publication have seen many attempts to disavow "orientalist" attitudes and replace them with anti- or post-Orientalist ones.

3. With the recent discovery of early texts in caches such as Mawangdui and Guodian, the challenges are real for all readers, not just those who approach China "from the outside": standard histories of Chinese thought and religion, since they emerge from two thousand or so years of subsequent history, prejudge many of the questions that these works raise.

4. Momigliano, "A Piedmontese View of the History of Ideas," in idem, *Essays in Ancient and Modern Historiography*, p. 6.

5. On recent transformations of the term, see Hartman, *The Fateful Question of Culture*, esp. pp. 26–42. The influence of culturalist anthropological models on everyday life and thought in the United States should be plain to anyone who considers how often, and with what effects, practices and attitudes are ascribed to a "culture" (regional, professional, ethnic, corporate, etc.). For a critique of cultural noninterventionism as facilitating certain kinds of harmful intervention in the lives of the members of a designated "culture," see Farmer, *AIDS and Accusation*. The resonance of the term "culture" (*wenhua* 文化) in Chinese contexts is somewhat unusual for a Euro-American observer: rather than connoting something constructed, arbitrary, and local, it announces a civilizational norm, and in the right hands it can have real coercive power (this is culture, that is not . . .).

6. As in *Luke* 10.30–37.

7. Hegel, *Enzyklopädie der philosophischen Wissenschaften*, par. 377, *Zusatz*, in idem, *Werke*, 10: 10 (my translation); see also idem, *Hegel's Philosophy of Mind*, pp. 1–2.

8. Hegel, *Enzyklopädie*, par. 243, *Zusatz*, in idem, *Werke*, 9: 14; see also Hegel, *Phänomenologie des Geistes*, in *Werke*, 3: 91, or *Phenomenology of Spirit*, p. 65.

9. Levinas, *Totality and Infinity*, p. 43; idem, *Totalité et infini*, p. 33. For a quick characterization of the "orientation towards the Other" from which Levinas derives both ontology and ethics and the place of language in this relation, see *Totality and Infinity*, pp. 50–51, 215–16.

10. Levinas, "Time and the Other," in Hand, *The Levinas Reader*, p. 48.

11. Levinas, *Totality and Infinity*, p. 73; idem, *Totalité et infini*, pp. 70–71.

12. The phrase 非我族類, inevitably cited by historians of ethnic consciousness and nationalism in China, stems from a speech in the *Zuo zhuan* (Cheng, 4th year; 26.7a). A consideration of the context, however, shows that even in the venerable source the ethnic theme is not obviously dominant:

秋, 公至自晉, 欲求成于楚而叛晉. 季文子曰. 不可. 晉雖無道, 未可叛也 . 國大, 臣睦, 而邇於我. 諸侯聽焉. 未可以貳. 史佚之志有之. 曰. 非我族類, 其心必異. 楚雖大, 非吾族也. 其肯字我乎. 公乃止.

In the autumn, the duke returned from Jin, desiring to seek alliance with Chu and to rebel against Jin [because the Jin court had shown him insufficient ritual respect]. Ji Wenzi said: "Although Jin lacks the Way, it is not yet right to rebel against it. The state is large, its officials are tightly knit, and it lies close to us. The many lords hearken to it. It is not yet permissible to break off. The historian Yi records [something relevant to] this, saying: 'Not being of our clan and group, they surely possess alien hearts [i.e., have different loyalties].' Although Chu is powerful, [the ruling house of] Chu is not of the same clan [as you and I]. How could they [be expected to] love us?" So the duke abandoned his plan.

Two things seem to be happening when the tag is invoked as a predecessor of modern ethnocentrism. First, modern usage tacitly understands *zu* not as "family" or "clan" (a group of individuals of princely rank, tied together in bonds of kinship and ritual observance) but as "race" (an indeterminately sized group of individuals of various ranks, putatively stemming from common ancestors in the remote past and often sharing linguistic, cultural, or political features). The context of the only other occurrence of the compound *zulei* in the *Zuo zhuan* (Xi, 31st year, 17.9b) is one of ancestor ritual and family prerogatives. Second, the discussion-context of the phrase is obliterated. Ji Wenzi admits that the rulers of Jin have shown themselves to be "without morality" (by showing discourtesy to the visiting Lu nobles), but he argues for preserving Lu's alliance with Jin on grounds of *Realpolitik*: Jin is a large, well-staffed, well-respected neighboring state. Ji's quotation from "the records of the scribe Yi" packages the power considerations in the guise of ritual. Citation converts all this into immemorial "tradition," repeating less guilelessly Ji Wen's opportunistic turning of texts to his advantage. This said, the cultural, ritual, and perhaps ethnic distinctiveness of Chu is often asserted or implied in classical texts (the *Shi jing* 詩經, for one, contains poems from almost every geographical area of the Zhou confederation but Chu), and interethnic warfare seems to have preceded the state system of the classical period. But states describing themselves as "Hua-Xia" 華夏 ("Chinese") made pacts with the "states of a different surname" according to their needs in the contemporary balance of power. I thank E. Bruce Brooks and Yuri Pines for illuminating the background of this passage.

13. On the "otherness" of Chinese pasts to Chinese presents, see the quotations on the basin of Tang at the beginning of Chapter 8; on the problems of constructing a transhistorical "subject" (race, nation, linguistic community, or other) to explain or compensate for current events, see above, pp. 89–90. A thoughtful, wide-ranging study of the relations between nation formation and historical linearism is Duara, *Rescuing History from the Nation*. R. Bin Wong's study of Chinese economic and po-

litical history over the last millennium, *China Transformed*, argues against Smithian and Marxian presumptions that reduce all possible courses of historical development to a small set of paths leading necessarily to the same destination. Generalizing from these studies, one sees how the Chinese past can become alien to members of the Chinese present; the relevant difference is, of course, not ethnic but conceptual.

14. Hegel, *Philosophie der Geschichte*, in idem, *Werke*, 12: 116, and *Lectures on the Philosophy of World History*, p. 152. Important forerunners of Hegel include Herder (*Ideen zu einer allgmeinen Menschengeschichte*) and Kant ("Idee zu einer allgemeinen Geschichte in weltbürgerlicher Absicht," in Kant, *Werke*, 9: 33–50; in English, "Idea for a Universal History with a Cosmopolitan Purpose," in Kant, *Political Writings*, pp. 41–53).

15. Hegel, *Philosophie der Geschichte*, in idem, *Werke*, 12: 96–97, and *Lectures on History*, p. 128 (the translator of the English version renders *Auslegung* as "expression"). For a critique of such spiritual geography, see March, *The Idea of China*.

16. Fabian, *Time and the Other*, p. 31. Fabian does not mention Levinas's essay "Le Temps et l'Autre," published in 1947, a preliminary sketch of *Totality and Infinity*; it is probably a case of parallel discovery.

17. Fabian, *Time and the Other*, p. 144.

18. Ibid., pp. 157, 159.

19. On Lattimore's career, see Newman, *Owen Lattimore and the 'Loss' of China*. On Fairbank's, see Evans, *John Fairbank and the American Understanding of Modern China*; and Fairbank, *Chinabound*.

20. On the reformist agenda shared by certain foreigners and Chinese, mainly housed in Shanghai's International Settlements, in the late 1800s, see Zhu Weizheng, "Daodu" 導讀 (Introduction), in Long Yingtai and Zhu Weizheng, *Wei wancheng de geming*, esp. pp. 57–63.

21. On the "end point of mankind's ideological evolution and the universalization of Western liberal democracy as the final form of human government" that was predicted to follow the disappearance of Soviet Russia, see Fukuyama's much-discussed article, "The End of History?"

22. Zhong Shuhe, *Zou xiang shijie congshu*.

23. "China is a much richer country than any part of Europe, and the difference between the price of subsistence in China and in Europe is very great. Rice in China is much cheaper than wheat is anywhere in Europe. . . . The difference between the money price of labour in China and in Europe is still greater than that between the money price of subsistence: because the real recompense of labour is higher in Europe than in China, the greater part of Europe being *in an improving state*, while China seems to be *standing still*" (Smith, *The Wealth of Nations* [1776], 1: 173; italics added). On the low cost of living in early nineteenth-century China as a bar to China's reception of foreign goods, see Karl Marx, "Trade with China" (1859), in

Marx and Engels, *Collected Works*, 16: 536–39. On the causal paths leading to these perceived economic states, see Wong, *China Transformed*.

24. On Weber's efforts to understand rationality both as a universal human endowment and as the outcome of specific European historical developments, see Schluchter, *The Rise of Western Rationalism*. I thank Chang Hao for reminding me of the rich analyses of "Oriental rationalism" in Weber and his successors. I apologize for failing to give that tradition an adequate consideration here.

25. Leibniz, "Preface to *Novissima Sinica*," in Cook and Rosemont, *Leibniz: Writings on China*, p. 45.

26. Jakobson, "Closing Statement: Linguistics and Poetics," in Sebeok, *Style in Language*, p. 358.

27. Fabian, *Time and the Other*, pp. 159, 158. For a specific example of such "cotemporality" (with a foregrounded reference to Hegel), see Marx, "Revolution in China and in Europe" (1853), in Marx and Engels, *Collected Works*, 12: 93–100.

28. Marx, *Pre-Capitalist Economic Formations*, pp. 97–98; see more particularly "The Future Results of the British Rule in India" (1853), in Marx and Engels, *Collected Works*, 12: 217–22.

29. For the classic formulation of the world-system approach to history, see Wallerstein, *The Modern World-System*. Others have proposed that a Euro-Asian world-system of closely integrated trade networks, subject to fluctuating political and biological conditions, was a reality from a far earlier date. For contributions to this approach emphasizing a closer and longer-term consideration of Asia, see Abu-Lughod, *Before European Hegemony*; Frank and Gills, *The World System*; Frank, *The Centrality of Central Asia*; and idem, *ReOrient*.

30. On the global "axial age," see Jaspers, *Origin and Goal of History*; and Eisenstadt, *Origins and Diversity of Axial Age Civilizations*.

31. For a perspective on contemporary history read in the light of the axial age inheritance, see Eisenstadt, *Fundamentalism, Sectarianism, and Revolution*.

32. Ferrari, *La Chine et l'Europe*, pp. 129–31. Ferrari first developed his theory of historical action and reaction from his study of medieval Italian city-states (*Histoire des révolutions d'Italie*, 1858). On Ferrari's development as a historian, see Bonnaud, *Y a-t-il des tournants historiques mondiaux?* Schemes of periodization are prominent in the tacit assumptions of Ferrari's time: see, e.g., Marx, "Introduction to the Critique of Hegel's Philosophy of Right," in idem, *Early Writings*, p. 245.

33. Ferrari, *La Chine et l'Europe*, p. 132.

34. For the revival of Hegelian eschatology in the climate of the late 1980s, see Fukuyama, "The End of History?" For an ethnographic argument paralleling Ferrari's, see Devereux and Loeb, "Antagonistic Acculturation."

35. Ferrari, *La Chine et l'Europe*, p. 118.

36. Ibid., pp. 374–75. Ferrari's acquaintance with Chinese history derives mainly from the same *Histoire générale de la Chine* (de Mailla's eighteenth-century translation of Zhu Xi's 朱熹 *Zizhi tongjian gangmu* 資治通鑑綱目) that later inspired Ezra Pound.

37. Ibid., pp. 536–37.

38. Ibid., p. 598.

39. The *Yi jing* 易經, or *Book of Changes*, provided the pattern for a massive work by Shao Yong 邵庸 (Kangjie 康節, 1011–77), *Huangji jingshi shu* 皇極經世書, correlating dates and tendencies in Chinese history with cyclical arrangements of the *Yi jing*'s hexagram patterns. On Shao's and related Chinese theories of ineluctable rise and fall, see Jullien, *La Propension des choses*, chap. 9.

40. Ferrari, *La Chine et l'Europe*, pp. 589–90.

41. See, e.g., Voltaire, "Entretiens Chinois," in idem, *Oeuvres complètes*, 27: 19–34.

42. These examples obviously relate more closely to American and European— but especially American—projects of improvement within China, than to alterations within Euro-American ideas or ways of living. Wells Williams sounds a note often repeated, writing in 1883 that the Chinese "have had up to this time no opportunity of learning many things with which they are now rapidly becoming acquainted. [But] the time is speedily passing away when the people of the Flowery Land can fairly be classed among uncivilized nations. . . . Soon railroads, telegraphs, and manufactures will be introduced, and these must be followed by whatsoever may conduce to enlightening the millions of the people of China in every department of religious, political, and domestic life" (*The Middle Kingdom*, 1: xv). Williams's picture of a one-way traffic of "reform" would hold, *mutatis mutandis*, for most popular accounts of beneficial exchanges between China and Euro-America. On the creation of such images and narratives, see Isaacs, *Scratches on Our Minds* (especially pt. II, chap. 5, "The Wards," on the theme of "how much they [the Chinese] needed to be helped and how receptive they were to the help," p. 130); Spence, *To Change China*; and Jespersen, *American Images of China*. Jespersen's main focus is, appropriately, Henry Luce and Time, Inc.

43. "Hybrid" is perhaps an unfortunate term, as it implies acceptance and fusion. For a searching analysis of anti-colonial nationalism in India, see Chatterjee, *Nationalist Thought and the Colonial World*. On the hybrid culture generated by modernization under external stimuli, see Leo Ou-fan Lee, *Shanghai Modern*; and the essays in Barlow, *Formations of Colonial Modernity in East Asia*; for the massive evidence of vocabulary change left behind by the process, see Lydia Liu, *Translingual Practice*. On the implications of the fact that capitalism and modernization reached China as an aggregate, suspended in colonialism, see Brook, "Capitalism and the Writing of History in Modern China," in Brook and Blue, eds., *China and Historical Capitalism*, pp. 110–57. Of course, China was never "colonized" in a formal sense: that is, it never

submitted as a whole to the rule of any foreign nation. The powerlessness of successive Chinese governments, extraterritoriality, foreign economic dominance, and the colonization or semi-colonization of bits of Chinese territory are the elements of Chinese experience of imperialism. That these facts add up to a China "not-colonized" is a sophism well castigated in Tani Barlow's essay "~~Colonialism's~~ Career in Postwar China Studies," pp. 373–411, in idem, *Formations of Colonial Modernity*. Rather than permitting scholars to quibble self-interestedly, the unclear distinction ought to open up further questions of distinction: what was the importance of foreign meddling at different times, in different regions, to observers occupying different social positions? How did the evolving concept of the nation-state affect Chinese observers' sense of their misfortune? How did colonial actions transform activities among Chinese? Was China between 1842 and 1949 perhaps not a poor example of colonialism but the first case of neo-colonialism?—all of which require patient inquiry rather than yes/no answers.

44. See, e.g., Teng and Fairbank, *China's Response to the West*; and Jerome Chen, *China and the West*. This insistent topic of the 1950s and 1960s eventually generated its dialectical opposite, the "China-centered approach." See Paul Cohen, *Discovering History in China*, for a sharp critique of theories of "response" and "modernization" and his proposal for a "China-centered history of China."

45. See Leo Ou-fan Lee, "In Search of Modernity," for an examination of this duality. Paul Cohen (*Discovering History in China*, pp. 94–95), speaking of historiography in words that can be applied to lived history, too, points out that "'modernity' is a fundamentally closed concept, with a built-in picture of historical process that is tightly unilinear and highly teleological in nature. . . . Only with open models of change, accompanied by open-ended questions, will historians be able to form a more empirically sensitive picture of the recent Chinese past." On Chinese debates about old and new circa 1920, see Huters, "Origins of Modern Chinese Spirituality."

46. Williams, *The Middle Kingdom*, 2: 74. Italics added.

47. See Duara, *Rescuing History from the Nation*; and p. 124 in this book. For a general discussion of the imputation of a history-less mode of existence to peoples outside the European area of influence, see Lévi-Strauss, *La Pensée sauvage*, pp. 324–57.

48. My comments here refer strictly to the anxious style of cultural comparison, strongly marked by Social Darwinism, best represented by Chen Duxiu 陳獨秀 and Du Yaquan 杜亞泉. For substantiation, see Chen Song, *Wu si qianhou dongxi wenhua wenti*, esp. pp. 3–137 (entitled "The Polemics of Same/Different, Superior/Inferior Regarding Eastern and Western Cultures"). On the role played in the historiography of civilizations by the commonplace of "the scientific West and the intuitive East," see Hart, "On the Problem of Chinese Science." On the perennial quality of such arguments, see Zhang Longxi, *Zou chu wenhua de fengbi quan*, pp. 4–11. For a pioneering comparative philosophical argument that does not assume antagonism

between East and West, see Tang Junyi, *Zhongxi zhexue sixiang zhi bijiao lunwenji* (original edition 1941). Tang Junyi's investigations should have been more fully taken into account in the present chapter, but the volume and complexity of his writings compel me to put that off for another project.

49. Northrop taught at Yale for many years; George H. W. Bush, visiting the Yale campus in 1989, recalled "Professor Northrop's lectures on logic." Northrop's interest in interdisciplinary and international perspectives earned him a place at the 1940s Macy Foundation conferences from which emerged the cybernetic program for biological and social science (he was not, however, an influential participant). *The Meeting of East and West* is dedicated to James Jesus Angleton, Northrop's student and early member of the Central Intelligence Agency. Suffice it to say that the work is very much part of its time, which is still in many respects our time. Fabian (*Time and the Other*, pp. 144–46) briefly discusses Northrop as "theoretician and apologist of a new international order." On the perception of Asia by policymakers in the early years of this new order, see Immanuel Wallerstein, "The Unintended Consequences of Cold War Area Studies," in Chomsky et al., *The Cold War and the University*, pp. 195–231. On Angleton as representative of the mixture of academics and espionage, see Saunders, *The Cultural Cold War*, pp. 238–49.

50. Northrop, *The Meeting of East and West*, p. 375.

51. Ibid., p. 328.

52. Ibid., p. 318.

53. Ibid. p. 459. The plan bears comparison with that proposed in Tang Junyi's *Zhonghua renwen yu dangjin shijie* (1975), in which the recovery of traditional Chinese humanism and an aesthetic participation in nature are described as the one possible path for the preservation of the human race.

54. See Northrop, *The Meeting of East and West*, pp. 470–72:

> *That conception of good conduct and the good state is the correct one, valid for everybody, which rests upon the conception of man and nature as determined by immediate apprehension with respect to the aesthetic component and by the methods of natural science with respect to the theoretic component.* . . . Before any individual or people can put forward one line of conduct as good or divine in the name of morality or religion, he or they must specify a positivistic aesthetic item immediately apprehendable and common to everybody, or a scientifically inferred and verified theoretical item in the nature of man or the universe which anyone can confirm; and show that without the conduct in question either the aesthetic or the theoretic factor in man's true nature would be falsely denied and not given expression with the precise degree of relativity or constancy which its character justifies.

55. Nakamura, *Ways of Thinking of Eastern Peoples*, pp. xvii–xx. I have intentionally

removed the association of these characteristics with particular "peoples," the better to show the generic "Orientalness" of the negations.

56. "The absolutely contrary contrary." The phrase is Emmanuel Levinas's, applied to "the feminine" as an instance of irreducible otherness; see *Le Temps et l'autre*, p. 77; "Time and the Other," in Hand, *The Levinas Reader*, p. 48.

57. Williams, *Shame and Necessity*, pp. 166–67.

58. Hall and Ames, *Thinking from the Han*, p. 9. Italics added.

59. See Hu Shi, *The Development of the Logical Method in Ancient China*; Liang Qichao, *Mo jing jiaoshi*; Feng Youlan, *A History of Chinese Philosophy*; Alfred Forke, *Lun Heng*; Graham, *Later Mohist Logic*.

60. Hall and Ames, *Thinking from the Han*, pp. 114, 134, 204, 212.

61. Jullien, *Un Sage est sans idée*, p. 9.

62. Ibid., p. 161.

63. See for example Jullien, *La Propension des choses*, p. 17: "In contrast to the development of Western thought, the originality of the Chinese consists in their lack of concern for any *telos*, any final destination of things, and in their attempts to interpret reality solely in its own terms, from the exclusive point of view of the internal logic of the processes taking place. . . . Let us recognize . . . that this way of thinking has an extreme underlying coherence, even if it has never emphasized conceptual formalization, and let us use it to decode from the outside our own intellectual history."

64. Jullien, *La Propension des choses*, pp. 228, 195, 188, 196, 214, 223, 231, 236, 238. For a rapid but typical linking of several of these predicates, see Jullien, *Un Sage est sans idée*, pp. 97–101, and for a similar table, ibid., pp. 122–23.

65. Jullien wisely warns us against "two common mistakes: naïve assimilationism, according to which everything can be directly transposed from one culture to another, and equally simplistic comparativism, which proceeds as though ready-made, suitable frameworks existed for apprehending the differences in question" (*The Propensity of Things*, p. 20). Indeed; Jullien deserves credit for this call for an unsimplistic comparativism.

66. One indication: Jullien's recent book *Un Sage est sans idée*, professing to speak of "the other of philosophy," fulfils the promise in the most traditional fashion, by contrasting the search for and love of wisdom (philosophy, the West) with its possession (sagehood, China). Indeed, that is the "other" that philosophy has had all along and can appeal to from any point on its network—as Socrates did when disavowing the predicate "wise," as the Arabs did when defining *falasafiya* in relation to theology, or as Alexandre Kojève did when he stopped lecturing on Hegel and became a negotiator for the GATT (see Kojève, "Les philosophes ne m'intéressent pas"). No one has to go to China to learn about *this* other. For further claims of the same type, see Jullien and Marchaisse, *Penser d'un dehors*.

67. Jullien, *La Propension des choses*, p. 214. One is reminded of the story about the astronomer Laplace, who, when asked by Napoleon why his *Mécanique céleste* (1802) said nothing about the Deity, answered, "Sire, I had no need of that hypothesis."

68. See the quotation from S. Wells Williams on p. 103 above for a sample of the missionary attitude, to which the insistence on the *uniqueness* of the West and its institutions, and the need to defend them, now often reads like a parallel (see, e.g., Huntington, *The Clash of Civilizations*). Is the West unique? If it is, the main thing Westerners have to learn from outsiders is how best to appreciate their own uniqueness. I wonder, though, whether uniqueness arguments are falsifiable or lead rather into the realm of the inexpressible (the incomparable). For a critical examination of the "Big Ditch" or "Great Divide" said to separate the West from its others, see Hart, "On the Problem of Chinese Science."

69. Jullien, *La Propension des choses*, pp. 223–24. Italics added, save for "genealogy."

70. Saussure (*Cours*, p. 162) gave this theory its classic expression in the words: "In all these cases, then, we encounter, not pre-existing *ideas* but *values* emanating from the system. When we say that these values correspond to concepts, it is understood that these concepts are purely differential, defined not positively by their content but negatively by their rapports with the other terms of the system. Their most exact characteristic is that of being what the others are not."

71. The phrase is Bateson's (*Steps to an Ecology of Mind*, p. 453) but stems from Shannon and Weaver (*The Mathematical Theory of Information*).

72. For a summation of the evidence, see Brooks, "Alexandrian Motifs in Chinese Texts."

73. James Peck's 1969 essay "The Roots of Rhetoric: The Professional Ideology of America's China Watchers" faulted American scholars for systematically ignoring or discounting the reality of imperialism; see Paul Cohen, *Discovering History in China*, pp. 98–111, on the essay and responses to it. See Bruce Cumings, *Parallax Visions*, pp. 124–27, for a model case of a North Korean "inscrutability" engendered simply by leaving out the U.S. stimuli to which the North Koreans were reacting.

74. Structuralism's dream was to transform knowledge in the human sciences into just such a "phonological" articulation. Here success is a sure sign of failure.

75. Teggart, *Rome and China*, pp. 236–39. For a rare recent discussion of Teggart, see Frank and Gills, *The World System*, pp. 11–13, 167–71. A recent attempt to provide the area between the empires with a comprehensive international history is Christian, *A History of Russia, Central Asia, and Mongolia*; on why a distinctive history of the region is necessary and neglected, see pp. ibid., 430–31. For the reconstruction of a Bronze Age "world-system" of exchange centered in Bactria and the Oxus Valley but extending to Mesopotamia and East Asia, see Gills and Frank, "The Cumulation of Accumulation," in Frank and Gills, *The World System*, pp. 81–114. On the dynamics of encroachment and involvement linking Chinese and their pastoralist

neighbors (the "barbarians") from an early date, see Barfield, *The Perilous Frontier*; and Nicola di Cosmo, "The Northern Frontier in Pre-Imperial China," in Loewe and Shaughnessy, *The Cambridge History of Ancient China*, pp. 885–966.

76. Teggart, *Rome and China*, p. x.

77. Ibid., p. viii; romanization modified and Chinese characters added.

78. Ibid., pp. ix, 240.

79. Ibid., pp. 241–42.

80. The spread of bubonic plague, too, is a consequence of Central Asian "world-system" building: see McNeill, *Plagues and Peoples*.

81. Teggart, *Rome and China*, pp. 225–35.

82. The chapters of the present book are submitted as possible cases in point.

Chapter 6

1. Since contemporary Chinese literature is not my main interest, I have relied on friends and colleagues for guidance through the dense bibliography on these questions. My biggest debts are to Zhang Kuan (who knew that I would disagree with him but generously supplied information nonetheless) and Wang Youqin 王友琴. Errors of fact and judgment can securely be lodged with me. Useful and variegated discussions of the topics treated here can be found in Rey Chow, *Writing Diaspora*, pp. 75–98; Liu Kang and Tang Xiaobing, *Politics, Ideology and Literary Discourse in Modern China*, particularly Tang Xiaobing, "The Function of New Theory" (pp. 278–99); Sheldon Lu, "Art, Culture, and Cultural Criticism in Post-New China"; Zhang Longxi, "Postmodernism and the Return of the Native," *Mighty Opposites*, pp. 184–212; Zhang Xudong, "On Some Motifs in the Cultural Discussion," in idem, *Chinese Modernism in the Era of Reforms*, pp. 71–99; and Henry Y. H. Zhao, "Post-Isms and Chinese New Conservatism."

2. A. C. Graham, discussing Derrida and Laozi in his historical work *Disputers of the Tao*, opened up this topic, on which see below, pp. 170–71.

3. All right, say I in response to my conscience, the argument is really that the two things differ *in the same respects* from the third thing; I maintain, however, that to say so leaves out a great many significant and deeply asymmetrical "respects" (such as the fact that the two "postmodernities" emerged from different needs and situations, and the later of the two came into existence under some degree of influence from the earlier); see chaps. 5 and 7, *infra*.

4. See, as an early report on this contrast, I. A. Richards's observations. Richards holds that "except for Mo Di 墨翟 and his followers, there seems to have been no problem of knowledge for Chinese thought," and speaks further of "the very absence in Mencius of anything which we can recognize as a theory of knowledge . . . his reflections are nearly all about action, its sources and control . . . his arguments are less demonstrations than instructions" (*Mencius on the Mind*, pp. 5, 61). More generally:

"Pragmatism, as a doctrine that ideas are tools to be judged by the work they do . . . is a fairly modern doctrine [in the West], a result of reflection and a result still treated in most European schools of philosophy as a heresy to be refuted. In Chinese philosophy, in its main streams at least, there seems to have been no Problem of Truth as such. Reflection has not exercised itself on the question 'What do we mean when we say that a statement is true?' The place of this problem has been taken by an assumption, so initial as to be unformulated, that what is true is what had better be accepted" (*Basic in Teaching,* pp. 24–25).

5. On the question of "colonial" or "translated" modernity, see above, Chapter 5, pp. 224–25*n*43.

6. On the identification, see Huters, "Origins of Modern Chinese Spirituality."

7. Two detailed and fascinating sociological studies are Gu, "Cultural Intellectuals"; and Lynch, *After the Propaganda State.*

8. An allusion to the title of the best-seller by Song Qiang, *Zhongguo keyi shuo 'bu'* (China can say no). For a brief but thoughtful discussion of such nay-saying, see Rey Chow, "Can One Say No to China?" See also Xu Ben, "Zai tan Zhongguo 'houxue' de zhengzhixing he lishi yishi," p. 135.

9. The ship *Yinhe* was pursued and boarded on the open seas by an American naval vessel, under the suspicion (unfounded) that it was carrying arms to Iraq.

10. Xu Jilin, "Wenhua rentong de kunjing," pp. 100–101.

11. Xu Jilin, "Bi pipan geng zhongyao de shi lijie," p. 131.

12. Rey Chow ("Can One Say No to China?" p. 151) names "the scarcely touched issues of *China's relation to those whom it deems politically and culturally subordinate.* I am referring, specifically, to *Tibet, Taiwan and Hong Kong*" (italics in original). Scarcely touched, indeed, because to discuss them would be to infringe the Four Great Principles that currently mark the boundaries of permitted debate within China.

13. Zheng Min, "Shijimo de huigu," p. 5; page numbers are henceforth cited in the text. In a study of Zheng's essay and the furore it aroused, Michelle Yeh surmises that the low estimate of modern Chinese poetry cited by Zheng mainly refers to Stephen Owen's review of Bei Dao, "The Anxiety of Global Influence: What Is World Poetry?" (see Michelle Yeh, "Chinese Postmodernism and the Cultural Politics of Modern Chinese Poetry," in Wen-hsin Yeh, *Cross-Cultural Readings of Chineseness,* pp. 100–127). On the issue of recognition, see Larson and Kraus, "China's Writers, the Nobel Prize, and the International Politics of Literature." The award of that prize to Gao Xingjian 高行健 in October 2000 set off a particularly shrill round of commentary in the "national insult" vein.

14. This picture of literary modernization closely corresponds to what Jean Paulhan called "Terror": the attempt to extirpate rhetoric and style in the name of an always elusive authenticity (see *Les Fleurs de Tarbes*).

15. The notion that the Chinese language (unlike Western languages) approximates, particularly in its poetic form, the processes of the unconscious is not, however, a misreading by Zheng of her sources: see Kristeva, *Des Chinoises*, pp. 60–62.

16. Zhao Yiheng, "'Houxue' yu Zhongguo xin baoshouzhuyi." The "conservative" source mentioned by Zhao is Lin Yü-sheng, *The Crisis of Chinese Consciousness*. Lin's analysis of "totalistic antitraditionalism" bears some resemblance to Zheng's description of May Fourth "binarism."

17. Zhao Yiheng, "'Houxue' yu Zhongguo xin baoshouzhuyi," pp. 5, 9–10.

18. Zheng Min, "Wenhua, zhengzhi, yuyan sanzhe guanxi de wojian," pp. 120, 124.

19. Zhang Kuan, "Zai tan Sayide," p. 9. In a characteristically condensed argument, Zhang states that "the cruelty of the German Fascists toward the Jewish people was the necessary consequence of the logic of Enlightenment discourse" and blames the May Fourth intellectuals for drinking at the same sources ("Wenhua xinzhimin de keng" 文化新殖民的可能 [The possibility of cultural neocolonialism], *Tianya*, Feb. 1996; cited in Lei Yi, "Shenme shi baoshou? Shei fandui minzhu?" p. 123). Zhang's reflection on the murder of the European Jews may be drawn from an unsubtle reading of Horkheimer and Adorno's *Dialectic of Enlightenment* (p. xiii; see also pp. 12–13, 180–181), a study of the "self-destruction . . . [and] the destructive aspect of progress." For another discussion of the historical problems surrounding colonialism and its relation to modernization, see Li Tuo, "Rang zhenglun fuchu haimian."

20. For examples of this narrative economy, see Zhang Kuan, "Oumeiren yanzhong de 'fei wo zulei.'"

21. Zhang, "Zai tan Sayide," p. 14. Most of Zhang's points have been adopted by Wang Ning ("Orientalism Versus Occidentalism?" pp. 59–61), who argues in this 1997 article that

the "Orient" does not merely refer to a geographical location. It also has a very profound political and cultural connotation. This "Orient" has become the "other" of the West, from which perspective Western people reflect its world. Thus it is absolutely necessary for them to have such an "other." . . . [But] Said's "Orient" or "Orientalism" also has its ideological and cultural limitations. . . . the "Western" idea or culture that we usually deal with in effect refers to the ideology or cultural concepts based on the bourgeois value standard prevailing in Europe and America, while those *contrary to them* are normally regarded as the "Oriental" concepts. It is on the basis of this striking difference in ideology and culture that *the East and the West* were in a state of opposition during the cold-war period after World War II . . . [and now, after the Cold War,] according to Samuel Huntington, "the great divisions among humankind and the dominating source of conflict will be cultural." (Italics added)

The sublime illogic of this bit of loose writing (Oriental concepts *the contrary to* Western concepts?) lays bare the truth about the invidious practice of cultural profiling. Like Zhang, Wang then cites Huntington on "the Confucian-Islamic connection that has emerged to challenge Western interests, values and power" and adds that Huntington, in a move beyond Edward Said, "has here correctly grasped the two origins of Oriental cultures, the Arab countries and China."

22. Cited in Zhang, "Zai tan Sayide," p. 12. I have been unable to find the exact passage to which Zhang refers. On the hollowness of rights talk as engaged in by governments, particularly the U.S. government, see Chomsky, *Powers and Prospects*. Zhang Longxi (*Mighty Opposites*, pp. 211–12) points out the inappropriateness of enlisting Said's name for nationalistic, race-based, or fundamentalist causes; see also Said, *Orientalism*, p. 322. For Said's own assessment of Huntington, see Said, "The Clash of Definitions," in idem, *Reflections on Exile and Other Essays*, pp. 569–90.

23. Huntington's *Clash of Civilizations* was an instant success in China. "His view that America should look on China as its greatest future antagonist was exciting to a number of Chinese, because it restored to the long-downtrodden Chinese the proud feeling of belonging to a great imperial power. Many people are still drawing advances on this pride, although I cannot see what it contributes to China's present progress" (Chen Xiaoming, "'Wenhua minzu zhuyi' de xingqi," p. 37). For a commentary on the exploitation of "alien threats" in the political environments of the various Pacific Rim countries, see Bruce Cumings, "The World Shakes China," in idem, *Parallax Visions*, pp. 151–71.

24. Cf. below, Chapter 7, pp. 159–60.

25. Foucault, "L'éthique du souci de soi comme pratique de la liberté," in idem, *Dits et écrits*, 4: 727–28.

26. Foucault, "Discourse on Power" (interview with Duccio Trombadori), in Foucault, *Remarks on Marx*, p. 171.

27. I have been unable to learn anything more about Wei Da.

28. Some of Wei Jingsheng's writings have been collected as *The Courage to Stand Alone*.

29. On the international trafficking in rights language, see Rey Chow, *Writing Diaspora*, pp. 178–79.

30. *Beijing ribao*, Apr. 2, 1979; *Zhongguo qingnian bao*, n.d., cited in Wei Da, *Gaige qianhou*, pp. 328–29. Identifying human rights activism and the Opium War is a cliché of long-standing: see, e.g., Deng Xiaoping, "First Priority Should Always Be Given to National Sovereignty and Security" (Dec. 1, 1985), in idem, *Selected Works*, 3: 335–37.

31. I borrow the phrase from Ngugi wa Thiong'o's *Decolonizing the Mind*.

32. Liu Kang, "Quanqiuhua yu Zhongguo xiandaihua," p. 145. The phrase "filling in the gaps" is ambiguous here—supplanting the Chinese Communist Party or

supporting it?—and not, I think, just a matter of style. On the round-trip journey of certain concepts from Chinese Maoism to French leftists and then back to Chinese post-ism, see Guo Jian, "Resisting Modernity." On the smooth transition from "communist" to "capitalist" ideology in China and the nature of the appeal of market economy there, see Billeter, *Chine trios fois muette*.

33. Zhao Yiheng, "Moxuyou xiansheng yu tamen de watiao," p. 137.

34. Xu Ben, "Zai tan Zhongguo 'houxue' de zhengzhixing he lishi yishi," p. 135. See also Zhang Longxi, *Mighty Opposites*, pp. 203–6, 210–11, on the question of collusion with the "official line." For a history of international human-rights negotiations in ultra-pragmatic detail, see Kent, *China, the United Nations, and Human Rights*. For a questioning of the language of rights talk, tied to a critique of economic globalization, see Farmer, *Pathologies of Power*, esp. chap. 9, "Rethinking Health and Human Rights."

35. In the early 1980s, according to Chen Xiaoming ("'Wenhua minzu zhuyi' de xingqi," p. 35), a number of scholars began to "have second thoughts about Western studies and return to national studies" (*fanxing xixue, huidao guoxue* 反省西學, 回到 國學). The term *guoxue* (national studies) first appeared in the late nineteenth century as a calque of the Japanese term *kokugaku* (itself based on a reference to the *Zhou li* 周禮: see Lydia Liu, *Translingual Practice*, p. 326). It bears the connotation of a celebratory account of national culture, often in the frame of a story about essential national characteristics (*guocui/kokusui* 國粹). The reported idols of the New National Studies or Post-National Studies are Zhang Taiyan 章太炎, Chen Yinque 陳 寅恪, Wang Guowei 王國維, Gu Jiegang 顧頡剛, Liang Shuming 梁漱溟, Zhang Junli 張君勱, Du Yaquan 杜亞泉 (Chen Xiaoming, "'Wenhua minzu zhuyi' de xingqi," p. 36)—anticolonialists to a man, but hardly cultural chauvinists. For similar lists, see Xu Ben, "Zai tan Zhongguo 'houxue' de zhengzhixing he lishi yishi," p. 136; and Zhang Yiwu, "Chanshi 'Zhongguo' de jiaolü," p. 134. On "national essence" thinking in the 1930s and 40s, see Lydia Liu, *Translingual Practice*, pp. 239–56.

36. Zhang Kuan, "Jiaqiang dui xifang zhuliu huayu de pipan" 加強對西方主流 話語的批判 (To strengthen the critique of mainstream Western discourse), *Zuojia bao*, June 24, 1995; cited in Lei Yi, "Shenme shi baoshou? Shei fandui minzhu?" p. 124.

37. Zhang Yiwu, "Chanshi 'Zhongguo' de jiaolü," p. 128.

38. Zhang Yiwu, "Hou xin shiqi wenhua: tiaozhan yu jiyu," pp. 112–14.

39. The dilemma of giving aid to the official doctrine is discussed in Lu Jia, "'Fan xifang zhuyi' huichao," pp. 17–18.

40. Zhang Yiwu, "'Xiandaixing' de zhongjie—yige wufa huibi de keti," p. 106.

41. Cited in He Jiadong, "Houxiandai pai ruhe nuoyong xiandaixing huayu," p. 74.

42. Zhang Yiwu, "Chanshi 'Zhongguo' de jiaolü," p. 128. The "overseas scholars" surely include Perry Link (*Evening Chats in Beijing*) and Merle Goldman (*Sowing the Seeds of Democracy in China*).

43. Zhang Yiwu, "Chanshi 'Zhongguo' de jiaolü," p. 129.

44. A widespread device, incidentally.

45. Zhang Yiwu, "Chanshi 'Zhongguo' de jiaolü," pp. 134–35. On "the Other of the Other," see also idem, "'Xiandaixing' de zhongjie," p. 109.

46. Barthes, *Mythologies*, pp. 144–46.

47. Zhang Yiwu, "Zai shuo 'Chanshi Zhongguo' de jiaolü," p. 125.

48. Zhang Yiwu, "Miandui quanqiuhua de tiaozhan," p. 140.

49. Zhang Yiwu, "'Xiandaixing' de zhongjie," p. 104. For a critical discussion of Zhang's essay, see Lei Yi, "Shenme shi baoshou? Shei fandui minzhu?"

50. Zhang Yiwu, "'Xiandaixing' de zhongjie," p. 105.

51. Ibid., p. 106.

52. Ibid., p. 107. Humanism (*rendao zhuyi* 人道主義, *renwen zhuyi* 人文主義) is a concept with a complex past in modern China, although its story is usually ignored by the "posthumanists." See Leo Ou-fan Lee, "Some Notes on 'Culture,' 'Humanism' and the 'Humanities.'"

53. Zhang Yiwu, "'Xiandaixing' de zhongjie," p. 108.

54. Zhang Yiwu, "Hou xin shiqi wenhua: tiaozhan yu jiyu," p. 112.

55. Zhang Yiwu, "'Xiandaixing' de zhongjie," p. 109.

56. One might compare the juggling of the franchise in "cultural democracy" with the "new democracy" and "new democratic culture" promoted by Mao Zedong. "The Chinese democratic republic that we are about to establish can only be a democratic republic of the joint dictatorship (聯合專政) of all anti-imperialist, antifeudal people under the leadership of the proletariat." "In China, we have a culture of imperialism, which reflects the imperialist countries' political and economic domination or semi-domination of China. Apart from those cultural institutions that act directly on behalf of imperialism in China, there are a few shameless Chinese who exalt that culture. Any culture that is tinged with a slave mentality belongs to this category. . . . If we don't abolish this sort of thing, our new culture can never be established" ("Xin minzhu zhuyi lun" 新民主主義論 [On new democracy; 1940], in Mao Zedong, *Xuanji*, pp. 635, 655). By pointing out the similarity of the two projects, I do not mean to classify Zhang Yiwu as a "Maoist"; rather, my intent is to call attention to the respectability, in some circles, of conceiving "democracy" to be an outcome, rather than a process, and of designing allegedly "democratic" policies in order to impose those outcomes. The design of "functional constituencies" and rosters of "national minorities" as quasi-representative institutions is a fairly transparent case of outcome direction.

57. As a matter of fact, the "Goddess" did not have the features of a "white woman." See *Tiananmen yijiubajiu*, pp. 155–56, for photos. The statue made, of course, a direct reference to an American national symbol, but ethnic phenotypes are not reliable indicators of political regimes.

58. Zhang Yiwu, "Chanshi 'Zhongguo' de jiaolü," p. 131, citing Rey Chow, "Violence in the Other Country," p. 27. An expanded version of Chow's article appears in Mohanty et al., *Third World Women and the Politics of Feminism*, pp. 81–100. For a critique, see Zhang Longxi, *Mighty Opposites*, pp. 151–83, 210. Chow's article shares with Zhang Yiwu the anger against the "intrusion" of foreign news media in the Chinese physical and political scene; she compares it to the colonial-period privilege of "extraterritoriality" granted to foreign residents in China. Like Zhang, too, Chow sees the term "democracy" as a stalking-horse for Western hegemony. "Don't they [the Chinese students of 1989] know what atrocities have been committed in the name of liberty and democracy?" she asks, citing as example "the way Margaret Thatcher's British government is treating the citizens of Hong Kong," namely, denying them any form of United Kingdom citizenship. Surely no definition of "democracy" is broad enough to contain the British government's behavior towards the resident of Hong Kong. (Proof again, if any were necessary, that democracy does not automatically come as a side effect of nationality.) I am unable to see in what way Chow's warnings address the problems of political and mediatic representation that concern most Chinese advocates of democratization.

Of the two, the allegation of "extraterritoriality" is the more serious tactical error. Certainly the privileges granted by a weak Qing court to the Great Powers, including the invulnerability of foreign citizens under Chinese law, were of the sort that any anticolonialist must repudiate. But in the context of 1989, when the legitimation of sovereignty was (ultimately) at issue, to categorize foreign news media as agents of a revived colonialism simply endorsed the Chinese Communist Party's claim to do what it liked with the land, the airwaves, and the people of China.

59. For a classic set of examples, see de Man, "Excuses," in idem, *Allegories of Reading*, pp. 278–301.

60. For the book that begat British cultural studies, see Hoggart, *The Uses of Literacy*. I am indebted to Virginia Farmer for discussions of the Winn-Dixie "culture." On what one might call, exasperatedly, "the culture of 'culture,'" see Hartman, *The Fateful Question of Culture*. For the background of the Chinese Communist Party's obsession with the direction of culture, see Mao Zedong, "Zai Yan'an wenyi zuotanhui shang de jianghua" 在延安文藝座談會上的講話 (Talks at the Yan'an forum on literature and art; 1942), in idem, *Xuanji*, pp. 804–35; trans. in Denton, *Modern Chinese Literary Thought*, pp. 458–84.

61. The leadership of May Fourth intellectuals in China corresponds to the moments of "departure" and "manoeuvre" in Chatterjee's analysis of the development of national consciousness; the moment of "arrival" is also the moment at which the elite lose control of the mass movement for which they had previously served as trailblazers. See Chatterjee, *Nationalist Thought and the Colonial World*, pp. 50–52, 151–53.

62. Zhang Yiwu, "'Xiandaixing' de zhongjie," p. 108. See also Liu Kang, "Quan-qiuhua yu Zhongguo xiandaihua," one of the few articles on post-ism to consider economic transformation. Chen Xiaoming, in *Shengyu de xiangxiang*, acknowledges that literature has lost its guiding function in a postideological era dominated by im-ages, where "peace and development" are the only items on the social agenda; that is his explanation for the formalism and political disengagement of the writers of the "post-new period."

63. 1919: May Fourth Movement, in response to China's envoys having accepted the unequal terms of the Treaty of Versailles. 1956–57: the "Hundred Flowers" campaign encouraging the expression of divergent views, followed quickly by the "Anti-Rightist" movement punishing as traitors those who had expressed such views. 1976: demonstrations after the funeral of Zhou Enlai 周恩來. 1979: Democracy Wall protests. 1989: demonstrations in support of political reform after the death of Hu Yaobang 胡耀邦. All five events brought to the surface dissatisfaction among educated people with the policies of the governments of the time; all five altered the course of "elite culture" and its relation to politics and mass culture. For a shrewd sociological analysis of intellectual nonconformity in 1989, see Gu, "Chinese Intellec-tuals and Politics," pp. 422–26.

64. For a study of how such exoticisms may operate in media representations and public discourse, see above, chap. 2; and also Chen Xiaomei, *Occidentalism*, esp. chap. 1.

65. "Whose motive?" might be a good place to begin, since the bombing is said to have resulted from the Central Intelligence Agency's one contribution to target se-lection in the campaign (see Eric Schmitt, "In a Fatal Error, CIA Picked a Bombing Target Only Once: The Chinese Embassy," *New York Times*, July 23, 1999). But the CIA's taking responsibility for the attack (as voiced by its director, George Tenet, in the House of Representatives on July 22), however satisfying to those who suspect that agency of running an independent foreign policy, may veil a decision taken by NATO on military grounds. For the position that "NATO deliberately bombed the Chinese embassy . . . after discovering it was being used to transmit Yugoslav army communications," see John Sweeney, Jens Holsoe, and Ed Vulliamy, "NATO Bombed Chinese Deliberately," *The Observer* (London), Oct. 17, 1999. Understanda-bly, neither the U.S. nor the Chinese government has confirmed this version of events.

66. See *People's Daily Online*, May 20, 1999: "Wangyou de shengyin: Wang Yizhou boshi da wangyou wen, xia" 網友的聲音, 王逸舟博士答網友問, 下 (Voices of our Internet community: Dr. Wang Yizhou responds to readers' questions, pt. 2), avail-able as of May 2000 at http://www.peopledaily.com.cn/item/wysy/199905/14/wyz-wy.html.

67. Wang Yizhou is actually unfair to Huntington (*The Clash of Civilizations*, pp. 310–12), whose recommendation is that the "Western civilizational bloc" avoid intervention in the affairs of the other blocs and seek merely to restrain the military potential of the "Islamic" and "Sinic" worlds. In objecting to "peaceful evolution toward democracy," Wang Yizhou is reprising an oft-repeated formula of Mao resurrected by Deng, equating peaceful evolution with surrender: see Deng, "Bourgeois Liberalism Means Taking the Capitalist Road," in idem, *Selected Works*, 3: 129–30.

The phrase "peaceful evolution" derives from the "containment" strategy toward the Soviet Union first abumbrated by George F. Kennan. Kennan saw the capitalist and socialist blocs reaching a state of "peaceful coexistence" (see his "Long Telegram" of Feb. 22, 1946, in *Foreign Relations of the United States, 1946*, pp. 696–709), a phrase that John Foster Dulles amended to "promoting peaceful evolution towards democracy" in speeches of 1957–58. According to Bo Yibo, a member of the Central Committee since 1945, Mao took "peaceful evolution" to be a serious policy threat, a "much more deceptive tactic" on the part of the United States to "corrupt" China. Dread of "peaceful evolution" arguably led Mao to his various radicalizing Rubicons: the break with the Soviet Union, the persecution of "revisionists" and "Rightists" within China, and finally the Cultural Revolution. (See Zhai Qiang, "Mao Zedong and Dulles's 'Peaceful Evolution' Strategy.") In light of Deng's constant reference to the Cultural Revolution and the "ten years of turmoil" as arguments against broadening freedoms of the press and the person, the renewal of a policy of refusing "peaceful evolution" is somewhat ironic.

68. See p. 231*n*21.

69. Apart from racial enmity, wartime emergencies have accounted for most of the notable infringements of citizens' rights in the United States—think of the "Red scares," the internment of Japanese-Americans, or the acquiescence of journalists and citizens in military management of news during our more recent conflicts far from home. Some of these shifts toward authoritarian rule have receded only partially with the coming of peace (every war has left the Executive Branch and security agencies stronger in the domestic balance of power). "Democracy American-style" would be far from a bad thing in almost any country, but it is not the definitive example of the species, nor is it automatically realized in "America."

70. For perspectives on the history of the term *quanli* 權利 (rights) since its introduction into Chinese in the nineteenth century, see Lydia Liu, "Legislating the Universal," pp. 148–52; and Jin Guantao and Liu Qingfeng, *Zhongguo xiandai sixiang de qiyuan*, pp. 369–80.

71. The phrase "civil rights" might be less confusing than "human rights," resting as it does on a more modest philosophical basis. The crucial distinction of vocabulary is that human rights tend to be ascribed to individuals *qua* humans and civic rights to individuals *qua* citizens. Universalism doesn't go away—the exemplary

civil-rights question is "Why should there be distinctions of privilege among citizens?"—but the historical specificity of particular constitutions is preserved well into the normative part of the discussion. "Civil rights" should not be confused with Jürgen Habermas's account of the emergence of modernity from an autonomous "public sphere" or "civil society," a theory much discussed in the Chinese 1980s but vitiated by its use to stand for another thing China "lacked." There is already an ample literature on the question of the existence (or not) of civil society in China, and an even larger one on the question of "Asian civilizations and human rights." On the former, see "Symposium: 'Public Sphere' / 'Civil Society' in China," *Modern China* 19 (1993); on the latter, see de Bary and Tu, eds., *Confucianism and Human Rights*; Sen, *Development as Freedom*; Anthony Yu, "Enduring Change"; Peerenboom, "The Limits of Irony"; Rorty, "Response to Peerenboom."

72. Tang Xiaobing, "The Function of New Theory," p. 292.

73. For a discussion and example of these dualities, see Wang Hui, "Fenqi jiujing zai nali?" pp. 114–16.

74. To single out a few newspaper stories from the summer of 2000, as China prepares its entry to the WTO—A "people's army" can indeed be sent to rescue members of the "people's government" under siege by infuriated farmers facing arbitrary levies and confiscations. Agencies of the "people's government" can operate profitable forced-labor camps, siphon earnings overseas, and recruit children to manufacture, for a pittance, the plastic toys that other, more fortunate children will joyfully extricate from their fast-food meals. A form of privatization (sometimes known as graft) has already taken place on a massive scale and without the imposition of an international banking regimen or structural-adjustment program. Under such conditions, the language of left and right is more than useless, it is positively harmful as long as its appearance of proposing "alternatives" fails to point out the undemocratic course taken by the "opening to the world market." If it sounds paradoxical or incoherent, in China today, to advocate both the reduction of inequality and the dismantling of the one-party state, that simply points to a problem in the language in which political demands are framed; or more properly, to a condition surrounding that language, namely the Party's startling success in imposing itself as the one unmoving pole of all political discourse. It has what amounts to hegemony over the conditions of capital investment and is simultaneously the supposed alternative to capitalism: an enviable market position, as the financial analysts would put it.

75. The parallel press conference conducted by Clinton and Jiang Zemin often took the following form: Clinton would urge the adoption of a right or principle; Jiang replied that the right in question already existed in China but followed this reassurance with a reminder that the inappropriate exercise of any right would be punished by the law. The talk of rights began to seem more and more a hollow exercise without the fashioning of means of recourse—these being beyond the concerns

of the diplomatic script. Thus the "rule of law" became the object of a particularly delicate and sustained (and no doubt intentional) misunderstanding: for one audience, "the rule of law" denoted legal protections, particularly as regards property, and for the other audience, "the rule of law" meant the obligation to obey the laws, whatever they might be. "Pluralism," indeed.

Chapter 7

EPIGRAPH: Cavafy, "Perimenontas tous varvarous" (Waiting for the barbarians) in *Poiēmata* (Poems), 1: 107–8. I have taken liberties with the nouns.

1. "Structure, Sign and Play in the Discourse of the Human Sciences," in Macksey and Donato, eds., *The Structuralist Controversy*, pp. 247–72. On the changing intellectual landscape of the years 1966 to 1971, see Macksey and Donato's preface to the second edition of their collection, "The Space Between," pp. ix–xiii.

2. As the following discussion will show, "deconstruction" is here taken rather broadly to indicate the forms of philosophy and human science that followed from the dissolution of the founding distinctions of structuralism (recounted in an exemplary manner in Derrida, *De la grammatologie*, pp. 145–202). For reasons of economy and also to distinguish the argument presented here from an exegetical one (expounding what "deconstruction" has already said about "China"), I present only a few readings from a vast corpus. For explicit discussions of "The East" as a poststructuralist locus, see Spivak, "Introduction" to Derrida, *Of Grammatology*; Spivak, *Critique of Postcolonial Reason*, pp. 279–81, 429–30; Zhang Longxi, *The Tao and the Logos*; Lowe, *Critical Terrains*; Hayot, "Chinese Dreams"; and Bush, "Ideographies." On the formation of a "Maoist" discourse in *Tel Quel* between 1970 and 1974, see Forest, *Histoire de "Tel Quel."* Hal Foster (*The Return of the Real*, p. 217) has recently inventoried the "epistemological exoticisms" of poststructuralism, as a prologue to questioning the identity of "difference" and "opposition" (I thank Ka-Fai Yau for alerting me to this reference).

3. Foucault, *Les Mots et les choses*, p. 10. My translation, as are all other translations in this essay unless otherwise marked. This passage follows on the quotation of Borges's imaginary "Chinese encyclopedia," a reference to which scholars of East-West literary relations seem unerringly drawn; see Zhang Longxi, *The Tao and the Logos*, p. 1.

4. Sollers, *Sur le matérialisme*, pp. 40–41 (the essay from which this passage is drawn was first presented to a *Tel Quel* workshop in May 1969). Barthes reprints the passage, interrupting his own text, at the center of *L'Empire des signes*. Is the figure of the Chinese calligrapher in some way the national anthem, the secret handshake of *Tel Quel*?

5. Jakobson, "Two Aspects of Language and Two Types of Linguistic Disturbances," in Jakobson and Halle, *Fundamentals of Language*, pp. 55–82. A few lines above the passage about Chinese spatiality, Foucault alludes to the cognitive distur-

bances observed in aphasics: "It is said that certain aphasics are unable to give a coherent ordering to hanks of multicolored wool laid out for them on a tabletop." These "hanks of multicolored wool" might be the texture of reality before it has been ordered into the warp and woof of paradigm and syntagm. For the imagery of paradigmatic verticality versus syntagmatic horizontality, see Lacan, "L'instance de la lettre dans l'inconscient ou la raison depuis Freud" (1957), in idem, *Ecrits*, p. 503.

6. Derrida, *De la grammatologie*, p. 119.

7. Ibid., pp. 15, 30.

8. Dante Alighieri, *Paradiso*, xxxiii, 85–90; trans. Singleton, *The Divine Comedy* 3.1: 377.

9. Gilles Deleuze's interest in China and its nomad neighbors has been generously reciprocated by scholars of East Asia; see, e.g., Dean and Massumi, *First and Last Emperors*; Connery, *The Empire of the Text*.

10. One of Sollers's collaborators reflects thirty years after: "The question of the winding-down of metaphysics and, therefore, the question concerning philosophy are what centrally occupied us then and it is in this perspective that, one day, the interest of Sollers and *Tel Quel* for the 'cultural revolution' and more generally Daoist China will have to be understood" (Pleynet, *Le plus court chemin*, p. 120).

11. On analogy and allegory, see above, pp. 31–32.

12. Zhang Longxi, *Mighty Opposites*, pp. 179–82.

13. The classic statement on this point is Gayatri Chakravorty Spivak's ("Introduction," *Of Grammatology*, p. lxxxii) questioning of "almost . . . a reverse ethnocentrism" in Derrida's association of logocentrism with the West alone: "the East is never seriously studied or deconstructed in the Derridean text."

14. As I have said in previous chapters, I can only understand "the West" as a boundary-marking concept produced by situations of contrast like this one. Likewise, when I say "we," I am vaguely invoking a set of people who are trying to interpret Chinese realities in a language like my own; I do not assume that this is a strongly coherent, self-similar, or structured community.

15. Marx, "Concerning Feuerbach," in idem, *Early Writings*, p. 423.

16. Saussure, *Cours*, pp. 151, 162, 166.

17. Ibid., pp. 164, 162, 168. On the history of the question of phonetic substance after Saussure and the related question whether the being of the phoneme is simply identical to the sum of its distinctive features, see S. Anderson, *Phonology in the Twentieth Century*.

18. I believe the repetition of this point is warranted, given the frequency of the sophism. Differential perception is (like common sense) well distributed. Marco Polo, in his report of his many years spent in China, never mentions the logographic writing system, which has struck many people as certain evidence that he never was in China: how could any Westerner spend twenty years there and not notice *that*?

But if he was illiterate in Italian (as he could very well have been and still done his trading effectively), then there would be nothing in Chinese writing to catch his attention, whether or not he ever learned to manipulate it. For him, then, there would be no relevant difference to point out.

19. See de Man, *Allegories of Reading*. On the definition of "text" ("the contradictory interference of the grammatical with the figural field"), see ibid., pp. 268–70. Note also that "deconstructive readings can point out the unwarranted identifications achieved by substitution, but they are powerless to prevent their recurrence even in their own discourse, and to uncross, so to speak, the aberrant exchanges that have taken place" (p. 242). Point taken.

20. "It is easy to observe the rigorous selectiveness and recurrence of the sounds used" in glossolalia, says Jakobson of one sample from Russia; they bear a determinate relation to sounds of the speakers' normal language in that they are loaded with "prevalently alien traits." The utterances may lack meaning, but their drive for order is clear; see Jakobson and Waugh, *The Sound Shape of Language*, pp. 211–15.

21. I take the term from David Porter (conversation, May 2000). Sinography, "writing about China," is not sinology—the latter assumes some expert knowledge, whereas sinographic texts can be revealing even in their naïveté. In a further extension, sinography is to sinology as historiography is to history, a textual examination of the bases of judgment.

22. In order to loosen the grasp of a purely historical inquest, then, I will have to make the methodological gesture of defining deconstruction vaguely and abstractly enough to allow for a critique, in the spirit of deconstruction, of ideas that have emerged from the space opened up by Jacques Derrida's work.

What do I mean by "deconstruction"? Too much specificity at the outset will cramp the investigation (it is startling how often the comparative conversation stumbles on the question of aperture). My Barefoot Doctor's definition, not very sophisticated but at least not crucially dependent on a complex infrastructure, holds that deconstruction is what happens when you set the wording of a text against its content, the means of persuasion against the persuasive agenda. This is a procedural definition only. Various consequences tend to follow from the choice and exploitation of a "difficult inch" (Wallace Stevens), but to define deconstruction by its predicted outcomes—by what it "achieves"—makes, I think, too optimistic and ideological a claim (does it always achieve them? must it always achieve them?).

23. A beautiful relic of this alignment is the anthology edited by Hollier, *Panorama des sciences humaines*. For the various partings of the ways in the years after 1968, see Forest, *Histoire de "Tel Quel,"* pp. 387–413 (Sollers-Derrida divergence, 1972); Foucault, "Mon corps, ce papier, ce feu" and "Réponse à Derrida," in idem, *Dits et écrits*, 2: 245–68, 281–95 (Foucault-Derrida divergence, 1972); Derrida, "Le Facteur de la vérité," in idem, *La Carte postale*, pp. 441–524 (Derrida-Lacan divergence, 1975).

24. Kristeva, *Des Chinoises,* pp. 59–62.

25. Kristeva, "Remarques sur le 'Mode de production asiatique,'" in idem, ed., *La Traversée des signes,* pp. 37–38.

26. See Freud, *Die Traumdeutung,* pp. 234–35: "The content of dreams appears to us as a translation of dream thoughts into another mode of expression . . . Dream content is given in a picture writing, the signs of which are to be translated one by one into the language of dream thoughts. One would often be led into error by trying to read these signs for their pictorial quality, rather than for their signifying relations."

27. Kristeva, *Des Chinoises,* pp. 62–63 ("happening" in English in the original).

28. Jullien, *La Propension des choses.* On the issue of screen memories, see Freud, "From the History of an Infantile Neurosis": Freud posits the view "that scenes from early infancy, such as are bought up by an exhaustive analysis of neuroses . . . are not reproductions of real occurrences, to which it is possible to ascribe an influence over the course of the patient's later life. . . . It considers them rather as products of the imagination, which find their instigation in mature life [and] which are intended to serve as some kind of symbolic representation of real wishes and interests" (in Gardiner, *The Wolf-Man by the Wolf-Man,* p. 192).

29. Kristeva, *Des Chinoises,* p. 63. The "separation" of modes of thought alludes to the narrator's feeling of uneasiness and alienness ("I feel like a monkey, a Martian, an other") under the gaze of a group of idle peasants (pp. 13–14), a bit of ethnographical frankness for which Kristeva has been scolded. For a thoughtful discussion of the "crossing of borders" of which her own work on China is an example, see her *La Révolution du langage poétique,* pp. 542–43.

30. On the rejection of Hegelian historical necessity, see Kristeva, *La Traversée des signes,* p. 23.

31. Sollers, *Sur le matérialisme,* p. 93.

32. Ibid., p. 40.

33. Ibid., p. 36.

34. Kristeva, *Des Chinoises,* pp. 220–21.

35. Barthes, "Alors, la Chine?" (*Le Monde,* May 24, 1974), in idem, *Œuvres complètes,* 3: 32–34. "Happenings" in English in the original. The *Tel Quel* mission to China (Roland Barthes, Julia Kristeva, Marcelin Pleynet, Philippe Sollers, and François Wahl) is chronicled in Kristeva's novel *Les Samouraïs.*

36. Kristeva, *Des Chinoises,* p. 228.

37. Foucault, "Sur la justice populaire: débat avec les maos" (1972), in idem, *Dits et écrits,* 2: 340–46. His interlocutors were Benny Lévy and André Glucksmann, representing the Gauche prolétarienne. The episode is discussed in Guo Jian, "Wen'ge sichao yu 'houxue'"; and idem, "Resisting Modernity."

38. Reckert, *Beyond Chrysanthemums*, p. 235. Among early reviewers of the book's English edition, Edmund White (*New York Times Review of Books*, Dec. 5, 1982, p. 34) was most sympathetic to its vision of "utopia." Lisa Lowe (*Critical Terrains*, pp. 188, 173) argues that Kristeva and Barthes perpetuated a certain Orientalist tradition: "The constructions of China . . . conjured the oriental Other not as a colonized space but as a desired position outside western politics, ideology, and signification." Yet they "continued to figure the Orient as Other," says Lowe, as "a fetish in both the psychoanalytic sense of being a fixation . . . and the sense of being reified, as Marx writes of the fetishism of commodities in capitalist society." On the Orient as one phase of a utopian strategy running through Barthes's career, see Célestin, *From Cannibals to Radicals*, pp. 134–74.

39. Barthes, *Empire of Signs*, p. 3; *L'Empire des signes*, p. 9 and in idem, *Œuvres complètes*, 2: 747. The original 1970 Skira publication includes color photographs and some juxtapositions of text and image that are no longer perceptible in the Howard and *Œuvres complètes* versions.

40. Compare Oscar Wilde: "In fact the whole of Japan is a pure invention. There is no such country, there are no such people. . . . The Japanese people are, as I have said, simply a mode of style, an exquisite fancy of art" ("Intentions," in Ellmann, *The Artist as Critic*, p. 315).

41. See Barthes, *Œuvres complètes*, 2: 1002–3, 1013–15, 1022–25. An important predecessor text is Baudelaire's ("De l'essence du rire," *Œuvres complètes*, 2: 525–543) description of "le comique absolu," a form of humor that achieves sublimity by breaking with all realism. One of Baudelaire's examples is English pantomime theatre.

42. My translation. Barthes, *L'Empire des signes*, p. 60, and in *Œuvres complètes*, 2: 778; for a different translation, see idem, *Empire of Signs*, p. 45.

43. My translation again. Barthes, *L'Empire des signes*, pp. 139–43, and in *Œuvres complètes*, 2: 818; for a different translation, see idem, *Empire of Signs*, pp. 103–6.

44. See passages added in the second edition of Kojève, *Introduction à la lecture de Hegel*, pp. 436–37.

45. Barthes, "Réponses," *Tel Quel* 47 (1971); in idem, *Œuvres complètes*, 2: 1319. For a perceptive analysis of the stages of Barthes's career, see Knight, *Barthes and Utopia*.

46. Barthes, "Sur S/Z et L'Empire des Signes," *Les Lettres françaises*, May 20, 1970 (interview with Raymond Bellour), in idem, *Œuvres complètes*, 2: 1015.

47. Barthes, "Entretien" (interview with Stephen Heath), in idem, *Œuvres complètes*, 2: 1294.

48. *The Empire of Signs* contains repeated allusions to Brecht. For the reforming semiology of Barthes's Brechtian period, see "Les Maladies du costume de théâtre" and "Les Tâches de la critique brechtienne," in idem, *Œuvres complètes*, 1: 1205–11, 1227–30. De Man (*Romanticism and Contemporary Criticism*, p. 169), somewhat

counterintuitively, reads *Mythologies* as discovering the already Brechtian nature of bourgeois reality-theater.

49. Barthes, *Empire of Signs*, pp. 61–62; for the original, see idem, *L'Empire des signes*, pp. 82–84, and in *Œuvres complètes*, 2: 789–90.

50. Barthes, Howard, *Empire of Signs*, p. 73; for the original, see idem, *L'Empire des signes*, p. 97, and in *Œuvres complètes*, 2: 797.

51. Kristeva, *La Révolution du langage poétique*, p. 529. The immediate subject is "seditious" Wagnerism in the French Third Republic.

52. On the history of the term, see Dahlhaus, *The Idea of Absolute Music*.

53. The plays presented in Moscow had been shortened and revised with an emphasis on dance and visual splendor by Mei in consultation with Zhang Pengchun 張彭春, a Columbia Ph.D. and professor of English at Nankai University, who also served as theatrical advisor and interpreter on the company's tours of America and the USSR. (Zhang subsequently served as a delegate to the United Nations commission that drafted the 1948 Universal Declaration of Human Rights; for his contributions to the discussions resulting in that document, see Glendon, *A World Made New*.) On Mei's Moscow tour and its aftereffects, see Mei Lanfang, *Wo de dianying shenghuo*, pp. 46–56; Mei Shaowu, *Wo de fuqin Mei Lanfang*, pp. 126–59; Cheng Pei-kai, "Mei Lanfang dui shijie jutan de wenhua chongji"; and idem, "Mei Lanfang zai Mosike." Mei Lanfang's memoirs (*Wutai shenghuo sishi nian*) go only as far as the early 1920s; a draft of some subsequent chapters was destroyed by Red Guards in 1966. Lars Kleberg's 1981 play "The Sorcerer's Apprentices" offers an imaginative reconstruction of the Moscow discussions around Mei Lanfang; nonetheless, a Chinese version of Kleberg's play in *Zhonghua xiqu* 中華戲曲 7 (1988) is presented as historical source material. For the play, see Kleberg, *Starfall*, pp. 23–49. Kleberg subsequently discovered and published an actual transcript of the discussions: see Kleberg, "Zhiv'ye impul'sy iskusstva."

54. Brecht, *Gesammelte Werke*, 7: 619–31; for a translation, see idem, *Brecht on Theatre*, pp. 91–99.

55. Brecht, *Brecht on Theatre*, pp. 91–95; for the original, see idem, *Gesammelte Werke*, pp. 620–26.

56. Brecht, *Brecht on Theatre*, p. 94; for the original, see idem, *Gesammelte Werke*, p. 623 ("beschränkt er sich darauf, die darzustellende Figur lediglich zu zitieren"). Cf. Barthes: "As Brecht observed, [Eastern drama] is dominated by *citation*, the pinch of writing, the fragment of code"; "What is our face if not a *citation?*"; "in his facial expressions, the actor does not play at being a woman, does not copy her, but merely signifies her" (translations mine; *L'Empire des signes*, pp. 75, 121, 122, and in *Œuvres complètes*, 2: 786, 808, 809; cf. *Empire of Signs*, pp. 53, 90, 89).

57. Well, almost nobody: see Wittfogel, *Oriental Despotism*.

58. Sergei Tretiakov, "A Great Mastery," *Pravda*, March 23, 1935; trans. Marilena Ruscica.

59. Andrei Tairov, comments in Kleberg, "Zhiv'ye impul'sy iskusstva," p. 135; trans. Marilena Ruscica.

60. Sergei Eisenstein, comments in Kleberg, "Zhiv'ye impul'sy iskusstva," pp. 136–37; trans. Marilena Ruscica. The invocation of "realism" (i.e., socialist realism) is merely strategic, since the aim of Eisenstein's remarks is to reject the current Zhdanovian guidelines for "realistic" plotting and representation.

61. See Banu, "Mei Lan-fang."

62. Ibid., p. 146; Cheng Pei-kai, "Mei Lanfang dui shijie jutan de wenhua chongji," pp. 42–43. Note, in Eisenstein's remarks, the poignant reference to "*our* time, the time of silent cinema"—the 1920s.

63. See Cheng Pei-kai, "Mei Lanfang dui shijie jutan de wenhua chongji," pp. 33–35.

64. On the status of "reading" in China, see above, Chapter 3, p. 207n30. Those who look for hieroglyphic tableaux will be happy to know that *nian* analyzes into two graphs, one meaning "now" and the other "mind," thus "reading" = "to hold present to the mind." A formula for the metaphysics of presence, in sum.

65. Graham, *Disputers of the Tao*, p. 227. Graham seems to draw on Wesling, "Methodological Implications of the Philosophy of Jacques Derrida," which in turn makes much use of Derrida's interview volume *Positions*.

66. The historiography of the "postmetaphysical" era owes much to Heidegger. See, e.g., Heidegger, "Der Spruch des Anaximander," in idem, *Holzwege*, pp. 296–343. For an argument connecting Nietzsche, Heidegger, and "the postmodern" generally, see Vattimo, "Nihilism and the Post-Modern in Philosophy," in idem, *The End of Modernity*, pp. 164–81.

67. On the comparative investigations of François Jullien, see above, Chapter 5, pp. 109–14.

68. Graham, *Disputers of the Tao*, p. 228.

69. Hall and Ames, *Thinking from the Han*, pp. 114, 134, 204. The description of Chinese thinking as one that dispenses with "substance" or "ontology" (*benti* 本體, *bentilun* 本體論) and achieves "inward transcendence" through art and contemplation, rather than "outward transcendence" in an alternate spiritual world, stems from Tang Junyi and Mou Zongsan (see, e.g., Tang's *Zhongxi zhexue sixiang zhi bijiao lunwenji*, pp. 140–66, reprising an essay first published in 1936; or Mou's *Zhongguo zhexue de tezhi*).

70. Hall and Ames, *Thinking from the Han*, p. 150. Cf. I. A. Richards, as cited on pp. 229–30n4 above.

71. For one of the most influential formulations of a difference between shame cultures and guilt cultures, see Benedict, *The Chrysanthemum and the Sword*, pp. 222–26. But the anthropology of "face" was an old chestnut of China Hand writing,

useful for framing Chinese habits as the inadequate equivalents of more complete and adult Western ones. (On travelers' dismissive descriptions of Chinese ritual as mindless outward behavior, see Zito, *Of Body and Brush*, pp. 51–57.) Benedict's cultural-relativist presentation, adopted by Dodds for the analysis of classical texts in *The Greeks and the Irrational*, surfaces again in Bernard Williams's recourse in *Shame and Necessity* to Homer and Aeschylus for the posing of ethical questions.

72. Hall and Ames, *Thinking from the Han*, pp. 271, 279, 281. For another analysis of the mainly non-verbal language of ritual, see Pocock, "Ritual, Language, Power: An Essay on the Apparent Political Meanings of Ancient Chinese Philosophy" in idem, *Politics, Language and Time*, pp. 42–79.

73. Hall and Ames, *Democracy of the Dead*, pp. 194–96.

74. The crucial articulations in this picture of rights, particularly the transformation of an "is" (the state is unable to compel conscience) into an "ought" (it should therefore leave conscience alone), derive from Spinoza; see *A Theologico-Political Treatise*, chap. 20, pp. 263–64.

75. Hall and Ames, *Democracy of the Dead*, p. 234.

76. Hall and Ames, *Thinking from the Han*, p. 271.

77. Ibid., p. 281.

78. Hall and Ames, *Democracy of the Dead*, p. 234.

79. Hall and Ames, *Thinking from the Han*, p. 279; very nearly the same language appears in their *Democracy of the Dead*, pp. 206–8.

80. Hall and Ames, *Democracy of the Dead*, p. 198. The ancient texts on ritual are less evasive than the postmodern communitarians. The ancients acknowledged with grudging respect that something already in people drives them to disobey—that people are not adequately constituted by their social relations but need to be controlled by them. The "Fang ji" 坊記 section of the *Records of Ritual* (*Li ji*), for example, begins: "The Master said this: 'The Way of a Gentleman, may it not be compared to the raising of dikes (*fang* 坊)? He hems in (*fang*) that wherein the populace is lacking [i.e., "benevolence" and "loyalty," according to the commentary]. He may make great efforts in the raising of dikes, but the people will still leap over them. So he uses ritual to hem in virtue, punishments to hem in excess, commands to hem in desires'" (*Li ji*, "Fang ji," 51/7b–8a.) All social institutions (in the "Fang ji" at least) are there to reinforce "dikes," categorical separators and hydraulic blockages. This happens whether or not the people are directly involved, since actions performed by nobles are done for show, as reminders:

> On the death of a father, three years' mourning; on the death of one's ruler, three years' mourning. This is done to show the people that there is no wavering [between the rival claims of father and ruler, or between self-interest and loyalty]. . . . While one's father and mother are alive, one may make ritual presents [to outsiders], but not of horses and carriages. This is to show the people that one does

not dare to consider one's property one's own. You may use this [exemplary be-
havior] to hem in the people, but the people will still disobey parents and show
disloyalty to rulers. (*Li ji*, 51/21b.)

The idealization by Hall and Ames of a groundless, self-generating complex of
relations omits precisely the resistance of the material on which ritual works, the
topic of the "Fang ji." The "Fang ji" shows "the people" as insufficiently schooled in
ritual: do they then have no "constitutive roles and relationships"? And yet it is to
these dubiously constituted humans that the gentleman must constantly display his
virtues. They are the audience who will judge the adequacy of his playacting. A slack
postmodernism can afford to neglect the referential and pragmatic obstacles to a
text's doing what it says it should do, but that is where the interrogation of ritual (as
a category and as a continued historical event) is most needed.

81. By "felicity" I refer to John Austin's (*How to Do Things with Words*, pp. 6–7)
observation that "performative" statements are evaluated not as true or false but as
felicitous (efficacious) or the contrary. Happy mythologies are felicitous ones.

82. Hall and Ames, *Democracy of the Dead*, p. 7. On the question of the cultural
presuppositions of human rights, see Glendon, *A World Made New*, pp. 72–78: a
group of philosophers convened by UNESCO in 1947 to seek the universal basis of
human rights legislation concluded that "consensus on foundations" was not necessary to expressing "common convictions." As Jacques Maritain humorously put it,
"we agree about the rights but on condition no one asks us why."

83. Ibid., pp. 52–56, 212. A more forthright proponent of ritual order might observe that the student representatives failed in their obligation to show due deference to their partners in harmony, the Central Committee: see the speech and attitudes of Wu'er Kaixi 吾爾開希 during his audience with Li Peng 李鵬, as recorded
in Carma Hinton's documentary *Gate of Heavenly Peace*. Hall and Ames present no
position from which one could justify the activists' "inappropriate role playing." Not
even the idea of a peaceful demonstration works in their ontology, for "the Chinese
have never recognized a severe theory/practice distinction, and have always considered not only 'saying' but 'thinking,' as well, as a kind of 'doing' . . . it is felt that the
government has a responsibility to prevent disrupting influences from damaging the
social fabric" (ibid., pp. 233–34). Hall and Ames try to turn the Cultural Revolution
to their advantage, too. They observe:

the real possibility of personal betrayal made taking other people, even family
members, into one's confidence, imprudent and sometimes dangerous. . . . This
decade of orchestrated national insanity forced Chinese persons into the mold of
self-sufficient, independent individuals. Within this Chinese experience, individuality, albeit in a skewed and aberrant form, was not a worthy ideal. Rather, it
was the consequence of repression. Liberation from this social malaise came with

the possibility of giving up the privation of privacy, to once again live shared, interdependent, and richly communal lives (ibid., p. 235).

The Cultural Revolution isolated people, and so a philosophy that brings people together will be as good as the Cultural Revolution was bad. The vague associative logic and its haphazard attempt to play a resemblance into an identity are worthy of the U.S. Senate floor. The more plausible case that the Cultural Revolution was a model of a ritual society, with an extraordinary level of "harmony" and participation in a "community defined by ritual activity" (marches, struggle sessions, "happenings," "invented games") is not remotely considered in *The Democracy of the Dead*.

84. Blackman, *Negotiating China*, pp. 51–52, 69, 71–72, 78, 58.

85. Ibid., p. 115.

86. For Hall and Ames on law, see *Democracy of the Dead*, pp. 216–20. Since all power lies with the collectivity, can the legitimacy of its actions ever be subjected to judicial testing? "Because the [PRC] constitution is primarily a compact of cooperation formulated on a premise of trust between person and community rather than a contract between potential adversaries, there are no independent provisions for the formal enforcement of claims against the state. . . . Resort to legal appeal is, by Chinese tradition, an admission of a failure to maintain communal harmony" (ibid., p. 218).

Contrast this "premise of trust" with the cross-border problems described by Ajay Kapur ("Puncturing Risk"), writing for bankers about the Chinese economy's current prospects. Kapur finds that

> an environment of capital scarcity and poor contract enforcement favors the relationship-based financial intermediation as seen in Asia, where power relationships substitute for contracts. However, this system suppresses price signals and misallocates resources. When abundant capital inflows from arm's-length investors meet this distorted system of resource allocation, it is rationally short-term in nature. These arm's-length investors have neither contracts nor local relationships as recourse—they want to keep their powder dry and the way to the exit clear. The implication—step up on transparency, contract enforcement, market-based information dissemination rather than deals in smoke-filled rooms to take advantage of the next (inevitable) wave of capital from arm's-length investors.

(I thank Charles de Trenck for providing me this study.) Bankers have their own reasons for believing what they do; here at least there is no talk of principles.

87. That rights are necessarily natural or intrinsic to the human person is by no means a universal doctrine of "Western" polities. In the early Republican era, the British constitutional model of a grant of freedoms emanating from the sovereign seemed to many Chinese thinkers preferable to the unlimited liberties retained, in the American theory, by "the people." See Price, "Constitutional Alternatives and Democracy."

88. For the classic presentation of a structural methodology based on the regulated oppositions of phonology, see Lévi-Strauss, *Anthropologie structurale*. For an indictment of structural functionalism as the ideology that applauds a system, any system, "because it functions," see Spivak, *In Other Worlds*, p. 134.

89. See Rémi Mathieu, "Postface" to Granet, *La Civilisation chinoise*, pp. 532–40.

90. Lévi-Strauss's *Les Structures élémentaires* contains an extended homage to Granet in the form of an elucidation and generalization of the "Chinese system" of marriage and kinship (see pp. 358–451).

91. Lévi-Strauss and Eribon, *De Près et de loin*, pp. 139–40, 63–64.

92. Linguistics can discover "no necessary relations at the level of vocabulary," observes Lévi-Strauss ("L'analyse structurale en linguistique et en anthropologie" [1951], in *Anthropologie structurale*, pp. 44, 57); "the error of traditional sociology, like that of traditional linguistics, is to have considered the terms, and not the relations among them." For the rejection of anecdotal, empiricist ethnography (analogous to phonetics) and the indispensable place of the zero sign in a method patterned on phonology, see Lévi-Strauss, "Introduction à l'œuvre de Marcel Mauss," esp. pp. xxxiii, xlix–li.

93. See, e.g., Derrida, *De la grammatologie*, pp. 54–55.

94. Derrida, "Le Puits et la pyramide," in idem, *Marges*, p. iii. My translation.

95. Ibid., p. 126.

96. De Man, "Sign and Symbol in Hegel's Aesthetics," in idem, *Aesthetic Ideology*, pp. 97–99.

97. Idem, p. 99.

98. Idem, p. 104.

Chapter 8

1. Legge, trans., "The Great Learning" (1861), in *The Chinese Classics*, 1: 361. Legge's note: "This fact about T'ang's bathing-tub had come down by tradition. At least, we do not now find the mention of it anywhere but here. It was customary among the ancients, as it is in China of the present day, to engrave, all about them, on the articles of their furniture, such moral aphorisms and lessons."

2. Pound, "Canto LIII" (1940), *The Cantos*, pp. 264–65.

3. Shaughnessy, *Sources of Western Zhou History*, p. 7.

4. Kircher, *China illustrata*, p. 164.

5. On the identity-building programs of Qing and subsequent governments, particularly in border regions, see Wong, *China Transformed*, pp. 166–77; Rawski, "Reenvisioning the Qing"; and Millward, *Beyond the Pass*.

6. Within China, the automatic opposition of "China" and "the world" now bears peculiar dialectical fruit, all the stranger for its implication that China is not part of "the world." (*Zhongguo yu shijie* 中國與世界 is a theme recognizable enough to have

generated multiple variants, as witness currently available book and journal titles: ancient *Zhongguo yu shijie*, seventeenth-century *Zhongguo yu shijie*, economic *Zhongguo yu shijie*, etc.)

7. By this I do not mean that literary or philosophical reading must submit to the authority of "history" as currently practiced in this (or any) country. Historians do not agree about what it is or how to talk about it. Rather, my sense is that if an existing argument gains plausibility from being phrased in a tenseless manner, one should test it by exploring temporal variations in its terms. One valuable effort to alter the conventional accounts that underlie most cultural soothsaying is the attempt to work out firm dates, segmentations, and interrelations for classical Chinese texts usually taken as self-consistent, self-contemporaneous wholes (as a consequence of their being treated as "classical," i.e., timeless). See Brooks and Brooks, *The Original Analects*, for an example of work in this vein.

8. Waldron, *The Great Wall of China*. A parallel investigation is Jensen, *Manufacturing Confucianism*. It would be a pity if these works were taken as mere positivistic exercises aimed at showing that there is "no such thing."

9. See Jakobson, *My Futurist Years*.

10. Cited in Lachterman, *The Ethics of Geometry*, p. 123. On the contradictions attending the Jesuit rendering of Euclid into Chinese, see Hart, "Translating the Untranslatable."

11. On "medical models" of philosophizing, see Nussbaum, *The Therapy of Desire*, particularly chap. 1, "Therapeutic Arguments."

Works Cited

Aarsleff, Hans. *From Locke to Saussure*. Minneapolis: University of Minnesota Press, 1982.

Abdel-Malek, Anouar. "Orientalism in Crisis." *Diogenes* 44 (1963): 102–40.

Abrams, M. H. *The Mirror and the Lamp: Romantic Theory and the Critical Tradition*. New York: Oxford University Press, 1953.

Abu-Lughod, Janet. *Before European Hegemony: The World System A.D. 1250–1350*. New York: Oxford University Press, 1989.

Agrippa, Cornelius. *De occulta philosophia*. Paris, 1567.

Albani, Piero, and Berlinghiero Buonarroti. *Dictionnaire des langues imaginaires*. Trans. Egidio Festa. Paris: Les Belles Lettres, 2001.

Albrow, Martin. *The Global Age*. Stanford: Stanford University Press, 1997.

Allen, Joseph R. *In the Voice of Others: Chinese Music Bureau Poetry*. Ann Arbor: University of Michigan, Center for Chinese Studies, 1992.

An Pingqiu 安平秋 and Zhang Peiheng 章培恒, eds. *Zhongguo jinshu daguan* 中國禁書大觀 (A survey of banned books in China). Shanghai: Shanghai wenhua, 1990.

Anderson, Benedict. *Imagined Communities: Reflections on the Origin and Spread of Nationalism*. London: Verso, 1991.

————. *The Spectre of Comparisons: Nationalism, Southeast Asia and the World*. New York: Verso, 1998.

Anderson, Stephen R. *Phonology in the Twentieth Century: Theories of Rules and Theories of Representations*. Chicago: University of Chicago Press, 1985.

Appadurai, Arjun. "Disjuncture and Difference in the Global Cultural Economy." *Public Culture* 2.2 (1990): 1–24.

Arendt, Hannah. *The Origins of Totalitarianism*. 2d ed. New York: Harcourt Brace Jovanovich, 1979.

Aristotle. *The Complete Works of Aristotle*. 2 vols. Ed. Jonathan Barnes. Princeton: Princeton University Press, 1985.

Austin, John. *How to Do Things with Words*. Ed. J. O. Urmson and Maria Sbisà. Cambridge, Mass.: Harvard University Press, 1962.

Bacon, Francis. *Of the Advancement of Learning*. 1605. Vol. 3 of *The Works of Francis Bacon*, ed. James Spedding, Robert Ellis, and Douglas Heath. London: Longmans, 1872.

Banu, Georges. "Mei Lan-fang: procès et utopie de la scène occidentale." *Revue d'esthétique* n.s. 5 (1983): 133–48. Trans. by Ella L. Wiswell and June V. Gibson as "Mei Lanfang: A Case Against and a Model for the Occidental Stage." *Asian Theater Journal* 3.2 (1986): 153–78.

Barfield, Thomas J. *The Perilous Frontier: Nomadic Empires and China*. Oxford: Blackwell, 1989.

Barlow, Tani E., ed. *Formations of Colonial Modernity in East Asia*. Durham, N.C.: Duke University Press, 1997.

Barthes, Roland. *L'Empire des signes*. Geneva: Skira, 1970. Trans. by Richard Howard as *Empire of Signs*. New York: Hill and Wang, 1982.

———. *Mythologies*. 1957; 2d ed., Paris: Seuil, 1970.

———. *Œuvres complètes*. Paris: Seuil, 1994.

Batchelor, Robert. "The European Aristocratic Imaginary and the Eastern Paradise: Europe, Islam and China, 1100–1780." Ph.D. diss., University of California, Los Angeles, 1999.

Bateson, Gregory. *Steps to an Ecology of Mind*. New York: Ballantine Books, 1972.

Baudelaire, Charles. *Œuvres complètes*. 2 vols. Ed. Claude Pichois. Paris: Gallimard, 1976.

Beck, Cave. *The Universal Character, by which all the Nations in the World may understand one anothers Conceptions, Reading out of Common Writing their own Mother Tongue . . . .* London, 1657.

Becker, Hans-Joachim. *Die frühe Nietzsche-Rezeption in Japan, 1893–1903*. Wiesbaden: Harrassowitz, 1983.

Benedict, Ruth. *The Chrysanthemum and the Sword: Patterns of Japanese Culture*. New York: Houghton Mifflin, 1947.

Benfey, Theodor. *Geschichte der Sprachwissenschaft und orientalischen Philologie in Deutschland*. Munich: Cotta, 1869.

Benjamin, Walter. *Gesammelte Schriften*. Ed. Rolf Tiedemann and Hermann Schweppenhäuser. Frankfurt am Main: Suhrkamp, 1980.

———. *Illuminations*. Trans. Harry Zohn. New York: Harcourt, Brace & World, 1968.

Berman, Antoine. *L'Epreuve de l'étranger*. Paris: Gallimard, 1984.

Bernal, Martin. *Black Athena*, vol. I. New Brunswick, N.J.: Rutgers University Press, 1987.

Biagioli, Mario. *Galileo, Courtier*. Chicago: University of Chicago Press, 1993.

Billeter, Jean-François. *Chine trois fois muette*. Paris: Allia, 2000.

———. *Li Zhi, philosophe maudit*. Paris: Droz, 1979.

Billings, Timothy. "Visible Cities: The Heterotopic Utopia of China in Early Modern European Writing." *Genre* 30 (1997): 105–34.

Blackman, Carolyn. *Negotiating China: Case Studies and Strategies.* St. Leonards, Australia: Allen & Unwin, 1997.

Blackmur, R. P. *Form and Value in Modern Poetry.* Garden City, N.Y.: Doubleday, 1956.

Bolton, Kingsley. "Language and Hybridization: Pidgin Tales from the China Coast." *Interventions* 2 (2000): 35–52.

Boltz, William G. *The Origin and Early Development of the Chinese Writing System.* American Oriental Series, vol. 78. New Haven: American Oriental Society, 1994.

Bonnaud, Robert. *Y a-t-il des tournants historiques mondiaux? La Chine, l'Europe et Ferrari.* Paris: Kimé, 1992.

Boodberg, Peter A. *Selected Works of Peter A. Boodberg.* Ed. Alvin P. Cohen. Berkeley: University of California Press, 1979.

Boone, Elizabeth Hill, and Walter D. Mignolo, eds. *Writing Without Words: Alternative Literacies in Mesoamerica and the Andes.* Durham, N.C.: Duke University Press, 1994.

Bopp, Franz. *Über das Conjugationssystem der Sanskrit-Sprache.* Frankfurt: Andreäische Buchhandlung, 1816.

Brecht, Bertolt. *Brecht on Theatre: The Development of an Aesthetic.* Ed. and trans. John Willett. New York: Hill and Wang, 1964.

———. *Gesammelte Werke.* 8 vols. Frankfurt am Main: Suhrkamp, 1967.

Brokaw, Cynthia. "Commercial Publishing in Late Imperial China: The Zou and Ma Family Businesses of Sibao, Fujian." *Late Imperial China* 17 (1996): 49–92.

———. *The Ledgers of Merit and Demerit: Social Change and Moral Order in Late Imperial China.* Princeton: Princeton University Press, 1991.

Brook, Timothy. "Censorship in Eighteenth-Century China: A View from the Book Trade." *Canadian Journal of History / Annales Canadiennes d'Histoire* 22 (1988): 177–96.

Brook, Timothy, and Gregory Blue, eds. *China and Historical Capitalism: Genealogies of Sinological Knowledge.* Cambridge, Eng.: Cambridge University Press, 1999.

Brooks, E. Bruce. "Alexandrian Motifs in Chinese Texts." *Sino-Platonic Papers* 96. Philadelphia: Sino-Platonic Papers, 1999.

Brooks, E. Bruce, and A. Taeko Brooks. *The Original Analects: Sayings of Confucius and His Successors.* New York: Columbia University Press, 1998.

Brown, John Seely, and Paul Duguid. *The Social Life of Information.* Boston: Harvard Business School Press, 2000.

Busch, Heinrich. "The Tung-lin Academy and Its Political and Philosophical Significance." *Monumenta Serica* 14 (1955): 1–163.

Bush, Christopher. "Ideographies: Figures of China and Japan in French Modernity." Ph.D diss., University of California, Los Angeles, 2000.

Bynner, Witter, and Kiang Kang-hu, trans. *The Jade Mountain: A Chinese Anthology, Being Three Hundred Poems of the T'ang Dynasty, 618–906*. New York: Knopf, 1929.

Cai Zong-qi. "Poundian and Chinese Aesthetics of Dynamic Force: A Re-discovery of Fenollosa and Pound's Theory of the Chinese Written Character." *Comparative Literature Studies* 30 (1993): 170–87.

Castells, Manuel. *End of Millennium*. Oxford: Blackwell, 1998.

Cavafis, Constantinos P. *Poiēmata (1896–1918)*. Athens: Ikaros, 1982.

Célestin, Roger. *From Cannibals to Radicals: Figures and Limits of Exoticism*. Minneapolis: University of Minnesota Press, 1996.

Champollion, Jean-François. *Grammaire égyptienne, ou principes généraux de l'écriture sacrée égyptienne appliquée à la représentation de la langue parlée*. 2 vols. Paris: Didot, 1836, 1841.

——. *Lettre à Monsieur Dacier relative à l'alphabet des hiéroglyphes phonétiques employés par les Egyptiens*. 1822. Reprinted—Montpellier: Fata Morgana, 1989.

Chatterjee, Partha. *Nationalist Thought and the Colonial World: A Derivative Discourse?* London: Zed Books, 1986.

Chen Ding 陳鼎. *Donglin liezhuan* 東林列傳 (Exemplary biographies of Donglin scholars). 1711. Reprinted—Beijing: Zhongguo shudian, 1991.

Chen, Jerome. *China and the West: Society and Culture, 1815–1937*. Bloomington: Indiana University Press, 1979.

Chen Song 陳崧, ed. *Wu si qianhou dongxi wenhua wenti lunzhan wenxuan* 五四前後東西文化問題論戰文選 (The controversy around the problem of Chinese and Western cultures, circa 1919: an anthology). Beijing: Zhongguo shehui kexue chubanshe, 1985.

Chen Xiaomei. *Occidentalism: A Theory of Counter-Discourse in Post-Mao China*. New York: Oxford University Press, 1995.

Chen Xiaoming 陳曉明. *Shengyu de xiangxiang—jiushi niandai de wenxue xushi yu wenhua weiji* 剩餘的想像—九十年代的文學敘事與文化危機 (Vestigial imagination: literary narration and the crisis of culture in the 1990s). Beijing: Huayi chubanshe, 1995.

——. "'Wenhua minzu zhuyi' de xingqi" '文化民族主義'的興起 (The rise of "cultural democracy"). *Ershiyi shiji* 39 (Feb. 1997): 35–43.

Cheng Pei-kai (Zheng Peikai 鄭培凱). "Mei Lanfang dui shijie jutan de wenhua chongji" 梅蘭芳對世界劇壇的文化衝擊 (The cultural impact of Mei Lanfang on world theater). *Dangdai (Con-Temporary)* 103 (1994): 26–43; 104 (1994): 66–90.

——. "Mei Lanfang zai Mosike" 梅蘭芳在莫斯科 (Mei Lanfang in Moscow). *Dangdai (Con-Temporary)* 105 (1995): 140–49.

Ch'ien, Edward T. *Chiao Hung and the Restructuring of Neo-Confucianism in the Late Ming*. New York: Columbia University Press, 1986.

Chomsky, Noam. *Cartesian Linguistics*. New York: Harper & Row, 1966.

———. *The New Military Humanism: Lessons from Kosovo*. Monroe, Maine: Common Courage Press, 1999.

———. *Powers and Prospects: Reflections on Human Nature and the Social Order*. Boston: South End Press, 1996.

Chomsky, Noam; Ira Katznelson; R. C. Lewontin; David Montgomery; Laura Nader; Richard Ohmann; Ray Siever; Immanuel Wallerstein; and Howard Zinn. *The Cold War and the University: Toward an Intellectual History of the Postwar Years*. New York: New Press, 1997.

Chow, Rey. "Can One Say No to China?" *New Literary History* 28 (1997): 147–51.

———. *Ethics After Idealism: Theory–Culture–Ethnicity–Reading*. Bloomington: Indiana University Press, 1998.

———. "Violence in the Other Country: Preliminary Remarks on the 'China Crisis,' June 1989." *Radical America* 22 (July-Aug. 1988 [sic]): 24–33.

———. *Writing Diaspora: Tactics of Intervention in Contemporary Cultural Studies*. Bloomington: Indiana University Press, 1993.

Chow Tse-tsung. "Ancient Chinese Views on Literature, the *Tao*, and Their Relationship." *Chinese Literature: Essays, Articles, Reviews* 1 (1979): 3–29.

Christian, David. *A History of Russia, Central Asia and Mongolia*, vol. 1, *Inner Eurasia from Prehistory to the Mongol Empire*. Oxford: Blackwell, 1998.

Cohen, Murray. *Sensible Words: Linguistic Practice in England, 1640–1785*. Baltimore: Johns Hopkins University Press, 1977.

Cohen, Paul A. *Discovering History in China: American Historical Writing on the Recent Chinese Past*. New York: Columbia University Press, 1984.

Cohen, Paul A., and Merle Goldman, eds. *Ideas Across Cultures: Essays in Honor of Benjamin Schwartz*. Harvard East Asian Monographs, 150. Cambridge, Mass.: Harvard University, Council on East Asian Studies, 1990.

Cohen, Warren. *East Asian Art in American Culture: A Study in International Relations*. New York: Columbia University Press, 1992.

Cohn, Bernard S. *An Anthropologist Among the Historians and Other Essays*. Delhi and Oxford: Oxford University Press, 1987.

Collange, Gabriel de, trans. *Polygraphie, et universelle escriture cabalistique de M. I. Trithème abbé*. Paris, 1561.

Collani, Claudia von. *Eine wissenschaftliche Akademie für China: Briefe des Chinamissionars Joachim Bouvet S.J.* Studia Leibnitiana Sonderheft 18. Stuttgart: Steiner, 1989.

Collingwood, R. G. *The Idea of History*. Oxford: Clarendon Press, 1946.

Collins, Randall. *The Sociology of Philosophies: A Global Theory of Intellectual Change.* Cambridge, Mass.: Harvard University Press, Belknap Press, 1998.

Connery, Christopher L. *The Empire of the Text.* New York: Rowan and Littlefield, 1998.

Cook, Daniel J., and Henry Rosemont, Jr., eds. and trans. *Gottfried Wilhelm Leibniz, Writings on China.* Chicago: Open Court, 1994.

Copenhaver, Brian P., trans. *Hermetica: The Greek Corpus Hermeticum and the Latin Asclepius.* Cambridge, Eng.: Cambridge University Press, 1993.

Creuzer, Friedrich. *Symbolik und Mythologie der alten Völker, besonders der Griechen.* Leipzig and Darmstadt: Heyer & Leske, 1819.

Cumings, Bruce. *Parallax Visions: Making Sense of American–East Asian Relations at the End of the Century.* Durham, N.C.: Duke University Press, 1999.

Da Dai Li ji 大戴禮記 (Records of ritual by the elder Dai). Ed. Wang Pinzhen 王聘珍. Beijing: Zhonghua, 1983.

Dahlhaus, Carl. *The Idea of Absolute Music.* Trans. Roger Lustig. Chicago: University of Chicago Press, 1991.

Davidson, Donald. *Inquiries into Truth and Interpretation.* Oxford: Clarendon Press, 1984.

Davie, Donald. *Articulate Energy: An Inquiry into the Syntax of English Poetry.* London: Routledge and Kegan Paul, 1955.

Davies, Anna Morpurgo. "Language Classification in the Nineteenth Century." In Thomas A. Sebeok, ed., *Current Trends in Linguistics*, vol. 12, *Historiography of Linguistics*, pp. 607–716. The Hague: Mouton, 1975.

Dean, Kenneth, and Brian Massumi. *First and Last Emperors.* New York: Autonomedia, 1990.

de Bary, William Theodore, and Tu Weiming, eds. *Confucianism and Human Rights.* New York: Columbia University Press, 1998.

D'Elia, Pasquale, S.J., ed. *Fonti Ricciane: Storia dell'introduzione del cristianesimo in Cina.* 3 vols. Rome: Libreria dello Stato, 1942–49.

De Francis, John. *The Chinese Language: Fact and Fantasy.* Honolulu: University of Hawaii Press, 1984.

de Man, Paul. *Aesthetic Ideology.* Ed. Andrzej Warminski. Theory and History of Literature, 65. Minneapolis: University of Minnesota Press, 1996.

———. *Allegories of Reading.* New Haven: Yale University Press, 1979.

———. *Blindness and Insight.* 2d ed. Minneapolis: University of Minnesota Press, 1983.

———. *Romanticism and Contemporary Criticism: The Gauss Seminar and Other Papers.* Baltimore: Johns Hopkins University Press, 1993.

Deng Xiaoping. *Selected Works.* Beijing: Foreign Languages Press, 1994.

Denton, Kirk A. *Modern Chinese Literary Thought: Writings on Literature, 1893–1945.* Stanford: Stanford University Press, 1996.

Derrida, Jacques. *La Carte postale: de Socrate à Freud et au-delà.* Paris: Galilée, 1980.

————. *De la grammatologie.* Paris: Minuit, 1967. Trans. Gayatri Chakravorty Spivak as *Of Grammatology.* Baltimore: Johns Hopkins University Press, 1976.

————. *Marges de la philosophie.* Paris: Minuit, 1972.

————. *Positions.* Paris: Minuit, 1972.

Derrida, Jacques, and Gianni Vattimo, eds. *La religion.* Paris: Seuil, 1996.

Descartes, René. *Œuvres philosophiques.* Ed. Ferdinand Alquié. Paris: Garnier, 1963.

Devereux, George. *From Anxiety to Method in the Behavioral Sciences.* The Hague: Mouton, 1967.

Devereux, George, and Edwin M. Loeb. "Antagonistic Acculturation." *American Sociological Review* 8 (1943): 133–47.

Dewey, John; Albert C. Barnes; Laurence Buermeyer; Thomas Munro; Paul Guillaume; Mary Mullen; and Violette de Mazia. *Art and Education.* Merion, Pa.: Barnes Foundation Press, 1929.

DeWitt, Bryce S., and Neill Graham. *The Many-Worlds Interpretation of Quantum Mechanics.* Princeton, N.J.: Princeton University Press, 1973.

Diderot, Denis, and d'Alembert, Jean le Rond, eds. *Encyclopédie ou Dictionnaire raisonné des sciences, des arts et des métiers.* 35 vols. Paris, 1740–55.

Dindorf, Wilhelm, ed. *Aristophanis Comœdiae.* 4 vols. Oxford: Oxford University Press, 1835–38.

Dodds, E. R. *The Greeks and the Irrational.* Berkeley: University of California Press, 1951.

Donato, Eugenio. "The Museum's Furnace: Notes Toward a Contextual Reading of *Bouvard and Pécuchet*." In Josué V. Harari, ed., *Textual Strategies: Perspectives in Post-Structuralist Criticism*, pp. 213–38. Ithaca, N.Y.: Cornell University Press, 1979.

Duara, Prasenjit. *Rescuing History from the Nation: Questioning Narratives of Modern China.* Chicago: University of Chicago Press, 1995.

Du Ponceau, Peter S. *A Dissertation on the Nature and Character of the Chinese System of Writing.* Philadelphia: American Philosophical Society, 1838.

Duret, Claude. *Thrésor de l'histoire des langues de cest univers.* Cologne, 1613.

Eco, Umberto. *Foucault's Pendulum.* Trans. William Weaver. New York: Harcourt Brace Jovanovich, 1988.

————. *The Search for the Perfect Language.* Trans. James Fentress. Oxford: Blackwell, 1995.

Egerod, Søren. "Typology." In Ming Wilson and John Cayley, eds., *Europe Studies China: Papers from an International Conference on the History of European Sinology*, pp. 280–96. London: Han-Shan Tang Books, 1995.

Ehrlich, Victor. *Russian Formalism: History–Doctrine.* The Hague: Mouton, 1955.

Eisenstadt, Shmuel Noah. *Fundamentalism, Sectarianism, and Revolution: The Jacobin Dimension of Modernity.* Cambridge, Eng.: Cambridge University Press, 1999.

Eisenstadt, Shmuel Noah, ed. *The Origins and Diversity of Axial Age Civilizations.* Albany: State University of New York Press, 1986.

Eisenstein, Elizabeth L. *The Printing Press as an Agent of Change: Communications and Cultural Transformations in Early-Modern Europe.* Cambridge, Eng.: Cambridge University Press, 1979.

Eisenstein, Sergei. *Nonindifferent Nature: Film and the Structure of Things.* Trans. Herbert Marshall. Cambridge, Eng.: Cambridge University Press, 1987.

Ellmann, Richard, ed. *The Artist as Critic: Critical Writings of Oscar Wilde.* Chicago: University of Chicago Press, 1969.

Elman, Benjamin A. *Classicism, Politics, and Kinship.* Berkeley: University of California Press, 1990.

————. *A Cultural History of Civil Examinations in Late Imperial China.* Berkeley: University of California Press, 2000.

————*From Philosophy to Philology.* Harvard East Asian Monographs 110. Cambridge, Mass.: Harvard University, Council on East Asian Studies, 1984.

Elvin, Mark. *The Pattern of the Chinese Past.* Stanford: Stanford University Press, 1973.

Emerson, Ralph Waldo. *Essays and Lectures.* New York: Library of America, 1983.

Encyclopædia Britannica. 28 vols. 11th ed. Cambridge, Eng.: Cambridge University Press, 1910–11.

Ershiwu shi 二十五史 (The twenty-five dynastic histories). Reprinted in 12 vols.— Shanghai: Guji, 1991.

Etiemble. *Les Jésuites en Chine: La querelle des rites (1552–1773).* Paris: Julliard, 1966.

————. *L'Europe chinoise.* Paris: Gallimard, 1988–1989.

Evans, Paul M. *John Fairbank and the American Understanding of Modern China.* New York: Blackwell, 1988.

Fabian, Johannes. *Time and the Other: How Anthropology Makes Its Object.* New York: Columbia University Press, 1983.

Fairbank, John King. *Chinabound: A Fifty-Year Memoir.* New York: Harper & Row, 1982.

Falkenhausen, Lothar von. "Inconsequential Incomprehensions: Some Instances of Chinese Writing in Alien Contexts." *Res* 35 (1999): 42–69.

Fan Ye 范曄. *Hou Han shu* 後漢書. Ed. Wang Xianqian 王先謙. Beijing: Zhonghua, 1982.

Fang Hao 方豪 (Maurus Fang). "Notes on Matteo Ricci's De Amicitia." *Monumenta Serica* 14 (1949–1955): 574–83.

Farmer, Paul. *AIDS and Accusation: Haiti and the Geography of Blame.* Berkeley: University of California Press, 1992.

————. *Pathologies of Power: Structural Violence and the Assault on Human Rights.* Berkeley: University of California Press, 2001.

Feng Youlan 馮友蘭. *Zhongguo zhexue shi* 中國哲學史. Shanghai: Shangwu, 1934. Trans. Derk Bodde as Fung Yu-lan, *A History of Chinese Philosophy.* 2 vols. Princeton: Princeton University Press, 1983 (1952, 1953).

Fenollosa, Ernest. "Chinese and Japanese Poetry. Draft of Lecture I. " Yale University, Beinecke Library, Pound Archive, catalogue number 3375.

————. *The Chinese Written Character as a Medium for Poetry.* Ed. Ezra Pound. Reprinted—San Francisco: City Lights Books, 1964.

————. "E. F. F. The Chinese Written Language as a Medium for Poetry. Oct 1909." Yale University, Beinecke Library, Pound Archive, catalogue number 3400.

————. "Synopsis of Lectures on Chinese and Japanese Poetry." Yale University, Beinecke Library, Pound Archive, catalogue number 3375.

Ferrari, Joseph. *La Chine et l'Europe: leur histoire et leurs traditions comparées.* Paris: Didier, 1867.

Fingarette, Herbert. *Confucius—The Secular as Sacred.* New York: Harper and Row, 1972.

Foreign Relations of the United States, 1946, vol. 6, *Eastern Europe and the Soviet Union.* Department of State Publication 8470. Washington, D.C.: Government Printing Office, 1969.

Forest, Philippe. *Histoire de "Tel Quel," 1960–1982.* Paris: Seuil, 1995.

Forke, Alfred, trans. *Lun Heng.* 2 vols. London: Luzac & Co., 1907–1911.

Foster, Hal. *The Return of the Real: The Avant-Garde at the End of the Century.* Cambridge, Mass.: MIT Press, 1996.

Foucault, Michel. *Dits et écrits 1954–1988.* Paris: Gallimard, 1994.

————. *Les Mots et les choses.* Paris: Gallimard, 1966.

————. *Remarks on Marx.* Trans. R. James Goldstein and James Cascaito. New York: Semiotexte, 1991.

Frank, André Gunder. *The Centrality of Central Asia.* Amsterdam: VU University Press, 1992.

————. *ReOrient: Global Economy in the Asian Age.* Berkeley: University of California Press, 1998.

Frank, André Gunder, and Barry K. Gills, eds. *The World System: Five Hundred Years or Five Thousand?* London: Routledge, 1993.

Franke, Otto. "Li Tschi und Matteo Ricci." *Abhandlungen der Preussischen Akademie der Wissenschaften* (Philosophisch-historische Klasse), no. 5. Berlin: de Gruyter, 1939.

Freud, Sigmund. *The Standard Edition of the Complete Psychological Works of Sigmund Freud.* 24 vols. Ed. James Strachey. London: Hogarth Press, 1953-66.

————. *Die Traumdeutung.* Frankfurt am Main: Fischer, 1977.

Fukuyama, Francis. "The End of History?" *The National Interest* 16 (1989): 3–18.

Fuller, Michael. "Pursuing the Complete Bamboo in the Breast: Reflections on a Chinese Image for Immediacy." *Harvard Journal of Asiatic Studies* 53 (1993): 5–23.

Gabelentz, Georg von der. *Chinesische Grammatik, mit Ausschluß des niederen Stiles und der heutigen Umgangssprache.* 1881. Reprinted—Halle: Niemeyer, 1960.

Gadamer, Hans-Georg. *Plato's Dialectical Ethics.* Trans. Robert M. Wallace. New Haven: Yale University Press, 1991.

Gallagher, Louis, S.J., trans. *China in the Sixteenth Century: The Journals of Matteo Ricci, 1583–1610.* New York: Random House, 1953.

Gardiner, Muriel, ed. *The Wolf-Man by the Wolf-Man.* New York: Basic Books, 1971.

Gelb, Ignace J. *A Study of Writing.* Chicago: University of Chicago Press, 1963.

Genette, Gérard. *Mimologiques: Voyage en Cratylie.* Paris: Seuil, 1976.

Gernet, Jacques. *Chine et christianisme: action et réaction.* Paris: Gallimard, 1982. Trans. Janet Lloyd as *China and the Christian Impact.* Chicago: University of Chicago Press, 1985.

————. *L'Intelligence de la Chine.* Paris: Gallimard, 1994.

Giehlow, Karl. *Die Hieroglyphenkunde des Humanismus in der Allegorie der Renaissance.* Jahrbuch der kunsthistorischen Sammlungen des allerhöchsten Kaiserhauses, 32.1. Vienna: Tempsky, 1915.

Glendon, Mary Ann. *A World Made New: Eleanor Roosevelt and the Universal Declaration of Human Rights.* New York: Random House, 2001.

Goldman, Merle. *Sowing the Seeds of Democracy in China.* Cambridge, Mass.: Harvard University Press, 1994.

Gombrich, E. H. *Symbolic Images: Studies in the Art of the Renaissance.* Chicago: University of Chicago Press, 1985.

Goodman, Howard L., and Anthony Grafton. "Ricci, the Chinese, and the Toolkits of Textualists." *Asia Major,* 3d ser., 3 (1990): 95–148.

Goodrich, Luther Carrington. *The Literary Inquisition of Ch'ien-lung.* 1935. Reprinted—New York: Paragon Books, 1966.

Goodrich, L. Carrington, and Chaoying Fang, eds. *Dictionary of Ming Biography.* 4 vols. New York: Columbia University Press, 1976.

Gourmont, Rémy de. *The Natural Philosophy of Love.* Trans. Ezra Pound. New York: Boni and Liveright, 1922.

Graham, A. C. "'Being' in Classical Chinese." In John W. M. Verhaar, ed., *The Verb 'Be' and Its Synonyms,* 5: 225–33. Dordrecht: Reidel, 1972.

————. *Disputers of the Tao.* Chicago: Open Court, 1989.

————. *Later Mohist Logic, Ethics and Science.* Hong Kong: Chinese University Press, 1978.

————. *Poems of the Late T'ang.* Harmondsworth, Eng.: Penguin, 1970.

Granet, Marcel. *Catégories matrimoniales et relations de proximité dans la Chine ancienne.* Paris: Alcan, 1939.

——. *La Civilisation chinoise.* 1929. Reprinted—Paris: Albin Michel, 1994.

——. *La Pensée chinoise.* 1934. Reprinted—Paris: Albin Michel, 1999.

Greimas, A. J. *Du sens.* Paris: Seuil, 1970.

Gu, Edward X. "Cultural Intellectuals and the Politics of Cultural Public Space in Communist China (1979–1989): A Case Study of Three Intellectual Groups." *Journal of Asian Studies* 58 (1999): 389–431.

Gu Yanwu 顧炎武. *Rizhi lu* 日知錄. Sibu beiyao. Shanghai: Shangwu, 1947.

Guéhenno, Jean-Marie. *La Fin de la démocratie.* Paris: Flammarion, 1993.

Guo Jian 郭建. "Resisting Modernity in Contemporary China: The Cultural Revolution and Postmodernism." *Modern China* 24 (1999): 343–76.

——. "Wen'ge sichao yu 'houxue'" 文革思潮與 '後學.' *Ershiyi shiji* 35 (June 1996): 116–22.

Guo yu 國語. Comm. Huang Pilie 黄丕烈. Sibu beiyao. Shanghai: Shangwu, 1947.

Guy, R. Kent. *The Emperor's Four Treasuries: Scholars and the State in the Late Ch'ienlung Era.* Harvard East Asian Monographs 129. Cambridge, Mass.: Harvard University, Council on East Asian Studies, 1987.

Hall, David L., and Roger T. Ames. *The Democracy of the Dead: Dewey, Confucius, and the Hope for Democracy in China.* Chicago: Open Court, 1999.

——. *Thinking from the Han.* Albany: State University of New York Press, 1998.

Hallen, Barry, and J. Olubi Sodipo. *Knowledge, Belief and Witchcraft: Analytic Experiments in African Philosophy.* Stanford: Stanford University Press, 1997.

Hand, Seán, ed. *The Levinas Reader.* Oxford: Blackwell, 1989.

Hansen, Chad. "Chinese Ideographs and Western Ideas." *Journal of Asian Studies* 52 (1993): 373–99.

——. *Language and Logic in Ancient China.* Ann Arbor: University of Michigan Press, 1983.

Harari, Josué V., ed. *Textual Strategies: Perspectives in Post-Structuralist Criticism.* Ithaca, N.Y.: Cornell University Press, 1979.

Harbsmeier, Christoph. "John Webb and the Early History of the Study of the Classical Chinese Language in the West." In Ming Wilson and John Cayley, eds., *Europe Studies China: Papers from an International Conference on the History of European Sinology,* pp. 297–338. London: Han-Shan Tang Books, 1995.

——. *Wilhelm von Humboldts Brief an Abel-Rémusat und die philosophische Grammatik des Altchinesischen.* Stuttgart / Bad Cannstatt: Frommann-Holzboog, 1979.

Hart, Roger. "Translating the Untranslatable: From Copula to Incommensurable Worlds." In Lydia H. Liu, ed., *Tokens of Exchange: The Problem of Translation in Global Circulations,* pp. 45-73. Durham, N.C.: Duke University Press, 1999.

————. "On the Problem of Chinese Science." In Mario Biagioli, ed., *The Science Studies Reader*, pp. 189–201. New York: Routledge, 1999.

Hartman, Geoffrey. *The Fateful Question of Culture*. New York: Columbia University Press, 1997.

Hayot, Eric. "Chinese Dreams: Pound, Brecht, *Tel Quel*." Ph.D. diss., University of Wisconsin-Milwaukee, 1999.

He Jiadong 何家棟. "Houxiandai pai ruhe nuoyong xiandaixing huayu: ping 'jingji minzhu' yu 'wenhua minzhu'" 後現代派如何挪用現代性話語—評 '經濟民主' 與 '文化民主' (How the postmodernists appropriate the discourse of modernity: a critique of "economic democracy" and "cultural democracy"). *Zhanlüe yu guanli* 27 (1998): 73–80.

Hegel, Georg Wilhelm Friedrich. *Hegel's Philosophy of Mind: Being Part Three of the 'Encyclopaedia of the Philosophical Sciences.'* Trans. William Wallace and A. V. Miller. Oxford: Clarendon Press, 1971.

————. *Lectures on the Philosophy of World History: Introduction*. Trans. H. B. Nisbet. Cambridge, Eng.: Cambridge University Press, 1975.

————. *Phenomenology of Spirit*. Trans. A. V. Miller. Oxford: Oxford University Press, 1979.

————. *Vorlesungen über die Geschichte der Philosophie*. Ed. Karl Ludwig Michelet. Berlin: Duncker & Humblot, 1833.

————. *Werke*. Frankfurt am Main: Suhrkamp, 1980.

Heidegger, Martin. *Holzwege*. Frankfurt am Main: Klostermann, 1950.

Heim, Steve J. *The Cybernetics Group*. Cambridge, Mass.: MIT Press, 1991.

Herder, Johann Gottfried. *Abhandlung über den Ursprung der Sprache: Text, Materialien, Kommentar*. Ed. Wolfgang Pross. Munich: Hanser, 1978. Trans. John H. Moran and Alexander Gode as *On the Origin of Language*. New York: Ungar, 1966.

————. *Ideen zur Philosophie der Geschichte der Menschheit*. Darmstadt: Melzer, 1966.

Hinton, Carma, producer. *Gate of Heavenly Peace* (film). Boston: Long Bow Productions, 1997.

Hjelmslev, Louis. *Nouveaux essais*. Paris: Presses Universitaires de France, 1985.

Ho, Ping-ti. *The Ladder of Success in Imperial China*. New York: Columbia University Press, 1962.

Hobbes, Thomas. *Leviathan*. Oxford: Oxford University Press, 1929.

Hoggart, Richard. *The Uses of Literacy*. London: Chatto & Windus, 1957.

Hollier, Denis, ed. *Panorama des sciences humaines*. Paris: Gallimard-NRF, 1973.

Hong Mingshui 洪銘水. "Mingmo wenhua lieshi Li Zhuowu de shengsi guan" 明末文化烈士李卓吾的生死觀 (The late-Ming cultural martyr Li Zhuowu on life and death). *Donghai xuebao* 39 (1998): 43–62.

Horapollo, attr. *The Hieroglyphics of Horapollo*. Trans. George Boas. New York: Pantheon, 1950.

Horkheimer, Max, and Theodor W. Adorno. *Dialectic of Enlightenment.* Trans. John Cumming. New York: Continuum, 1989.

Hu Shih 胡適. *The Development of the Logical Method in Ancient China.* Shanghai: Commercial Press, 1922.

Huainan zi 淮南子. Ed. Gao You 高誘. Sibu beiyao. Shanghai: Shangwu, 1947.

Huang, Ray. *1587: A Year of No Significance.* New Haven: Yale University Press, 1981.

Huang Tsung-hsi (Huang Zongxi 黃宗羲). *The Records of Ming Scholars.* Ed. and trans. Julia Ching and Chao-ying Fang. Honolulu: University of Hawaii Press, 1987.

Hucker, Charles O. *The Censorial System of Ming China.* Stanford: Stanford University Press, 1966.

Humboldt, Wilhelm von. *Gesammelte Schriften.* 15 vols. Ed. Albert Leitzmann. Berlin: Behr, 1903–20.

———. *Sur l'origine des formes grammaticales.* 1823. Reprinted—Bordeaux: Ducros, 1969.

Hummel, Arthur W., ed. *Eminent Chinese of the Ch'ing Period.* 2 vols. Washington, D.C.: Government Printing Office, 1943, 1944.

Huntington, Samuel. *The Clash of Civilizations and the Remaking of World Order.* New York: Simon & Schuster, 1996.

Huters, Theodore. "On the Origins of Modern Chinese Spirituality." Unpublished ms.

———. "Yubo: 1910 nian Zhongguo wenhua lun zhan" 餘波: 1910 年中國文化論戰 (In the wake: controversies over Chinese culture circa 1910). *Jintian (Today)* 45 (1999): 261–78.

Isaacs, Harold R. *Scratches on Our Minds: American Images of China and India.* New York: John Day, 1958.

Iversen, Erik. *The Myth of Egypt and Its Hieroglyphs in European Tradition.* 1961. Reprinted—Princeton: Princeton University Press, 1993.

Jakobson, Roman. *My Futurist Years.* Ed. Bengt Jangfelt. Trans. Stephan Rudy. New York: Marsilio, 1998.

Jakobson, Roman, and Morris Halle. *Fundamentals of Language.* The Hague: Mouton, 1956.

Jakobson, Roman, and Linda Waugh. *The Sound Shape of Language.* Bloomington: Indiana University Press, 1979.

Jaspers, Karl. *The Origin and Goal of History.* Trans. Michael Bullock. New Haven: Yale University Press, 1953.

Jensen, Lionel. *Manufacturing Confucianism: Chinese Traditions and Universal Civilization.* Durham, N.C.: Duke University Press, 1997.

Jespersen, Otto. *Progress in Language: With Special Reference to English.* 1894. Reprinted—Amsterdam: Benjamins, 1993.

Jespersen, T. Christopher. *American Images of China, 1931–1949*. Stanford: Stanford University Press, 1996.

Jin Guantao 金觀濤 and Liu Qingfeng 劉青峰. *Zhongguo xiandai sixiang de qiyuan: chaowending jiegou yu Zhongguo zhengzhi wenhua de yanbian, di yi juan* 中國現代思想的起源: 超穩定結構與中國政治文化的演變(第一卷) (The origins of modern Chinese thought: The evolution of Chinese political culture from the perspective of ultrastable structure, vol. 1). Hong Kong: Chinese University Press, 2000.

Jones, Owen. *A Grammar of Ornament*. London: Day & Son, 1856.

Jowett, Benjamin, trans. *The Dialogues of Plato*. Oxford: Clarendon Press, 1871.

Julien, Stanislas. *Syntaxe nouvelle de la langue chinoise, fondée sur la position des mots*. 2 vols. Paris: Maisonneuve, 1869–70.

Jullien, François. *Fonder la morale*. Paris: Grasset, 1995.

———. *La Propension des choses*. Paris: Seuil, 1992. Trans. Janet Lloyd as *The Propensity of Things: Toward a History of Efficacy in China*. New York: Zone Books, 1995.

———. *Traité de l'efficacité*. Paris: Grasset, 1997.

———. *Un Sage est sans idée, ou l'autre de la philosophie*. Paris: Seuil, 1998.

———. *La Valeur allusive*. Paris: Ecole Française d'Extrême-Orient, 1985.

Jullien, François, and Thierry Marchaisse. *Penser d'un dehors (La Chine): Entretiens d'Extrême-Occident*. Paris: Seuil, 2000.

Kadir, Djelal. *Columbus and the Ends of the Earth: Europe's Prophetic Rhetoric as Conquering Ideology*. Berkeley and Los Angeles: University of California Press, 1992.

Kant, Immanuel. *Kant's Political Writings*. Ed. Hans Reiss. Cambridge: Cambridge University Press, 1977.

———. *Werke*. 10 vols. Ed. Wilhelm Weischedel. Darmstadt: Wissenschaftliche Buchgesellschaft, 1983.

Kao Yu-kung and Mei Tsu-lin. "Syntax, Diction, and Imagery in T'ang Poetry." *HJAS* 31 (1971): 49–136.

Kapur, Ajay. "Puncturing Risk, Accumulating Courage and Buying Equities." Memorandum, Hong Kong: Morgan Stanley Dean Witter, April 23, 1999.

Keightley, David N. *Sources of Shang History: The Oracle-Bone Inscriptions of Bronze Age China*. Berkeley: University of California Press, 1985.

Kennedy, George A. "Fenollosa, Pound and the Chinese Character." In *Selected Works of George A. Kennedy*, pp. 443–462. New Haven: Far Eastern Publications, 1965.

Kenner, Hugh. *The Pound Era*. Berkeley: University of California Press, 1971.

Kent, Ann. *China, the United Nations, and Human Rights: The Limits of Compliance*. Philadelphia: University of Pennsylvania Press, 1999.

Kern, Robert. *Orientalism, Modernism and the American Poem*. Cambridge, Eng.: Cambridge University Press, 1996.

Kiparsky, Paul. "From Paleogrammarians to Neogrammarians." In *Studies in the History of Linguistics*, ed. Dell Hymes, pp. 331–345. Bloomington, Ind.: Indiana University Press, 1974.

Kircher, Athanasius. *China monumentis, quà sacris quà profanis, nec non variis naturae & artis spectaculis, aliarumque rerum memorabilium argumentis illustrata.* Amsterdam, 1667.

———. *Polygraphia nova et universalis ex combinatoria arte detecta.* Rome, 1663.

Kleberg, Lars. *Starfall: A Triptych.* Trans. Anselm Hollo. Evanston, Illinois: Northwestern University Press, 1998.

———. "Zhiv'ye impul'sy iskusstva" (The live impulses of art). *Isskustvo kino* 1 (1992): 132–139.

Klein, Jacob. *Greek Mathematical Thought and the Origin of Algebra.* Trans. Eva Brann. Cambridge, MA: MIT Press, 1968.

Knight, Diana. *Barthes and Utopia: Space, Travel, Writing.* Oxford: Clarendon Press, 1997.

Knowlson, James. *Universal Language Schemes in England and France, 1600–1800.* Toronto: University of Toronto Press, 1975.

Kojève, Alexandre. *Introduction à la lecture de Hegel.* Second edition. Paris: Gallimard, 1968.

———. "Les philosophes ne m'intéressent pas, je cherche des sages." (Interview with Gilles Lapouge.) *La Quinzaine littéraire,* 1–15 July 1968.

Kristeva, Julia. *Des Chinoises.* Paris: Editions des femmes, 1974.

———. *La Révolution du langage poétique.* Paris: Seuil, 1974.

———. *Les Samouraïs.* Paris: Fayard, 1990.

Kristeva, Julia, ed. *La Traversée des signes.* Paris: Seuil, 1975.

Küng, Hans, and Julia Ching. *Christianity and Chinese Religions.* New York: Doubleday, 1989.

Kumarajiva (Jiumoluoshi 鳩摩羅什). *Sanshi'er zhuanti Jin'gang jing* 三十二篆體金剛經. Ming Chongzhen period ed. Reprinted—Tianjin: Guji shudian, 1985.

La Barre, Weston. *Muelos: A Stone Age Superstition About Sexuality.* New York: Columbia University Press, 1980.

Lacan, Jacques. *Ecrits.* Paris: Seuil, 1966.

Lachterman, David Rapport. *The Ethics of Geometry: A Genealogy of Modernity.* New York: Routledge, 1989.

Larson, Wendy, and Richard Kraus. "China's Writers, the Nobel Prize, and the International Politics of Literature." *Australian Journal of Chinese Affairs* 21 (1989): 143–60.

Ledderose, Lothar. *Ten Thousand Things: Module and Mass Production in Chinese Art.* Princeton: Princeton University Press, 2000.

Lee Kuan Yew 李光耀. "Culture Is Destiny." *Foreign Affairs* 73 (1994): 109–26.

Lee, Leo Ou-fan. "In Search of Modernity: Some Reflections on a New Mode of Consciousness in Twentieth-Century Chinese History and Literature." In Paul A. Cohen and Merle Goldman, eds., *Ideas Across Cultures: Essays on Chinese Thought in Honor of Benjamin I. Schwartz*, pp. 109–35. Harvard East Asian Monographs, 150. Cambridge, Mass.: Harvard University, Council on East Asian Studies, 1990.

———. *Shanghai Modern: The Flowering of a New Urban Culture in China, 1930–1945*. Cambridge, Mass.: Harvard University Press, 1999.

———. "Some Notes on 'Culture,' 'Humanism' and the 'Humanities' in Modern Chinese Cultural Discourse." *Surfaces* 5 (1995): 6–29.

Legge, James, ed. and trans. *The Chinese Classics*. 1861–72. Reprinted—Taipei: Southern Materials Center, 1991.

Lei Yi 雷頤. "Shenme shi baoshou? Shei fandui minzhu?" 甚麼是保守? 誰反對民主? (What is conservativism? Who opposes democracy?). *Ershiyi shiji* 40 (April 1997): 122–25.

Lessing, Gotthold Ephraim. *Laokoön, oder, Über die Grenzen der Malerei und Poesie*. 1766. Trans. Edward Allen McCormick as *Laocoön: An Essay on the Limits of Painting and Poetry*. Baltimore: Johns Hopkins University Press, 1984.

Lévi, Jean. "Le Mythe de l'âge d'or et les théories de l'évolution en Chine ancienne." *L'Homme* 17 (1977): 73–103.

Levinas, Emmanuel. *Le Temps et l'autre*. Montpellier: Fata Morgana, 1979.

———. *Totalité et infini: essai sur l'extériorité*. Paris: Librairie Générale Française, 1998. Trans. Alphonso Lingis. *Totality and Infinity: An Essay on Exteriority*. Pittsburgh: Duquesne University Press, 1969.

Lévi-Strauss, Claude. *Anthropologie structurale*. Paris: Plon, 1958.

———. "Introduction à l'œuvre de Marcel Mauss." In Marcel Mauss, *Sociologie et anthropologie*, pp. ix–lii. Paris: Presses Universitaires de France, 1950.

———. *La Pensée sauvage*. Paris: Plon, 1962.

———. *Les Structures élémentaires de la parenté*. 1947; 2d ed., The Hague: Mouton, 1967.

———. *La Vie familiale et sociale chez les indiens Nambikwara*. Paris: Société des Américanistes, 1948.

Lévi-Strauss, Claude, and Didier Eribon. *De Près et de loin*. Paris: Editions Odile Jacob, 1988.

Lewis, Mark Edward. *Writing and Authority in Early China*. Albany: State University of New York Press, 1999.

Li ji 禮記 (Records of ritual). In Ruan Yuan 阮元, ed. *Shisanjing zhushu* 十三經注疏. 1815. Reprinted—Taipei: Dahua, 1987.

Li Tiangang 李天綱. *Zhongguo liyi zhi zheng: lishi, wenxian he yiyi* 中國禮儀之爭: 歷史, 文獻和意義 (The Chinese Rites Controversy: its history, documents, and meaning). Shanghai: Guji, 1998.

Li Tuo 李陀. "Rang zhenglun fuchu haimian" 讓爭論浮出海面 (Let the debates rise to the surface). *Dushu* (Dec. 1997): 52–59.

Li Zhi 李贄. *Fen shu, Xu fen shu* 焚書, 續焚書 (A book for burning; Another book for burning). Beijing: Zhonghua shudian, 1975.

Li Zhizao 李之藻, ed. *Tianxue chuhan* 天學初函 (A first compendium of celestial [i.e., Catholic] studies). 1628. Reprinted—Taipei: Xuesheng, 1965.

Liang Qichao 梁啟超. *Mo jing jiaoshi* 墨經校釋 (The Mohist canon, edited and annotated). Shanghai: Shangwu, 1922.

Lin Yü-sheng. *The Crisis of Chinese Consciousness.* Madison: University of Wisconsin Press, 1979.

Link, Perry. *Evening Chats in Beijing.* New York: Norton, 1992.

Liu, James J. Y. "The Study of Chinese Literature in the West: Recent Developments, Current Trends, Future Prospects." *Journal of Asian Studies* 35 (1975): 21–30.

Liu Kang 劉康. "Quanqiuhua yu Zhongguo xiandaihua de butong xuanze" 全球化與中國現代化的不同選擇 (Globalization and the alternative choice of Chinese modernization). *Ershiyi shiji* 37 (Oct. 1996): 140–45.

Liu Kang and Tang Xiaobing, eds. *Politics, Ideology and Literary Discourse in Modern China: Theoretical Interventions and Cultural Critique.* Durham, N.C.: Duke University Press, 1993.

Liu, Lydia H. "Legislating the Universal." In idem, ed., *Tokens of Exchange*, pp. 127–64. Durham, N.C.: Duke University Press, 1999.

———. *Translingual Practice: Literature, National Culture, and Translated Modernity—China, 1900–1937.* Stanford: Stanford University Press, 1995.

Liu, Lydia H., ed. *Tokens of Exchange: The Problem of Translation in Global Circulations.* Durham, N.C.: Duke University Press, 1999.

Liu Xie 劉勰. *Wenxin diaolong* 文心雕龍. Ed. Zhou Zhenfu 周振甫. Taipei: Liren chubanshe, 1983.

Loewe, Michael, and Edward Shaughnessy, eds. *The Cambridge History of Ancient China: From the Origins of Civilization to 221 B.C.* Cambridge, Eng.: Cambridge University Press, 1999.

Long Yingtai 龍應台 and Zhu Weizheng 朱維錚, eds. *Wei wancheng de geming: wuxu bainian ji* 未完成的革命—戊戌百年紀 (The incomplete revolution—one hundred years after the Reform Movement of 1898). Taipei: Shangwu, 1998.

Lowe, Lisa. *Critical Terrains: French and British Orientalisms.* Ithaca, N.Y.: Cornell University Press, 1991.

Lu Jia 陸家. "'Fan xifang zhuyi' huichao" '反西方主義'回潮 (The return of anti-Westernism). *Zhongguo shibao zhoukan* (Hong Kong), Jan. 2, 1994. pp. 16–19.

Lu, Sheldon Hsiao-peng. "Art, Culture, and Cultural Criticism in Post-New China." *New Literary History* 28 (1997): 111–33.

Luhmann, Niklas. *Essays on Self-Reference*. New York: Columbia University Press, 1990.

Lun yu 論語 (Analects of Confucius). In Ruan Yuan 阮元, ed. *Shisanjing zhushu* 十三經注疏. 1815. Reprinted—Taipei: Dahua, 1987.

Lundbæk, Knud. *The Traditional History of the Chinese Script, From a Seventeenth Century Jesuit Manuscript*. Aarhus, Denmark: Aarhus University Press, 1988.

Lynch, Daniel C. *After the Propaganda State: Media, Politics and 'Thought Work' in Reformed China*. Stanford: Stanford University Press, 1999.

Ma Jianzhong 馬建忠. *Ma shi wen tong* 馬氏文通 (The comprehensive grammar of Mr. Ma). Beijing: Zhonghua shuju, 1961.

Macksey, Richard, and Eugenio Donato, eds. *The Structuralist Controversy: The Languages of Criticism and the Sciences of Man*. Baltimore: Johns Hopkins University Press, 1972.

Mailla, Joseph-Anne-Marie de Moyriac de. *Histoire générale de la Chine, ou Annales de cet empire, extraites du Tong-kien-kang-mou*. 13 vols. Paris: Pierres & Clousier, 1777–85.

Mair, Victor. "Ma Jianzhong and the Invention of Chinese Grammar." In Chaofen Sun, ed., *Studies in the History of Chinese Syntax*, pp. 5–26. *Journal of Chinese Linguistics* monograph series, no. 10. Berkeley: Journal of Chinese Linguistics, 1997.

Malraux, André. *The Psychology of Art*. 3 vols. Trans. Stuart Gilbert. New York: Pantheon, 1949–50.

Mao Zedong. *Mao Zedong xuanji* 毛澤東選集 (Selected works of Mao Zedong). Beijing: Zhongguo renmin jiefangjun zhanshi chubanshe, 1967.

March, Andrew L. *The Idea of China: Myth and Theory in Geographic Thought*. New York: Praeger, 1974.

Marx, Karl. *Early Writings*. Trans. Rodney Livingstone and Gregor Benton. New York: Vintage Books, 1975.

———. *Pre-Capitalist Economic Formations*. Trans. Jack Cohen. New York: International Publishers, 1965.

Marx, Karl, and Friedrich Engels. *Collected Works*. London: Lawrence and Wishart, 1980.

McDermott, Joseph P. "Friendship and Its Friends in the Late Ming." In *Jinshi jiazu yu zhengshi bijiao lishi lunwenji* 近世家族與政治比較歷史論文集 (English title: *Family Process and Political Process in Modern Chinese History*), ed. Zhongyang yanjiu yuan, Jindaishi yanjiu suo 中央研究院近代史研究所, 1: 67–96. Taipei: Zhongyang yanjiu yuan, 1992.

McNeill, William H. *Plagues and Peoples*. Oxford: Blackwell, 1977.

Mei Lanfang 梅蘭芳. *Wo de dianying shenghuo* 我的電影生活 (My life in the movies). Beijing: Zhongguo dianying chubanshe, 1984.

———. *Wutai shenghuo sishi nian* (Forty years on the stage). Ed. Xu Jichuan 許姬傳. Beijing: Zhongguo xiju chubanshe, 1987.

Mei Shaowu 梅紹武. *Wo de fuqin Mei Lanfang* 我的父親梅蘭芳. Tianjin: Baihua wenyi chubanshe, 1984.

Mill, John Stuart. *A System of Logic.* London: Longmans, 1872.

Millward, James A. *Beyond the Pass: Economy, Ethnicity and Empire in Qing Central Asia, 1759–1864.* Stanford: Stanford University Press, 1998.

Minamiki, George. *The Chinese Rites Controversy from Its Beginning to Modern Times.* Chicago: Loyola University Press, 1985.

Mohanty, Chandra Talpade; Ann Russo; and Lourdes Torres, eds. *Third World Women and the Politics of Feminism.* Bloomington: Indiana University Press, 1991.

Momigliano, Arnaldo. *Essays in Ancient and Modern Historiography.* Middletown, Conn.: Wesleyan University Press, 1987.

Montesquieu, Charles-Marie Secondat de. *Oeuvres complètes.* Paris: Seuil, 1977.

Morgan, Evan. *A Guide to Wenli Styles and Chinese Ideals: Essays, Edicts, Proclamations, Memorials, Letters, Documents, Inscriptions, Commercial Papers.* Shanghai: Christian Literature Society for China, 1912.

Morohashi Tetsuji 諸橋轍次, chief ed. *Dai Kanwa jiten* 大漢和辭典. 13 vols. Tokyo: Taishūkan, 1955–60.

Morris, Charles W. "Foundations of the Theory of Signs." In *International Encyclopedia of Unified Science*, vol. 1, ed. Otto Neurath, Rudolf Carnap, and Charles W. Morris, pp. 78–137. Chicago: University of Chicago Press, 1955.

Mote, F. W. *Imperial China, 900–1800.* Cambridge, Mass.: Harvard University Press, 1999.

Mou Zongsan 牟宗三. *Zhongguo zhexue de tezhi* 中國哲學的特質 (The distinctive features of Chinese philosophy). Hong Kong: Rensheng chubanshe, 1963.

Mulder, Jan W. F., and Sándor G. J. Hervey. *The Strategy of Linguistics.* Edinburgh: Scottish Academic Press, 1980.

Müller, Max. *Lectures on the Science of Language.* New York: Charles Scribner's Sons, 1884.

Mungello, David. *Curious Land: Jesuit Accommodation and the Origins of Sinology.* Honolulu: University of Hawaii Press, 1989.

———. *Leibniz and Neo-Confucianism: The Search for Accord.* Honolulu: University of Hawaii Press, 1977.

Nagy, Gregory. *Comparative Studies in Greek and Indic Meter.* Cambridge, Mass.: Harvard University Press, 1974.

Nakamura Hajime. *Ways of Thinking of Eastern Peoples: India, China, Tibet, Japan.* Ed. Philip P. Wiener. Honolulu: University of Hawaii Press, 1964.

Natorp, Paul. *Platos Ideenlehre.* Leipzig: Meiner, 1903.

Newman, Robert P. *Owen Lattimore and the 'Loss' of China.* Berkeley: University of California Press, 1992.

Ngugi wa Thiong'o. *Decolonizing the Mind.* London and Portsmouth, N.H.: James Currey / Heinemann, 1986.

Nietzsche, Friedrich. *Nietzsches Werke.* 15 vols. Leipzig: Naumann, 1899–1904.

———. *Sämtliche Werke: Kritische Studienausgabe.* 13 vols. Ed. Giorgio Colli and Mazzino Montinari. Munich and Berlin: DTV / de Gruyter, 1988.

Nock, A. D., ed. *Corpus Hermeticum.* Trans. A.-J. Festugière. Paris: Les Belles Lettres, 1973.

Northrop, F. S. C. *The Meeting of East and West: An Inquiry Concerning World Understanding.* New York: Macmillan, 1946.

Nussbaum, Martha C. *The Therapy of Desire: Theory and Practice in Hellenistic Ethics.* Princeton: Princeton University Press, 1994.

Nylan, Michael. "Calligraphy, the Sacred Text and Test of Culture." In Cary Y. Liu, Dora C. Y. Ching, and Judith G. Smith, eds., *Character and Context in Chinese Calligraphy,* pp. 17–77. Princeton, New Jersey: Princeton University, Art Gallery, 1999.

Owen, Stephen. "The Anxiety of Global Influence: What Is World Poetry?" *New Republic,* Nov. 19, 1990, pp. 28–32.

———. "Poetry and Its Historical Ground." *Chinese Literature: Essays, Articles, Reviews* 12 (1990): 107–18.

———. *Readings in Chinese Literary Thought.* Harvard-Yenching Institute Monograph Series, 30. Cambridge, Mass.: Harvard University, Council on East Asian Studies, 1992.

———. *Traditional Chinese Poetry and Poetics: Omen of the World.* Madison: University of Wisconsin Press, 1985.

Paulhan, Jean. *Les Fleurs de Tarbes ou la terreur dans les lettres.* 1941. Reprinted—Paris: Gallimard, 1990.

Peerenbohm, Randall. "The Limits of Irony: Rorty and the China Challenge." *Philosophy East and West* 50 (2000): 56–89.

Peirce, Charles Sanders. *Values in a Universe of Chance: Selected Writings.* Ed. Philip P. Weiner. Stanford: Stanford University Press, 1958.

People's Daily Online. "Wangyou de shengyin: Wang Yizhou boshi da wangyou wen, xia" 網友的聲音, 王逸舟博士答網友問, 下 (Voices of our Internet community: Dr. Wang Yizhou responds to readers' questions, part 2). May 20, 1999. Available at http://www.peopledaily.com.cn/item/wysy/199905/14/wyz-wy.html.

Petry, Michael John, trans. *Hegel's Philosophy of Nature.* London: George Allen & Unwin, 1970.

Pinot, Virgile. *La Chine et la formation de l'esprit philosophique en France.* Paris: Geuthner, 1932.

Pleynet, Marcelin. *Le plus court chemin: De "Tel Quel" à "L'Infini."* Paris: Gallimard, 1997.

Plotnitsky, Arkady. *Complementarity: Anti-Epistemology After Bohr and Derrida.* Durham, N.C.: Duke University Press, 1994.

Pocock, J. G. A. *Politics, Language and Time: Essays on Political Thought and History.* New York: Atheneum, 1971.

Porter, David. *Ideographia: The Chinese Cipher in Early Modern Europe.* Stanford: Stanford University Press, 2001.

Pound, Ezra. *ABC of Reading.* 1934. Reprinted—New York: New Directions, n.d.

———. *The Cantos of Ezra Pound.* New York: New Directions, 1979.

———. *Confucius: The Great Digest & Unwobbling Pivot.* New York: New Directions, 1951.

———. *Literary Essays of Ezra Pound.* Ed. T. S. Eliot. London: Faber & Faber, 1954.

Price, Don C. "Constitutional Alternatives and Democracy in the Revolution of 1911." In Paul Cohen and Merle Goldman, eds., *Ideas Across Cultures: Essays in Honor of Benjamin Schwartz,* pp. 199–260. Harvard East Asian Monographs, 150. Cambridge, Mass.: Harvard University, Council on East Asian Studies, 1990.

Puett, Michael. "Nature and Artifice: Debates in Late Warring States China Concerning the Creation of Culture." *Harvard Journal of Asiatic Studies* 57 (1997): 471–518.

Qian, Zhaoming. *Orientalism and Modernism: The Legacy of China in Pound and Williams.* Durham, N.C.: Duke University Press, 1995.

Qiu Xigui 裘錫圭. *Chinese Writing.* Trans. Gilbert L. Mattos and Jerry Norman. Berkeley, Calif.: Society for the Study of Early China and Institute of East Asian Studies, 2000.

Quilligan, Maureen. *The Language of Allegory: Defining the Genre.* Ithaca, N.Y.: Cornell University Press, 1979.

Quine, W. V. *Ontological Relativity and Other Essays.* New York: Columbia University Press, 1969.

Ramsey, S. Robert. *The Languages of China.* Princeton: Princeton University Press, 1989.

Rawski, Evelyn S. "Reenvisioning the Qing: The Significance of the Qing Period in Chinese History." *Journal of Asian Studies* 55 (1996): 829–50.

Reckert, Stephen. *Beyond Chrysanthemums: Perspectives on Poetry East and West.* Oxford: Clarendon Press, 1993.

Reuchlin, Johann. *On the Art of the Kabbalah / De Arte cabalistica.* 1517. Trans. Martin Goodman and Sarah Goodman. New York: Abaris, 1983.

Richards, I. A. *Basic in Teaching: East and West.* London: Kegan Paul, Trench and Trubner, 1935.

———. *Mencius on the Mind.* London: Kegan Paul, 1932.

Riddel, Joseph. "Decentering the Image: The 'Project' of 'American' Poetics?" In Josué V. Harari, ed., *Textual Strategies: Perspectives in Post-Structuralist Criticism*, pp. 322–58. Ithaca, N.Y.: Cornell University Press, 1979.

Robins, R. H. *A Short History of Linguistics.* Bloomington: Indiana University Press, 1968.

Rorty, Richard. *Philosophy and the Mirror of Nature.* Princeton: Princeton University Press, 1979.

———. "Response to Randall Peerenboom." *Philosophy East and West* 50 (2000): 90–92.

Rossi, Paolo. *Clavis Universalis: arti mnemoniche e logica combinatoria da Lullo a Leibniz.* Milan and Naples: Ricciardi, 1960.

Rousseau, Jean-Jacques. *Essai sur l'origine des langues.* 1759. Ed. Charles Porset. Bordeaux: Ducros, 1968.

Ruan Yuan 阮元, ed. *Shisanjing zhushu* 十三經注疏. 1815. Reprinted—Taipei: Dahua, 1987.

Said, Edward W. *Culture and Imperialism.* New York: Knopf, 1994.

———. *Orientalism.* New York: Random House, 1978.

———. *Reflections on Exile and Other Essays.* Cambridge, Mass.: Harvard University Press, 2000.

Salmon, Vivian. *The Study of Language in Seventeenth-Century England.* Amsterdam Studies in the Theory and History of Linguistic Science, 3.17. Amsterdam: Benjamins, 1979.

Saunders, Frances Stonor. *The Cultural Cold War: The CIA and the World of Arts and Letters.* New York: The New Press, 2000.

Saussure, Ferdinand de. *Cours de linguistique générale.* Ed. Tullio de Mauro. Paris: Payot, 1972.

Saussy, Haun. "*China Illustrata*: The Universe in a Cup of Tea." In Daniel Stolzenberg, ed., *The Great Art of Knowing: The Baroque Encyclopedia of Athanasius Kircher*, pp. 105–14. Stanford: Stanford University Libraries, 2001.

———. *The Problem of a Chinese Aesthetic.* Stanford: Stanford University Press, 1993.

———. "Writing in the *Odyssey*: Eurykleia, Parry, Jousse, and the Opening of a Letter from Homer." *Arethusa* 29 (1996): 299–338.

Scaglione, Aldo. *The Classical Theory of Composition from Its Origins to the Present: A Historical Survey.* Chapel Hill: University of North Carolina Press, 1972.

Schlegel, Friedrich von. *Über die Sprache und Weisheit der Indier.* Heidelberg: Mohr & Zimmer, 1808.

Schleicher, August. *Die Sprachen Europas in systematischer Übersicht.* Bonn: H. B. König, 1850.

Schluchter, Wolfgang. *The Rise of Western Rationalism: Max Weber's Developmental History.* Trans. Guenther Roth. Berkeley: University of California Press, 1981.

Sebeok, Thomas A., ed. *Style in Language.* Cambridge, Mass.: MIT Press, 1960.

Secret, François. *Les Kabbalistes chrétiens de la Renaissance.* Paris: Dunod, 1964.

Segalen, Victor. *Essai sur l'Exotisme.* Montpellier: Fata Morgana, 1986.

Sen, Amartya. *Development as Freedom.* New York: Knopf, 1999.

Shang shu 尚書 (The book of documents). In Ruan Yuan 阮元, ed. *Shisanjing zhushu* 十三經注疏. 1815. Reprinted—Taipei: Dahua, 1987.

Shannon, Claude E., and Warren Weaver. *The Mathematical Theory of Information.* Urbana: University of Illinois Press, 1949.

Shaughnessy, Edward L. *Sources of Western Zhou History: Inscribed Bronze Vessels.* Berkeley: University of California Press, 1991.

———. *Before Confucius: Studies in the Creation of the Chinese Classics.* Albany: State University of New York Press, 1997.

Shaughnessy, Edward L., ed. *New Sources of Early Chinese History: An Introduction to the Reading of Inscriptions and Manuscripts.* Berkeley, Calif.: Society for the Study of Early China and Institute of East Asian Studies, 1997.

Shih, Vincent Yu-chung, trans. Liu Xie, *The Literary Mind and the Carving of Dragons.* Hong Kong: Chinese University Press, 1983.

Siku quanshu zongmu tiyao 四庫全書總目提要. 5 vols. Taipei: Shangwu, 1983.

Singleton, Charles S., trans. Dante Alighieri, *The Divine Comedy.* 6 parts in 3 vols. Princeton: Princeton University Press, 1970–75.

Sivin, Nathan. "Why the Scientific Revolution Didn't Take Place in China—Or Didn't It?" *Chinese Science* 5 (1982): 45–66.

Slaughter, Mary M. *Universal Languages and Scientific Taxonomy in the Seventeenth Century.* Cambridge, Eng.: Cambridge University Press, 1982.

Slonimsky, Nicholas. *Lexicon of Musical Invective: Critical Assaults on Composers Since Beethoven's Time.* 2d ed. Seattle: University of Washington Press, 1969.

Smith, Adam. *The Wealth of Nations.* London: J. M. Dent & Sons, 1934.

Sollers, Philippe. "La Chine sans Confucius." *Tel Quel* 59 (1974): 12–15.

———. *Sur le matérialisme.* Paris: Seuil, 1974.

Song Qiang 宋強, Zhang Zangzang 張藏藏, Qiao Bian 喬邊. *Zhongguo keyi shuo 'bu'* 中國可以說不 — 冷戰後時代的政治與感情抉擇 (China can say no: political and emotional choices for the post-Cold War period). Beijing: Zhonghua gongshang lianhe chubanshe, 1996.

Spence, Jonathan D. *To Change China: Western Advisers in China, 1620–1960.* Harmondsworth, Eng.: Penguin, 1969.

———. *The Chan's Great Continent: China in Western Minds*. New York: Norton, 1998.

———. *The Memory Palace of Matteo Ricci*. Harmondsworth, Eng.: Penguin, 1983.

Spinoza, Benedict de. *A Theologico-Political Treatise and A Political Treatise*. Trans. R. H. M. Elwes. New York: Dover, 1955.

Spivak, Gayatri Chakravorty. *A Critique of Postcolonial Reason: Toward a History of the Vanishing Present*. Cambridge, Mass.: Harvard University Press, 1999.

———. *In Other Worlds*. New York: Routledge, 1987.

Sproat, Richard. Review of Peter T. Daniels and William Bright, eds., *The World's Writing Systems*. *Written Language and Literacy* 1 (1998): 79–82.

Standaert, N. *Yang Tingyun, Confucian and Christian in Late Ming China: His Life and Thought*. Leiden: Brill, 1988.

Stevens, Wallace. *The Collected Poems of Wallace Stevens*. New York: Knopf, 1954.

Stillman, Robert E. *The New Philosophy and Universal Languages in Seventeenth-Century England: Bacon, Hobbes and Wilkins*. Lewisburg, Pa.: Bucknell University Press, 1995.

Sullivan, Michael. *The Meeting of Eastern and Western Art*. Berkeley: University of California Press, 1989.

Tang Junyi 唐君毅. *Zhonghua renwen yu dangjin shijie* 中華人文與當今世界 (Chinese humanism and the contemporary world). 1975. Reprinted—Taipei: Xuesheng, 1988.

———. *Zhongxi zhexue sixiang zhi bijiao lunwenji* 中西哲學思想之比較論文集 (Essays in comparative philosophical thought, Chinese and Western). 1941. Reprinted—Taipei: Xuesheng, 1988.

Tang Xiaobing. "The Function of New Theory: What Does It Mean to Talk About Postmodernism in China?" In Liu Kang and Tang Xiaobing, eds., *Politics, Ideology, and Literary Discourse*, pp. 278–99. Durham, N.C.: Duke University Press, 1994.

Teggart, Frederick J. *Rome and China: A Study of Correlations in Historical Events*. Berkeley: University of California Press, 1939.

Teng, Ssu-yu, and John Fairbank. *China's Response to the West: A Documentary Survey, 1839–1923*. Cambridge, Mass.: Harvard University Press, 1954.

Tiananmen yijiubajiu 天安門一九八九. Taipei: Lianjing chubanshe, 1989.

Tianxia bianyong wenlin miaojin wanbao quanshu 天下便用文林妙錦萬寶全書 (A complete book of ten thousand treasures, with the precious brocade of the literary grove, in a convenient form for all the world to use). Ming woodblock ed. Bibliotheca Apostolica Vaticana, Barb. orient. 139.

Toury, Gideon. *In Search of a Theory of Translation*. Tel Aviv: Porter Institute for Poetics and Semiotics, 1980.

Trithemius, Johannes. *Polygraphia*. Oppenheim, 1518.

Tsien, Tsuen-hsuin. *Paper and Printing.* Vol. 5, pt. I, of Joseph Needham, ed., *Science and Civilisation in China.* Cambridge, Eng.: Cambridge University Press, 1985.

Tu Weiming, ed. *The Living Tree: The Changing Meaning of Being Chinese Today.* Stanford: Stanford University Press, 1994.

Twitchett, Denis. *Printing and Publishing in Medieval China.* New York: Fredric Beil, 1983.

Unger, James Marshall. "The Very Idea: The Notion of Ideogram in China and Japan." *Monumenta Nipponica* 45 (1990): 392–411.

———. "Rejoinder to Chad Hansen." *Journal of Asian Studies* 52 (1993): 949–54.

V.-David, Madeleine. *Le Débat sur les écritures et l'hiéroglyphe aux XVIIe et XVIIIe siècles.* Paris: SEVPEN, 1965.

Valéry, Paul. "Le Retour de Hollande." In idem, *Variété II*, pp. 19–41. Paris: Gallimard, 1930.

Vandermeersch, Léon. "Écriture et langue graphique en Chine." *Le Débat* 62 (1990): 61–73.

Vattimo, Gianni. *The End of Modernity.* Trans. Jon R. Snyder. Baltimore: Johns Hopkins University Press, 1991.

Vigenère, Blaise de. *Traicté des chiffres.* Paris, 1586.

Voltaire. *Œuvres complètes de Voltaire.* Paris: Garnier, 1879.

Waldron, Arthur. *The Great Wall of China: From History to Myth.* Cambridge, Eng.: Cambridge University Press, 1990.

Wallerstein, Immanuel. *The Modern World-System, I: Capitalist Agriculture and the Origins of the European World-Economy in the Sixteenth Century.* New York: Academic Press, 1974.

———. *The Modern World-System, II: Mercantilism and the Consolidation of the European World-Economy, 1600–1750.* New York: Academic Press, 1980.

———. *Unthinking Social Science: The Limits of Nineteenth-Century Paradigms.* Cambridge, Eng.: Polity Press, 1995.

Wang Hui 汪暉. "Fenqi jiujing zai nali?–' Sihui chongwen' xu" 分歧究竟在那裡？《死灰重溫》序 (Wherein lies the disagreement? A preface to *Old Ashes Rekindled*). *Shijie* 視界 1 (2000), 112–21.

Wang Ning 王寧. "Orientalism or Occidentalism?" *New Literary History* 28 (1997): 57–67.

Wang Wei 王維. *Wang Youcheng ji jianzhu* 王右丞集箋注 (Poetry-collection of Vice-Minister Wang, annotated). Ed. Zhao Diancheng 趙殿成. Shanghai: Guji chubanshe, 1984.

Warburton, William. *The Divine Legation of Moses.* London, 1738–41.

———. *Essai sur les hiéroglyphes des Egyptiens.* 1744. Reprinted—Paris: Aubier-Flammarion, 1977.

Weale, B. L. Putnam. *The Vanished Empire.* London: Macmillan, 1926.

Wei Da 威達. *Gaige qianhou lüewang lu—julong fusu* 改革前後略忘錄—巨龍復蘇 (A chronicle of the reform process—the giant dragon revives). Chengdu: Chengdu keji daxue chubanshe, 1993.

Wei Jingsheng. *The Courage to Stand Alone*. Trans. Kristina M. Torgeson. New York: Viking Penguin, 1998.

Weinberger, Eliot, ed. *Nineteen Ways of Looking at Wang Wei: How a Chinese Poem Is Translated*. Mount Kisco, New York: Moyer Bell Limited, 1987.

Weinreich, Uriel. *Languages in Contact: Findings and Problems*. The Hague: Mouton, 1968.

Welsh, Andrew. *Roots of Lyric: Primitive Poetry and Modern Poetics*. Princeton: Princeton University Press, 1979.

Wesling, Donald. "Methodological Implications of the Philosophy of Jacques Derrida for Comparative Literature: The Opposition East-West and Several Other Oppositions." In John J. Deeney, ed., *Chinese-Western Comparative Literature: Theory and Strategy*, pp. 79–111. Hong Kong: Chinese University Press; and Seattle: University of Washington Press, 1980.

Whitney, William Dwight. *Language and the Study of Language*. New York: Charles Scribner & Company, 1868.

Whorf, Benjamin Lee. *Language, Thought and Reality*. Cambridge, Mass.: MIT Press, 1956.

Wiener, Norbert. *Cybernetics, or Control and Communication in the Animal and the Machine*. New York: Wiley, 1948.

———. *The Human Use of Human Beings: Cybernetics and Society*. New York: Avon, 1967.

Wilkins, John. *An Essay Towards a Real Character, and a Philosophical Language*. London, 1668.

Wilkinson, Endymion. *Chinese History: A Manual, Revised and Enlarged*. Harvard-Yenching Institute Monographs Series, 52. Cambridge, Mass.: Harvard University Asia Center, 2000.

Williams, Bernard. *Shame and Necessity*. Berkeley: University of California Press, 1993.

Williams, S. Wells. *The Middle Kingdom*. 2d ed. New York: Scribners, 1895.

Wilson, Ming, and John Cayley, eds. *Europe Studies China: Papers from an International Conference on the History of European Sinology*. London: Han-Shan Tang Books, 1995.

Wittfogel, Karl A. *Oriental Despotism: A Comparative Study of Total Power*. New Haven: Yale University Press, 1957.

Wittkower, Rudolf. *Allegory and the Migration of Symbols*. New York: Thames and Hudson, 1987.

Wong, R. Bin. *China Transformed: Historical Change and the Limits of European Experience.* Ithaca, N.Y.: Cornell University Press, 1997.

Wu Xiangxiang 吳相湘, ed. *Tianzhujiao dongchuan wenxian* 天主教東傳文獻 (Documents on the eastward transmission of Catholicism). Zhongguo shixue congshu series. Taipei: Xuesheng shuju, 1952.

Xie Yunfei 謝雲飛. *Zhongguo wenzixue tonglun* 中國文字學通論 (A survey of Chinese grammatology). Taipei: Xuesheng, 1984.

Xu Ben 徐賁. "Zai tan Zhongguo 'houxue' de zhengzhixing he lishi yishi" 在談中國 '後學' 的 政治性和歷史意識 (Again on Chinese postmodernism's political character and historical consciousness). *Ershiyi shiji* 39 (Feb. 1997): 132–37.

Xu Jilin 許紀霖. "Bi pipan geng zhongyaode shi lijie" 比批判更重要的是理解 (Understanding is more important than critique). *Ershiyi shiji* 30 (Aug. 1995): 130–36.

———. "Wenhua rentong de kunjing—90 niandai Zhongguo zhishijie de fanxihua sichao" 文化認同的困境—90 年代中國知識界的反西化思潮 (The difficulties of cultural identity: the anti-Western trend in Chinese intellectual life of the 1990s). *Zhanlüe yu guanli* 18 (1996): 100–3.

Xu Shen 許慎. *Shuowen jiezi [zhu]* 說文解字注 (The explication of graphs and analysis of characters, with annotations). Ed. and annot. Duan Yucai 段玉裁. Taipei: Liming, 1976.

Yang Tingyun 楊廷筠. *Dai yi pian* 代疑篇 (A treatise for removing doubts). In Wu Xiangxiang 吳相湘, ed., *Tianzhujiao dongchuan wenxian* 天主教東傳文獻 (Documents on the eastward transmission of Catholicism), pp. 471–631. Zhongguo shixue congshu series. Taipei: Xuesheng shuju, 1952.

Yang Zhen'e 楊振鄂. *Yang Qiyuan xiansheng nianpu* 楊淇園先生年譜 (A chronological biography of Mr. Yang Qiyuan). Zhongguo gongjiao zhenli xuehui congshu series. Shanghai: Shangwu, 1946.

Yeh, Wen-hsin, ed. *Cross-Cultural Readings of Chineseness: Narratives, Images, and Interpretations of the 1990s.* China Research Monographs, 51. Berkeley, Calif.: Institute of East Asian Studies, 2000.

Yi jing 易經 (The Book of Changes). In Ruan Yuan 阮元, ed., *Shisanjing zhushu* 十三經注疏. 1815. Reprinted—Taipei: Dahua, 1987.

Yip, Wai-lim. *Ezra Pound's "Cathay."* Princeton: Princeton University Press, 1969.

———. *Hiding the Universe: Poems by Wang Wei.* New York: Mushinsha/Grossman, 1972.

Yourcenar, Marguerite. *Nouvelles orientales.* Paris: Gallimard, 1963.

Yu, Anthony C. "Enduring Change: Confucianism and the Prospect of Human Rights." *Lingnan Journal of Chinese Studies* 2 (2000): 27–70.

Yu, Pauline. *The Poetry of Wang Wei.* Bloomington: Indiana University Press, 1980.

———. *The Reading of Imagery in the Chinese Poetic Tradition.* Princeton: Princeton University Press, 1987.

————. "Wang Wei: Recent Studies and Translations." *Chinese Literature: Articles, Essays, Reviews* I (1979): 219–40.

Zhai Qiang. "Mao Zedong and Dulles's 'Peaceful Evolution' Strategy: Revelations from Bo Yibo's Memoirs." *Cold War International History Project Bulletin*, 6–7 (1995–96): 29–32; also available through http://cwihp.si.edu/cwihplib.nsf.

Zhang Hanliang 張漢良. "Dexida, shuxie yu Zhongwen" 德希達, 書寫與中文 (Derrida, writing, and the Chinese language). *Dangdai* (Con-Temporary) 4 (1986): 30–33.

Zhang Kuan 張寬. "Oumeiren yanzhong de 'fei wo zulei'" 歐美人眼中的 "非我族 類" (The ethnic other in the eyes of Europeans and Americans). *Dushu* (Sept. 1993): 3–9.

————. "Zai tan Sayide" 再談薩伊德 (On Said again). *Dushu* (Oct. 1994): 9–14.

Zhang Longxi 張隆溪. *Mighty Opposites: From Dichotomies to Differences in the Comparative Study of China.* Stanford: Stanford University Press, 1998.

————. *The Tao and the Logos: Literary Hermeneutics, East and West.* Durham, N.C.: Duke University Press, 1992.

————. *Zou chu wenhua de fengbi quan* 走出文化的封閉圈 (Beyond cultural isolationism). Hong Kong: Shangwu, 2000.

Zhang Xudong. *Chinese Modernism in the Era of Reforms.* Durham, N.C.: Duke University Press, 1997.

Zhang Yingjin, ed. *China in a Polycentric World: Essays in Chinese Comparative Literature.* Stanford: Stanford University Press, 1998.

Zhang Yiwu 張頤武. "Chanshi 'Zhongguo' de jiaolü" 闡釋"中國"的焦慮 (The anxiety of interpreting "China"). *Ershiyi shiji* 29 (June 1995): 128–35.

————. "Hou xin shiqi wenhua: tiaozhan yu jiyu" 後新時期文化: 挑戰與機遇 (Post-new period culture: challenge and opportunity). *Zhanlüe yu guanli* 2 (1994): 112–14.

————. "Miandui quanqiuhua de tiaozhan" 面對全球化的挑戰 (Facing the challenge of globalization). *Ershiyi shiji* 38 (Dec. 1996): 138–42.

————. "'Xiandaixing' de zhongjie—yige wufa huibi de keti" '現代性' 的終結——一個無法迴避的課題 (The end of "modernity," an unavoidable topic). *Zhanlüe yu guanli* 3 (1994): 104–9.

————. "Zai shuo 'Chanshi Zhongguo' de jiaolü" 再說 '闡釋中國'的焦慮 (Again about the anxiety of "interpreting China"). *Ershiyi shiji* 34 (Apr. 1996): 121–26.

Zhao, Henry Y. H. (Zhao Yiheng 趙毅衡). "'Houxue' yu Zhongguo xin baoshouzhuyi" '後學'與中國新保守主義 ("Post-ism" and Chinese neo-conservatism). *Ershiyi shiji* 27 (Feb. 1995): 4–15.

————. "Moxuyou xiansheng yu tamen de watiao" 莫須有先生與他們的蛙跳 (The Incroyables and their leapfrogging). *Ershiyi shiji* 38 (Dec. 1996): 135–37.

————. "Post-Isms and Chinese New Conservatism." *New Literary History* 28 (1997): 31–44.

Zheng Min 鄭敏. "Shijimo de huigu: Hanyu yuyan biange yu Zhongguo xinshi chuangzuo" 世紀末的回顧:漢語語言變革與中國新詩創作 (Retrospect at century's end: The transformation of the Chinese language and modern Chinese poetic creation). *Wenxue pinglun* 3 (1993): 5–20.

————. "Wenhua, zhengzhi, yuyan sanzhe guanxi de wojian" 文化, 政治, 語言三者關係的我見 (The relations among culture, politics and language as I see them). *Ershiyi shiji* 29 (June 1995): 120–29.

Zhong Shuhe 鍾叔河, ed. *Zou xiang shijie congshu* 走向世界叢書 (English title: *From East to West: Chinese Travellers Before 1911*). 10 vols. Changsha: Yuelu, 1985.

Zhou li 周禮 (Rituals of Zhou). In Ruan Yuan 阮元, ed. *Shisanjing zhushu* 十三經注疏. 1815. Reprinted—Taipei: Dahua, 1987.

Zhou Mi 周密. *Qidong yeyu* 齊東野語 (Conversations of a rustic from eastern Qi). Beijing: Zhonghua shuju, 1982.

Zhu Xi 朱熹. *Zhuzi yulei* 朱子語類 (Conversations of Master Zhu, arranged by topic). Shanghai: Guji chubanshe, 1992.

Zhuang Zhou 莊周. *Zhuangzi* 莊子. Ed. Guo Qingfan 郭慶藩. Taipei: Hanjing, 1985.

Zito, Angela. *Of Body and Brush: Grand Sacrifice as Text/Performance in Eighteenth-Century China*. Chicago: University of Chicago Press, 1997.

Zuo zhuan 左轉 (The Zuo commentary to the *Annals of Lu*). In Ruan Yuan 阮元, ed. *Shisanjing zhushu* 十三經注疏. 1815. Reprinted—Taipei: Dahua, 1987.

Index

Harvard East Asian Monographs
(* out-of-print)

Harvard East Asian Monographs

Harvard East Asian Monographs

Harvard East Asian Monographs

Harvard East Asian Monographs

Harvard East Asian Monographs

133. Paul A. Cohen, *Between Tradition and Modernity: Wang T'ao and Reform in Late Ching China*

134. Kate Wildman Nakai, *Shogunal Politics: Arai Hakuseki and the Premises of Tokugawa Rule*

135. Parks M. Coble, *Facing Japan: Chinese Politics and Japanese Imperialism, 1931–1937*

136. Jon L. Saari, *Legacies of Childhood: Growing Up Chinese in a Time of Crisis, 1890–1920*

137. Susan Downing Videen, *Tales of Heichū*

138. Heinz Morioka and Miyoko Sasaki, *Rakugo: The Popular Narrative Art of Japan*

139. Joshua A. Fogel, *Nakae Ushikichi in China: The Mourning of Spirit*

140. Alexander Barton Woodside, *Vietnam and the Chinese Model: A Comparative Study of Vietnamese and Chinese Government in the First Half of the Nineteenth Century*

141. George Elison, *Deus Destroyed: The Image of Christianity in Early Modern Japan*

142. William D. Wray, ed., *Managing Industrial Enterprise: Cases from Japan's Prewar Experience*

143. T'ung-tsu Ch'ü, *Local Government in China under the Ching*

144. Marie Anchordoguy, *Computers, Inc.: Japan's Challenge to IBM*

145. Barbara Molony, *Technology and Investment: The Prewar Japanese Chemical Industry*

146. Mary Elizabeth Berry, *Hideyoshi*

147. Laura E. Hein, *Fueling Growth: The Energy Revolution and Economic Policy in Postwar Japan*

148. Wen-hsin Yeh, *The Alienated Academy: Culture and Politics in Republican China, 1919–1937*

149. Dru C. Gladney, *Muslim Chinese: Ethnic Nationalism in the People's Republic*

150. Merle Goldman and Paul A. Cohen, eds., *Ideas Across Cultures: Essays on Chinese Thought in Honor of Benjamin L Schwartz*

151. James Polachek, *The Inner Opium War*

152. Gail Lee Bernstein, *Japanese Marxist: A Portrait of Kawakami Hajime, 1879–1946*

153. Lloyd E. Eastman, *The Abortive Revolution: China under Nationalist Rule, 1927–1937*

154. Mark Mason, *American Multinationals and Japan: The Political Economy of Japanese Capital Controls, 1899–1980*

155. Richard J. Smith, John K. Fairbank, and Katherine F. Bruner, *Robert Hart and China's Early Modernization: His Journals, 1863–1866*

156. George J. Tanabe, Jr., *Myōe the Dreamkeeper: Fantasy and Knowledge in Kamakura Buddhism*

157. William Wayne Farris, *Heavenly Warriors: The Evolution of Japan's Military, 500–1300*

158. Yu-ming Shaw, *An American Missionary in China: John Leighton Stuart and Chinese-American Relations*

159. James B. Palais, *Politics and Policy in Traditional Korea*

160. Douglas Reynolds, *China, 1898–1912: The Xinzheng Revolution and Japan*

161. Roger Thompson, *China's Local Councils in the Age of Constitutional Reform*

162. William Johnston, *The Modern Epidemic: History of Tuberculosis in Japan*

Harvard East Asian Monographs

Harvard East Asian Monographs

190. James Z. Lee, *The Political Economy of a Frontier: Southwest China, 1250–1850*

191. Kerry Smith, *A Time of Crisis: Japan, the Great Depression, and Rural Revitalization*

192. Michael Lewis, *Becoming Apart: National Power and Local Politics in Toyama, 1868–1945*

193. William C. Kirby, Man-houng Lin, James Chin Shih, and David A. Pietz, eds., *State and Economy in Republican China: A Handbook for Scholars*

194. Timothy S. George, *Minamata: Pollution and the Struggle for Democracy in Postwar Japan*

195. Billy K. L. So, *Prosperity, Region, and Institutions in Maritime China: The South Fukien Pattern, 946–1368*

196. Yoshihisa Tak Matsusaka, *The Making of Japanese Manchuria, 1904–1932*

197. Maram Epstein, *Competing Discourses: Orthodoxy, Authenticity, and Engendered Meanings in Late Imperial Chinese Fiction*

198. Curtis J. Milhaupt, J. Mark Ramseyer, and Michael K. Young, eds. and comps., *Japanese Law in Context: Readings in Society, the Economy, and Politics*

199. Haruo Iguchi, *Unfinished Business: Ayukawa Yoshisuke and U.S.-Japan Relations, 1937–1952*

200. Scott Pearce, Audrey Spiro, and Patricia Ebrey, *Culture and Power in the Reconstitution of the Chinese Realm, 200–600*

201. Terry Kawashima, *Writing Margins: The Textual Construction of Gender in Heian and Kamakura Japan*

202. Martin W. Huang, *Desire and Fictional Narrative in Late Imperial China*

203. Robert S. Ross and Jiang Changbin, eds., *Re-examining the Cold War: U.S.-China Diplomacy, 1954–1973*

204. Guanhua Wang, *In Search of Justice: The 1905–1906 Chinese Anti-American Boycott*

205. David Schaberg, *A Patterned Past: Form and Thought in Early Chinese Historiography*

206. Christine Yano, *Tears of Longing: Nostalgia and the Nation in Japanese Popular Song*

207. Milena Doleželová-Velingerová and Oldřich Král, with Graham Sanders, eds., *The Appropriation of Cultural Capital: China's May Fourth Project*

208. Robert N. Huey, *The Making of 'Shinkokinshū'*

209. Lee Butler, *Emperor and Aristocracy in Japan, 1467–1680: Resilience and Renewal*

210. Suzanne Odgen, *Inklings of Democracy in China*

211. Kenneth J. Ruoff, *The People's Emperor: Democracy and the Japanese Monarchy, 1945–1995*

212. Haun Saussy, *Great Walls of Discourse and Other Adventures in Cultural China*